P. C. Headle

Evangelists in the Church

Anatiposi

P. C. Headley

Evangelists in the Church

Reprint of the original, first published in 1875.

1st Edition 2024 | ISBN: 978-3-38283-199-8

Anatiposi Verlag is an imprint of Outlook Verlagsgesellschaft mbH.

Verlag (Publisher): Outlook Verlag GmbH, Zeilweg 44, 60439 Frankfurt, Deutschland
Vertretungsberechtigt (Authorized to represent): E. Roepke, Zeilweg 44, 60439 Frankfurt, Deutschland
Druck (Print): Books on Demand GmbH, In de Tarpen 42, 22848 Norderstedt, Deutschland

EVANGELISTS IN THE CHURCH

FROM

PHILIP, A. D. 35, TO MOODY AND SANKEY, A. D. 1875.

WITH SIXTEEN PORTRAITS.

BY REV. P. C. HEADLEY,

AUTHOR OF "COURT AND CAMP OF DAVID," "JOSEPHINE," ETC.

BOSTON:
HENRY HOYT,
No. 9 CORNHILL.
1875.

TO

REV. J. M. MANNING, D. D.,

PASTOR OF THE OLD SOUTH CHURCH,

WHICH WELCOMED GEORGE WHITEFIELD TO BOSTON,

This Volume is Inscribed,

AS AN EXPRESSION OF RESPECT AND REGARD,

BY HIS

FRIEND AND PARISHIONER,

THE AUTHOR.

PREFACE.

In this first attempt to group together the leading evangelists of various denominations, in their relations to each other and to the progress of Christ's kingdom in the world, the author has aimed at impartiality in his treatment of them and their work.

Many of them are here sketched for the first time; of others the only authentic record is given; and while all the methods are not endorsed or peculiarities commended, no one can fail to see the legitimate, scriptural position of the true evangelist. A few who are not in the list, or are scarcely more than mentioned, either did not furnish the necessary facts in time, or do not desire the publication of personal history.

The narrative of Mr. and Mrs. Boardman, from the lateness of the material, is very brief; but we regret it the less because it will soon be issued entire, in a neat volume, from the press of the Willard Tract Society. For the lives of Jacob Knapp, Thomas S. Sheardown, A. B. Earle, Jabez S. Swan, Daniel Baker, and E. P. Hammond, we are indebted to very full biographies of them, published several years since.

The engraving of Council Hall will have special interest as the crowning and favorite enterprise of President Finney's life-work, erected in sight of his home, and to him the pledge of future prosperity to Oberlin.

It was the animating hope, while collecting and sifting a large number of volumes, papers, and letters, that the cause of truth and the salvation of men would be promoted by the appearance of these condensed narratives of so many of the workers for Christ, honored with the name of Evangelist.

In another volume we hope to present sketches of the Christian workers, not formally evangelists, especially those connected with Young Men's Christian Associations.

CONTENTS.

CHAPTER I.

CHAPTER II.

CHAPTER III.

CONTENTS.   vii

CHAPTER X.

CHAPTER XI.

CHAPTER XII.

CHAPTER XVIII.

CHAPTER XIX.

CHAPTER XX.

CHAPTER XXI.

CHAPTER XXII.

CHAPTER XXIII.

ILLUSTRATIONS.

EVANGELISTS.

FROM A. D. 35 TO A. D. 1875.

CHAPTER I.

THE ANCIENT CHURCH. — THE FIRST EVANGELIST. — HIS LABORS AND
SUCCESS. — A CALL TO LEAVE SAMARIA. — THE ETHIOPIAN. — PHILIP
AT AZOTUS. — TAKES UP HIS RESIDENCE AT CESAREA. — ENTERTAINS
PAUL AND HIS COMPANY. — THE AGES OF SECULAR CHRISTIANITY AND
DECLINING SPIRITUALITY. — THE OFFICE OF EVANGELIST OF DIVINE
APPOINTMENT. — ITS RELATIONS TO THE PASTORAL WORK. — OBJEC-
TIONS ANSWERED. — ESSENTIAL ELEMENTS IN THE CHARACTER OF AN
EVANGELIST. — TESTIMONY. — BOGATZKY A CENTURY AGO.

IN the ancient church, there were men whose special
call and labors were to save her decaying life from extinc-
tion, and reinforce it with fresh spiritual power.

Moses, cradled on the waters of the Nile, and summoned
from the Egyptian palace to the wilderness to receive his
high commission from Jehovah, was sent, not only to rescue the Hebrews from merciless slavery, but to go before
them in the ministry of the Word to the land of religious
freedom and greater spiritual blessings. It was indeed. a
revival, when the Israelites, led by Jehovah out of bondage,
through the sea and the desert, went up to the mount of
God to form the Jewish Church into a "theocratic nation."
The man and the means were extraordinary, because demanded by the emergency.

Moses stands at the head of that order of men who
were really the evangelists of the old dispensation, — the

prophets. The foretelling of future events was only a single special endowment. The word "prophet" is from a Hebrew root which means "to boil or bubble over," in other words to give forth from a fountain God had poured into the soul. The synonymes of prophet were, "the interpreter," "the messenger of Jehovah," "the man of spirit," "the man of God." Lyman Abbott says in his authoritative work, "Dictionary of Religious Knowledge," "These preachers had neither church nor pulpit nor salary; they gathered their congregations where they could find them, — in the street, the field, the highways. They depended on the hospitality of the pious for their support." He then refers to their poetic discourses, recited with the accompaniment of *music* on "the rude instruments of their age." Moses was the first of the line of these seer-evangelists sent to the house of Israel, and Samuel was the founder of the distinct order and of the earliest "training college" of these independent servants of God. Prophets and priests came into marked contrast. When the interference of the former was called for, they appeared to encourage or threaten. Elijah before Ahab, "like the ghost of the murdered Naboth in the vineyard of Jezreel," is an illustration; and that he was a princely herald of Jehovah to this backsliding people — the White-field of the period in which he lived — is evident from the honor bestowed upon him and his worthy predecessor Moses at the transfiguration.

Ezra and Nehemiah called to new faith and restored covenant mercies the captive people of the Most High. Isaiah, Jeremiah, Ezekiel, and Joel were examples of a fearless, independent ministry among the Hebrews, — flaming messengers of the Lord to an unfaithful church. Their rebukes and appeals stirred to penitence or hostility the hearts of the people. They were all preachers apart from the established priesthood, and did not hesitate to resort to unusual measures to arouse and move to obedience those to whom they delivered the testimony of God.

The Pentecostal ingathering of Christian disciples was the beginning of the revival movement in the world, as distinguished from national deliverances, the growth of Jehovah's visible kingdom by the increase of population, and the unrecognized operations of the Holy Spirit in the use of the appointed sacrifices and services of Hebrew ritualism. It was the earliest of those harvest seasons of the Spirit which have since marked the increase in numbers and godliness of the churches. The glorious work spread through the capital of Judea, until the "disciples were greatly multiplied." Among these were many Hellenistic or Grecian Jews, who read the Scriptures in their own tongue instead of the Hebrew dialect. They did not hold the first rank in the aristocracy of the Abrahamic line, and thought, possibly with reason, that on this account there was partiality in the distribution of the poor fund, at least that part of it given to the needy widows.

The apostles', whose spiritual duties made it quite impossible to look after these details, called together the representative men or leaders among the converts, and suggested the appointment of seven deacons, to have this charity in charge. Of these were Stephen, the first martyr under the new dispensation, and Philip, the first evangelist.

Saul of Tarsus, the gifted and dashing leader in the persecution of the disciples awakened by their aggressive faith, had spread terror throughout Jerusalem and its suburbs; and Philip, who may have witnessed the violent death of his co-worker, the transfigured Stephen, with many others who were recognized preachers of the new faith, fled from the metropolis. He went to the capital of Samaria, where Christ had planted the "seed of the kingdom," preparing the way for Philip. His labors moved the entire population, bringing to the surface all the elements of opposition to the gospel. Among these he confronted the Spiritualism of that day, whose favorite prophet was Simon Magus. This Simon had everything at stake. His genius and mysterious power had won for him a position of extraordinary honor; he walked before the people with a god-like authority, the recipient of homage and fortune. He evidently resisted the religious excitement until his adherents were subdued by the wonder-working Spirit, and he could no longer withstand the sweeping movement. He also renounced his sorceries, and joined the disciples of the crucified Nazarene. The tidings of the great revival in Samaria soon reached Jerusalem. The apostles immediately sent Peter and John to the aid of Philip. Upon their arrival they communicated to the believers in Samaria, by the laying on of hands, the Pentecostal endowment of the Holy Ghost. This impressive scene brought to the surface the superficial conversion and hidden hypocrisy of the sorcerer: he desired to purchase the gift of God with money. The sacrilege was fearfully rebuked, and the terrified, convicted man begged for mercy. The apostles, with Philip, seemed to have felt no surprise that such spurious conversion should attend a great religious excitement.

It is probable, although not recorded, that during this visit of Peter and John, Philip was appointed by them to the permanent work of an evangelist. Peter and John returned to Jerusalem, leaving the Samaritan field to to Philip. Soon after, by some token of his will unknown to us, God commanded the evangelist to travel southward, without giving a reason for this advance into the desert country. Loyalty to his King required unquestioning obedience, and he went forward; when lo! a chariot slowly rolled over the plain, and in it, reading a parchment page, sat an Ethiopian from the court of his queen, where he stood nearest her throne in authority.

Philip put himself in the way of the traveller, who invited him to a seat by his side. The royal messenger was musing with wonder over the fifty-third chapter of Isaiah, and asked the evangelist concerning Him who "was led like a lamb to the slaughter." When the world's Redeemer was presented to him for loving trust, he believed and was baptized by the fountain or stream. After the outward seal of his faith had been received from Philip, and before he could entreat him to return to the chariot, the evangelist mysteriously disappeared, — "caught away by the Spirit,"—and is next heard of at Azotus, an old Philistine city. Turning his face towards Jerusalem, he held meetings wherever he could get an audience along the path of travel. Of his subsequent labors we have no record. He took up his residence in Cesarea, the political capital of Judea, seventy miles from Jerusalem. Here Peter by divine command first preached the gospel to a Gentile household, — that of Cornelius, a Roman centurion in the proconsul's life-guard called the "Italian band." A century and a half later, Origen, one of the fathers, preached there, and collated the different versions of the Septuagint; it was also the home of the great historian Eusebius.

Thirty years after Philip began his evangelistic work, he entertained at Cesarea the venerable Paul and his party during a tour of pastoral visitation among the churches.

With his brief history, that of the distinctive office of the evangelist disappears for ages. We have no further record of this co-worker with the local and established ministry, during the period succeeding that covered by the sacred annals. The early bishops of Rome had a widening circle of missionary labors around the Eternal City, until her growing power attracted to her, weak princes for her protection, and then the mightiest for her approval. At length her supreme temporal sovereignty, supporting

her corrupt spiritual life, threw upon the gloom of the
Dark Ages the lurid glare of the martyrdom of the disciples of a primitive Christianity.

It is true that in the middle of the fourth century the
Greek pulpit orator, Chrysostom, swayed multitudes
with his denunciation of certain abuses, and St. Augustine, after his reform in morals, preached and wrote burning words upon gospel themes; but no large spiritual
harvests were reaped.

Fulgentius in the North African Church, Germanus
among the Franks, who visited Britain, Cæsarius of Arles,
St. Patrick, born in Scotland and taken to Ireland as a
slave while a youth, were all ecclesiastics of glowing zeal
in the evangelistic service of the ruling hierarchy of the
fifth and early part of the sixth centuries. They were
illustrations of the necessity of this form of labor in all
ages. Later, Serverinus, along the Danube, among the
tribes desolated by the merciless Attila, a mysterious, holy
man, of unknown origin, was a very remarkable, self-
denying, and devoted evangelist. Neander, in his " Memorials of Christian Life in the Early and Middle Ages,"
gives sketches of these, and of others who did the evangelistic work of their times. Nearly a thousand years after
the Messiah's birth, Peter the Hermit summoned papal
Europe to the great crusade for the rescue of Jerusalem
from the Turkish infidels, with the awakening shout,
" God wills it ! " Although a military enterprise attended
with untold suffering and waste of life, the beneficent
results, in many lines of human progress, are seen and felt
to-day.

Catholic missionaries visited all climes, with a self-sacrificing zeal worthy of imitation by the professors of a
purer faith.

The Mystics quietly sought communion with God; and
the Alpine Vaudois "formed a long-continued chain of

witnesses for the truth." The Lyonese merchant, Pierre Valdo, the latter part of the twelfth century, sold his possessions, and became substantially a lay evangelist in behalf of declining Christianity. There were other glowing centres of aggressive spirituality in the lives of devout men, who were solitary, practical evangelists of vital truth and godliness. The German Tauler, the Bohemian Huss, the English Wickliffe, in the fourteenth century, "reformers before the Reformation," were God's messengers to a heartless church, preparing the way for Martin Luther, whose voice, sounding over Europe the denunciations of Rome and the doctrine of justification-by faith, echoes still around the world.

The *spirit* of evangelism has thus distinguished all great moral and religious crises and all progress in the past.

The word "evangelist" is from the Greek ἐυαγγελίστιοὶ, that is to say, "the bringer of good tidings." Its application has been limited by modern usage to preachers without any particular charge.

The scriptural testimony to the distinctive and unrepealed appointment of evangelists is very emphatic; it is mentioned in order of importance before that of pastors and teachers, while not a hint is anywhere given that it is of inferior importance, and may be accepted or rejected according to the approval or prejudice of the churches.

Let any one, with proper reverence for God's Word, study this aspect of the subject, and he may safely abide by the decision to which he is led by the oracles of God.

Albert Barnes says, "The office was distinct from that of the pastor, the teacher, and the prophet, and was manifestly an office in which preaching was the main thing."

Prof. Hackett, in his "Notes on the Acts," says, "The title of evangelists appears to have been given to those who had no stated pastoral charge, but travelled from place to place as they had opportunity."

This has been, substantially, the view of the permanent office in the Church, held by the ablest divines of Europe.

Bengel, in his "Gnomon of the New Testament," says, "The evangelist was fitted for an office of the highest importance by a gift superior to that of pastors and teachers."

Dr. Scott says, "They were preachers of the gospel, without full, apostolical authority and without any stated charge; going among the heathen to found churches or visiting churches already formed to set in order the things that were wanting, to supply the deficiencies or aid the labors of the stated pastors, and to stimulate them to greater earnestness in discharging their duties. When zeal for propagating the gospel subsided, this office fell into disuse; but in one form or other the office of evangelist, or something of the same nature, must revive along with the work of evangelizing the nations." And Dr. Scott even went so far as to say that evangelists were "superior in dignity to diocesan bishops." This testimony is the more emphatic from the pen of a clergyman of the Church of England.

Olshausen, who, in scholarly and spiritual discernment, has perhaps no rival as a commentator, held that "evangelists are such teachers as, journeying about, labored for the wider extension of the gospel."

Kuiœvel affirms that "evangelists, in the age of the apostles, were not settled pastors of any Christian congregation, or resident at any stated place, but were itinerant presbyters."

We reverently affirm that Jesus, whose herald-evangelist was John, filled this office. He was not a pastor, nor, in the popular use of the term, was he a missionary. His labors were confined to what, in his day, corresponded

to our churches, his scattered "chosen people," sometimes preaching in their synagogues, but generally in the
open air, the "acceptable year of the Lord."

We think that upon a little reflection it will be apparent
to any one that, from the very nature of his work, the position of our Lord was more nearly that of the true evangelist of the last hundred and fifty years, than any other
order of gospel messengers. He employed and thus
authorized the means they have used with success; he
proclaimed the truth on mountain-slopes, at the sea-side,
and wherever he could have the hearing ear; he protracted the services without any rule, but a wise adaptation of them to desired results; he was thronged with
superficial adherents, who left him when the test of loyalty
came; he was misunderstood, criticised, condemned, and
slandered. It is easy enough to make his preaching and
treatment exceptional, in our judgment; but the difference
between his experience, with that of the apostles also, and
of such men as Whitefield, Wesley, and others, was only
of time and place.

That the appointment of evangelists has never been withdrawn from the church needs no further proof than that the
same demand exists now as when Philip labored with the
apostles who had joined him in Samaria; and even when
such assistance, as in Dr. Edwards's time, has not been
at hand, pastors have left their parishes, and for weeks
done precisely that kind of work among the churches
visited by the subduing presence of the Holy Ghost.

While discretion in his conduct, charity without compromise with error, sound common-sense, knowledge of
men, and reliance on the Holy Spirit, are indispensable
qualities for the highest success, on the other hand, an
evangelist should never be invited to a parish without
considerate regard for his peculiarities and methods, and
hearty co-operation. To rely upon him is one thing, to

make the most of his assistance under God is another; and what should be done. That he will have a plan of his own, and sometimes appear and indeed be too tenacious of it, is to be expected; and he may be called dictatorial, and even wilful, when he is only working in his own natural way, and could succeed only by this general method of labor.

In the year 1845, President Finney, through the "Oberlin Evangelist," addressed a letter to ministers on "Fanatical Excitement." His object was to emphasize the caution, in revivals especially, against a "dash of bitterness and vituperation," to which the indifference or opposition of those who had no sympathy with unusual efforts to save men exposed those engaged in them. He frankly confessed that he had formerly sometimes felt the stirrings of this natural irritation. He particularly condemned " sectarianism, which in all its forms is only a modified species of fanaticism," and may even distinguish one hostile to revival measures. The timely communication was the admonitory voice of a warrior for Christ, whose ripening experience would guard every point of attack by the enemy upon the leaders of Immanuel's host.

The sources of power in this instrumentality are simple and practical, humanly considered, in addition to that need of it in extremity, when aid in a particular field of harvest is indispensable. The very decision to call in such aid increases the prayerful spirit where it already exists, and creates public interest. It is recorded by an eminent minister of the revival in the early part of this century, when there were no evangelists: "As one means of extending the work, ministers who had enjoyed the presence of God among their own people were selected by some ecclesiastical body and sent forth, generally two together, on preaching tours among the neighboring churches. The *expectation* of their coming drew together

large audiences wherever they preached." He then speaks
of the preparation made for their coming, and the animating, awakening effect of their presence and appeals,
which were followed by the outpouring of the Spirit.
Many scores of places in the Eastern and Middle States
were thus visited, and blessed with seasons of refreshing.
Again there are excellent pastors who do not know how to
bring their work to harvest, and a good evangelist is just
the help the state of things requires. Whatever attending, subordinate errors and loss there may be, God's gracious designs of redeeming mercy in the world are plainly
thus fulfilled.

We shall not enter into an extended discussion of the
question of Evangelism, but let the authentic narratives
answer it better than any measure of abstract reasoning
or contrasted prejudices and general statements could do.

God, in his providence and grace, is bringing the subject before the churches as never before. We have seen
an editorial in a religious paper of twenty-five years ago
entitled " The End of Evangelists."

The contrast between the wisdom, judgment, and plans
of even Christian people, when not taught by the Spirit,
has rarely a stronger illustration than in such an infer-
ence proclaimed as a prophecy, followed by the present
unequalled popularity of evangelism, which is likely to
increase rather than decline. Unsanctified self in a good
man is rebuked with humiliating emphasis by the declara-
tion, " My thoughts are not your thoughts, nor my ways
your ways, saith the Lord."

Evangelism is a vital question to be met at the altar of
believing prayer and before the cross of Christ, that we
may learn simply and clearly the mind of the Spirit. The
life of the church depends on this attitude, in whatever
direction the light is poured upon the path of conquest.

We shall only consider briefly objections which are

made directly against evangelists, without discussing
others whose force has equal strength when applied to
revivals under any management. Those who feel no interest in special seasons of refreshing, reveal the unscriptural position they occupy in the legitimate results. We
think history will show that no church whose pastor took
the responsibility of such an attitude, approved by his
church, was ever a great spiritual power in the world, nor
his charge an aggressive company of the Lord's " Sacramental host."

We shall notice the general reasons offered for opposition to evangelistic efforts, leaving others to be answered
by the narratives which follow of the representative characters in this service among the churches.

It has been affirmed that the assistance of the evangelist
often disturbs the harmony between pastor and people.

We find the testimony of pastors in regard to the results
of the labors of evangelists recognized by the churches to
be the *reverse* of this. But granting that from causes beyond
the pastor's control, or that of the evangelist, sometimes a
pastor is transferred subsequently to another charge, does
the fact prove at all that the salvation of scores, it may be
of hundreds, with the general effect upon the community
and Christ's kingdom, was not " a result out of all proportion," in the language of Dr. Hall of New York, " to any
incidental evils "? Is a pastor's continuance in a particular field, without harvest, his personal relations and comfort, the one great overshadowing consideration to the
Redeemer of the world?

There are those who do not question the scriptural argument, but direct their opposition against the abuses of
evangelism, especially the resort to unusual measures to
promote a revival. The injudicious manner and methods
are the great objections, and a sufficient reason for not
venturing on the experiment of asking the aid of an evan-

gelist. The fallacy of this position must be seen when we reflect upon the fact that, in *all* enterprises affecting the popular feeling, there is always a considerable allowance for inevitable defects, — a margin of waste, to be charged to the imperfections of human agency and the action of undisciplined minds.

The simple inquiries are, first, Looking over a given period of history, does the good accomplished exceed any incidental regretted results? and second, Does God clearly set his seal upon the work? The latter includes the former, for the Holy Ghost makes no mistakes, whatever the judgment of men on immediate appearances.

Another objection made is, that the unusual methods, with the prevailing excitement created by the repeated appeals, are attended with spurious conversions, and a reaction to deeper spiritual declension than that which existed before the awakening. Under no guidance, even in the most quiet condition of things, can fatal compromises be prevented in the concerns of the soul; nor can it be shown that the number of such cases is greater in a revival under a sound evangelist than under any other saving means of grace. Besides, Jesus had this sad experience, in his brief ministry, of stony and thorny ground hearers. It is written that on one occasion, when he applied a searching test of character to his converts, a great number left him, and "followed no more with him." The apostles recognized and lamented the same result. The most striking instance of conversion to all appearance, under the first evangelist, Philip, was a startling illustration of this peril to souls when God is working.

Nothing has brought the work of the evangelist more into disfavor in all the past than the occasional imitators of the men who were called of God to the work. We shall have occasion to allude to some of these. And yet how strange that good men should seize upon an incidental result as a decisive objection against this divine appointment, any more than against the pastorate itself. Will any competent judge affirm that a larger proportion of evangelists, including the most eccentric and transient in their meteoric course, than of pastors, have made a partial success or an entire failure of their career? In the former, unwise and harmful action is more conspicuous than in the quiet life of utter inefficiency or disastrous management of the latter; but if the fact in the one case should set aside a most useful instrumentality, surely its force lies with equal justness against the other ministrations of the gospel.

We have recently learned the history of a pastorate so injudicious and selfish in its general character that an old and harmonious church was nearly wrecked, and will require years of wise spiritual culture to recover it from the wretched condition in which it was left by a conservative pastor. But who, excepting the captious and unbelieving enemies of the church, for a moment adduce such a failure as an argument against the settlement of ministers or the preaching of the Word at all? Instead of this, prayerful caution is the lesson taught, with all the training of seminaries and ordaining, and oversight of the brethren by installation; while no provision is made for the evangelist's preparation for his calling, and no fraternal relations for counsel and co-operation established. The marvel is that no more irregular and injurious men and measures have been among the churches. But the inquiry may meet us here, How is it in regard to those churches which were "burnt over" with religious excitement under the guidance of imprudent itinerants, called evangelists? Such exceptions only prove the rule we have stated. For the world has nothing so good, especially if on a large and popular scale, which has not glaring abuses and attractive and damaging counterfeits. The point is not whether flames

destroy in careless keeping and handling, but, Is the fire
indispensable, warming unnumbered homes with its glowing heat? No more necessary to our human life are
the rekindled fires, than are revivals to the vitality of the
church; and these are not generally known where the
attitude of a decided hostility to evangelistic labors is
taken by pastor and people. The only position, it seems
to us, God can approve and bless is, without pet theories or
measures, waiting upon Him, — neither substituting human
machinery for divine power, nor refusing to use means
the Spirit will bless.

In the late civil war, when national life and liberty were
at stake, the enthusiasm of philanthropy was often sadly
and disastrously misdirected, and the waste of life and
treasure immense; but what patriotic heart would have
preferred an inglorious peace, if possible? And shall we
choose tranquillity and established order, when the choice
lies between them and moving upon the enemies of
God's kingdom and winning glorious victories, with some
mistakes in judgment and methods of attack upon the
"powers of darkness"? Certainly, Jehovah answers the
question, as he did that of the terrible struggle of the
nation, by giving the seal of his saving might and songs
of rejoicing over the wonders of his power.

Again, pastors often shrink from the work demanded
by the Lord's command, "Break up the fallow ground."
The friendships and intimacies of a pleasant pastorate,
with, it may be, a sensitive, unaggressive nature, make it
wellnigh impossible fearlessly and faithfully to deal with
the hearts of their hearers.

Further still, as a popular minister intimated not long
since, a cultivated, wealthy parish wants instruction and
entertainment, and feel it a "great tax" to even look after
and support mission-chapels for the "common people."
How humiliating and ominous of future failure in the

settled ministry, and how emphatic the defence of God's order of evangelists, is such a statement! The "protracted meetings," which are inseparable from evangelism, have very ancient authority. Pentecost and the continuous labors of the apostles were of the same general character, and first reappeared in modified form in this country at the South, the history of which will be elsewhere given. "Meetings of Days," or religious convocations for churches of a large district, were held at some convenient centre, and the usual variety of Sabbath services enjoyed for a week, with intervals of social intercourse. When such repeated services were adopted in connection with evangelistic effort, the conservative piety of the churches was greatly alarmed; human machinery was usurping the place of sovereign grace in the salvation of men. The fact was overlooked that, in all affairs of great personal and at the same time public interest, multiplied meetings were employed to awaken attention and concentrate thought upon the subject, and that the supernatural power of the Holy Spirit did not change at all the laws of mind and of social influence. To keep before the awakened thought the great question of eternal life, till a decision is reached, is plainly a wise adaptation of means to the end.

There is a responsibility, not often presented in the strong light it should be on the part of pastors and laymen, in gathering the fruit of revival work, whatever the particular means used. We were impressed with the remark of a leading and conservative Methodist layman, in criticising somewhat a popular evangelist, to the effect that the very waste attending a brief period of concentrated labor would be greatly diminished were it not for the neglect by the resident ministers, and Christians around them, to maintain a high type of piety, and follow up with faithful care and effort the labors of harvest-time. This failure is not a *necessary* reaction: it is seen in the most quiet times. "No man cared for my soul" could fitly express, as we all know, the prevailing inatten- tion to the souls of the people, both within and without the church.

Professor Porter, of the Theological Seminary at Ando- ver, in his "Letters on Revivals," classifies the pastors who opposed special activity in saving souls under the following heads : —

"A was one of those good men who are under the dominion of a sluggish temperament. To travel from one side of his parish to another cost him as much self-denial as it cost Cæsar to cross the Alps and subdue kingdoms.

"B was a man of literary taste, an idolater of books. He laid down his favorite author with reluctance to attend a prayer-meeting. He was so fond of reading, especially works of genius and popular literature, that the spirituality of his heart was gradually impaired.

"C was fond of social avocations, giving the energy of his being to the lighter forms of social intercourse.

"D overloaded himself with secular cares.

"These were a few who preached the *sovereignty of God* in such a way as to provide a refuge for sloth in Christians and ministers."

While the statements are undeniably true of almost every period of great religious interest especially, when the ordinary routine must be abandoned and such means and assistance employed as the emergency demands, there is something fearful about them if we reflect upon the nature of the preacher's calling and the infinite issues at stake.

And then, in respect to the evangelists themselves, much of the attendant loss of desired good, and disrespect shown them by the world, has arisen from the opposition and denunciation with which they have been met by Christian people, — treated often without a private or public hear- ing, as if, instead of being brethren whose sincere desire

2

and purpose was the salvation of men, they were unworthy of confidence. The wicked have loved to have it
so, and have joined in the denunciation of Christ's servants.

We have only to remember that Wesley, Whitefield, the
Haldanes, Kirk, Finney, and nearly every other successful
evangelist, has run the gauntlet of this severe criticism and
unfraternal hostility. Even the extremely cautious, pastoral Nettleton in his methods did not entirely escape.

In each particular case, the cause of complaint and hostility has been sufficient and imperative to those opposing,
if not in the sight of God and of all the people. Not only
so, but it will be seen that innovations upon previous
ecclesiastical views and methods have frequently, without
further test of the movement than this application of
traditional and denominational precedents, been met at
once by distrust and denunciation in the name of the Lord.
There may have been a providential design of wholesome
discipline in the permitted conflict, compelling attention
to tendencies of evil character, and so, in the end, aug-
menting the ultimate good results.

The necessity of caution in assuming a hostile position is
very forcibly suggested in the rule adopted by Dr. Hopkins'
Church, in Auburn, which will appear on another page,
— to drop criticism, seek to know personal duty, and
watch the tokens of the Holy Spirit's working.

Said one of New England's ablest and most highly
esteemed pastors to the writer, "I hope you will answer
one question in your book : why it is that some evangelists,
whose manner of life, in certain respects, was question-
able, especially their social freedom at picnics, and in other
circles, which did not indicate a high degree of spirituality, were so successful. I have asked ministerial brethren,
and the reply has been, The sovereignty of God."

We were surprised at this answer ; as if there were not
always a connection between the human responsibility and

the work of the Spirit, — a reason for the successful labor as clear as that in the natural world.

The reply we think is simple and twofold. First, granting that the evangelist whose labors are blessed is not even a Christian, there is no mystery. If the truth be presented. and pressed upon the attention with adaptation to the people addressed, in an atmosphere of believing prayer, it must take effect.

The instrument may be a Baalam, and God make him a rich blessing. We will illustrate : We knew a pastor, and editor of a leading religious paper, whose labors were uniformly attended with revival interest, and who once came from the house of dissipation to preach a melting preparatory lecture, and at length fell beyond recovery. His explanation of the mystery was, that he was evangelical, imaginative, earnest, and knew men, and he preached, while others prayed. He was once settled near an intellectual, literary, and very conservative brother, who was content with the peace of the cemetery; his soundness in doctrine was never questioned, nor his purity of character : and yet conversions rarely occurred during many years of his pastorate, while Death reaped down his harvest. No other results were expected, and these only were seen.

We do not mean to intimate that any evangelist honored of God in our knowledge, was unconverted; but we would present the matter in the strongest light. On the other hand, a minister may be eccentric and apparently trifling, and yet have in exercise that which God has bound himself to honor, — the first and chief thing in personal experience and in the work of God for others, — *faith*, believing, prevalent prayer. And if, like Whitefield and Wesley, and others, he be a consecrated soul, in communion with Christ, he will have power alone, both with God and man. He is at the same time in Geth-

semane, which is the way to Calvary where Jesus bled,
and also the herald of the cross, to whose base he will lead
many souls.

An inquiry from the opposite standpoint might be
pressed with equal force, to which the "sovereignty of
God" is usually, we think, the only answer.

Why is it that there have been sound and gifted pastors,
free from all eccentricities and irregularities, who preached
for many years without conversions, or with very few, and
these, perhaps, having no recognized connection with their
ministration? There may be financial prosperity and social
pleasures. No one will venture to charge this orthodox
fruitlessness upon divine sovereignty in the interpretation
of it as his purpose and will; therefore, that churches, with
self-complacency and grateful acquiescence in the spiritual
dearth, should dismiss anxiety. Surely, there is another
and truer explanation. We recollect a very suggestive
illustration of the different ways of "waiting upon God."

A good and able pastor, who for a long time had this
quiet pastorate, was succeeded by a young man no less
cultivated and judicious, but in downright earnest to see
harvest, resolved to use such means as the condition of
progressive feeling which he *expected* might clearly indicate. A few months later, youthful hearers were weeping
around him, and a glorious revival swept through his rural
parish. He went into the work believing in the promises of Jehovah, and tenderly calling upon his people
to bring in their tithes and prove him; and they obeyed
the Spirit's voice, and went tearfully to the altar of consecration, while from Heaven's uplifted window was poured
down the priceless blessing.

In no other service for the church, or for humanity dis-
connected directly with it, are eccentricities or weaknesses which do not prevent, on the whole, desired
achievements, a fatal or grave objection. A commander,

a statesman, a professional man, and even a mechanic, is judged by the measure of *permanent success*. What *remains* after attending and transient incidents have passed from immediate criticism, is the only *just and safe test*.

The committee appointed by the Oneida Association in 1827 to report on the revival within their bounds, put on record the following testimony: "The preaching and other labors of evangelists have been a very obvious and efficient means of originating and carrying forward the work. The opinion of some — that there ought to be evangelists in the church, whose principal business should be to aid settled ministers — is strengthened by their usefulness in this revival. Whether provisions should be made for their support by societies formed for the purpose, or whether it should be left to the liberality of churches and individuals benefited by their labors, is a question which the committee feel incompetent to decide."

The revolution on the whole subject of revivals within a century is wonderful, and the beneficent result is very apparent in the new energy breathed into the various religious denominations, giving birth to missionary enterprises and manifold agencies for the conversion of souls unemployed before.

Dr. E. N. Kirk, whose great success as an evangelist we shall record in its proper place, very cautiously and judiciously says: —

"Should a pastor or church employ such helpers? and, if so, when? Some have resolved never to employ them. I should not dare make that resolution, but I would be sure the time and the man had come before employing such assistance. When one is employed, the pastor should hold the reins, giving the helper full scope within prescribed limits. Do not depend on him, or any other man, to do your work; nor look in ordinary circumstances for help except to your own flock or to a neighboring pastor, but chiefly to your ascended Lord.

" What are the indications that an evangelist should be employed? They may be these, — one or all : The pastor feels an impulse which he is conscious his own labors cannot follow successfully. This must be felt : description cannot make it known unless you have felt it. The church has the same impulse, which the pastor also knows ; he cannot work effectively. Then, again, an evangelist can be procured who has substantially the qualifications which the field and the times demand. Employ him."

The above are general suggestions to pastors, which cannot cover all the crises in churches,. with or without settled ministers, which may demand the labors of the evangelist ; for they clearly were not designed as a *dernier ressort*, but as additional forces in the harvest-work of the Holy Spirit.

Sabbath evening, June 13, 1875, we attended a meeting of great interest in Dr. Robinson's Memorial Church, on Fifth Avenue, New York, called to discuss " Evangelistic Labors at Home and Abroad." Dr. Hall, of the 5th Avenue Church, and Dr. Ganse, Dutch Reformed, were the principal speakers. The address of the former was very eloquent and impressive. He said, " We ought to be thankful for the spirit of evangelism which is abroad, and that the churches are striking out to reach the masses. A Christian ought to be grateful for any agency, however defective, which breaks up the incrustation of worldliness and brings men to Christ. Some good people see difficulties in the way of employing such instrumentalities, but practically they do not exist. We, as ministers, should not fear them. No earnest, true worker can do us any harm." He alluded to the work of Mr. Hammond the past year in California, and to the isolated cases of injudicious efforts, cited in the newspapers, while ministers and churches on the ground were the best judges, and their testimony to the spiritual results was unanimous : these results were out of all proportion to any defects. With hearty sympathy he outlined the wonderful achievements abroad of more recent activity, and emphasized the necessity of such agencies supplementing the pastoral relation.

Dr. Ganse remarked that this restoration of apostolic success was a sufficient answer to modern infidelity, whose exponents were such gifted men as Herbert Spencer and Tyndale ; it was God appearing in the midst of scepticism. He said, further, that any Sabbath day, in two hours enough people passed by the corner near his church, on their way to Central Park, a few blocks beyond, to fill all the sacred temples in the neighborhood ; and very forcibly inquired, " How are we to reach these multitudes ? " The question was the more startling in connection with the fact that the earnest, popular Dr. Hall's sanctuary was exclusive of all but the rich because of its expensive sittings, the pews costing hundreds, and some thousands of dollars annually.

Surely, never were evangelists more demanded, nor the prospect of their future usefulness greater than now.

We have just had an illustration of traditionary, ecclesiastical prejudices in the face of God's own wonder-working, when, by a large majority, the Presbyterian and other clergymen in Philadelphia voted to invite Mr. Moody there. Some of the pastors objected because the evangelist was *not ordained*, and therefore not only irregular, so that to ask him to labor with them would be a dangerous precedent, but he was not connected with any clerical body that could try him, if the necessity arose.

Said a layman in the Congregational Church very recently, who had been thrown in such relations to a number of vacant churches that he was desired to secure candidates, "After the endeavor to meet their wants, I was requested not to send men whose idea of the ministry was apparently professional mainly, but those who ' believed and felt the truths of the gospel.' " He expressed surprise. We think the present movements of evangelists abroad, and some already made here, with the financial depression teaching its lessons, and other providential voices, are all turning the thoughts of thoughtful Christian persons to the stern and yet affecting realities of our Evangelical faith, and they will demand instrumentalities which will reach and move the hearts of the people.

Another truth no less interesting, is the marked crisis in Christian experience passed by most if not all of those men whose influence was hallowed and abiding. From doubt and legal bondage they escaped, usually through deep spiritual tribulation, into the prevailing light and joy and peace of victorious faith, — a rest and delight of soul in Jesus. They had that enduement from on high which the gospel offers to every believer on the conditions of unreserved surrender, by simple, unwavering trust, to Him who proclaims himself to be "wisdom, righteousness, sanctification, and redemption." An unconverted preacher who declares the truth of God may be made, in answer to the prayers of the saints, the means of saving many; but he alone who knows the deep things of Christ experimentally can wield the sword of the Spirit with its divinest power.

There is an aspect of the far-reaching influence of evangelists which has been an impressive surprise to the writer, — the harmonious plan and divine order in their use, instead of an irregular, erratic agency resembling the occasional appearance of the comet among the unchanging stars upon the nightly sky. It is wonderful to notice how timely and natural have been the advent and service of the successful workers in this department of the world's redemption. To change the illustration to one which has been used with reference to God's providential dealings : we have looked upon the wrong side of unfinished embroidery, and all has seemed without system, — fragmentary ; but the true view is upon the other surface, where the beautiful figure appears.

The Wesleys and Whitefield, the Haldanes, Nettleton, Finney, Knapp, Kirk, Baker at the South, with subsequent evangelists, were and are as clearly a part of a vast and glorious system of saving forces, interworking and supplementing each other, as any movements of the "church universal," and without which its very life would have decayed to the point of threatened death. What might have been accomplished if, instead of opposing Jehovah's plan, the churches had accepted it, and prayerfully taken it into their care, providing for its highest legitimate power, cannot be told. When it is, as it must be erelong, thus recognized, and adjusted to the other means of grace in their spiritual activity, the people of God will learn what they and the world have lost.

There is now unwonted interest among Christians on this subject of evangelistic labor. It is strongly expressed in a note recently received from a venerable, highly-gifted, and successful evangelist of a generation passing away : —

NEW BRUNSWICK N. J., April 16, 1875.

DEAR BROTHER, —

I do wish you success in your proposed volume, and pray that it may be made a blessing to many. The churches are waking up to the importance of reviving the ancient order of evangelists. They are much needed throughout the land as helpers to the pastors, who in many places are struggling hard to arouse the masses, with no very great success. One of these heaven-sent and heaven-kindled torches or firebrands, appearing at a *crisis*, might set all the works of the devil in a blaze!

Most affectionately, in Jesus Christ our Lord,

JAMES CAUGHEY.

It will be seen in the course of our history that in the earlier years of evangelistic work in this country, the denominational lines were sharply drawn; but gradually these disappeared in the progress of Christian union, until now a sectarian evangelist is quite unknown.

We close this brief discussion of a far-reaching, infinitely important topic, with a single stanza from the poem of the devout and earnest Bogatzky, written more than a hundred years ago, on the thrilling prayer of the prophet Isaiah: "Oh! that thou wouldst rend the heavens, that thou wouldst come down; that the mountains might flow down at thy presence . . . to make thy name known to their adversaries, that the nations may tremble at thy presence": —

> "Oh! haste to help, ere we are lost.
>   Send forth evangelists in spirit strong,
> Armed with Thy Word, — a dauntless host,
>   Bold to attack the rule of ancient wrong.
> And let them all the earth to Thee reclaim
> **To be Thy kingdom and to know Thy name.**"

CHAPTER II.

The Reappearance of the Evangelist. — The First Open-Air Sermon. — George Whitefield and John Wesley. — Charles Wesley. — The Holy Club. — Methodists. — Whitefield in the American Colonies. — Opposition from Ministers and Colleges. — Successes. — Wonderful Scenes. — Results.

It was Saturday afternoon, the seventeenth day of February, 1739, when a young man, just past his twenty-fourth year, stood on an elevation at Rose Green, Kingswood, near Bristol, his native city, preaching the first sermon in the open air which had fallen on English ears The grounds around had been a "royal chase," but only the few trees scattered among the opened coal-mines remained to remind the spectator of the once green avenues beneath interlocking boughs, along which had sped the sportsman's steed beneath his rider of noble blood. It was a strange scene : two hundred grim colliers had gathered to hear the youthful preacher, who, with fervid eloquence, presented to them the Saviour of the world. They listened, and went away to return at the next service with a multitude, which a few days later increased to twenty thousand, — a vast sea of humanity, largely without any means of grace besides. Referring to these great occasions, he writes of one : "The day was fine, the sun shone very bright ; and the people, standing in such awful manner around the mount, in the profoundest silence, filled me with holy admiration. Having no righteousness of their own to renounce, they were glad to hear of Jesus, who was a friend to publicans, and came to call not the righteous but sinners to repentance. The first discovery of their being affected was to see the white gutters made by their tears, which plentifully fell down their black cheeks as they came out of their coal-pits."

That young herald of the cross, distrustful of power, untried in extempore preaching, swaying the throng circling away to a distance which only a voice of such compass and richness could reach, was George Whitefield. How came he there, suddenly startling an empire, like the unexpected appearance of a splendid comet in the heavens, and, not unlike that celestial visitant, an object of varied speculation and strange alarm?

At the same time two other youthful heralds of the cross, disregarding the stereotyped order of the national church, and eloquently proclaiming the simple gospel, were becoming famous among the masses in the English metropolis. One of these was the rising preacher whose parish was to include children of God in every land; and the other was he who, with Isaac Watts, was to lend the wings of sacred song to devotions in the Protestant temples of the world.

John and Charles Wesley were these co-workers with George Whitefield. John, at the earnest request of the latter, went to his aid in Bristol; and on Monday, May 2, 1739, two months and a half after Whitefield preached in the open air, Wesley followed his example, addressing three thousand people near that city, from the appropriate text, Isaiah lxi : 1. A few days afterwards he proclaimed in the hearing of thousands, from Hannam Mount, Kingswood, — Whitefield's first pulpit beneath the bending heavens, — the entreaty of the same seraphic seer, — " Ho, every one that thirsteth, come ye to the waters!"

Who were these evangelists, in the prime of manhood, whose names were already sounding through the sea-girdled realm of George the Second?

George Whitefield was born December 16, 1714, in the old city of Gloucester, England. His father, Thomas Whitefield, was proprietor of the Bell Inn, having left for it the lucrative calling of a wine-merchant in Bristol. He was the eldest of fourteen children, and although the family lived upon a valuable estate, he was early sent to business, both to reduce the expenses of so large a household and to prepare himself for remunerative employment. George was the youngest of six sons of the inn-keeper, and had one sister, the eldest of the seven children. His father died when he was two years of age. His mother's pet because he was the orphaned "baby," she spared no sacrifice to give him an education. She told him, with prophetic appreciation, that she expected more comfort from him than from any of the other children, — a remark which he said stimulated to earnest endeavor in his youth to make good her fond anticipations; and yet he yielded to the temptations of his age and the pleasure-loving times, an experience over which later he deeply mourned. His mother married again, but unhappily, and home lost its charms for him.

While at school in his native city his oratorical powers, especially in dramatic entertainments, made him very popular, and his teacher prepared plays to encourage him in the culture of his genius. He exchanged study for the Bell Inn, to assist his mother. Here he was often deeply convicted of his need, as a lost sinner, of Christ, reading the Bible till dead of night. A youthful friend urged him to go to Oxford and renew his studies; his brief answer was, "I wish I could!" Disagreement arose between him and a married brother about the affairs of the inn, and George went to live with his mother, who had given up the unpleasant complications in business for residence in another part of the city. And now a new danger arose from the influence of attractive and irreligious

young men; but God saved him from the threatening
peril. Convictions returned, and he gave himself with the
absorbing devotion of an anchorite to the appointed services of the Church, and was quite indifferent to all other
objects of thought.

At this crisis an Oxford student, who had paid his way in
the position of servitor, called upon Whitefield's mother,
and mentioned the fact, when she exclaimed, as if a new
revelation from her faithful Lord had come to her, " This
will do for my son "; and turning to him, inquired, " Will
you go to Oxford, George ? " The prompt reply was,
" With all my heart." Application was accordingly made,
urged by influential friends, and he was entered. No more
diligent, blameless young man was then in those halls
of learning. For one only in his eighteenth year, his
influence was widely felt when he took the place of
servitor in Pembroke College, Oxford. Resisting the
formalism and immoralities of a university which had
ejected two thousand Non-Conformists, he had his earliest
experience in persecution by the "riotous students,"
because he declined the solicitations to join them, a course
which compelled him sometimes to shut himself in his
room to escape their insults till his decision of character conquered an honorable peace. The tutor of young
Whitefield became his warmest and a most serviceable
friend.

Before this period in his history, the "Holy Club" had
been formed, composed of John and Charles Wesley, Kirk-
ham, Merton, and Morgan of Christ Church. These students were devoted Christians amidst prevailing laxness of
religious principle, and reduced their devout living to such
undeviating system, that they were called "Methodists."
Others joined them; but Whitefield, who had heard of
them and felt drawn towards them with a growing sympathy, modestly kept himself apart, hoping that some-

thing might occur to introduce him to the charmed circle. Providence interposed as follows : —

A pauper had attempted suicide, and Mr. Whitefield sent a poor woman to request Mr. Charles Wesley to visit this forlorn being and administer to her spiritual instruction. The messenger. was charged not to say who sent her, but she chose to disobey ; and Mr. Wesley, who had often seen him walking alone and had heard something of him, invited him to breakfast on the following morning. An introduction to the select society of these despised students soon followed ; and Mr. Whitefield now, like them, "began to live by rule, and to pick up the very fragments of time, that not a moment of it might be lost." Nothing, perhaps, contributed more to the formation of this union than the advice given to Mr. John Wesley by a plain Christian whom he had travelled many miles to visit. "You wish, sir," said the good man, "to serve God and go to heaven. Remember that you cannot serve Him alone : you must, therefore, find companions or make them. The Bible knows nothing of solitary religion." Wesley never forgot this, and he used his utmost exertions to promote Christian fellowship and united effort.

The club now numbered fifteen noble young men, whose high purpose it was to cultivate earnestly, systematically, the intellect and heart. But there was a Romish legality and penance mingled with their frequent devotions. Whitefield gave himself to such protracted fasting and prayer, that he could not walk from bodily weakness. His tutor called a physician, who found him sinking into a nervous fever.

The blessing which came to his soul during this lingering sickness made it a memorable and priceless discipline. The inflowing of that perfect love which casts out fear, a baptism of the Holy Ghost marking a new and more blessed experience, filled him with "joy unspeakable and

full of glory," which never for any length of time left him.
He alludes to a great spiritual insight into God's Word,
while, in his own language, "The partition-wall of bigotry
and sect-religion was broken down. I loved all, of whatever denomination, who loved the Lord Jesus in sincerity.'

He now attracted the attention of his bishop, Dr. Benson,
who sent for him, encouraged him with a fatherly interest,
and gave him five guineas, "when he had not a dollar in
the world." This dignitary made a rule to ordain no candidate for orders under twenty-three years of age, but
proposed to make Whitefield, although only twenty-one,
an exception, and urged him to enter the ministry. After
much self-examination and hesitancy he consented to accept
the bishop's offer. The evening before that appointed for
his ordination in the cathedral of Gloucester, he spent two
hours in prayer for himself and those who were to set
him apart to an office whose sacredness and responsibilities almost appalled him ; and rising early the next morning repeated the solitary communion with his Lord and
Redeemer. The light of the 20th of June, 1736, streamed
through the windows of the old cathedral upon the fair,
flushed, and spiritual face of the candidate for holy orders.
He records of the occasion : —

"I trust I answered every question from the bottom of
my heart, and heartily prayed that God might say ' Amen ! '
And when the bishop laid his hands upon my head, if my
vile heart do not deceive me, I offered up my whole spirit,
soul, and body to the service of God's sanctuary. Let come
what will, life or death, depth or height, I shall hencefor-
ward live like one who, this day, in the presence of men
and angels, took the holy sacrament upon the profession
of being inwardly moved by the Holy Ghost to take upon
me that ministration in the church. I call heaven and
earth to witness that, when the bishop laid his hands upon
me, I gave myself up to be a martyr for Him who hung

upon the cross for me. Known unto Him are all future events and contingencies. I have thrown myself blindfold, and I trust without reserve, into His Almighty hands. When I went up to the altar, I could think of nothing but Samuel's standing, a little child, before the Lord, with a linen ephod."

He declined a flattering call to a London parish, while he engaged with rare devotion to clerical duties among the poor and unlettered in Mr. Kinchin's charge at Dumner, as his assistant. But his heart was enlisted with holy enthusiasm in a pilgrimage to the American colony of Georgia, where two of his associates in the "Holy Club" had gone before him, whom he was invited to join.

While holding meetings before his departure, his experiences of the divine presence were so great that he says, " My soul would make such sallies that I thought it would go out of my body." He describes a terrific storm, when the thunder-peals filled with their reverberations the heavens, and the "lightning ran upon the ground," sending affrighted people from their beds, while he and a "poor, pious countryman were in the field, praying, praising, and exulting in God, and longing for that time when Jesus shall be revealed in a flame of fire." At Bristol he was thronged; the people "hung upon the rails, others climbed up the leads of the church, and all together the church was so hot with their breath that the steam would fall from the pillars like drops of rain." It was the same at Bath and other cities. But he also began to feel the discipline of persecution. Some of the clergy called him a "spiritual pickpocket, and others thought he made use of a charm to get the people's money." He was thus driven to more fervent prayer, spending whole nights in supplication and praise. What a spectacle was such apostolic zeal and success in a youth twenty-two years of age!

3

He embarked December 28, 1737, in the "Whita-ker," for the New World, making the ship's company his parish of devoted, fearless service for his Master. Less than a year he labored to establish an Orphan House in Georgia and to bring his countrymen and the natives to Christ, when, with comparatively small results, he returned to England to be ordained priest in the Church of England. This additional form of admission to clerical duties was extended to him by his bishop on Sunday, January 14, 1739. Wherever he preached the power of God was with him, and multitudes hung upon his lips. And now came the greatest trial, and, as it proved, the greatest blessing of his ministry, — the open conflict of the gospel with the traditions and formalism of the established church. The churches were closed against him in Bristol, whither he had gone to preach,— the beginning of similar troubles . everywhere with the established clergy. But prohibitions increased his popularity with the people. This desertion by his brethren determined him to resort to open-air preaching. In his own words, "I thought I might be doing the service of my Lord, who had a mountain for his pulpit and the heavens for his sounding-board, and who, when his gospel was refused by the Jews, sent his servants into the highways and hedges." He was no less tenacious of church order and decorum than Wesley; but God led them both to throw off ecclesiastical fetters and venture boldly upon a new method of the dispensation of a free gospel.

This co-worker with Whitefield, to whom the latter owed much of his own success, was more favored in his early history. John Wesley was born at Epworth, Lincolnshire, England, June 17, 1703, Old Style. His father, Samuel Wesley, was the rector of this parish, and his mother, Susanna Annesley, was the daughter of a leading Non-Conformist divine; she was very beautiful and highly educated. The system, thorough discipline, and religious nurture and general culture of her large family, numbering in all nineteen children, was very extraordinary, and probably never surpassed in a Christian household. And yet the rector, who had a mania for poetical composition, was always fighting 'the wolf from his door. He was imprisoned for debt, and died insolvent.

Susanna, by her independence and advanced position in service for Christ, came near sacrificing John. In the absence of her husband, she would open her doors for worship, conducted by herself. Even her husband protested against this innovation. She proposed to obey him if he commanded her to desist from a work which was greatly blessed, but others must continue it. Persecution followed; and to it was added repeated strokes of death and the crushing weight of debt. Twice was the incendiary fire kindled in the rectory, and the last time it was consumed. The family apparently escaped, when John was found in the burning dwelling. The flames beat back the agonized father, when the waking boy fled from his smoking bed to the window, and was taken from his place of peril by two peasants, one on the shoulders of the other, just as the roof fell in crushing the chamber to the earth. The glad father exclaimed, "Come, neighbors, let us kneel down; let us give thanks unto God! He has given me all my eight children! Let the house go, I am rich enough." He little dreamed that unborn millions would say to his grateful ascription, Amen.

It is a singular fact that Epworth Rectory should have been disturbed by the very "manifestations" which more than a century later founded the widely-extended system of a false revelation, — modern Spiritualism. The whistling of winds around the house when none were abroad, the clattering of windows, and the sounding of metallic furniture, opening of doors, etc., bewildered the inmates, as did similar exhibitions a hundred years before the people of Salem, until they executed their neighbors for witchcraft. For two months those sounds were heard and then died away, without any other result than the amusement of the family. No sufficient explanation was given of what the gifted and learned Isaac Taylor regarded as "neither celestial nor infernal, but extra-terrestrial intruding upon our sphere occasionally, as the Arabian locust is sometimes found in Hyde Park." This experience had evidently influence upon the character of John, in stimulating his faculty of belief, and preparing the way for the reception of phenomena, however mysterious, which wore the impress of divine power. He entered Christ Church College, Oxford, in 1720, at the age of sixteen. His brother Charles went to the Westminster School. While there Garret Wesley, of Ireland, related only by name, afterwards Baron Morrington, desired to adopt him. He declined the honor, and Richard Colley, who took it instead, became the grandfather of Marquis Wellesley, Governor-General of India, and of Duke of Wellington. This was an escape from worldly promotion to hymn-making and preaching, scarcely less suggestive than his brother's from the flames.

John now turned his inquiring thought to the doctrine of sanctification as taught in the Scriptures. His mother urged him to make an entire consecration to God. Here was the dawn of his "later doctrine of the witness of the Spirit," and at the same time, of divergence from the prevailing tenet of the "final perseverance of the saints."

Passing through great spiritual conflicts, he was soon after admitted to orders, preaching occasionally, and retaining his connection with Lincoln College, to which he had removed. He was conspicuous in the classics and in logic, shining in the daily disputations which were held. Still, such was his desire for tranquil thought to settle his

views and mental habits, he entertained the purpose of
seeking the life of a recluse, — a contrast surely to that of
the active service of the founder of Methodism. Returning to Oxford, he found congenial spirits, and the Holy
Club was soon followed by the epithet which is forever
embalmed in ecclesiastical history, — " Methodists," on
account of the rigid simplicity and system of the lives of
this small company of devout young men. John's father,
when dying at Epworth, earnestly desired him to be his
successor ; but already his eye looked over the sea to the
aborigines of the English possessions in America. He and
Charles, with Ingham and Delamotte, embarked October
14, 1735. On the same ship were twenty-six German
Moravians, whose wonderful experience of trust and peace
had a very great influence on the Wesleys, awakening afresh
the inquiry into "perfect peace"; especially so by their
joyful singing amid a storm which threatened to founder
the vessel and bring speedy death to all on board, followed
by the testimony they gave, and the following questions :
"Have you the witness within yourself? Does the Spirit
of God bear witness with your spirit that you are a child
of God?"

The mission to the Indians was a failure through
inexperience ; but a deeper insight into spiritual things
by both proved a divine preparation for future usefulness.

February 1, 1738, the Wesleys were again in England ;
and soon after John went to Herrnhut, — "Watch of the
Lord," — where the Moravian Brotherhood had settled on
the estate of Count Zinzendorf, a friend of God and His
people. After receiving a great blessing through these
simple yet intelligent Christians, he returned to England in
September, 1738, and immediately commenced preaching
to the little " societies " already formed in the metropolis,
and holding "love feasts," which were often "attended
with Pentecostal power." At length, conquering his

instinctive love of the established order of the church, he
listened to Whitefield's urgent call, and sounded the gospel
trumpet from the green hill-top at Kingswood, "crossing
the Rubicon" in the face of the frowning Church of England.   He was thenceforth to preach the gospel with
unfettered freedom, and addressed the gathering crowds
in cities and towns around London with marvellous effect.
May 12, 1739, he took a new and advanced position in his
career of independent religious organization, and laid the
corner-stone of the first Methodist chapel in the world at
Bristol.   Then followed the friendly separation from the
Moravians, with whom he had been so intimately associated, and the opening for regular public worship of the
foundery in Moorfields, — the future headquarters of the
new denomination in London.   Later came the controversy
with Whitefield on Calvinism, and necessarily their diver-
ging careers of usefulness.   The evangelistic itineracy and
successes of the Wesleys, and the spread of their doctrines
and polity, are familiar to all who have read the annals of
a branch of the church universal, unrivalled in its steady
and rapid prosperity from the date of its birth.

Lady Huntington, the daughter and wife of an earl, who
was born at Chartley in 1807, soon after her marriage, at
the age of twenty-one, became deeply anxious respecting
her religious state through the faithful words of Margaret
Hastings, a convert under Rev. Mr. Ingham, a most
earnest, fearless, and itinerating preacher, who "went
from town to town, from hamlet to hamlet, and house to
house preaching 'repentance towards God and faith towards
our Lord Jesus Christ.'"   So intense were the convictions
and protracted the struggles of Lady Huntington that she
was entirely prostrated, and lay in helpless terror at the
gates of death.   At length she cast herself on Jesus with
joyful faith, and sent immediately for the Wesleys.   From
that hour her mansion became the home — the hallowed

Nazareth—of these brothers when persecuted and despised, and later of Whitefield, and of their friends, Doddridge, Watts, and kindred spirits.

Said Doddridge, referring to the rising evangelists, " I cannot but think that, by the success of some of these despised men, God is rebuking the madness of those who think themselves the only wise men, and in a remarkable manner laying bare His mighty arm."

The Tabernacle, in which President Finney preached more than a century later, is worthy of special notice. Moorfields, where it was built, was just beyond the old city wall, — a marshy tract, on which the first brick of London was made, and which in the time of Whitefield was filled and graded into the City Mall for archery,— a resort of the sporting, riotous rabble. When, in April, 1739, the evangelist determined "to beard the lion in his den," and preach there, "many told him he would never come out of the place alive." He left his coach, with an escort which the surging crowd swept from him, but allowed him to pass till he reached the spot where a table had been crushed by the crowd, leaving him only a wall, which he mounted, and preached with subduing power. A weather-shed was erected by his dissenting friends, which in the summer of 1753 disappeared before the brick edifice, eighty feet square, holding four thousand people.

Standing in Kingswood with our evangelists, one hundred and thirty-six years ago, in the bright spring-time, with the verdure and bloom of an English landscape in the distance beyond the surging throng, the inquiry is natural and pertinent, What demand was there in the moral and spiritual condition of the people of a proud empire for this innovation upon the ordinary services and routine of the church? Why did God send these young men forth to awaken the sympathy or the hostility of millions in two hemispheres? A glance at the religious aspect of England will answer the questions, and pour a flood of light on a providential interposition which was as clearly such as the work of the great reformer when he went from a monk's cell to confront the hierarchy of Europe.

Ryle forcibly says, in his admirable lecture on White-field, " In forming your opinion of the comparative merits of Christian men, never forget the old rule, ' Distinguish between times.' Place yourself in each man's position."

Since the Reformation England had not seen, morally, a darker period. The formularies and services of the established church were observed, but the power of the gospel had disappeared. The clergy were, as a body, worldly and heartless in official duties. Corrupt litera-ture alone could command the principal place in court and castle. Shameless licentiousness was an accomplish-ment, and pure religion was scorned. Dissenters had shared with churchmen the common declension after per-secution ceased.

Doddridge and Watts preached and sang the " faith once delivered to the saints," and bewailed the increasing ungodliness which threatened to sweep away the fruits of Luther's mighty achievements for a decaying Christianity. The Georges successively fostered the irreligion and reek-ing immoralities, which not only disgraced the nobility but dishonored the very altars of God. Such universal profligacy and scepticism called for extraordinary men and means. Zion's rejected King had prepared both to vindi-cate his own glory and answer the prayers which rose from the elect few who had "not bowed the knee to Baal." We have followed these " divine links " in the preparatory dis-cipline and nurture of the young evangelists till they pro-claimed the despised truth from Mount Hannan, beneath the dome of unclouded light, to the wondering and awak-ened multitudes. Under Wesley, Methodism has become a mighty fact and force in the world, while the evangelist of two hemispheres, from the same spiritual movement, has entered fully upon his wonderful career.

August 14, 1739, Whitefield embarked again for America, taking with him, for his Orphan House, five thousand dollars, which the people had cheerfully contributed. He was nine weeks on the deep, landing at Philadelphia. The churches were immediately opened to him, and thronged; but he was soon compelled to make the "court steps his pulpit," from which, in the chill winds of November evenings, he unweariedly preached to the equally unwearied multitudes.

Among the hearers from a distance was the venerable Mr. Tennant, of Neshaminy, Penn., the father of Gilbert and William, all of them just the men for this crisis. They were gifted, fearless, and popular, and had suffered persecution. They entered heartily into Whitefield's views, visiting with him fields of harvest, and were themselves "sons of thunder." The sermons of Gilbert, who in another chapter will be noticed more at length, Mr. Whitefield warmly approved. He said: "Never before had I heard such searching sermons. I found what a *babe* and *novice* I was in the things of God."

Here again, with Whitefield on the threshold of his first American campaign among the churches, the inquiry is suggested, What was the religious condition of our own colonies, especially at the North, whose early settlers were the sifted seed of the Old-World churches, that made a great spiritual revolution necessary or possible? To answer the momentous question, we have only further to outline the marvellous achievements of him who, still adhering to the church of his fathers, went forth to restore with primitive power the office and work of the evangelist.

CHAPTER III.

THE GREAT AWAKENING IN NEW ENGLAND. — WHITEFIELD'S VISIT AND
LABORS. — EVANGELISTIC PASTORS. — EDWARDS. — THE TENNANTS. —
PARSONS WHEELOCK, POMEROY, BUEL, BARBER, DAVENPORT. — WHITE-
FIELD'S SECOND TOUR IN NEW ENGLAND. — OPPOSITION IN HIGH PLACES.
— PREVAILING CONVICTION. — HIS DEATH. — RESULTS. — LESSONS.

THE churches of the land, which, in the early part of
the eighteenth century, were largely Presbyterian, Congregational, and Episcopal, had generally, like those across
the sea, little spirituality. Revivals were comparatively
unknown. In New England were generally entertained the
ideas, common in Europe, that baptism made those who
were not guilty of immoralities communicants if they
desired the sacrament, while only church members could
vote or hold office, which views multiplied nominal believers, and made the ministry, to an alarming extent, powerless beyond the routine of parish duties and secular affairs.
A darker period has never been known, spiritually, in our
country, worldliness and frivolity prevailed, and the very
principles of the Puritans seemed to be departing from
their descendants.

Among the select few who communed with God, and
became alarmed at the threatening declension, was Dr.
Edwards, of Northampton, the gifted, scholarly, and logical theologian of his day. He began in 1734· to preach,
with the definite purpose of breaking up the lethargy of
the people, Luther's great message, "justification by faith
alone." He laid his massive blows upon the foundations
of false hope, — whether "outward morality, owning the

covenant and partaking the Lord's Supper, or any other
means of grace." The sinner's lost condition, his personal
guilt which left him justly at the sovereign mercy of God,
and his absolute dependence on the Holy Spirit, were proclaimed with searching clearness and fearless warning. Very
soon a change in the aspect of the people was visible. A
profound impression was made by the conversion of a young
lady, "notorious as a leader in scenes of gayety and rustic
dissipation." The work went on with tremendous power ;
"the noise among the dry bones waxed louder and
louder," and converts in and out of the church multiplied
till their number under his immediate ministry reached
three hundred. It was a marvellous thing amid the universal moral slumber and startled surrounding towns.
From them many flocked to Northampton to see what the
strange commotion meant, and returned to kindle the
celestial flame on their own altars. South Hadley, Suffield, Sunderland, Deerfield, Hatfield, and other places
caught the Pentecostal awakening, until it went over the
boundary of the present Commonwealth of Massachusetts
into Connecticut, sweeping through Lebanon, Durham,
Stratford, Ripton, and New Haven, and onward still to
towns beyond. New Jersey joined New England under
the preaching of the Tennants. The subjects of this widely
extended work were of all ages, "from the child of four
years to the man of seventy." The interest continued in
many places two years or more. Dr. Colman, of Boston,
wrote Dr. Edwards for an account of it, which he forwarded
to Drs. Watts and Guise in London.

In the wake of these revivals, which had blessed a number of important towns in the colonies now forming the
New England and Middle States, came to our shores
George Whitefield, by pre-eminence the evangelist. He
landed at Philadelphia in November, 1739. After preaching to thousands in the city surging around him wherever

he opened his lips to proclaim the gospel message, he visited with growing popularity, notwithstanding the hostility
of many church officials, the principal towns in that part
of Pennsylvania and also in New Jersey.

He was invited to New York, but the bishop's commis-
sary hastened in anger to refuse him the use of the house of
worship in his charge; for it must be borne in mind that
Mr. Whitefield was everywhere a recognized clergyman
of the Church of England, and naturally went to his own
denomination whenever received by them. Denied admission to the bishop's sanctuary, he resorted to the fields
or open lots, preaching to the crowds who flocked around
him. Returning to Philadelphia he sent his family forward
to Savannah by ship, and he set out by land, followed sixty
miles by people from that city. At Charleston, South
Carolina, he met both bitter opposition and cheering success. Pushing on to Savannah, he found old friends had
changed front on account of his irregular ministry in the
open air. But with singular equanimity for the yet youthful orator, he might be seen one day among the orphans
speaking to them tenderly, and superintending the building
of their "Bethesda"; and the next, with the spell of his
holy eloquence, holding the throng gathered beneath the
shade of Nature's earliest temples.

At length, enfeebled in health, his spirits depressed,
in consequence, he went to Newcastle on his way to the
North, where he preached two and three times daily for
two months. When he reached Philadelphia, the churches
were closed against him, and his clarion voice rang out
upon the free air of Him whose world-wide, redeeming
love was the message in its utterance often choked with
weeping. Praying circles multiplied, and a church was
organized.

A few months later he is again in Savannah, engaged
in his favorite charity, prostrated physically by the exces-

sive heat and varied toil for his ever-present Lord. At
this crisis he gladly accepted an invitation from Dr. Colman, of Boston, and other influential citizens, to visit the
land of the Puritans, whose character he greatly admired.

After preaching a farewell sermon to four thousand
people, he embarked for New England the latter part of
August. On Sunday, September 14, the ship was in sight
of the shores of Rhode Island, beating against a contrary
wind. Desiring to be in time for religious services at
Newport, he called together in the cabin the Christian
passengers to pray for this blessing and a place of entertainment. When they came on deck again the wind was
favorable, and the vessel glided in good time into the
harbor. Upon landing, Mr. Whitefield and his party
repaired to the sanctuary; and at the close of the exercises, a gentleman went directly to him and asked him if
his name was Whitefield, and then told him his party
would be provided with lodgings. After deeply interesting meetings in Newport he left for Boston, and was met
four miles out of the city by the governor's son and his
party of representative men. We have no space for even
a notice of the mighty movement here.

In Brattle Street place of worship; First Church and New
North, at the corner of Clark and Hanover Streets; Mr.
Checkley's, in Summer Street, where a panic from apprehended danger of a crash killed several, and drove the
throngs to the Common; in Roxbury; at Cambridge, where
he had seven thousand hearers; and then again in Boston,
where, with "most of the pastors, he dined with the governor, who invited him to his private apartment, and, weeping, wished him good success, and recommended himself,
ministers, and people, to his prayers"; at Charlestown,
where a "gracious melting was discernible through the
whole congregation"; then again, in Boston, he was the
same gospel magician, entrancing the people with the sim-

ple "truth as it is in Jesus." There was a repetition of like scenes at Marblehead, Salem, Ipswich, and Newbury, while contributions for his Orphan House poured into the treasury. Returning to Boston, with undiminished interest, he preached his farewell sermon in the New England metropolis upon the Common to *thirty thousand* persons, October 12, 1740. He says of his visit, "Boston people are dear to my soul. They were greatly affected by the Word, followed night and day, and were very liberal to my dear orphans."

He now journeyed to Northampton to meet Dr. Edwards. The governor, accompanying him in his own "coach to the ferry, blessed him, and with tears bade him farewell," only to intercept and join him at Marlborough and go in company with him to Worcester. His revival labors, and his communion with the leading mind of New England at Northampton, were memorable experiences in the life of the evangelist. They labored and wept together with sacred delight. The only ripple on the surface of the deeply-flowing tide of sympathy was the cautionary criticism of the pastor upon the danger of following impulses instead of divine impressions.

Whitefield had his usual success at Westfield, Springfield, Suffield, East Windsor, Middletown, Wallingford, New Haven, and other towns along the route to New York. He wrote in his journal very warmly of his tour in New England, which, he thought, "for the establishment of religion, exceeded all other parts of the world."

After very wonderful personal experiences of divine things, and scenes of conviction and conversion, he once more went by way of Charleston to Savannah, sailing for England January 24, 1741. He also went to Scotland, which he visited fourteen times. At Cambuslang, several miles from Edinburgh, on a "green brae," a natural amphitheatre, from all quarters gathered a multitude estimated as high as *fifty thousand* people, day after day, moved by the breath of the Spirit till sobs, prayers, and hymns were heard throughout the vast concourse, sometimes during all the night. The communion tables were spread for many hours, until *three thousand* had partaken of the sacred symbols.

We now leave Whitefield encountering opposition at home, having painful disagreements with Wesley, while both were advancing the common cause of Christ, and turn to the conflicting opinions in New England after his departure. The nervous affections, sometimes apparently contagious, attending the powerful effusions of the Holy Spirit, prostrating persons in helpless unconsciousness, and which had occurred in England and lately in Ireland, without any explanation beyond physical conditions peculiar to the times, together with the extravagances of some evangelists who entered the field, created decided and demonstrative opposition to Whitefield and his labors.

The most influential evil of this crisis was the career of Rev. James Davenport, of Southold, L. I., at first a favorite of Whitefield, and a zealous, successful evangelist. He at length fell into the same fatal mistake that the brilliant Edward Irving of England did, of making impressions his guide, and, under fancied revelations of the divine will, doing work for the adversary of God and man. He came to New England, declaring his power to discern unrenewed ministers, condemning such with censorious judgment, and depending for guidance upon visions and even dreams of the night. In New London, Connecticut, he marched at the head of a band of converts at night, shouting in the streets, "Come to Christ!" He was presumptuous, extravagant, and schismatic, yet evidently at heart a good man, as his humble confessions of Satanic delusion and human weakness very clearly indicated.

There were others, young men called "exhorters," who

entered the field of revival effort regardless of pastoral rights, and assumed leadership of religious activity to multiply converts. These outgrowths of an extraordinary spiritual revolution were incidental, and to be expected from the devil's agency wherever God shakes his kingdom of darkness, and the frailties and passions of men. The "Separatists," who went off from the half-way covenant churches, with all their irregularities, were almost a necessary reaction, and not an integral part of "the great awakening."

Two of New England's foremost colleges, through the action of their Faculties, condemned Whitefield as an enthusiast, and were sustained in their position by several distinguished pastors. Indeed, the division of opinion was wide-spread, although the great evangelist and orator had largely the confidence of the ministry and churches. It was made a grave charge that he sang hymns along the highway while passing from one town to another.

In Connecticut, laws against itinerancy were enforced, and devoted ministers were sent from parishes as vagrants; others were imprisoned. We now look back with amazement upon the bitter hostility of good men to the great movement which with all its attending defects was plainly the interposition of God to save his church from heartless formalism and set in motion divine forces felt to-day over the world.

There was one result of the grand movement which revealed the necessity of sound evangelists : it was the itinerancy of the settled pastors. Edwards, those "sons of thunder" the Tennants, Parsons, Wheelock, Pomeroy, Buel, and Barber went from one parish to another, and not unfrequently were absent for weeks, assisting their brethren in the harvest seasons of the Holy Ghost. The absence of any independent preachers of ability to supplement Whitefield drove these ministers into the waving fields, whose ripened grain must suffer infinite loss unless helpers came to the rescue.

With the additional experiences in England, Scotland, and Ireland, attempted assassination, and an atrocious assault in bed at Biddeford, Whitefield, enfeebled by his exhausting efforts, again embarked, August, 1744, for America. His glowing zeal made the ship his parish, where for eleven weeks he prayed for the crew and pointed them to the Lamb of God. He arrived at York, Maine, October 19, and was taken ashore dangerously ill. Providentially and happily his host was a physician, once a "noted sceptic, but now one of his spiritual children."

The greeting of Moody, the worthy minister, was characteristic and emphatic: "Sir, you are first, welcome to America; secondly, to New England; thirdly, to all faithful ministers in New England; fourthly, to all the good people in New England; fifthly, to all the good people of York; and lastly to me, dear sir, — less than the least of all." Whitefield next preached at Portsmouth, N. H., when apparently near death, by a wonderful dispensation of divine power, after which he was pronounced dead, but gradually recovered. The people were so moved that their cries and lamentations followed his almost lifeless form to the place of his abode.

November 24, very feeble, he reached Boston once more. He was soon preaching to such crowds, "you might have walked on the people's heads," in the principal churches of the city. But organized opposition began to appear, in the form of protests by associations, against his extempore preaching, itineracy, and his influence on the settled ministry. He was also accused of intemperate zeal and great egotism; published sermons by several prominent pastors condemned his work; with an apparent zeal for divine truth and order, they denounced Whitefield as an enthusiast and slanderer of his brethren.

4

Dr. Chauncy and Dr. Prince, of Boston, were arrayed against each other. In strength and numbers, the friends of the evangelist were largely in the majority.

While in the metropolis of New England occurred one of the most memorable scenes in his unexampled career, — perhaps never equalled in moral grandeur in any religious assembly before or since. While preaching in a crowded church, with his usual power, a blaze of lightning filled the house, followed by a thunder-clap, which rolled with deafening roar over the startled assembly. This was the prelude of a storm, which flamed and thundered amid the sudden night till the hushed assembly trembled before the terrific war of the elements. Mr. Whitefield kneeled by the desk, and with that majestic uplifting of his hands peculiar to him, with almost unearthly pathos and power, repeated : —

> " Hark ! the Eternal rends the sky !
>   A mighty voice before Him goes, —
>   A voice of music to His friends,
>   But threatening thunder to His foes.

> " Come, children, to your Father's arms !
>   Hide in the chambers of His grace
>   Till the fierce storm be overblown,
>   And the avenging fury cease."

Rising, he added, " Let us devoutly sing to the praise and glory of God this hymn in Old Hundred." The congregation rose, and for the moment drowned the echoing voice of the tempest with the sounding anthem, which moved the vast throng as a gale bows the green forest. The benediction fell with lofty simplicity upon their attentive ears as the blinding flashes grew fainter and the reverberations died away around the weeping, sobbing worshippers. Few were the words spoken by the agitated processions a moment later moving along the aisles towards the open doors.

The "Old South" has nothing more creditable in its historic records than the noble position taken upon the arrival of Mr. Whitefield with the gifted pastor, Dr. Prince. This excellent and conspicuous divine was the unwavering friend of the evangelist, and his pulpit was freely offered him, while his pen was mighty in the defence of the Lord's persecuted messenger.

Rev. Gilbert Tennant came to the assistance of the Boston pastors, after Mr. Whitefield's departure to make excursions to outlying towns, — in March, going as far as Berwick, Maine, and then to Exeter, New Hampshire. Whitefield went to Georgia, but was again in Boston the following July, and the succeeding month went to Philadelphia, and itinerated in the Middle and Southern States till March, 1748, when he sailed for Bermuda to re-establish his health. He arrived in England in June. Six years later he revisited New England; again in 1764; and in 1770 made his last tour in the colonies there. On Saturday, September 29, he rode from Portsmouth to Exeter, where, when told he looked more fit to go to bed than preach, he replied, "True, sir!" then clasping his hands together and looking upward, he said, "Lord Jesus, I am weary *in* Thy work, but not *of* Thy work. If I have not yet finished my course, let me go and speak for Thee once more in the fields, seal Thy truth, and come home and die." He died at Newburyport from asthmatic suffocation at 6 o'clock, A. M., September 30, 1770, more generally and deeply mourned than perhaps any preacher of the Word in any age of the world. The epitaph on his monument at Newburyport, where he desired to be buried, is a condensed history of his life, labors, and death.

𝕿𝖍𝖎𝖘 𝕮𝖊𝖓𝖔𝖙𝖆𝖕𝖍

Is erected, with affectionate veneration,

𝕿𝖔 𝖙𝖍𝖊 𝕸𝖊𝖒𝖔𝖗𝖞

OF

THE REV. GEORGE WHITEFIELD,

Born at Gloucester, England, December 16, 1714.
Educated at Oxford University ; ordained 1736.
In a Ministry of Thirty-four Years,
He crossed the Atlantic Thirteen times,
And preached more than Eighteen Thousand Sermons.
As a Soldier of the Cross, humble, devout, ardent,
He put on the whole Armor of God,
Preferring the Honor of Christ to his own Interest, Repose,
Reputation and Life.
As a Christian Orator, his deep Piety, disinterested Zeal, and
Vivid Imagination,
Gave unexampled Energy to his look, utterance, and action.
Bold, fervent, pungent, and popular in his Eloquence,
No other uninspired man ever preached to so large assemblies,
Or enforced the simple Truths of the Gospel by Motives
So persuasive and awful, and with an influence so powerful,
On the Hearts of his Hearers.

HE DIED OF ASTHMA, SEPTEMBER 30, 1770,

Suddenly exchanging his Life of unparalleled Labors

FOR HIS ETERNAL REST.

Dr. McFarland, in his records of the wonderful scenes at Cambuslang, warmly adds of the great orator for the Master, "England gave him birth, America retains his bones, and one of Scotland's best men had the honor to write his life."

The wonder has been expressed that George Whitefield did not raise the protest of his eloquent appeal against slavery. The subject was not discussed in the colonies, and its future extension and overshadowing influence in politics unthought of by the people. His absorbing object, to which God called him, was a religious revolution, attended with no less opposition and persecution than was the cause of antislavery nearly a century later. He was the Luther of modern revivals. It was his great work and honor to restore Pentecostal faith in the Holy Ghost to the churches.

George Whitefield's grand success was in the pulpit. To this was he called. His personal counsels were given as he had opportunity, and were wisely adapted to the states of mind among inquirers after truth; but he had little time for these details of Christian labor. His high employment, for which he was pre-eminently qualified by natural endowments and divine graces, was to sway, in the name and love of Christ, vast audiences, and through these stir continents upon the one commanding concern, human salvation.

However glorious the power and its achievements, how could it be otherwise than that manifold elements, from the highest to the lowest, in awakened thought and feeling, should come into a movement of so great extent and of such revolutionary force?

Writes a biographer : "There was nothing in the appearance of Whitefield which would lead you to suppose that a Felix could tremble before him. He was something above the middle stature, well proportioned, and remarkable for a native gracefulness of manner. His complexion was very fair, his features regular, and his dark blue eyes small and lively; in recovering from the measles he had contracted a squint with one of them; but this peculiarity rather rendered the expression of his countenance more rememberable than in any degree lessened the effect of its uncommon sweetness. His voice excelled both in melody and compass; and its fine modulations were happily accompanied by that grace of action which he possessed in an eminent degree, and which has been said to be the chief requisite for an orator. To have seen him when he first commenced, one would have thought him anything but enthusiastic and glowing; but as he proceeded, his heart warmed with his subject, and his manner became impetuous and animated, till, forgetful of everything around him, he seemed to kneel at the throne of Jehovah, and to beseech in agony for his fellow-beings.

"On one occasion after he had finished his prayer, he knelt for a long time in profound silence; and so powerfully had it affected the most heartless of his audience, that a stillness like that of the tomb pervaded the whole house. Before he commenced his sermon, long, darkening columns crowded the bright, sunny sky of the morning, and swept their dull shadows over the building in fearful augury of the storm.

" His text was, 'Strive to enter in at the strait gate; for many, I say unto you, shall seek to enter in, and shall not be able.' 'See that emblem of human life,' said he, pointing to a shadow that was flitting across the floor. 'It passed for a moment, and concealed the brightness of heaven from our view; but it is gone. And where will you be, my hearers, when your lives have passed away like that dark cloud? O my dear friends, I see thousands sitting attentive, with their eyes fixed on the poor, unworthy preacher. In a few days we shall all meet at the judgment seat of Christ. We shall form a part of that vast assembly that will gather before the throne; and every eye will behold the judge. With a voice whose call you must abide and answer, he will inquire whether on earth you strove to enter in at the strait gate; whether you were supremely devoted to God; whether your hearts were absorbed in him. My blood runs cold when I think how many will then seek to enter in, and shall not be able. Oh, what plea can you make before the Judge of the whole earth? Can you say it has been your whole endeavor to mortify the flesh, with its affections and lusts? that your life has been one long effort to do the will of God? No! you must answer, I made myself easy in the world by flattering myself that all would end well; but I have deceived my own soul, and am lost.

"'You, O false and hollow Christian! of what avail will it be that you have done many things; that you have read much in the sacred Word; that you have made long prayers; that you have attended religious duties, and appeared holy in the eyes of men? What will all this be, if, instead of loving Him supremely, you have been supposing you should exalt yourself in heaven by acts really polluted and unholy?'

"'And you, rich man, wherefore do you hoard your silver? wherefore count the price you have received for Him whom you every day crucify in your love of gain? Why, that, when you are too poor to buy a drop of cold water, your beloved son may be rolled to hell in his chariot pillowed and cushioned around him.'

"His eye gradually lighted up, as he proceeded, till, towards the close, it seemed to sparkle with celestial fire.

"'O sinners!' he exclaimed, 'by all your hopes of happiness, I beseech you to repent. Let not the wrath of God be awakened. Let not the fires of eternity be kindled against you. See there!' said he, pointing to the lightning which played on the corner of the pulpit. ''Tis a glance from the angry eye of Jehovah! Hark!' continued he, raising his finger in a listening attitude, as the distant thunder grew louder and louder, and broke in one tremendous crash over the building. 'It was the voice of the Almighty as he passed by in his anger.'

"As the sound died away, he covered his face with his

hands, and knelt beside his pulpit, apparently lost in inward and intense prayer. The storm passed rapidly away, and the sun, bursting forth in his might, threw across the heavens a magnificent arch of peace. Rising and pointing to the beautiful object he exclaimed, ' Look upon the rainbow, and praise Him that made it. Very beautiful it is in the brightness thereof. It compasseth the heavens about with glory, and the hands of the Most High have bended it.' The effect was astonishing; many shaded their eyes when he pointed to the lightning, and knelt as they listened to the approaching thunder, and some burst into a flood of tears."

However remarkable were the outward elements of Whitefield's popularity, — the fine form and face, the graceful gesture and pathos, — that he possessed also the mental and moral qualities for the highest oratory is evident, not only from the fact that the throngs including every rank never tired of his eloquence, but the testimony of such critical hearers as Hume, Lords Chesterfield and Bolingbroke, and the pre-eminently observing and practical Franklin. The principal sources of his unequalled success as a preacher were his consecration to soul-saving, his prayerfulness, the pure gospel he declared, the simple and lucid style of delivery, the boldness and directness of his appeals, his marvellous vividness of description, and his " thundering earnestness." We add an illustration of his word-painting which some of our readers will recollect to have heard. He was describing the lost sinner under the figure of a blind, wandering beggar whom even his guiding dog had left to the darkness of night, among pitfalls and precipitous steeps; and he made so lifelike his unconscious approach to the edge of the abyss that when he reached it, Lord Chesterfield, who listened spell-bound, exclaimed audibly, " He's gone ! he's gone ! " Like his Master while in the flesh, he had, besides this graphic delineation, unrivalled facility in the illustrative use of natural phenomena and incidents of daily life. And yet he was self-forgetful, self-denying, unostentatious, and catholic in spirit. Sometimes, it is true, he erred in judgment and manner, and showed, as in his not very courteous letter on Arminianism to Wesley, consciousness of power and success : in other words, he was not exempt from the frailties of our common humanity. It is enough to say that, while Wesley, in his chosen path of usefulness, has no rival, George Whitefield, the chief of evangelists, has had no peer as a popular orator in the ministry of God's grace towards men.

The number of conversions in New England, during less than three years, was estimated at fifty thousand, with an augmentation of one hundred and fifty Congregational Churches, besides a corresponding accession to the Presbyterian body. The Baptists also were largely increased in membership. The ingathering of more than a million of souls now would not be a greater work of grace, in proportion to the number of inhabitants from which they were taken.

The clergy, who, on account of the prevailing laxness in discipline and in the terms of admission to the churches, and also in the required qualifications for ordination, were to an alarming extent unconverted. The undeniable fact was doubtless too severely handled by Whitefield, the Tennants, and less gifted, erratic itinerants. Nor is it strange if, in such a spiritual revolution, there was often rashness and errors of judgment amid conflicting forces. "But what is the chaff to the wheat, saith the Lord?" And who now in the church of Christ does not smile at the unbelief that feared and prophesied disaster to Christianity in America, and indeed all over the earth, from the irregularities, measures, and controversies of 1742 and the few subsequent years? "We forget that the powers of darkness are entirely under the control of the Father

of lights, and are permitted to make no movement which
He will not overrule for the advancement of His cause."

The serious mistake, it seems to us, on the part of those
who criticised and condemned the whole movement, was
in not waiting in faith and holy love upon God, whose
cause alone was concerned, and who has promised wisdom
to realize the largest blessing possible, while they guarded
with patience and discriminating charity against evil results. It is not enough that men act conscientiously, to
make them safe in their judgment of means which the
Holy Spirit deigns to attend with His renewing energy:
they need to lay aside previous conclusions formed by
education and pride of position, and, with self-forgetful
consecration, to inquire of God, who is never troubled
about the issue of any crisis in the affairs of His kingdom and does not require us to be. There is deep meaning in the prophetic rule of Christian conduct, — "He
that believeth shall not make haste." When the agency
is clearly not of the Lord, and the good done is merely
incidental, He will not leave his humble and trustful
ones in doubt; and the course adopted will command the
sober second thought of the people, whatever the first
impressions. How clearly was this true of the "Great
Awakening"! How steadily the hostility, sometimes passionate, died away before the seals of Jehovah's presence
and glory in it! Nor can we question that, if all religious
persons, especially the ministers, had prostrated themselves
before the Lord and sought with singleness of purpose to
know His will, and have His interposing grace and providence defeat the devices of Satan, still greater blessings
would have been bestowed, and poignant regrets spared
many of the servants of Christ.

We have repeated the history of the days of Whitefield
because of the light it sheds upon the whole question of
evangelism, and all succeeding estimates of its place and

value in the aggressions of Zion. For while, as already suggested, unmistakably bad tendencies in revival efforts, when they exist, should be resisted, the past shows us that timidity, love of peace, of ease, and self-assertion in interfering with the methods of the divine working, are the greater dangers.

Theological dogmas and ecclesiasticism; moulding habits of thoughts and feeling, have quite as often refused to follow the Spirit as mere enthusiasm has gone before. Among the most unpopular divisions of that day, the Separatists, whatever erratic action attended their movements, contributed strength to the advancing kingdom of our Lord by holding forth the true test of communion. The Presbyterian ministry, in Pennsylvania and Delaware alone, had nearly doubled, and the number of churches increased in about the same ratio. The increase of population in the colonies had some share in this growth. But the latter fact is more than balanced by the number of conversions in the churches, the large percentage of those who went to the Lord's table upon the easy terms of the " half-way covenant," acknowledging the privileges of believers and maintaining lives free from scandal. Not a few ministers were renewed, while the additions to the number of students worthily preparing to preach were considerable. A fatal blow was given to the doctrine that an unconverted ministry was consistent or to be allowed.

Can any one doubt that a similar division of opinion, counsel, and action would attend a work, now universally acknowledged to be of God, and fraught with blessings scarcely less precious in results of their kind than the Reformation under Luther, were it to appear again in New England? We think not. Good men even would be alarmed at both the human and Satanic manifestations incidental to a movement so deep and of such magnitude, and for the time believe the evils to be far greater than any possible good.   So natural is it to magnify immediate effects, which our judgment condemns, and stretch forth our hands to steady the ark of God, when jostled before our finite gaze, as if we were called upon to save it from an inglorious fall, when the same power that permitted the oscillations has appointed their limitations.

CHAPTER IV.

Co-workers with Whitefield, and His Successors in Evangelistic Labors. — The Tennants. — Rev. Samuel Finley, d. d. — Rev. William Robinson.

WE think that next to Whitefield in power and success among the leading human agencies which were visible in the " Great Awakening " of the last century, the Rev. Gilbert Tennant will have a place in history. He was the son of Rev. William Tennant, who was educated at Trinity College, Dublin, became an Episcopal clergyman in 1706, and later chaplain to an Irish nobleman. He emigrated to this country about 1716, when Gilbert was twelve years of age. After a brief pastorate in the province of New York he removed to Bucks County, Pennsylvania, and was pastor of the Presbyterian Church at Neshaminy, where he established the famous " Log College." The school received this name from its enemies because of the architecture of the building, humble pretensions as a private enterprise, and yet high standard of culture. It was the first Presbyterian institution in America whose special object it was to train young men for the ministry, and was the germ of the well-known College of New Jersey.

Gilbert studied with his father, finishing his course at the time the plan of the school was fully matured, and was immediately officially connected with it.

An extract from Mr. Whitefield's journal affords an interesting glimpse of the Tennant family at Neshaminy, and their relation to the great revival movement in our

land. "At my return home from visiting a family, was
much comforted by the coming of one Mr. Tennant, an old
gray-headed disciple and soldier of Jesus Christ. He
keeps an academy about twenty miles from Philadelphia,
and has been blessed with four gracious sons, three of
which have been, and continue to be, eminently useful in
the church of Christ. He brought three pious souls along
with him, and rejoiced me by letting me know how much
they had been evil spoken of for their Master's sake. He
is a great friend of Mr. Erskine of Scotland, and, so far
as I can learn, both he and his sons are secretly despised
by the generality of the synod, as Mr. Erskine and his
friends are hated by the judicatories of Edinburgh, and as
the Methodists preachers (as they are called) are by their
brethren in England."

Dr. Archibald Alexander adds, "This testimony of Mr.
Whitefield, the celebrated evangelist, whose popularity
and success have never been equalled by any other, goes
to show that the course pursued by old Mr. Tennant and
his sons was different from that of other ministers of the
synod, to whom he stood in the same relation as Whitefield, Wesley, and their coadjutors to the great body of
the clergy in England."

When George Whitefield left Boston, in 1740, Dr.
Alexander says, "He persuaded and urged Mr. Gilbert
Tennant to make a preaching tour through New England,
as far as Boston, to water the good seed which he had
sown by his preaching on his late visit. At that time
there was but little intercourse between the Middle and
Eastern Colonies ; and no ecclesiastical connection between
the Presbyterian and Congregational Churches. Among
Mr. Whitefield's opposers were reckoned, both in this
country and in Great Britain, a majority of the clergy
and professors of religion ; thus verifying the words of
our Lord, 'If they have persecuted me, they will also

persecute you; if they have kept my sayings, they will keep yours also.'"

Mr. Tennant, inflamed with a very ardent zeal, set off in the depth of winter to preach to a strange people, among whom he probably had not a single acquaintance. Mr. Whitefield made no journeys without several attendants, men who cheerfully ministered unto him, as did Timothy and Luke and Silas and Mark and others to Paul. But Mr. Tennant appears to have gone on his self-denying evangelical tour alone. He reached Boston December 13, 1740, and for nearly three months preached daily with extraordinary power and success. Dr. Prince gave him a cordial welcome to his pulpit, and has recorded in his "Christian History" his own views of the noble stranger's preaching. "It was both terrible and searching. It was for matter justly terrible, as he, according to the inspired oracles, exhibited the dreadful holiness, justice, law-threatenings, truth, power, and majesty of God, and his anger with rebellious, impenitent, and Christless sinners; the awful danger they were in every moment of being struck down to hell, and damned forever with the amazing miseries of that place of torment. By his arousing and scriptural preaching, deep and pungent convictions were wrought in the minds of many hundreds of persons in that town, and the same effect was produced in several scores in the neighboring congregations. And now was such a time as we never knew. The Rev. Mr. Cooper was wont to say that more came to him in one week, in deep concern, than in the whole twenty-four years of his preceding ministry. I can say also the same as to the numbers who repaired to me. Mr. Cooper had about six hundred different persons to visit him on the concerns of their souls, in three months' time. And Mr. Webb, another of the pious Boston ministers, informs me he has had in the same space above a thousand."

Rev. Dr. Finley, after expatiating on the learning, heroic character, and intelligent, glowing zeal of Mr. Tennant, writes of his sermons, "As Mr. Tennant's preaching was very alarming and awakening to careless sinners, so it was much blessed to this end wherever he preached. And it was not only rendered effectual in producing conviction of sin and exciting desires to flee from the wrath to come, but also to comfort mourners in Zion, and to encourage the timid and diffident. The atoning blood of the Redeemer, that only sovereign balsam, was applied to their recent or festering wounds. For while at one time, when he thundered the terrors of the law, the heavens seemed to gather blackness and a tempest of wrath appeared to be hurled on the heads of the guilty, at other times, when he exhibited the riches of the grace and provisions of the gospel, the heavens seemed to smile, the clouds were dispelled, and the sky became serene. The Almighty God was shown to be their refuge, and underneath were the everlasting arms. Then his exhilarating words dropped upon them as dew."

Mr. Tennant's own account to Mr. Whitefield of his labors is brief and interesting : —

"Dear Brother, — On my return I have been preaching daily ; ordinarily three times a day, and sometimes oftener ; and through pure grace have met with success much exceeding my expectations. In the town of Boston, there are many hundreds, if not thousands, as some have judged, under soul-concern. When I left the place, many children were deeply affected about their souls and several had received consolation. Some aged persons in church communion and some open opposers were convinced. Divers young and middle-aged were converted, and several negroes. The concern was rather more general in Charlestown. In Cambridge also, in the town and in the college, the shaking among dry bones was general."

He names over twenty towns into which the revival extended. In New Haven, including the college, these scenes were repeated, students coming " on foot twenty miles to hear the Word of God." At Milford thousands were awakened. Mr. Tennant exclaims, "Glory to God on high ! I thank you, sir, that you did excite me to this journey." He then refers to the success of his brother William, at Burlington, N. J., and Mr. Robinson in " New York government," and to the spreading interest in the Connecticut Colony under Mr. Mills, Mr. Blair in Pennsylvania, and Mr. Cross on Staten Island.

The Tennants were a remarkable family, felt in their generation beyond our possible appreciation at this distance. They were the " right-hand men " of George Whitefield in the Middle States, as Dr. Prince and Dr. Edwards were in New England. Without these mighty defenders and co-laborers, it is difficult to see how he could have had more than a partial success. Mr. Tennant's position in regard to revivals, and ministerial qualifications in connection with them, brought him into an intensely bitter conflict with his synod, ending in its division. That he was too sweeping and uncharitable in some of his denunciations cannot be doubted ; but he was also a mighty man in saving souls. After visiting England in 1753-4, he was settled in Philadelphia, where, changing his manner of preaching without notes to written sermons, he lost much of his power. He calmly and triumphantly died there in 1764, in his sixty-second year.

Rev. Samuel Finley, D. D., born in the County of Armagh, Ireland, was one of seven brothers, all of whom became godly men. His parents were of Scotch descent. He came to this country September, 1734, and subsequently entered the " Log College." He was licensed in 1740, and became a zealous, wise, and greatly useful evangelist. He labored in West Jersey ; in Connecticut,

5

where, at New Haven, he was seized as a vagrant under
the statute against itinerants, and carried beyond the colonial limits; and finally settled, in 1744, at Nottingham,
Maryland. Here he established a school of similar character to the "Log College," which sent forth a constella-
tion of distinguished men. In 1761 he was President of
New Jersey College. His death, which occurred July
16, 1766, in his fifty-first year, was one of the most triumphant on record. Among his exultant expressions were
those to Rev. Elihu Spencer, who said to him, "I have
come, dear sir, to see you confirm by facts the gospel you
have been preaching. Pray, sir, how do you feel?" He
replied, "Full of triumph! I triumph through Christ.
Nothing clips my wings but the thoughts of my dissolu-
tion being prolonged. O that it were to-night! My very
soul thirsts for eternal rest." He was asked what he saw
in eternity to excite such vehement desires. "I see the
eternal love and goodness of God. I see the fulness of the
Mediator. I see the love of Jesus. Oh, to be dissolved
and be with Him!"

Dr. Finley was a coadjutor of the Tennants in carrying forward the spiritual revolution which saved a powerful branch of Zion from hopeless formalism, and in
moulding the character of his generation and that which
followed him.

Rev. William Robinson, another evangelist who studied
at "Log College," was the son of a wealthy English Qua-
ker, and came to America when a young man. But little
is known of his early history. The immediate cause of
his conversion was an evening ride under a magnificent
sky, which flooded the rural scene around him with its
glory. Conscience inquired of his admiring thought,
"What do you know of this God? Have you ever sought
His favor or made Him your friend?" The question drew
him to Christ, the refuge for his soul. After finishing his

course of studies, he was licensed by the presbytery of New Brunswick as an evangelist. He at once turned his attention to the neglected places, — the dispersed settlements of Presbyterians in the States south of New Jersey.

The Presbyterians from the north of Ireland, compelled by the hostile incursions of the Indians to fly from their first settlements on the frontier of Pennsylvania, went to western Virginia and North Carolina. Whole congregations with their ministers had removed. This wild region was Mr. Robinson's chosen field, into which he entered with apostolic devotion, heroism, and success. Threatened by the civil authorities because an itinerant, but allowed by the kind-hearted sheriff to go on his way, he became a "bright and a shining light" amid the darkness upon the southern borders. He achieved a glorious work for Christ in extending there the "Great Awakening."

Says Dr. Alexander, "Probably Mr. Robinson, during the short period of his life, was the instrument in the conversion of as many souls as any minister who ever lived in this country. The only circumstance relating to his person which has come down to us is that he was blind of one eye, so that by some he was called 'the one-eyed Robinson.'" The circumstances of his death are unknown.

These noble, self-denying men, suffering persecution even among Christian people, were not alone in their holy labors and trials of faith for the advancement of the greatest, grandest movement of the century, a movement without which the whole aspect of the civil and martial conflict which followed would have been greatly changed. Nor may we affirm that the final triumph of liberty could have been secured without the moral force and the power of prayer which was given by it to the people of the Colonies. Names not a few, on the Lord's roll of honor, will not be known to the world until their hastening coronation day.

CHAPTER V.

The "tidal wave" of religious interest which attended the preaching of the evangelists of the eighteenth century subsided before that of the rising political conflict between the Colonies and the royal usurpation of the home government, which at length swept them into a long and sanguinary war. The decade of years which followed the proclamation of peace were dark with moral decadence, and yet, to clear-eyed Faith, brightened with signs of preparation for God's appearing in behalf of Zion. The disbanded armies and French infidelity together poisoned nearly every community. In the West and South, over large sections, "there was no other vestige of the Christian religion than a faint observance of Sunday, and that merely as a day of rest for the aged and a play-day for the young"; on the other hand, on the borders, lawless Indians and "renegade white men" kept the settlers in perpetual alarm; and the entire population of the new republic had passed through the discipline of eight years of bloodshed, with their trials, anxieties, and mourning.

The great experiment of freedom, amid conflicting views and interests, made thoughtful people feel that the "God of armies" alone who had given them the victory, could garner for future generations its precious fruits. The

intrigues of infidel politicians thickened around even
Washington, and without the interposition of the God of
the fathers, the fate of their emancipated children had a
clouded future. The religious outlook, while the shouts of
"Independence now and forever!" were ringing over the
fresh graves of the fallen in freedom's battles, was dismal
indeed; religion and morality, which the nation's chieftain, in his farewell address, affirmed were its "indispensable supports," were never at a lower ebb.

There were professionally no evangelists, nor could that
period produce them. The churches were many of them
decimated by war, and had sunk into unaggressive apathy.
There were no "schools of the prophets"; no Whitefield
or Wesley to come to the rescue from England chafing
against the humiliating decision of the "arbitration of the
sword" in the settlement of her colonial difficulties.

But the time had arrived when the comparatively few of
the "seed of Jacob," the wrestler, prevailed in prayer. God
must employ the only means possible, without a miraculous
interposition, to gather a harvest for His kingdom. We
shall briefly sketch some of the wonderful scenes of this
second mighty work of God, mainly in the South, as the
first was at the North. It will be seen that the pastors
were compelled to do the work of evangelists, and the
churches to resort to unusual means and measures, while
they were attended with outbursts of feeling even beyond
the exciting manifestations of Whitefield's time.

And yet the revival, in which "protracted meetings" had
their origin, were warmly approved by the presbyteries
and synods of the influential and conservative denomination within whose bounds the interest largely prevailed.
It is a singular fact that, in the awakening which went over
the North and South, a quarter of a century later, when
again the evangelist was a conspicuous instrumentality,
similar measures and emotional demonstrations of much

milder form should awaken in the same and other denominations very decided opposition, both in churches and
their representative ecclesiastical bodies.

From 1778, when Joseph Patterson, a layman, "whose
zeal had not waned in the storm and terrors of war," was
the means employed by the Spirit to bless the inmates of
Fort Vance with a precious harvest of souls, occasionally similar seasons were enjoyed in the country, especially
in Pennsylvania. The effect of these is apparent in the
"Report of the Committee of the Washington County
Presbytery" on the mighty movement which distinguished
the dawn of the nineteenth century : —

"About the latter end of the year 1801 and beginning
of 1802, there was a remarkable attendance upon ordinances ; meetings for the worship of God, both public and
social, were generally crowded, and there appeared an increasing attention to the Word and great solemnity in the
assemblies. The people of God became more sensible of
and affected with the low state of religion, and the dangerous, perishing condition of sinners. It appeared that God
made use of the intelligence we had of the revival of religion in other places to excite a longing and praying for the
Lord's returning with power to our languishing churches,
that we might experience the displays of his power.

"In the month of September, 1802, the Lord began in
a glorious manner to show His stately steppings in the sanctuaries of His grace. At several sacramental occasions in
that month there were considerable evidences of the gracious presence of God and of the operations of His Holy
Spirit. But the first extraordinary manifestations of the
divine power were made in the congregation of the Three
Springs, part of the charge of the Rev. Elisha Macurdy,
at the time of the administration of the Lord's Supper, on
the fourth Sabbath of September, 1802. Christians had
entered into an agreement to spend a certain time, about

sun-setting, on each Thursday, in secret prayer, each by himself, to plead with God for His gracious presence and the outpouring of His Spirit on that occasion. This was done for some weeks before the Sacrament. On the Sabbath immediately preceding the communion there was considerable evidence of the powerful presence of God, particularly towards the close of the afternoon sermon. When the congregation was dismissed, about fifty persons continued upon the ground, appeared unwilling to go away, and spent the most of the night in social worship.

"The last Saturday in the month was a time of gracious influences; many more were brought under concern. Most of that night was spent in social worship, and the work remarkably increased until Monday morning. When the congregation was dismissed, some hundreds remained; several attempts were made to part, but all in vain. They remained all night on the ground; and this night far exceeded any that had been before. About the break of day on Tuesday morning there were six persons who gave evidence of obtaining hope in Jesus. About eleven o'clock the assembly dispersed. On the Thursday following, the people of the Cross Road congregation, the other part of Mr. Macurdy's charge, met for social worship, it being their monthly society day. This was also a time of God's power. There were many instances of new awakening. They continued all the night in religious exercises.

"On Tuesday, the 5th of October, 1802, the day of concerted prayer, the Lord appeared, by the powerful operation of the Spirit, in the congregation of Cross Creek, the charge of the Rev. Thomas Marquis. The people were solemn and attentive through the day, and in the evening, when dismissed, they appeared backward to go away. After part were gone and many standing about the doors, one of the elders who was in the house went to the door and spoke a few words respecting their situation, and in a

few minutes the young people were all in tears. They
then joined in singing a hymn and in prayer. By this time
some of those who had gone away returned. They went
all again into the house, candles were brought, and the
night was spent in prayer, conversation, and praise, until
two o'clock in the morning. During this time many cried
out in the anguish of their souls, bitterly lamenting their
misimprovement of time and abuse of mercies. On
another occasion when the congregation was dismissed the
effects of God's power more visibly appeared. Many then
cried out in great agony of soul; many more expressed
their concern by a desire of social worship that night, in
which they were gratified. The exercises of prayer and
praise, with frequent exhortations, continued the whole
night, except two short intervals spent in conversation with
the distressed This was a very solemn season; the people were almost universally bowed, while some appeared
to be on the brink of despair. A goodly number, who since
that time have been admitted to the table of the Lord, have
dated their first deep and abiding convictions from that
season. It was a night to be had in everlasting remem-
brance, for which it is hoped many will praise God eter-
nally. At this time some began to speak the language of
Canaan with solemn, sweet serenity of mind, and in
heavenly, heart-affecting accents.

"On the Sabbath, the tenth day of October, 1802, the
Lord's Supper was administered at the charge of the Rev.
Joseph Patterson. As many as the house could contain
attended to social worship and preaching throughout the
night. Divine worship was also carried on a considerable
part of the night at the tent. Many new awakenings took
place through the night, and the social exercises continued
until the public worship began on Monday. Through this
day many more were made to cry out in agony of soul,
unable to sit or stand; some of them, very notorious in

vanity and profanity, were struck to the ground, and con-
strained to cry out aloud in bitter anguish of soul, 'Undone!
undone! forever undone!'

"The last Sabbath in October the Lord's Supper was
administered at Cross Roads. A great multitude of people
collected; many from a great distance, accommodated with
provisions to continue on the ground during the whole of
the solemnity. There were thirty-two wagons On Sabbath day and night there was much rain and snow; yet the
people mostly continued at the place night and day until
Tuesday morning.

"Ministers still preached successively in the house
throughout the day. Prayers and exhortations were continued all night in the meeting-house, except at short intervals, when a speaker's voice could not be heard for the
cries and groans of the distressed.

"On Monday three ministers preached at different places,
one in the house and two out in the encampments. This
was a very solemn day, particularly in the house. After
public worship was concluded and the people were preparing to remove, the scene was very affecting. The house was
thronged full, and when some of those without were about
to go away, they found that part of their families were in
the house, and some of them lying in distress, unable to
remove. This prevented a general removal; and though
a number went away the greater part remained. About
the time of the departure of those who went away, the
work became more powerful than it had been at any time
before, and numbers who had prepared to go were con-
strained to stay. It was a memorable time of the displays
of divine power and grace through the whole night. Many
of the young people were remarkably exercised, and frequently addressed others about the perishing condition
they were in, the glories of the Saviour, the excellency
and suitableness of the plan of salvation, and warned,

invited, and pressed sinners to come to Christ, — all this in a manner quite astonishing for their years. Numbers of old experienced Christians also were particularly exercised, were much refreshed and comforted, and affectingly recommended the Lord Jesus and his religion to those around them. About sunrise, after a time of solemn, sweet exercise, the congregation was dismissed, and soon after dispersed.

"On Saturday, the thirteenth day of November, 1802, a greater concourse of people than had ever been seen before at a meeting for divine worship in this country assembled at Upper Buffalo meeting-house, in the congregation of the Rev. John Anderson, and formed an encampment in a semicircle around the front of the tent, in a shady wood. The greater part had by this time learned from experience the necessity of coming prepared to encamp on the ground during the solemnity, as so many persons in distress could not be removed to lodgings in the evening ; nor could such a multitude be accommodated in a neighborhood of the most hospitable inhabitants, taking all home to lodgings. On this occasion it would have required one hundred houses, with perhaps one hundred persons to each house. But the people had been so engaged that they were not disposed to separate in the evenings ; therefore many brought wagons (about fifty of them) with their families and provisions, with a great number of tents, which they pitched for their accommodation. The public exercises of devotion commenced at two o'clock, with sermons both in the meeting-house and at the tent, and were continued, with but short intermissions, until Tuesday evening. Fifteen ministers were present, all members of the synod of Pittsburg, and with cordial harmony took part in the various labors of the solemn season. The administration of the Word and ordinances was accompanied with an extraordinary effusion of divine influence on the hearts of the hearers. Some hundreds were, during the season, convicted of their sin and misery. Preaching, exhortations, prayers and praises, were continued alternately throughout the whole night in the meeting-house, which was crowded full, and also part of the night at the tent.

" On the Sabbath morning, action sermons were preached in the meeting-house and at the tent ; and after the way was prepared at both places, the communicants from the house repaired to the communion table at the tent, where the holy ordinance was administered to about nine hundred and sixty communicants.

"This night was spent as the former had been ; perhaps the only difference that appeared was in the numbers who were visibly pierced to the heart, and made to cry out, ' What shall we do ? ' and in the degree of their exercise, both of which greatly exceeded those of the preceding night.

" Between midnight and day-break, after a short intermission of public worship, an exhortation was given to the distressed, directing them to Christ, and setting forth the fulness of His grace and suitableness to all their wants.

" On Monday the whole assembly was addressed by one speaker from the tent. They were composed, solemn, and attentive during the time of public worship ; but after the blessing was pronounced many were struck down in all parts of the congregation, and many more sat still, silently weeping over their miserable state as sinners exposed to eternal wrath. Many of God's dear children were filled with peace in believing. They saw the spiritual glory which the gracious presence of God had given to the solemnity ; they rejoiced in hope, and waited to see and feel more of the efficacy of free grace. Others, sorrowful and thirsting for the water of life, wished to stay a little longer at the pool. The ministers, therefore, determined not to leave them, but to labor with diligence while God

was making the Word and ordinances effectual to the conviction and conversion of sinners. Not a few were awakened to a lively sense of their sin during the evening and
night who have since, we hope, obtained pardon and
peace with God through our Lord Jesus Christ. The
exercises were continued until after sunrise on Tuesday
morning, when the assembly was solemnly dismissed, and
began with apparent reluctance to prepare to disperse.
Notwithstanding that they had continued so long and
rested little, it appeared to be very difficult to separate and
leave the place. After some time the most removed,
except the people of the congregation, who still tarried,
lingering at the place where so much of God's power had
been manifested to their eyes and in their consciences.
Numbers who had gone home to provide refreshments for
their friends, returned. Still they could not part. All
again collected in the meeting-house, where this day also
was spent till evening in preaching, exhortation, and prayer.
The exercise was very powerful, and numbers were affected
who appeared to be unmoved before."

Adds a chronicler, "One of the most powerful sermons on this Pentecostal occasion was an exposition of the
second Psalm, by Rev. Elisha Macurdy, which was long
known in the region round as 'Macurdy's war sermon.'
'The scene,' said Rev. Thomas Hunt, who was in the
wagon from which it was preached, 'appeared to me like
the close of a battle in which every tenth man had been
fatally wounded. The recollection thrills through my
soul while I write.'

"The churches from Lake Erie southward along the
western side of the Allegheny Mountains, and through the
few settled portions of the Northwest Territory, which
about this time were formed into the State of Ohio, felt
the swelling of the river of waters of life.

"Some of the scenes witnessed in Kentucky are almost

beyond our conception. Rev. J. B. Finley, an eye-witness
of a vast meeting at Cane Ridge, in August, 1801, to which
people had come from all quarters of the State, even the
distance of two hundred miles, and from the settlements
north of the Ohio, thus describes it: "We arrived upon
the ground, and here a scene presented itself to my mind,
not only novel and unaccountable, but awful beyond description. A vast crowd, supposed by some to have
amounted to twenty-five thousand, was collected together.
The noise was like the roar of Niagara. The vast sea of
human beings seemed to be agitated by a storm. I counted
seven preachers, all preaching at one time, some on stumps,
others on wagons. The religious exercises on the ground
were continued from Friday morning until the ensuing
Wednesday evening, day and night, without intermission.
Heavy rains fell during that time, apparently without
being noticed by the people, though few were protected
by any covering.

"From such a tempest of religious emotions, evils have
resulted. Campbellism and Universalism have been cast
forth like a scum. The Presbyterian Church itself was
rent asunder, and the 'Cumberland' branch of it, holding
semi-Arminian doctrine, and licensing uneducated men to
preach, arose there. And these masses of people were
convulsed by inexplicable nervous affections of a spasmodic
nature. Still from the inflammable chaff much wheat was
sifted, which has borne precious seed and been gathered
with rejoicing."

A fair conception of the meetings in the more sober
parts of the Southwest may be obtained from the following
letter, written by Rev. James McGready, descriptive of
some held in Tennessee : —

"The present summer has been the most glorious time
that our guilty eyes have ever beheld. All the blessed
displays of Almighty power and grace, all the sweet gales

of the Divine Spirit and soul-reviving showers of the blessings of heaven, which we enjoyed before, and which we considered wonderful beyond conception, were but like a few scattering drops before the mighty rain which Jehovah has poured out like a mighty river upon this our guilty, unworthy country. The Lord has indeed showed Himself a prayer-hearing God; He has given His people a praying spirit and a lively faith, and then He has answered their prayers far beyond their highest expectations. This wilderness and solitary place has been made glad; this dreary desert now rejoices and blossoms like the rose; yea, it blossoms abundantly, and rejoices even with joy and singing.

"At Gaspar River, in early summer, ministers and experienced Christians were everywhere engaged praying, exhorting, conversing, and trying to lead inquiring souls to the Lord Jesus. In this exercise the night was spent till near the break of day. The Sabbath was a blessed day in every sense of the word. The groans of awakened sinners could be heard all over the house during the morning sermon, but by no means so as to disturb the assembly. It was a comfortable time with many at the table. Mr. McGee preached in the evening upon the account of Peter's sinking in the waves. In the application of his sermon the power of God seemed to shake the whole assembly. Towards the close of the sermon the cries of the distressed arose almost as loud as his voice. After the congregation was dismissed, the solemnity increased till the greater part of the multitude seemed engaged in the most solemn manner. No person appeared to wish to go home; hunger and sleep seemed to affect nobody: eternal things were the vast concern. Here awakening and converting work was to be found in every part of the multitude, and even some things strangely and wonderfully new to me. Sober professors, who had been communicants for many years, now lying prostrate on the ground, crying out in such language as this : 'I have been a sober professor, I have been a communicant. Oh, I have been deceived, I have no religion!' The greater part of the multitude continued at the meeting-house all night, and no person appeared uneasy for food or sleep.

"On Monday a vast concourse of people came together. This was another day of the Son of man. With propriety we could adopt the language of the patriarch, and say, 'The Lord is here : how dreadful is this place! It is none other but the house of God and the very gate of heaven!' Two powerful sermons were preached by Messrs. McGee and Hodge. The almighty power of God attended the Word to the hearts of many, and a universal solemnity overspread the whole assembly. When the congregation was dismissed, no person seemed to wish to leave the place. The solemnity increased, and conviction seemed to spread from heart to heart. Little children, young men and women, and old, gray-headed people, persons of every description, white and black, were to be found in every part of the multitude, pricked to the heart with clear, rational, scriptural convictions, crying out for mercy in the most extreme distress; whilst every now and then we could find one and another delivered from their burden of sin and guilt by sweet, believing views of the glory of God in the face of Jesus Christ. In such exercises the multitude continued at the meeting-house till Tuesday morning after sunrise, when they broke up after they were dismissed by prayer, and indeed the circumstance of their parting added to the solemnity of the occasion. The number that, we hope, were savingly brought to Christ on this occasion were forty-five persons."

It is a very suggestive circumstance that Dr. Gardiner Spring, who feared the influence of Mr. Finney's "protracted meetings," should have written of the scenes which we have noticed: "I marvel not a little that, after all our eyes have seen and our ears have heard, there should be good men among us who look with suspicion upon these days of mercy, and who do not rather hail them, even in this midnight of our national tribulations, as the harbinger of that predicted period ' when the light of the moon shall be as the light of the sun, and the light of the sun shall be seven-fold, as the light of seven days.' This is a ruined world; I should give up all for lost unless God did thus appear in his glory, and build up Zion. There is no other helper, there is no other hope!"

The Rev. Dr. Samuel Ralston, of Alleghany County, Pennsylvania, a laborer amidst the harvest scenes, in his "Letters," showing, in opposition to certain enemies of the work, that it was "agreeable to the Word of God" and kindred with the great revivals in Scotland and in New England, testifies that "this work was begun and carried on in this country under the preaching and influence of the doctrines contained in the Confession of Faith of the Presbyterian Churches. That this work is a gracious work of the Spirit of God is apparent to me from the effects it has produced. It has reclaimed the wicked and the profligate, and transformed the lion into a lamb. It has brought professed deists to become professed Christians, and turned their cursings into blessings and their blasphemies into praises. Many who could not relish any religious conversation are now only delighted when talking about the plan of salvation and the wonders of redeeming love; and many, very many, give evidence by their life and conversion that they are born of God.

In a sermon preached before the synod of Kentucky, expressing sympathy with the revival and its results, Rev. David Rice recognizes the advanced Christian experience which is now awakening a very deep interest. He says, "The subjects of this work appear to be very sensible of the necessity of sanctification as well as justification,

and that 'without holiness no man can see the Lord'; to
be greatly desirous that they themselves and 'all that
name the name of Christ should depart from iniquity,'
should recommend the religion of Jesus to the consciences
and esteem of their fellow-men, that the light of their
holy conversation should so shine before men that they,
seeing their good works, might give glory to God. A
heaven of perfect purity and the full enjoyment of God
appears to be the chief and ultimate object of their desire
and pursuit."

The General Assembly of the Presbyterian Church in
1803 appointed a committee, consisting of Rev. Messrs.
Samuel Miller, Archibald Alexander, and James Welsh,
"to draw up a statement as the result of the free conversation on the state of religion." To favorable testimonies which it had given in previous years it added the
following : —

"The Assembly heard at more than usual length and
with more than common satisfaction the accounts received
from their members of the state of religion within the
bounds of the Presbyterian Church. Since an inquiry of
this nature has become a part of the annual business of the
Assembly, it may be confidently asserted that no result
was ever presented to our body so favorable and so grati-
fying to the friends of truth and piety.

"There is scarcely a presbytery under the care of the
Assembly from which some pleasing intelligence has not
been announced, and from some of them communications
have been made which so illustriously display the triumphs of evangelical truth and the power of sovereign
grace as cannot but fill with joy the hearts of all who
love to hear of the prosperity of the Redeemer's kingdom."

The sound, able, and eloquent Rev. William Spear,
D. D., of Brooklyn, N. Y., in his comments on the

revival of 1800, has the following closing summary and
appeal : —

" When we compare the three great revivals of American history, we may observe a progression in their character.

" The first was one of colonization. It made the dead
formalism of Europe intolerable, and placed a renovated
and free people upon a new, unoccupied, and suitable
continent. This was the digging up and the transfer of
the ore.

" The second was one of ' awakening,' as it was well
termed at the time. It was one of doctrinal instruction,
of spiritual quickening; and it is wonderful how the holy
influence of Jonathan Edwards, David Brainerd, and others
of that day is to be traced at the root of the revival and
missionary efforts of all sects and lands. This was the
melting and fining of the metal.

" The third was one of evangelic organization. It girded
and arrayed the followers of Christ, some of them in general societies, some of them in the establishment of separate ecclesiastical agencies, for the great work of giving
the gospel to mankind. This was the advancement to the
building of engines and machinery.

" The fourth must be one of dissemination. It must
employ the numerous membership and the vast resources
of the Church in conveying the knowledge of salvation
' to every creature.' This must supply fuel, kindle the
fires, man and load the trains and vessels, and send the
freights of mercy over land and sea, to every inhabitant
of this land, and to every mortal and immortal descendant
of those who were driven from Eden for their sin. ' They
shall obtain joy and gladness, and sorrow and sighing shall
flee away.' "

" Now again, ' the kingdom of heaven is at hand ! ' Shall

we mumble over our phylacteries, cleanse our cups and platters, and garnish the tombs of dead prophets? Shall we hold our peace? Or shall we haste with our best gifts to the King, wake our sons and daughters to proclaim His approach, and sound the glad tidings to the meek, the broken-hearted, the captives?"

CHAPTER VI.

THE PROGRESS OF EVANGELISM IN AMERICA. — WESLEY'S INFLUENCE
GROWING INTO DISTINCT FORM AND IN POWER. — EMBURY AND
BARBARA HECKER. — THE BRITISH OFFICER. — JOHN SUMMERFIELD,
THE YOUTHFUL EVANGELIST.

WESLEY'S profoundly developed and organized movement, including both vital godliness and ecclesiastical
reform, reached this country "without observation," but
was destined to enter into all its future life.

In 1765 a family of German descent, from a Protestant
colony in the County of Limerick, Ireland, which had
been visited by John Wesley, landed in New York. This
disciple of Christ, in ecclesiastical relations of Mr. Wesley, was Philip Embury. Among those who came in the
same ship were Paul Heek and his wife Barbara. The
neighborhood was without a church or religious services;
backsliding and worldly amusements prevailed. Mr. Embury, a carpenter, licensed to preach, was a good, but
diffident and retiring man. Barbara Heek was the opposite in qualities of character; and one day, finding a company playing cards, she seized the pack, and throwing
them into the fire, turned to Mr. Embury, and said,
"Brother Embury, you must preach to us, or we shall all
go to hell, and God will require our blood at your hands."
She overcame his objections and hesitation, and he
preached his first Methodist sermon, in the metropolis of
this country, to half a dozen hearers. The attendance
steadily increased. On a February day, 1767, the secluded
assembly were surprised by the entrance of a British offi-

eer in full uniform; but anxious surprise soon passed into confidence and fellowship, while the stranger joined in the devotions. He was the brave Captain Webb, who had lost an eye, and nearly his life, on the Plains of Abraham, in the campaign of 1758. He barely lived, and eight years later was awakened at Bristol, England, under the appeals of John Wesley, who soon after licensed him to preach. He was sent to Albany, N. Y., Master of the Barracks, where he also established a meeting. Hearing of Mr. Embury and his religious movement, he hastened to a fraternal greeting. Nearly at the same time Robert Strawbridge, a flaming evangelist from Drumnsah, near the Shannon River, Ireland, was planting the standard in the wilds of Maryland.

Meanwhile Mr. Embury's congregation compelled a removal, first to a hall, and soon after to a rigging-loft of larger dimensions. Barbara's faith now rose to the emergency. She went to the Lord for a chapel, and with radiant face came from the altar with this answer ringing in her inward ear, "I the Lord will do it." In 1768 the site of John Street church was located, and Mr. Embury, a carpenter by trade, worked unweariedly upon the structure, building with his own hands the pulpit, in which, October 30, he preached the dedication sermon.

The beginning was fairly made, the visible fortress of an aggressive faith established, with the human weaknesses and surface-work incident to all earthly agencies in extending the kingdom of Christ.

The Methodist Episcopal Church was not intended at the outset by its founder to be a radically new and separate sect, but a reform movement to carry the gospel to the masses. This was apparent when, after the Revolutionary War, the unaggressive position of the mother communion, along with the alarming decline of religion in this country, led the followers of Wesley to send over the sea for laborers in the wide harvest-field of the perishing people. A delegation of three ordained clergymen of the Church of England came, one of them Thomas Coke, late Doctor of Civil Law in Oxford University, as superintendent, with authority to appoint Francis Asbury to the same office in America. This action was ratified at a General Conference in Baltimore, and the Methodist Episcopal Church on this continent took its place in the ecclesiastical history of a republic fresh from its "baptism of blood," in its independence of the British Crown.

So far from anticipating, however, the result which inevitably followed, Mr. Wesley was surprised and promptly emphatic in his protest when he heard that his superintendents had assumed the title of bishops.

But the Methodists were born of evangelism, and practically could have no sympathy, nor long any connection, with the English Church. Their ministers were missionary evangelists, and nobly entered upon their work in the wilds and wastes of a hemisphere. The two great evangelists of England had thus extended their influence over two continents, which will be felt to the end of time. The "circuit-rider" went his round, and in our cities unostentatious Methodist sanctuaries gathered earnest congregations.

At the close of the eighteenth century, there appeared in the field of world-wide itineracy the most eccentric preacher, perhaps, of any period. Lorenzo Dow was born in Coventry, Conn., Oct. 16, 1777, and died in Georgetown, D. C., February, 1834. He was an independent Methodist preacher, or as he styled himself, a "cosmopolite," travelling with his devoted wife Peggy, in all possible ways, in all seasons and weather, and in both America and the British Empire. With flowing hair and beard and carelessly peculiar dress, he was an original, uncultured, shrewd, self-sacrificing, godly, and evidently useful evangelist.

Anecdotes of his ready wit and strange methods of reaching the common people are current in nearly every Protestant community of the land. He often made his appointments one or two years in advance, and uniformly promptly fulfilled them. Many thousands were hopefully converted under his preaching. Still, marked eccentricity is undesirable in the ministry, and the history of the Christian church has had, we think, not even an imitation of Lorenzo Dow in his extraordinary possession of it, and success in its religious use.

There died in Dublin, Ireland, five years after Mr. Dow, a somewhat singular yet very devoted itinerant among his own countrymen. Gideon Ouseley was descended from a highly respectable family in Dunmore, County of Galway, and was quite successful among the Catholics. He was a plain, earnest, godly man. Cotemporary with him were those zealous itinerating servants of the Lord, the Rev. Thomas Walsh, the Rev. Charles Gorham, and Bartholomew Campbell. During their faithful labors in Ireland, God was preparing there a remarkable genius for his service in America, the opposite in gifts and graces to the wandering " cosmopolite."

Nearly forty years after the Baltimore. convocation, while Dr. Nettleton was at the meridian of his life and usefulness, March 17, 1821, John Summerfield, the "young Wesley" as he was called, landed in the city of New York. He was a handsome young man from Cork, Ireland, only twenty-three years of age, whose fame had gone before him, principally among his own denomination, by whom he was warmly welcomed. However saving the influence of his sermons, his special work seemed to be to introduce the denomination he represented to the older and then more cultured and established churches.

On the 10th of May, 1821, the American Bible Society held its fifth anniversary in the City Hotel. The venerable and honorable Elias Boudinot, the president, over fourscore years of age, occupied the chair. Rev. J. M. Matthews, D. D., late chancellor of the University of New York, was chairman of the committee to procure speakers. He wrote of his success as follows : "A respectable gentleman of the Methodist Church called upon me and mentioned that a young preacher of great promise of their denomination had just arrived from England, whom he would like to have invited to speak at the approaching anniversary. I readily consented, and when after receiving my note he called, I was much struck with his appearance, and so well satisfied that he was no common man that I proposed to him to take the post of honor and speak last."

Summerfield did speak. "Just at that moment Dr. Boudinot, unable to remain longer on account of his great weakness, was helped off the stage leaning on his staff. The speaker, with admirable felicity, seized upon that beautiful incident, and as he compared him to old Jacob, leaning upon his staff and blessing his sons, the effect was perfectly overwhelming. From that hour Summerfield was the admiration of New York, and, as he became known, the admiration of the whole country."

Although no printed page can give a just impression of his oratory, a passage from a report of this address may afford a fair specimen of his general style : —

"In seconding the motion of thanks to the venerable president, I am assured of the consentaneous feeling of every heart around me. When I beheld him enter the room, I felt a thrill strike through my soul, but which I cannot describe. I believe it was the generous throb of every individual here present at the sight of Boudinot; it was sympathetic, and every heart vibrated in perfect unison with my own. My imagination involuntarily recognized in him a resemblance to pious Jacob; and ' finding the time draw near when he must die,' I fancied that he had said in his heart, 'Gather yourselves together that I may bless you before I die!' And when one told Jacob and said, ' Behold thy sons come unto thee, Israel strengthened himself, and sat upon the bed,' and said, ' Hear ye sons of Jacob, and hearken unto Israel, your father.' Instead of urging upon you anything as a motive to your unanimously seconding the motion, I leave it to yourselves, and the best feelings of your hearts ; nor am I at all apprehensive for the result. At the same time, you will present your thanks to Almighty God for having raised up such a father to your society, for having put it into his heart to ' come to the help of the Lord against the mighty,' and as the best way of expressing your gratitude to this servant of the Lord, remember him sincerely at the throne of grace, and pray that whenever it shall please the Head of the Church, and God of the Bible, to remove him hence, his last hours may be peace ; pray that God would speak to his heart the word which once cheered the fainting mind of Israel of old, — ' Fear not to go down into Egypt; I will go down with thee into Egypt, and I will also surely bring thee up again '; and that, borne up under this assurance, he may be able to say to his surviving friends, with a heavenly smile, ' Whither I go ye know, and the way ye know.' "

This "prodigy " was born at Lancashire, January 31, 1798. His father and mother, who had nine children, were devoted Christians. " Previously to the birth of this child, his father had frequently been heard to say that there was nothing that he desired more in early life than that he should have a son ; that that son should be a minister of the gospel ; and that his name should be called John. And truly, as he and his wife, like Zacharias and

Elisabeth of old, 'were both righteous before God, walking in all the commandments and ordinances of the Lord blameless,' so likewise his prayer was heard: a man-child was born; and his father, in the spirit of the venerable priest of Jerusalem, 'praised God' that He had given him a son. And at the time of the birth of the babe his father solemnly dedicated him to the work of the ministry."

William Summerfield was a millwright, machinist, and iron-founder, successively; and at one time a local preacher. Amelia, his wife, died at Liverpool, in 1811. John was a remarkably precocious, attractive boy, and petted by all who knew him. When only six years of age he was sent to the celebrated Moravian school at Fairfield, near Manchester, where he remained five years, surprising and delighting even the bishop by his proficiency in the classics, while he was superficial in nothing. The failure of his father in business compelled him to leave Fairfield, and he opened successfully soon after, although only twelve years of age, a night-school, the income from which, with filial devotion, he gave to his mother. When fifteen he was French correspondent in a mercantile house at Liverpool, where he continued till its financial embarrassment.

In 1812 the family removed to Dublin, where John's premature intelligence attracted to him companions several years older than himself, by whom he was led into fashionable vices. The religious impressions made at home, and in the Moravian school, would at times return, and send him, with agonizing remorse, to his closet of prayer, for mercy. In his better moments he corresponded with Rev. Dr. Raffles respecting preparation for the ministry. Of this crisis he says: —

"I had a strong desire to return to England, having opened a correspondence with the Rev. Mr. Raffles, a

Calvinist minister, with a view of obtaining permission
to enter their seminary at Hoxton, to be prepared for
the ministry, which, if I had done, I should probably
now have been a preacher of the everlasting gospel to
that people. I poured out my prayers to God; and if
ever I felt power with the Almighty, it was then. I am
assured He smiled on me in all I did, and when I had
wept before Him on the reflection of the awfulness of the
work, and my own youth, I have experienced such a sense
of His presence and promises of assistance, that I could
not for a moment doubt it was His will.

"From what I experienced at that time, I am convinced
that there are as good men in that body of Christians as
in any other, for I was strongly rooted in their opinions,
but suffered no diminution in love to God on that account.
Since then, the Almighty, in a great measure, withdrew
His presence from me; and when my father directed my
pursuits to worldly objects, He thwarted me in every
undertaking."

The reading of the memoir of the youthful William·
Spencer, whom he had heard, and whose brief life reminds
us of Summerfield, was the direct means of his deeper
religious emotions. His passion for fine speaking led him
to the best preaching efforts in the forum, and even acting
on the stage. His habits were irregular, and his constitution suffered seriously. The coal-trade was selected for
him by his father. A more uncongenial employment was
scarcely possible; it was like binding down the wounded
young eagle with a clanking chain to the barren rock.
Dispirited and careless, he got into debt by "accepting
bills for the accommodation of friends," and was thrown
into prison, where he was confined for seven months.
Here he drew up memorials for fellow-prisoners, under
the Insolvent Act, — a business which he continued after
his release with remunerative success. Frequenting the

courts, he was once a witness, when his examination was
so clear and mature, the judge asked him what was his
profession. He replied, "I have n't any." The judge
exclaimed, "No profession, no profession, sir!" The
witness answered, "No, my lord." Complimenting him,
the official added, "Depend upon it, you'll one day or
other be a shining character in the world!"

The year 1817 was memorable in his experience. In an
agony of despair, he was tempted to commit suicide. One
day, while weeping, he met a mechanic, who, learning his
condition, invited him to a prayer-meeting held for soldiers
from the barracks, when he was the subject of earnest supplication till he found peace in believing. Learning that
those to whose prayers he owed so much were ridiculed and
roughly treated by ungodly comrades, he began his labors
among these wicked men, as the best expression of grateful regard to the persecuted saints. He was greatly blessed
in his efforts. Patrick French, his first class-leader, from
this time had a wonderful influence in moulding Summerfield's character; he was a holy, loving, devout man of God.

The young disciple now joined the "Praying Association," and was called upon to exercise his gifts by
speaking in the chapels. The first attempt greatly agitated him, but he passed the ordeal with composure
and impressiveness, the date of his public ministrations, in
which no real failure ever cast a shadow upon his brilliant career. He discovered the secret of success as an
ambassador of Christ, *the study of the Scripture, and the
closet of protracted communion with God*, from which he
came forth filled with the Holy Ghost. In April, 1818,
not yet twenty-one, he was licensed as a local preacher.
His father requested him to join him in a manufactory at
Cork. He did so only to leave soon, with the call of his
Master, to enter this "field of the world," heard above the
din of machinery and all the voices of Mammon.

His popularity, wherever he declared the gospel message, was immediate and universal. He was in Dublin in 1819, and thronged by its excited people. His health was too uncertain to hazard an appointment upon the circuit, and he commenced his evangelistic itineracy. He visited England in the spring of 1820, on business for his father and for religious objects, and partly also to recruit his health, returning to Cork in August. Perhaps no part of his work was more valuable in Ireland to his own denomination than his signal success in healing a division on a question which had previously distracted the society in England, but which was amicably settled in America in the year 1784, and was then legally mooted in Ireland, — the propriety of administering the sacrament of the Lord's Supper in the Methodist chapels, and by ministers not regularly ordained according to the formula of the Church of England.

A passage from Mr. Holland's biography will shed clear light on his peculiar work both abroad and in this country : —

" So interesting was the appearance and so fascinating the eloquence of this young evangelist, that many persons who had never heard a Methodist preacher, and probably would not have been prevailed upon to hear any other, attended the preaching of Mr. Summerfield in the neighborhood of Cork. Whether, however, these were churchmen or Catholics, persons bigoted against Methodism or mere men of the world, all were delighted and edified by the fervor and simplicity of his sermons. While he labored to acquit his conscience in speaking faithfully to all who heard him, with the meekness of wisdom he sought to turn to profitable account even the slanders of foolish or wicked men : ' Oh, how happy we should be when we hear our faults from our enemies. Our friends seldom tell them to us, — too seldom.' "

We add a few extracts from his private journal : —
" For these last two days I have been in Gethsemane.
I long for the time of refreshing. Come, my Lord, come
quickly ! ' I cried unto the Lord : He heard me, and delivered me from all my troubles.' I seldom had such a pouring out of the divine glory. Bless the Lord, O my soul !
magnify His great name. Applied myself to reading
principally in *the* Book."

On the first Sunday morning in the year 1820 he
preached in Cork to a large assembly. " I was peculiarly
affected," says he, 'under the first prayer. The Lord gave
to my eyes refreshing tears, and I could only sob my
petition to His throne. He caused all his goodness to pass
before me and to reveal to me His name ! I felt Him
passing by. He put His hand on me, and then revealed
His glory ; He covered me : I was lost in the ocean of
His goodness."

It is true, it was not always so with him. His consuming zeal wore out his nervous system, and he knew seasons
of great depression and temptation ; but his faith rarely
failed him. Riding one week " forty-one miles and
preaching ten times," and during seven weeks " travelling
three hundred and sixty-two miles and preaching fifty
times," in the light of human wisdom, seems a suicidal
waste of life. But God only can trace moral and spiritual
influences and estimate the usefulness of any devoted
soul, however brief the mortal toil. From the hour of
his introduction to the religious public in this country, his career was uninterruptedly and growingly popular. Although he brought with him no credentials, his
standing at home was known ; and he was appointed at the
meeting of the New York Conference at Troy, in June,
1821, to the metropolis, where he had preached his first
sermon in America. He gave the annual discourse before
the Marine Church, and the anniversary address, three

days later, in Dr. Romyn's church. Wherever he spoke, for hours before the service commenced the place was overflowing, and on one occasion he was obliged to gain access to the pulpit through a window. He visited Philadelphia, Baltimore, and Washington. What a spectacle was that, when this youth of twenty-three stood in the National Capitol, holding the throng crowding the edifice in wrapt attention! At Philadelphia he was attacked with hemorrhage. June, 1822, his case was thought to be hopeless, and he rejoiced in the prospect of his departure. While writing with unnatural rapidity his messages, he suddenly stopped, and fell into a profound slumber, which continued sixteen hours. When he awakened, the crisis was passed for the time, and he slowly regained his former strength.

By the advice of his physician, he went to New Jersey, when Princeton College honored him with the degree of A. M. Returning to New York, he sailed, December 25, as delegate of the American Bible Society to the Protestant Bible Society of France, to be present at the anniversary of the latter the following April. He reached Paris safely, but with no improvement in health. His public address, March 16, translated into French, was a fine effort, and the same admiring attentions he had received here followed him there. He visited England, and sailing soon after for the New World, he arrived once more, to die, in his adopted America. May 19, at the Conference in Baltimore, he was ordained elder, with the permission to travel wherever his health might require. He went as far north as Montreal, with no improvement in health. On his return he served the Missionary Board of Philadelphia a few weeks, with the highest success, especially in the treasury department. In the spring of 1824 he assisted in forming the American Tract Society, and his last public act was the delivery of its first address,

— an eloquent discourse, which seemed to have in it echoes of the heavenly world to which he was so near.

Dropsy set in a month later; and June 13, 1825, at the age of twenty-seven, with loving words to his friends, and of sweetest trust in his Redeemer, he fell asleep. The funeral was held in John Street Church, and his remains buried in Brooklyn.

Among the various occasions of special interest was the meeting in behalf of the deaf and dumb. He closed his address with thrilling power. He said among other things, "Turn away from these children of affliction, and when the Lord says, 'Inasmuch as ye did it unto the least of these, ye did it unto me,' you too may be dumb and speechless in shame."

Wrote Dr. Beman, of Troy, Presbyterian, "It is impossible to impress upon canvas or steel the holy sweetness irradiating his pale, worn features when he talked of the love of Jesus from the pulpit or the platform or the fireside. It is said he was a man of prayer, but he was no less a man of the Bible."

Jehovah sent this extraordinary young evangelist to our country, evidently, because his voice could reach savingly, not only many individual souls, but to throw over all denominations a softening, elevating, spiritual influence, bringing them closer in Christian sympathy, while laying the foundations of some of our leading unsectarian institutions for spreading the gospel of a common Saviour through our own borders and over the globe.

CHAPTER VII.

EARLY LAY EVANGELISTS. — INDIA AND SCOTLAND. — THE SPIRITUAL DE-
CLENSION AND DEATH. — THE HALDANE FAMILY. — ROBERT AND JAMES.
— THEIR YOUTHFUL HISTORY, — CONVERSION. — ENTER UPON THE
WORK OF EVANGELISTS.

IN the year 1795, a quarter of a century after George
Whitefield's death, a gifted, refined, and wealthy young
Scotchman, in the house of Rev. Greville Erving, Rose
Court, Edinburgh, proposed to devote his life and fortune to the missionary enterprise in India, just then awakening interest in Scotland, selling for this object his fine
estate. The rich and luxurious Oriental metropolis, Benares, with its Pagan magnificence, was the fortress of
spiritual darkness, within whose walls the glowing, chas-
tened enthusiasm of that visitor purposed to plant the flag
whose glory was the star of Bethlehem. The boldness of
the projected advance upon the stronghold of an ancient
heathenism displayed the grand heroic nature of the man.

But no missionary could then enter India without the
consent of the company that ruled that vast empire ; and
after an unfavorable correspondence with it and the British government, the scheme was abandoned. Thirty
years later this attempt to occupy Benares was pronounced
by Bishop Heber to be "Utopian." But the praises of
Christian converts have long since floated out of missionary chapels upon the air rent with the outcries of idol-
atrous orgies.

At this very time another, no less noble in gifts and
graces, was fixing his tearful eye upon the throngs moving

7

in unbroken ranks, under the very shadow of sanctuary spires, to the gate of eternal night.

These soldiers of the cross, in the freshness of manliest manhood, favorites in society and the admiration of the world, were the brothers Robert and James Haldane. They were henceforth to be spiritual forces unknown in Scotland since the visits of the great evangelist of both continents and the preaching of Wesley in England. A new emergency in the churches of Christ found His saving instrumentalities ready to meet it.

The revivals in Scotland, on account of divisions among Dissenters, were limited in extent and power when Whitefield was there, and had been followed by deeper moral slumber. The religious condition in the home of Knox was called "the midnight of the church."

The infidelity of Hume and Adam Smith had poisoned the literature, and through that had infected the ministry. The term "moral sermons," applied to those of the distinguished Dr. Blair, described the prevailing style of the best preaching, whose popular representatives were more at home in convivial circles than in their pulpits. Rev. Dr. Hamilton, of Strathblane, sketches them with terrible sarcasm: "To deliver a gospel sermon or preach to the hearts and consciences of dying sinners was as completely beyond their power as to speak in the language of angels. The coldness and indifference of the minister, while they proclaimed his own aversion to his employment, were seldom lost upon the people. The congregations rarely amounted to a tenth of the parishioners, and the one half of this small number were generally, during the half hour's soporific harangue, fast asleep. They were free from hypocrisy: they had no more religion in private than in public."

While the devil was thus apparently supreme in the land reddened often with martyr-blood, God, "without observation," had prepared leaders in Israel to rally His saints and win victories which should be felt to the end of time and through the eternal ages.

Where and how were these brothers trained for their great work? With an ancestry whose unbroken line extended a thousand years in the past, Captain Haldane, a successful seaman, with his devout wife, lived near Dundee, Scotland. Many earnestly Christian families maintained the reverent domestic worship so beautifully described in "The Cotter's Saturday Night," — an exercise so varied by the Shorter Catechism, questions, brief explanations, prayer, and psalm, that the children even " were never weary of the service, while the Sabbath was sacredly kept as holy time, with such cheerful serenity that they never thought the home morose or gloomy."

The saintly mother left the boys she had consecrated wholly to the Lord in 1774, when Robert, the eldest son, was ten, and James six years of age. They were now removed to the care of their maternal grandmother, Sadie Lundie. Here Robert showed the bent of his genius by preaching to the domestics of the Lundie house in their common hall. Three years later they were both sent to the High School of Edinburgh, and boarded with the rector, Dr. Adam, the well-known author of "Roman Antiquities."

Favoring circumstances led Robert, at the age of sixteen, to the British navy, and he joined the war-ship "Monarch" at Portsmouth. James remained at the school, and to the great delight of Dr. Adam became *Dux*, or first in his class. He accompanied the distinguished principal, in 1784, in a tour through England. Upon his return he entered upon an engagement in the East India service, in the capacity of midshipman on board the "Duke of Montrose," declining for it the splendid offer of a place with and share in the business of Mr.

Coutts, the great banker. God had a different destiny for him than that of a financial millionaire. After twice escaping threatened death by perils of the deep, the serious impressions of childhood were deepened by Doddridge's "Rise and Progress," which, under the lashings of conscience, he "read as a task." Notwithstanding, he fought a duel with an insulting cavalry officer returning to England in the same ship, while touching at the island of St. Helena; his pistol burst, and that of his challenger missed fire.

He became wild and daring, and was admired by men of the world for his spirit and bravery. His last voyage in the "Duke of Montrose" terminated June, 1793, when, at the age of twenty-five, passing examination for commander, he was nominated for the first officer of an Indiaman. The honor gave him the title of Captain Haldane. At this crisis of affairs he visited Airthney in Scotland, where he met Miss Joass, only daughter of Major Alexander Joass, and an engagement soon after followed. Objections to his sea life were overcome, and he was married to her a few months afterwards, repairing with his bride to London. This excellent lady brought to the new home a sweet but decided Christian life, which was immediately felt by the now sceptical, careless husband. Arrangements to sail in the "Melville Castle" were completed, but the Government detained the vessel for several months. Meanwhile he not only determined to quit the sea, but became deeply interested in his own personal salvation. He settled in Edinburgh. Here the Holy Spirit awakened him to deep convictions of guilt and peril, and revealed Christ as his only and sufficient hope.

Before we sketch the entrance of James upon the work of an evangelist, soon to be his cherished employment, we will follow Robert to this date in his career.

In the spring of 1781 he was transferred from the

"Monarch" to the "Foudroyant," which lay for some time after at Spithead. This was a divine ordering not then understood by young Haldane. It led to frequent visits to Gosport, where he, and afterwards his brother James, were brought under the moulding influence, intellectually and spiritually, of Rev. Dr. Bogue, an able and most worthy Scotch Presbyterian. He counselled them, directed them in their course of reading, and was an example of noble Christian benevolence, having originated the London Missionary Society. The peace declared in 1783 between Britain and her American Colonies had a decisive effect upon Robert's plans of life. He resumed collegiate studies in Edinburgh the next year, 1784, and went with Dr. Bogue to Paris and Flanders. The following year he married Katharine Cochrane Oswald, and soon removed to his residence at Airthney, where ten years were spent in beautifying his grounds.

Twice he came near death by drowning, in the charming lake he constructed : once slipping from a rock he barely grasped a post ; and at another time, in winter, he went down with the breaking ice. No decided religious impressions upon his character were made by these startling providences.

With culture and all the refinements and luxuries of his elegant establishment, the earthly prospects of Robert Haldane were brilliant ; he was already mentioned for Parliament and universally a favorite. But the French Revolution at this period, crumbling thrones and altars, was attracting the discussion of a wondering world. The discriminating mind of Haldane, under the influences of the Holy Spirit, unconsciously passed from the surface agitation to the underlying principles, and was led, with the human aid of devoted clergymen whose friendship he enjoyed, to the foundation of all true liberty and peace for nations or individual souls,— faith in the Lord Jesus Christ.

The Christian man who was the most distinctly and gratefully recognized in the manifold agencies that brought him to the Cross was one of his own masons, with whom he had an extended conversation on the "finished work of Christ," while walking in the woods of his own Airthney. How little thought the humble mechanic of the mighty work given him to do for his Lord during that single hour of fidelity to his employer, between whom and himself the social position was so wide!

And now these brothers, by family ties and in Jesus, looked upon the world for which He died with new spiritual vision and lofty purposes, before which the honors and glory of time lost their fascination forever.

James Haldane preached his first lay-sermon at Gilmerton in the west of Scotland, May 6, 1797, whither he had gone in company with John Aikman, a young gentleman of means, who, after living several years in Jamaica, and yielding to the prevalent dissipation, returned so remorseful on account of sins that reason reeled. Soon after he found Christ and peace. The brothers were kindred spirits, and went forth with burning zeal to "seek and save the lost." The people flocked to hear the "sea-captain" and his companion. The parish minister was indignant at this invasion of his charge, and closed against them the schoolhouse, when a godly tradesman offered them a "spacious loft"; from which the multitude were soon compelled, for lack of room, to resort to a large barn, filling it in every part. The tocsin of alarm over the heresy of lay-preaching sounded from Gilmerton to Edinburgh, and good pastors joined bad ones in the excited protest against its toleration. The modest, truthful answer of Captain Haldane was a defence of his course.

His calm utterances were the announcement of his divinely appointed mission, upon which he now entered with all his heart, with his friend Aikman. "Having heard

of the deathlike state of the north of Scotland, and the
carelessness and immorality of the ministers there, they
resolved to examine personally into the state of religion,
and to preach in its different towns and populous villages."
What a spectacle of sublimest moral significance was the
going forth of those young men, their light carriage
laden with tracts and pamphlets for distribution to the
number of twenty thousand, with the rising murmur of
opposition from the "regular clergy" around them!

At Aberdeen the whole city seemed moved, and the
throng "almost trod upon each other," to hear the "preaching captain," whose first text of a sermon of great power
was, "I am not ashamed of the gospel of Christ." At a
village near Banff the *tuck* (beat) of a drum, by which a
sermon was announced, gathered the people "on the green
banks of the gently-flowing Dovern."

"He was about thirty years of age at that time, and
had on a blue greatcoat. He also wore powder, and his
hair tied behind, as was then usual for gentlemen." His
clarion voice was heard at a great distance, and his appeals
to the conscience and heart were like those of Peter on
the day of Pentecost. He extended the tour to Orkney
Islands where among the converts, was an old man, ninety-
two, who did not know when the evangelist arrived who
Jesus was, and who, when a "lad, herding cattle, under a
sense of darkness as to his future state, prayed to God
that some teacher might be sent to enlighten his ignorance."
After eighty years that soul's cry was answered by sending thither James Haldane. The two messengers of grace
penetrated to the northernmost borders of Scotland. At
Thurso the "town was in an uproar over the remarkable
preacher, who was very zealous, preaching in the open
air." Though the rain poured down, no one left till the
sermon was ended, and then, with lingering, reluctant
steps, turned away to seek their homes. The next day,

the Sabbath, from the crowd rose the shout, "Stone him!"
"Stop him!" But no one ventured to obey the mad outcry. From Caithness, the northern county, he went to
Sutherland, "preaching in chapels, town-halls, at market-
crosses, by the sea-shore, or by the river's side," sometimes
addressing six thousand hearers.

The day when "Christ shall make up His jewels" alone
will reveal the number of conversions. Perhaps the greatest result to His cause was the impulse given to churches
of all denominations, even where denied, and felt to this
day in the widening circles of its saving power. One of
the grandest immediate fruits was the formation at Edinburgh, January 11, 1798, of a committee of twelve laymen
to establish what is termed, nowadays, a "lay college,"—
the first of which we have any knowledge.

Capt. Haldane and Mr. Aikman, in the autumn of 1798,
preached in the south and west of Scotland with undiminished success. In the ancient town of Ayer Mr. Haldane
was arrested while delivering the gospel message, which
only increased his unsought popularity. At the County
Fair of Langholm, where they went to preach, they met
the distinguished Rev. Rowland Hill, who entered heartily
into their work, and who was himself a pastor-evangelist;
and who soon after, through the influence of the evangelists, was called by the party of gentlemen who were the
financial supporters of the enterprise, to the "Circus
Church," in Edinburgh, which was suggested by the
Tabernacle in London. Thus a circus became a sanctuary,
where thousands of the "common people" listened to the
gospel of a full and free salvation every Sabbath day.
More wildly romantic and heroic scenes never were known
than some which transpired in the glens of Scotland
during the progress of this great religious movement.

In Glenlyon the people were compelled to assemble at
night beneath the sombre firs of the forest, lighting the

weird spot with lamps, hung upon the branches swaying in the chill autumnal winds. The prayers, in which were no idle words, died away in sobbing echoes along the rocky ravines, followed by the sounding psalms of praise, which went as directly to the throne of light. The preaching was with such an unction from the Lord that often, when Christ was the theme, the strong Highlanders wept like children, and the whole assembly seemed to be moved by a resistless, invisible presence, which had complete mastery of them. Whole families went twenty miles on foot, starting in the night, to reach in time the place of meeting, and after the services returned as they came. The open doors and hearts of the people residing near the church or woods in which they worshipped provided for the temporal wants of these gospel pilgrims.

While James Haldane was thus prosecuting his evangelistic labors with entire consecration of his powers and worldly means, Robert, resigned to the great disappointment of not securing the missionary's post of duty, which was then next to the stake of martyrdom in the offering of all things to Him " who gave *Himself* for us,"was preparing for equally self-denying, holy activity for Christ.

The beautiful estate of Airthney, his charming home, was now given up that he might be free for any service. He says of this step : " I gave up a place and a situation which continually presented objects calculated to excite and to gratify the lust of the eye and the pride of life." He assembled his domestics, gardeners, and laborers in the tenants' hall where supper was prepared, and after stating the provision made for them, asked forgiveness for any failures in his duties as a master, and spoke to them tenderly on the concerns of the soul. One aged member of the household could not bear the separation, and died the day the loved proprietor left it in other hands.

Of this (to all but his own consecrated heart) extra-

ordinary sacrifice of temporal good, Divie Bethune, Esq.,
of New York, records in a letter to his friend, Rev. John
Mason, D.D., dated at Edinburgh, July 17, 1801, " He has
sold his fine landed estate for twenty thousand guineas, and
bought into the funds, for the purpose of being ready to
appropriate his money for promoting the interests of religion ; and out of an income of six or seven thousand pounds
a year, limits his family to five hundred pounds sterling.
All the rest goes to building tabernacles, educating and
sending missionaries everywhere. He has them in Den-
mark, and feels interested for America." The most of
these missionaries were simply evangelists, engaged in the
same service for Christ to which James gave his life, and
to which Robert also devoted largely his lips, his pen, and
his wealth.

Three hundred young men from various social conditions were educated by Robert Haldane, at a cost of one
hundred thousand dollars. We think the last of that army
of workers was the venerable, learned, and excellent Dr.
Henderson, President of a London College, who died a
few years ago. He spent a year and a half in Iceland,
including the summer of 1814–15, with the intervening
winter, in behalf of the British Bible Society, distributing
through the different parishes the Scriptures in the ancient
dialect of the island. Beyond all human estimate has
gone abroad the mighty work of those brothers, whose best
service for Christ was, directly or indirectly, in the line
of evangelistic labor.

A little later Robert is occupied with " George Whitefield's plans for the revival of religion in England, and he
resolved to build a number of houses of worship in Scotland, and to educate young preachers to labor in them."
It will be remembered that Whitefield scattered " tabernacles " over England, and built several in the American
Colonies for the unsectarian preaching of the Word of

life. He gave the Lord's treasury, in different ways, more than three hundred and fifty thousand dollars.

Here we strike again divine links in the world's redemption, — the Haldanes and their co-workers touching the circle of Whitefield's and Wesley's labors. James Haldane was called now to the pastoral charge of the Circus Church, which had grown out of the movement already noticed. He accepted, after much reflection and prayer, with the express stipulation that it should not prevent his laboring as an evangelist. The very same year he set out again for the north of his own dear peninsula. In four weeks he preached over sixty times, many of these in the open air, with such transforming effect that the historian of John Knox draws a vivid contrast between the region visited by the evangelists and other parts of Scotland.

Those faithful servants of the Lord went to the Shetland Islands, where, with few exceptions, all classes gave them a cordial welcome. James Haldane had now preached in every part of Scotland, distributing tracts, "from the Solway Frith in the south round about to the Tweed, and thence beyond Caithness and the clustering Orkneys and Shetlands even to the *Ultima Thule* of the Romans. He had also skirted the fastnesses of the islands from Dunkeld to Sutherland."

Persecution of the Haldanes began to appear in the highest places of power. Under pretence of political ends in the religious movement, legislative prohibition of lay preaching was invoked, and even Mr. Pitt introduced a bill into Parliament for its suppression. This stirred the spirit of Robert Haldane, whose vigorous pen answered the charge, while James fearlessly prosecuted his calling among the people eager to hear the gospel along the "beautiful shores of Bute, and sailing over to Arran, preached in all its villages."

Like Whitefield, James Haldane seemed endowed with

supernatural strength for the accomplishment in a few years of what would occupy the life of an ordinary man.

We need not follow in detail the further unwearied labors of the brothers to their death, — James confining himself mainly to preaching, and Robert devoting himself to literary work for his Master and a missionary tour of the continent. At Geneva, Switzerland, he lectured to the students of theology, and formed the friendship of Merle D'Aubigne and kindred minds. His Bible readings and wisely-directed zeal for the revival of primitive piety in Switzerland and France were widely felt, and the results were great and permanent in their value to Protestant, spiritual Christianity.

December 12, 1842, he triumphantly fell asleep in Jesus. Among his latest utterances were Paul's victorious words, "I have fought a good fight, I have kept the faith, and there is henceforth laid up for me a crown of righteousness which the Lord, the righteous Judge shall give me at that day, and not to me only, but unto all them also that love his appearing." His faintest farewell testimony was, "Forever with the Lord! forever!"

February 8, 1851, James closed his wonderful career as evangelist and pastor no less gloriously. Some of the expressions which fell from his dying lips were, "When Christ, who is our life, shall appear, we also shall appear with him in glory"; "Exceeding great and precious promises." He then said, "But I must rise"; and when Mrs. Haldane said, "You are not able to get up," he smiled, and replied, "I shall be satisfied when I awake in His likeness." This ascension to glory was the thought of his immortality fluttering amid the ruins of its crumbling prison in its flight to the celestial hills. No servant of our Lord, excepting Dr. Chalmers, in Scotland, was evermore highly honored in death.

Rev. Dr. Lindsay Alexander, in his funeral sermon, said,

"Of all the influences which have been operating upon our people during the last half-century just closed, none, perhaps, has been more powerful and extensive in all its bearings than that which commenced when God touched the heart of James Haldane with evangelical fire, and sent him from secular operations to the streets and highways of his native country to proclaim to his fellow-men 'the unsearchable riches of Christ.'

"It needed such a man to accomplish such a work as he had to undertake. Men educated in the retirement of colleges, men of timid, sensitive, or delicate tastes and temperaments, men infirm of purpose or hesitating in action, would have been bent or scattered before the storm which interest and prejudice and the old hatred of the human heart to all that is earnest in religious life, everywhere stirred up against the itinerant preachers. It needed a man who had been trained up amid scenes of danger and of strife, and whose spirit was accustomed to rise with opposition, to encounter and brave the tempest. Such a man was found in Mr. James Haldane. The habits he had acquired at sea, in battling with the elements and with the untamed energy of rude and fearless men, stood him in good stead when called to contend for liberty of speech and worship in opposition to the bigoted and tyrannical measures of those who would have slain the authors of the new system. He was not the man to quail before priestly intolerance or magisterial frowns. Dignified in manner, commanding in speech, fearless in courage, and unhesitating in action, he everywhere met the rising storm with the boldness of a British sailor and the courtesy of a British gentleman, combined with the uprightness and inoffensiveness of a true Christian. To the brethren who were associated with him he was a pillar of strength in the hour of trial, while upon those who sought to put down their efforts by force or ridicule, it is difficult to say

whether the manly dignity of his bearing or the blameless
purity of his conduct produced the more powerful effect
in paralyzing their opposition when he did not succeed in
winning their applause."

Rarer men than they ought to be, were those congenial
brothers, who were genial, social, and even playful in their
true Christian cheerfulness and joy. The means which
the evangelists employed, in addition to the clear, discriminating preaching of the gospel, then comparatively
unknown to the masses; disregarding forms which ob-
scured and hindered the force of truth, was the introduction into Scotland of field-preaching, after the example
of Whitefield and Wesley in England and her colonies,
which was the principal fact and offence of their awakening career. They followed appeals in public with personal
counsel and prayer when opportunity offered, but he depended mainly upon the proclamation of the uncompromising gospel. Nothing else was thought of, so far
were they in advance of the stereotyped and powerless
order of things around them.

That more might have been accomplished in harvest-
work by greater concentration of saving influences which
personal contact in the inquiry-meeting and in the home
affords, we may not doubt from the laws of mind and
the immediate decisions demanded by all the voices of
God to the human soul.

The mighty impulse given to a pure Christianity by
these men of " new measures " for their times and country was not confined to a kingdom nor a continent. The
dying embers of the sacred fires kindled in Europe and
America by the Wesleys and Whitefield were fed and
fanned into a flame, which warmed afresh the bosom of
the church, and lit up the horizon of her future with
cheering promise of the coming glories of new conquests
to the praise of her waiting King. How constantly

repeated is the humiliating lesson which is now taught
us across the Atlantic in the triumphs of grace there,
that aggressive, fearless men and measures meet with
their greatest opposition among the nominal people of
God.

CHAPTER VIII.

THE AMERICAN EVANGELIST. — RELIGIOUS CONDITION OF THE CHURCHES. — REV. ASAHEL NETTLETON, D. D. — HIS EARLY YEARS. — COLLEGE LIFE. — RELIGIOUS STRUGGLES AND DELIVERANCE. — WITH MILLS, LOOKS TO THE MISSIONARY FIELD. — VISITS WASTE PLACES AT HOME. — BECOMES AN EVANGELIST. — HIS LABORS. — MEASURES. — PREACHING. — DEATH. — HIS SPECIAL WORK.

IN the summer of 1809, among the graduates of Yale College was a young man of pleasing yet serious aspect, whose soul was fired with a lofty purpose. Born on a farm in North Killingworth, Connecticut, April 21, 1783, Asahel Nettleton quietly continued in agricultural pursuits with his father till he reached his majority. He was trained to habits of strictest morality and taught the catechism by his parents, who were communicants in the Congregationalist Church on the half-way covenant plan. His leisure hours were improved in the study of such books as he was able to procure preparatory to entering college. The convictions of sin and of the need of Christ, to which he was not a stranger, in 1800, after a struggle extending through ten months, culminated in a clear conversion. For two years before, revivals, which for nearly half a century had gradually declined, again became more frequent; his native town was blessed with a gracious visitation, and his strong will surrendered to God. His experience was a marked one, from the conflict with legality and doctrines. He was "slain by the law and made alive by Christ."

With Samuel I. Mills, who was born on the same day,

without any knowledge by either of the other's feelings, he had a strong desire and purpose to be a missionary to pagan lands. No board of missions had then been formed in America. These congenial spirits were drawn together, communing first through correspondence and later in "goodly fellowship" at Yale, to which Mills journeyed on purpose to see his friend, who still remained in college in the position of butler. But by singular providence neither was to preach Christ to the heathen.

After waiting with hope deferred for an opening, Mr. Nettleton was licensed in the summer of 1811, and immediately sought waste places of Zion with the cherished expectation of erelong transferring his service to a distant and darker land. His attention was turned to the destitute towns on the borders of Rhode Island, in the eastern part of his native State, where religious meetings were held only by travelling ministers, and itinerants of small attainments, self-appointed to their circuits of limited activity. They were often injudicious and disorderly, finding fault with the settled ministry, and introducing novel methods of their own. Women were invited to exhort the assemblies, and an irreverent freedom encouraged.

Mr. Davenport's erratic, fanatical course was fresh in the minds of the people of that region where he began his career. Pamphlets setting forth in glowing language the evils attending the mighty work under Edwards and Whitefield were on the book-shelf of many a home. The gifted and earnest young preacher at once met these facts, which moulded his whole method of labor afterwards. The condition of New England churches generally was that of preparation for more of the aggressive preaching and movements of half a century previous, in which he was destined soon to engage.

The Lord had raised up and endowed intellectually and

spiritually such leaders in Israel as Griffin, Dwight, the younger Edwards, Hooker, and others. Under their ministry revivals were enjoyed which saved the dying life of true religion, and prepared the way for a new era of evangelistic laborers and their wide-spread influence in the land.

While the results of Mr. Nettleton's labors in eastern Connecticut were not visibly large, mainly from the hinderances suggested and the want of believing prayer among the people of God by profession, personally it was useful discipline for his special work. In the autumn of 1812 he was invited to preach in South Salem, New York, where there was no pastor and no spiritual concern. A visit on his way thither to the Rev. Bennet Tyler, D. D., of South Britain, was the commencement of a lifelong and very "endeared friendship," which, after the evangelist's death, made the survivor his appreciative, admiring biographer. The deep religious feeling in the town induced him, at the earnest desire of Mr. Tyler and others, to remain a week. The description by the latter of Mr. Nettleton's manner at this beginning of his career will make an interesting portrait of him as he appeared before the public assembly : —

"His manner at this time was somewhat peculiar, but not so much so as to injure his usefulness. His address at the first meeting which he attended will not soon be forgotten by those who heard it. It was in a school-house crowded with people, not a few of whom were under deep conviction of sin. As he rose, being an entire stranger, every eye was fixed upon him, and a breathless silence pervaded the assembly. With great solemnity he looked upon the congregation, and thus began : ' What is that murmur which I hear ? I wish I had a new heart. What shall I do? They tell me to repent. I can't repent. I wish they would give me some other direction.' He thus went on for a short time, personating the awakened sinner, and bringing out the feelings of his heart. He then changed the form of his address, and in a solemn and affectionate manner appealed to the consciences of his hearers, and showed them that they must repent or perish; that it was their reasonable duty to repent immediately; and that ministers could not direct them to anything short of repentance without being unfaithful to their souls. The address produced a thrilling effect, and served greatly to deepen the convictions of those who were anxious.

"During the week he remained in South Britain he took a lively interest in the revival which was in progress, and he left the place with his heart glowing with love to souls and with ardent desires that God would give him grace to be faithful to the people among whom he was going to labor. From that time, for ten years, it was his happy lot to be employed almost constantly in revivals of religion."

Dr. Nettleton's work at first was almost wholly with parishes without pastors, where there was great spiritual declension, strengthening the things which remained of former blessing and rebuilding the walls of Zion. He often stayed several months in a place to accomplish this result. He was equally adapted, by the same qualities which made him successful there, to aid pastors needing assistance in time of revival, or because they failed, whatever the cause, to awaken savingly those whom they may have faithfully instructed. At South Salem, New York, his method was to preach on the Sabbath, hold one or two meetings during the week, and converse with persons as he had opportunity. Very soon there was apparent great solemnity. At the end of two weeks, several young people, after an evening meeting, went to the house where he boarded, deeply anxious. The following day he found in the families he visited the same evidence that a work of grace had commenced in the town.

And now appeared Mr. Nettleton's conservative spirit, made intensely so by the facts we have noticed. He never encouraged hope, but warned converts of the danger of self-deception, and dwelt much upon the distinguishing marks of genuine conversion. If he erred, it must be confessed that it was on the safe side ; and yet it may be a question how far, in this crisis of religious feeling, the process of testing and holding back the hopeful disciple, to make him know, if possible, by certain evidences, whether he is one or not, may be scriptural and wise.

The revival spread with great power, and many expressed a saving interest in Christ. For two months his labors were crowned with increasing success, when, the parish agitating the subject of calling him to the pastorate, he suddenly took his departure. The same plan of effort, with like results, was repeated in Danbury. In 1813 he enjoyed similar seasons of harvest in Lyme, in Milton, and near Litchfield, where Dr. Lyman Beecher was pastor. This gifted and faithful preacher, in connection with a neighboring minister, raised funds, and indirectly secured this evangelist. Mr. Nettleton's peculiar tact in the wise adaptation of means to a given result was noticeable here. The place was almost prayerless in the deep sleep of all classes over spiritual realities. He had, before he came there, requested the people of God to pray for that place. Upon stating, at the close of one of his earliest meetings, that he had come to labor for a revival, and urging them to seek it at the mercy-seat, he added, "Whether you do or not, it is possible there may be one, for Christians in other places have agreed to pray for you." The effect was electric, and there were cases of pungent conviction on the spot.

There was an incident in the progress of the precious season of refreshing, interesting from its similarity to the phenomena of the "Great Awakening." A meeting

was so pervaded by the Holy Ghost that all present
were bowed under His presence, and some cried out in
"such horror of mind that it became necessary to remove
them to a neighboring house." The scene was new to
Mr. Nettleton, and for a few moments the usual quiet
was disturbed. His executive ability, together with his
habitual self-possession, restored order, and he addressed
the assembly in the following cautious, judicious language : —

"It may, perhaps, be new to some of you that there
should be such distress for sin. But there was great distress on the day of Pentecost, when thousands were
pricked in the heart, and cried out, 'Men and brethren,
what shall we do?' Some of you may, perhaps, be ready
to say, If this is religion, we wish to have nothing to do
with it. My friends, this is not religion. Religion does
not cause its subjects to feel and act thus. These individuals are thus distressed, not because they have religion,
but because they have no religion and have found it out.

"It was so on the day of Pentecost. The thousands who
were pricked in their heart had found that they had no
religion, and were unprepared to meet their God. They
had made the discovery that they were lost sinners, and
that their souls were in jeopardy every hour."

Mr. Nettleton constantly aimed, by the calmness of his
manners in his management of public services, to prevent what he had learned to dread, — any extraordinary
effects or highly emotional expressions. The arrangement
of his meetings very essentially aided him in this purpose.
Excepting on the Sabbath, they were held only on occasional evenings, and all of them in churches and school-
rooms. Over them he presided with an ever-watchful
eye and with unruffled serenity and solemnity.

He remained at Milton four months, according to a rule
he had adopted to finish the work he commenced, when

possible to do so, before leaving it to other hands. When
he felt that, for the time, the harvest was comparatively
garnered, he left for another field. Meanwhile, he assisted,
with very visible effect, the pastor at Hadlyme, then went
to South Farms, in Litchfield, where occurred several of
the most striking cases of conversion in any revival during
his ministry.

When exhausted, he took his departure for rest in his
native town. He refused, in his disinterested devotion to
the service of Him who "had not where to lay His head,"
to accept the money tendered him by Dr. Beecher. Having no family, his thought never went beyond the immediate supply of his wants.

In the autumn of 1814 he resumed his favorite employment, which was the cultivation of waste places, beginning
at East Granby. At Bolton, Manchester, New Haven,
Salisbury, Bridgewater, Torrington, Waterbury, and other
towns in Connecticut; in Pittsfield, Lenox, Lee, Taunton,
and other places in Massachusetts; Saratoga, Schenectady,
including the college, Brooklyn, and elsewhere in New
York; and in Newark, New Jersey, his methods of labor
and success were the same in general character and fruits.

Saratoga, where Mr. Nettleton went expressly to recruit
his strength, became the centre of a glorious revival
throughout the county. In Pittsfield, Berkshire County,
Mass., he saw the same outgoing of the Holy Spirit among
the people. Perhaps no place was the arena of greater
conflict and excitement, on account of opposition, than
Pittsfield. On the Fourth of July, while the revival was
in progress, the enemies of the work were parading the
streets with martial music and firing salutes. Dr. Hum-
phrey preached through it all with remarkable power,
while Christians trembled for the ark of God, and prayed.
God heard their petitions, and turned the boasted triumph
of the wicked, under the patriotic disguise of a celebra-

tion, into inglorious defeat. The inquiry meeting that evening, before sermon, was largely attended, and the Holy Ghost fell upon the assembly. Mr. Nettleton took the pulpit, and rose quite above himself in resistless force of argument and appeal. His subject was, "Up, get you out of this place!" When, in his description of Lot's escape from Sodom, he reached the outbursting storm of fire, "he turned the heads of the audience completely towards the windows. They involuntarily looked round to see the conflagration — to see Sodom in flames!" The scene reminds us of Whitefield's great occasions.

In 1822 he contracted a typhoid fever and was brought very low, while visiting at the house of his friend, Rev. Mr. Parmele, at Bolton, who, in turn, took the disease and died. For nearly two years the evangelist seldom preached. Feeling the need of a collection of hymns better adapted to revivals than any then in use, while at Bolton he compiled the "Village Hymns." They were widely popular, and used by many parishes for ordinary chapel and vestry services. In Virginia and North Carolina, whither he went for his health, he was the same earnest herald of the Cross, winning souls to the crucified One.

Mr. Nettleton, after having preached with considerable success in the spring of 1825 in Brooklyn, N. Y., and in the summer of that year in Taunton, Mass., went to the city of New York early in the winter in feeble health. He remained here until February, when he repaired to Jamaica, L. I. He found there a divided church; but by his remarkable tact and patient love he united the members, and entered into a rich spiritual harvest. The following winter he was in Albany, and physically so weak he thought death was near. In the spring he visited Durham, and although scarcely able to preach was instrumental in the conversion of many souls. After spending

a few months at Lexington Heights, among the Catskill
Mountains, in the autumn of 1827 he journeyed southward, and passed the winter in Virginia.

At this time Rev. Charles G. Finney had become famous
in conducting great revivals in the Middle States, and
awakened the fears of Mr. Nettleton that his boldly
aggressive methods were leading to dangerous extravagance in theological views and in the means employed.
While pre-eminently calm and cautious in his work, a
pastor in the staid Old Dominion wrote of him: " His
measures — if it be proper thus to characterize the means
which he used in connection with revivals of religion —
were new in this region, and excited great interest." This
suggestive statement indicates clearly the danger of an
unconsciously false bias and unsound judgment upon
innovations which supplement or supplant established
usages and favorite theories.

In 1829, Mr. Nettleton again labored in New England
with precious but diminished results. With the approach
of winter he was compelled to return to the South. He
assisted Drs. Spring, Dickenson, and Snodgrass, of New
York, in revivals during the winter of 1830–31. With the
opening spring he made a voyage to England, where he met
the wild rumors of American religious excitements, and
felt called upon to condemn them, and vindicate the ministry from the odium all had to bear for the errors of a few.
In this he was honest, but needlessly alarmed, as we have
since learned in the light of history. Upon his return
from Europe he only preached occasionally, retiring soon
after to East Windsor, where he spent most of the remainder of his life in comparative quiet. Upon the organization
of the Theological Institute of Connecticut, he was chosen
Professor of Pastoral Duty.

In 1839 he received the honorary title of D. D. from
Jefferson College in Pennsylvania, and Hampton Sidney

College, Virginia. He remonstrated against the compliment when proposed at an earlier date by a New England institution. In his new trouble he sought counsel of an esteemed brother, who replied by relating the following anecdote : "A man once said to an aged clergyman, 'My neighbors are slandering me, and what shall I do?— " Do your duty,' said the minister, 'and think nothing about it. If they are disposed to throw mud, let them, but do not attempt to wipe it off; lest you should wipe it all over you.'"

He decided, upon reflection, to emulate the example of Dr. Porter, of Andover, in a like dilemma. " What shall a sober man do? If he refuses this title on general principles, because it is inconsistent with the spirit of the gospel, he charges a long list of worthies, such as Watts, etc., with bearing a public mark of pride or folly. If he refuses on principles which respect himself only, he is liable to be charged with the ostentation of humility, and really needs much prayer and heart-searching to be sure that cursed pride is not at the bottom. For much noise to get rid of this contemptible honor resembles ocean into tempest wrought, to waft a feather or to drown a fly. A wise man would not kill a gnat by a blow that might fracture his leg."

Albert Barnes, the commentator of world-wide, well-earned fame, seems to have declined successfully the distinction, escaping both Scylla and Charybdis.

We now come to the scenes which precede the "inevitable hour." Mr. Nettleton never recovered fully from the prostration of his whole system by the fever of 1822 ; but by the visits South secured comfortable health till the summer of 1841, when he was prostrated with that painful disease, gravel. He gradually sank, after repeated surgical operations. With great submission, he often alluded to the small importance he always attached " to the manner in

which persons die." He had not the least solicitude
respecting the issue of his sickness. By the pressure of
his hand, when too weak to speak, he assured those who
watched the ebbing life, that all was peace. He serenely
departed this life on the morning of May 16, 1844, a few
weeks over fifty-eight years of age.

It is impossible to estimate the number of hopeful conversions under the ministry of Dr. Nettleton. He kept
no journal for several years; but several thousands united
to the different churches, scattered over the extensive
region of his faithful ministry. Of the peculiar qualities
of his character for his chosen calling, and his methods,
some hints have been given already, incidentally, in the
brief narrative of his labors.

Dr. Nettleton was an uncompromising Calvinist, holding, without the Antinomian element, with deepest conviction, the doctrines of grace as presented in the Edwardian
system of theology. He was jealous of the least departure from them. They were the substance of his preaching, in which he pressed home, with great emphasis, the
guilt and responsibility of the impenitent, along with his
entire dependence upon the Holy Spirit in every step of
recovery from an utterly lost condition. He could therefore labor harmoniously and successfully only with Christians of similar views, and did not attempt to do so in any
other relations, never once thinking of "union meetings,"
now becoming common in and out of revivals. His own
experience, also, had much to do with his ministerial
methods. His conversion was preceded by a long and
fearful struggle, during which he had very humbling
views of his own condition by nature, and his indebtedness
to sovereign grace. He was therefore very careful to
guard against superficial convictions and any doubts respecting the doctrines which he had learned in the Shorter
Catechism while a child; nor did he see that there was

the danger of extreme views in the direction of his own
convictions; of discouraging weak faith, and of exalting
divine sovereignty at the expense of human responsibility. He opposed with equal decision and fervor measures
which were novel and apparently unsafe in their tendency. Rising for prayer and "anxious seats" were in
his view altogether human contrivances, which, by foster-
ing reliance on means, would hinder and not help the convicted sinner in his unyielding rebellion. Presenting the
ability, and obligation therefore, of the unconverted to
become Christians by the act of their own will, to Dr.
Nettleton was making conversion a mere promise of obedience, a purpose to obey God, and consequently a most
dangerous heresy. As one of our ablest and most devout
theological professors said to the writer, "Standing alone,
some of these methods and statements might have led to
serious results; but in connection with the intelligent
piety and sound common-sense of the laity generally,
and with an educated ministry, the dreaded evils were
only incidental and temporary."

Dr. Kirk says truly, that no evangelist, probably, in
his own way, which displayed, it cannot be denied, great
wisdom, had more management and measures in the successful promotion of his work.

Dr. Edward Beecher writes : —

"He often deliberately resorted to a frequent repetition of the leading ideas, till they were deeply rooted
in the mind. He once illustrated to me his theory on
this subject by the following similitude: 'A shepherd, driving before him a large flock of sheep, does
not go straight on in the path in the centre of the
road. If he did he would soon leave most of the flock
behind. To avert this he often stops and turns, now to
the right and now to the left, so as to keep the whole
flock before him. Some preachers,' he said, 'drive a few

of the audience before them, but soon outrun and leave
behind, straggling to the right hand and the left, a large
portion of their flock.'

"He said, also, that a large class of minds were awakened and convinced of sin, not by any connected train of
reasoning, but by some one sentence or word which smites
and penetrates them like an arrow. He illustrated this
remark by a reference to a sermon that I had heard on the
parable of the lost sheep. In one part of the sermon he
came to a point in his description of the state of the
sinner where he rose to the climax of emotion and impression by ringing out, in clear and thrilling tones, the
words, '*Lost*, LOST, LOST.' It startled and electrified
me at the time, but I did not know how great was its
practical power until he told me that those words had
been the arrows of the Almighty to many in the various
places in which the sermon had been delivered."

Dr. Sprague, in his annals of the American pulpit,
referring to his prejudice against new revival methods,
records very truly of him : —

"There was, after all, something that gave character and
effect to his measures, which has not been, and perhaps
cannot be, described. He had a manner of doing little
things that was perfectly inimitable ; another, in attempting the same, might not only defeat his end but render
himself absolutely ridiculous. He knew how to meet
every case with the most appropriate counsels, and not
unfrequently he produced the deepest impression by absolute silence, when he knew that the individual had expected
to be personally addressed. When it is said that he had
no machinery in connection with the ordinary means of
grace beyond an inquiry meeting, it is due to truth also to
say that everything that he said and did was so peculiar as
to form what might almost seem a distinct system of
measures."

"He aimed at the average common mind, and not at leading minds. He sought also to fix a few truths deeply in one sermon, rather than to go over a wide field of thought."

No single fact illustrates the very conservative views which gifted and good men then entertained more forcibly than the apology offered by Dr. Nettleton's biographer for his *extemporaneous preaching*, a style of address not only indispensable in revival interest, but urged now upon the attention of theological students by the masters in Israel. "Dr. Nettleton rarely had any manuscript before him, unless it were a brief outline of his discourse, — a course circumstances compelled him to adopt," (referring to the occupation of his time in meetings and private conversation). Even he was "exceedingly tried on the subject," but after prayerful reflection and taking counsel of his brethren, he decided "that it was his duty to persevere in that course which God was crowning with such signal success. But notwithstanding these disadvantages he was an instructive preacher."

We smile over this vindication of the only true method, with the proper training always assumed, of pulpit instruction and appeal, no less than forensic pleading. Thus does the Lord use varied and inharmonious workmen, in their views of particular methods, to keep the balance of forces and reach all classes of minds and conditions of feeling.

Dr. Nettleton had a grand work to do, and did it well. He went over fields — once more or less under the divine influence — that were largely to such cultivation as irresponsible, occasional itinerants might give them. He turned up the fallow ground, ploughing deep, sowing sifted seed, and waiting on God for harvest. Beyond their prayers, he trusted little to laymen ; and nothing at all in the hands of the saintly women, whom he thoroughly believed, and in the strictest interpretation of the words, should "keep silence in the churches," excepting in meetings exclusively for their own sex.

Only such a worker could have been welcomed by most of the pastors with whom he labored, whose views coincided precisely with his own.

The Divine call and mission of this evangelist and the great secret of his power are impressively stated in the language of President Dwight, of Yale College, who used to say to his classes as they went out from under his care, " Young men, it is not great talent or great learning that is to enable you to do good ; it is abiding in Christ. The young man of whom we expected least all the way through college attained to the greatest usefulness, and did the most for the Master's cause. That man was A. Nettleton. His abilities were not striking, but he pre-eminently lived with the Lord, and wherever he went Christ went with him."

CHAPTER IX.

Rev. Charles G. Finney. — His Nativity. — School Days. — Studies Law. — Large Promise — Religious Character. — Criticisms of Preaching and Prayer-Meetings. — Conversion. — Characteristic Decision. — Prepares to Preach. — Licensed. — Ordained as an Evangelist. — Labors in Jefferson and St. Lawrence Counties. — Campaign in Central New York — Rome. — Utica. — Opposition. — Testimony of Pastors. — Auburn. — Troy. — Delaware. — Pennsylvania. — New York City — Providence. — Boston, etc. — Chatham Street Theatre purchased for a Church. — Mr. Finney called to it. — Great Success. — Pastor of Broadway Tabernacle.

WONDERFUL is God's providential order in His redeeming work, although, to superficial observation, there is often no connection between great events and changes in the spiritual world. Dr. Nettleton began with neglected places, a solitary evangelist, gradually working into the best rural parishes of what was then the most accessible part of New England. But the influence of his glorious work went abroad over the country, awakening Christian thought and earnest prayer. Just as his strength began to fail, and there was the preparation for a wider and more aggressive evangelism, Christ's ambassador appeared in the Empire State, to lead the churches into the field of conflict and victory.

In the quiet and beautiful village of Adams, Jefferson County, N. Y., in the year 1823, a young man of thirty, a law-student in the office of Judge Wright, came from a grove not far distant, with tearful yet lighted face, and closing with a will his law books, said, substantially,

"There is an end of law, and henceforth it is the gospel of Christ." There had been for some time a deep religious interest in the community, which he had resisted, and by his commanding influence hindered its progress among the youthful hearts around him. With a keen discernment of inconsistencies, he had sharply criticised ministers and laymen. Sometimes, when the bell rang for prayer-meeting, he would say to his fellow-student: "Come, W——, let us go to meeting." At its close, returning to his office, he entertained his friend with an analysis of the petitions offered, in remarks like the following: "Did you notice T——'s prayer? He did n't know what he wanted; his part was Orthodox *duty*. But there was L——, he got hold; he meant something, and believes in God." And so he went round the circle, with a discriminating, if not always just, estimate of the prayers to which he had listened.

To the pastor he once said, after service, "Mr. G——, you don't believe what you preach; were I in your place, holding the truth you declare, I would ring the church-bell, and cry in the streets, 'Fire! fire!'"

His unsettled religious views were adjusted upon an evangelical basis while engaged in the study of law, which led him to a thoughtful examination of the Bible. This brought on an intellectual and spiritual conflict, which terminated in his conversion, to the great astonishment of all his friends and acquaintances, and, we might add, to his own also. In that grove, where we have stood with strange and deep emotions, he knelt to settle the question of submission to the Spirit before he left it. Suddenly the terrible struggle ceased; the storm passed, and a shout of victory and joy burst from his lips. He bounded like a freed captive to his place of study, and renounced prospective legal honors and a fortune for the reproach and triumphs of Christ.

This was the beginning of the remarkable religious history of the Rev. Charles G. Finney. When he announced the change in the public assembly, his first utterance was, while his large expressive eyes glanced over the surprised audience, "My God, is it I!" Yes, it *was* he; and from that hour, his testimony to the power of God's truth and grace, without an uncertain sound, has been growing in richness of experience and the area of its saving influence. He learned subsequently that among those who ceased not to pray for him, were devout women who had, for a long time, made him the burden of believing supplication, to which he always felt his conversion was to be directly attributed.

The evening of the day of his conversion, Mr. Finney received that baptism of the Holy Spirit which carries the soul far beyond the peace of justification into manifestations of Christ and the glories of redemption, which no language can portray. There is in this experience the power of a conscious union and communion with the Father, Son, and Holy Ghost, and also a vivid realization of all spiritual verities. The next morning brought a fresh flood of glory from the Divine Comforter over his whole being. It is to these repeated blessings he attributes his success in saving others, and leading Christians to accept their privilege of victorious faith, and its continuous rest in Jesus.

We add his own testimony on this subject: —

"I was powerfully converted on the morning of the 10th of October, 1821. I was too ignorant to appreciate or define the change that had come over me. As I hastily retired from the spot where I had knelt, and for the first time believed God, I exclaimed aloud, 'If I am ever converted, I will preach the gospel.' God took me at my word. The remainder of that day was spent in business; but my peace of mind was perfect. It was new. I did

9

not understand it. I could have no consciousness of sin. My sense of guilt was all gone, and I could not revive my conviction of sin. I thought I must have quenched the Holy Spirit; and, remembering the boldness of my language when I in the morning closed with God's promises, I suspected I had committed an unpardonable sin. But this thought did not trouble me, and I could not be troubled about anything. The moment I turned from business that evening, my whole soul seemed to swell within me, and I was filled with an inexpressible longing to pour my whole being out to God. I rushed into a dark room, which, however, seemed perfectly light. I met the Saviour as I entered. He seemed to approach to meet me. His look broke my heart all to pieces in a moment. I fell at His feet overcome. I confessed, and wept aloud like a child, and must have remained in this posture for two hours. It did not even occur to me at that time, nor for months afterward, that I did not see Jesus with my fleshly eyes.

"When I rose and returned to the office, a mighty baptism of the Holy Spirit came upon me, and seemed to go through me, soul and body. Words can never adequately describe it. It seemed to descend upon me like a mighty shower, and then to glow over and through me like successive waves of love and power. I felt as if my whole being was filled to its utmost capacity with the life and love and power of God. The fulness was so great, I seemed pressed to bursting and beyond endurance with divine love and power. This lasted until I was exhausted. The next morning, as I arose, it came upon me again in the same manner and measure. The evening before, just described, while the waves of love were passing over me, a young man came in; and, as I attempted to tell what ailed me, he fell upon the floor and cried out, in deep anguish, 'Pray for me.' Immediately after this baptism,

I found myself filled with an endowment of power before which sinners could not stand.

"I can now only give an outline in this short article. I have had many similar baptisms since, with like results, but cannot give an account of them here. I dare not conceal these great works and mercies of God."

Mr. Finney was born in Warren, Litchfield County, Conn., August 29, 1792. His parents were not religious people till after his own conversion. They removed to a farm in Henderson, Jefferson County, N. Y. Here he was master of his first school, when in his eighteenth year. Later he taught in New Jersey, alternating between giving and receiving instruction in the schools, till he commenced his legal course in the year 1818, which was God's beginning with him of decisive preparation for the great work before him. In the chamber of a store in Adams he began his theological studies. He commenced preaching during an extensive revival at Evans Mills, where the church earnestly desired him to remain. But he was not permitted to settle anywhere, being pressed by the Spirit and Providence of God from place to place, and was thus led to the work of an evangelist without any plan or design of his own.

His license by the presbytery of St. Lawrence was dated March, 1824; and the same year he was ordained. During this and the next year he was constantly conducting revivals in the county of his home and the adjoining one, St. Lawrence.

In 1825 he entered the wide, and ever after widening, arena of his labors, which drew to him the growing interest of the American, and even English Dissenting churches. Leaving the quieter fields of uninterrupted success in northern New York, he accepted an invitation to the central and prosperous village of Rome, a few miles from Utica. About this time he removed his ecclesias-

tical relation from the presbytery of St. Lawrence to that
of Oneida.

It seems quite remarkable, in contrast with the present
accounts in detail of revival meetings, that, even in the
religious press of Mr. Finney's time, no full reports of the
stirring scenes which attended his labors should have
appeared. The reason seems to have been the fear of
public sentiment, which set strongly against what was
clearly the mighty power of God abroad among the people.
It was Whitefield's fearless and awakening proclamation
of truth over again, with substantially the same effects.
The presbytery of Oneida was evidently, as a body, in
advance of their ministerial brethren generally. Through
a committee composed of Rev. John Frost, Rev. Moses
Gillett, and Rev. Noah Coe, an extended narrative of the
revivals in the county was published. Mr. Gillett, pastor
of the Presbyterian Church in Rome, reported under date
of Oct. 30, 1826, as follows : —

"A revival prevailed in the town of Western, under the
preaching of Mr. Finney, the influence of which was felt
here. The latter part of last November, the presence of
the Spirit was visible in the conviction of sinners in the
eastern part of the town, called Wright's Settlement.
Meetings soon became very solemn. In about four weeks
forty might be numbered as hopeful converts to Christ.

"Monday evening, the last week in December, a meeting
of inquiry was held for convicted sinners. Mr. Finney
came here that evening and remained four weeks, and was
a distinguished instrument in promoting the revival. The
meeting of inquiry was at a private house, and a prayer-
meeting at a school-house was held at the same time. The
room was filled with inquiring sinners. After prayer, personal conversation, and a short address, we dismissed them.
Instead of retiring they partly fell upon each other, and
gave vent to their feelings in sobs and groans. It was with

difficulty we prevailed upon them to retire. From this time the excitement became general in the village. Meetings were held for about five weeks in the church every evening, and most of the time the house was crowded. Sometimes there was preaching, and sometimes only prayers, with short addresses. Meetings of inquiry were now held in the day-time, and in some instances, three hundred and upwards have attended. Great stillness and solemnity prevailed till the close, when sometimes there would be a burst of feeling in groans and loud weeping. We urged them to retire, telling them that they must look to Christ; that their impenitent tears would not save them. When not engaged in meeting we visited from house to house. We often found sinners in great agony of mind, and Christians in almost equal agony praying for them. Although constantly engaged, it seemed we had little to do, except to look on and see the salvation of the Lord.

" Worldly business was, to a great extent, suspended. Religion was the principal subject of conversation in our streets, stores, and even taverns. At two different times, it appeared that more than twenty were hopefully converted in twenty-four hours. All classes of people were affected. Many who had regularly attended public worship for twenty years, and lived through revivals unmoved, were now made to tremble and bow to the Cross. Four lawyers, four physicians, all the merchants who were not professors before, and men of the first respectability in the place, were hopeful converts.

" During the greatest excitement there was but little open opposition. Scoffers were confounded; Universalists trembled. Some renounced their sentiments, and were brought to repentance. The moralist was stripped of his vain covering, and led to beg for mercy. Great is the change. ' It is the Lord's doing, and it is marvellous in our eyes.' In March, one hundred and sixty-seven were received into the church upon profession of faith. The whole number received is two hundred and eighty-four. Upwards of thirty have united with the Methodist Church, and some with the Baptists and Episcopalians. The number of hopeful converts cannot be accurately stated, — probably not far from five hundred. Some of them were from adjacent towns. A number who have expressed hopes here have not yet united with any church.

" For eleven months there has been no time when sinners were not under conviction, and but few weeks without instances of hopeful conversion. Meetings of inquiry are continued, and a spirit of fervent prayer still prevails.

" There has been such wrestling and agony in prayer as we had never before witnessed. Christians viewed their impenitent connections and neighbors as standing on the brink of hell, and that nothing but the mercy of God could save them. They prayed as though they could not be denied. They seemed to take hold of the promises of God to prayer with strong faith. In little praying circles intercessions were made for individuals by name. Striking answers appeared to be given. In the language of the prophet it might be said, ' As soon as Zion travailed she brought forth her children.' Christians seemed to plead with God, as a child would plead with his parent ; and they found Him more ready to give the Holy Spirit, than earthly parents to give good gifts to their children. Indeed, the great instrument in this glorious work has been *prayer.* Christians seemed to believe both the promises and threatenings of God, and in view of them have wrestled at the throne of grace until they prevailed. The word of God, in sermons, short addresses, at prayer-meetings, and in private conversation, has had a powerful effect in convicting sinners of their great guilt, and desert of eternal punishment. The truths brought into view are such as have generally been termed the doctrines of grace.

"The command was urged, 'Make you a new heart and a new spirit, for why will ye die?' No allowance was given to wait God's time. They were told, ' Now is the accepted time, now is the day of salvation'; that the longer they continued impenitent the greater their guilt, the more danger of becóming hardened, of grieving the Spirit, and of dying without hope.

"Meetings of inquiry have apparently been a powerful means of bringing sinners to repentance. When hundreds have attended there would be a death-like stillness, and great solemnity in almost every countenance. They were conversed with individually, and such instruction given as their case seemed to require. In many instances, convicted sinners have apparently been born again while praying.

"It will doubtless be asked, with no ordinary interest, What are the fruits of this revival?' In general, the subjects appear as well, if not better, than in former revivals which I have witnessed. A marked reformation in morals is too apparent to be denied. The Sabbath is more strictly observed. Intemperance and profane swearing are checked. More good feeling in neighborhoods and families prevails. The church is blessed with peace and harmony. It may be said, in truth, these Christians love one another."

The following account is from the Rev. Mr. Aikin, pastor of the First Presbyterian Church, Utica : —

" Rev. Mr. Finney came to Utica ; and, as in other places, his plain and pungent and faithful preaching was attended with evident and wonderful success. Christians had been told of their departures from God, their backslidings in heart, their lukewarmness, their love of the world and conformity to it, and of the necessity of a broken spirit of deep and thorough repentance, before they could reasonably expect a general revival of religion. It was not long before the work became powerful. Places of worship were thronged ; and the stillness of the sepulchre reigned,

broken occasionally by a deep sigh from some heart that
was writhing under the condemning influence of divine
truth. Instead of noise and confusion, the meetings were
solemn, and sometimes awfully so, by the presence of God,
which made sinners afraid, and Christians humble and
still. True, there has been noise; there has been no
small stir about these things, but it has been on the other
side — among the enemies of the revival, as it was in the
days of the Apostle.

"The general features of this revival are the same as
have always marked every genuine outpouring of the
Spirit, since the apostolic age. I shall, therefore, not
repeat them; but would here observe that it has been
confined to no particular class in the community. Its sweet
and saving influence has fallen upon the rich and the poor,
the ignorant and the learned, and moulded into its own
lovely image, as we humbly trust, the proud moralist and
the polluted debauchee. It has made "new creatures"
of gamblers and drunkards, and swearers and Sabbath-
breakers, and brought the self-righteous Pharisee, the
deluded sceptic, deist, and Universalist, to abandon their
dreams of happiness and heaven without a holy heart,
and to fly for cleansing to the blood of the Lamb.

"The probable number of converts in Utica is about
five hundred. The number of hopeful converts in a population like this, it is not easy definitely to ascertain. Not
far from sixty persons, some of whom were travellers, who
'turned in to tarry but for a night,' or day, or week,
others belonging to the towns around, experienced, as we
trust, the grace of God. More than a hundred, the subjects
of the revival, have united with the First Presbyterian
Church; numbers with the Methodist and Baptist, the
Second Presbyterian and Welsh Congregational Churches.
Many children, from seven to thirteen years of age, give
evidence of piety. Nor has this good work of the Lord

ceased. The spirit of prayer still continues, though in a less degree; and consequently conversions are less frequent than they were last winter. Scarcely a week has passed during the last summer, when one or more has not been brought into the kingdom of Christ. For the last six weeks, twenty have hopefully experienced the grace of God.

"Besides Mr. Finney, who has been signally owned and blessed, important services have been rendered by the Rev. D. Nash, Mr. N. Smith, and other brethren in the ministry, who are remembered with gratitude both by the church and their pastor.

"With regard to the means used in this revival, I should say nothing, were it not for the gross misrepresentations that have gone abroad. They are substantially the same as were employed by Whitefield, Edwards, Brainard, and by some still living, whose praise is in all the churches. The grand means, and that into which all others are resolved, has been the *Word of God:* the doctrines of salvation; the depravity of the heart, consisting not merely in the negative want of love to God, but in positive hatred to him; the law of God, its extent, purity, perfection, and binding influence; the sovereignty of God, illustrated and enforced, not so much by abstract reasoning as by matters of fact; the nature and necessity of regeneration by the Holy Spirit, and justification by faith alone, — these truths have been preached *constantly*, both in the pulpit and out of it. Nor have we failed to urge sinners to repent and submit to Jesus Christ, and that immmediately, as the only condition of forgiveness; warning them, at the same time, that, so long as they refused to comply, all their tears and prayers and efforts are not only vain, but sinful.

"Believing it to be duty to use every lawful and proper measure to render effectual divine truth, we have, and we trust in humble dependence on God, visited from house to house, conversed freely with individuals, and fearlessly declared the truths in the street, in the grocery, the counting-room, and private dwelling. We have also had various small circles for prayer, as well as stated and public prayer-meetings ; and, in the former, females, in some cases, though more seldom than we could wish, have taken a part. Never, in the same space of time, I am confident, was the Bible so much read in Utica, as it has been for twelve months past. Besides these means, discipline, meetings of inquiry, days of fasting and prayer, and conference meetings for the church, have been very useful.

"Never was so large a church more happily united than we have been during this revival ; and it is so still. I verily believe there is here the ' unity of the spirit in the bond of peace.' Some few individuals may have differed from their brethren with regard to the propriety of some measures ; but I have seen none who were blind to the mighty hand of God that was bowing down rebel sinners on every side, and none so hardened in unbelief as not to adore and rejoice in it."

In Troy and New Lebanon, Rev. Mr. Finney was blest with rich displays of divine glory in the salvation of the people. In a letter lately received from Dr. Richard Steele, who has been a "ruling elder" in the First Presbyterian Church, Auburn, fifty-one years, a sound, spiritual, active layman, widely known in central New York, he says of Mr. Finney : "He first came in the summer of 1826 ; preached with great power and marked success, although strongly opposed by some good people. In the winter of 1831, he came again from Rochester on his way to Boston. There was at the time considerable religious interest among us, and he was prevailed upon to stay over four or five days and preach a few times ; and, although he had paid his fare in the stage and directed the driver to call for him at two o'clock the next morning, at the house where

he stopped (a private residence) a petition was got up
signed by non-professors, some of whom were among the
most prominent citizens of the place, urging him not to
leave. That request was sent to his room, after he
had retired to bed; and it is said he uttered a groan, and
after a while sent word down to those who were waiting,
' Go to the stage office, and withdraw my name from the
list of passengers.' He then remained for say three or
four weeks. This was the most glorious revival under the
labors of any evangelist that has ever visited Auburn: the
fruits of these two revivals are among the most abiding
and decisive of any that we have enjoyed. The first
above named, you may say, continued two years; and
numbers were added to our church. Of the second, about
one hundred and forty were added to the First Church at
one time, and sixty to the Second Presbyterian Church;
also numbers to the Baptist and Methodist Churches, of
those who were converted under his preaching in our place
of worship. In those days also 'the brethren had a mind
to work,' by much prayer and continued labor."

In Rochester, N. Y., Mr. Finney saw one of the most
signal displays of divine power he was permitted to
witness, during all the years of his extraordinary success
in revivals. His discourses on moral government were
irresistible in their logic; and, in an atmosphere pervaded
by the Divine Spirit, did execution rarely seen since the
day of Pentecost. The leading minds of the city bowed
before the truth; and the heart of the Empire State was
stirred, and permanently blessed, as never before.

Similar scenes in character, if not always in degree,
attended his visits to Providence, R. I., and Boston,
having spent three winters in the latter city. His latest
effort here was under the pastorate of Rev. Dr. Stone,
Park Street Church, now at San Francisco. In several
places he repeated his labors the second and third time.

With reference to his itinerant labors and some of
their results, one who was intimately associated with him
says : —

"He has always spoken of the three great revivals in
Rochester, in which he labored, as among the most interesting ones he has ever seen. A large number of prominent lawyers were converted in that city, and a goodly
number of the converts in each of those revivals became
ministers of the gospel. The revivals in Oneida County
resulted in the conversion of many, a multitude of whom
entered the ministry, and some were foreign missionaries.
Dr. Garrett Judd and his wife, and Mrs. Gulick (the
mother of the missionary Gulicks), of the Sandwich Island
Mission, were converted in the revival at Utica and its
vicinity. The work all through central New York and
elsewhere had similar results. The revivals in Auburn,
N. Y., in 1826, and again in the spring of 1831, were
revivals of mark in their power and results : in Philadelphia and the one in Reading, Pa., in the years 1828 and
1829, were very powerful and permanent in their results.
Prayer and instruction, public and private, were the means
upon which he always relied. Prayer-meetings and meetings for inquirers were held, and such measures only were
employed as were calculated and required to bring the
awakened to immediate decision, and to accept Christ on
the spot. Instruction was the great instrument used, and
prayer to secure the teaching of the Holy Spirit. He
never resorted to any measures to create an excitement,
but only used such as seemed demanded by the necessities
of the work in every place. He laid great stress upon
secret prayer. He has never made any formal profession of
sanctification in the sense of living without sin, but has
long believed and taught that Christ is able in this life to
save his people from their sins ; that he is as willing as
he is able to do this : and he does not believe that those

who fall short of inculcating this doctrine preach the whole gospel. As to the fact whether A or B lives without sin, he does not pretend to judge or know, except by their fruits."

Dr. Steele gives us interesting details respecting the mighty work of God in Rochester and New York City :

AUBURN, N. Y., June 21, 1875.

MY DEAR BROTHER, —Your letter of the 18th inst. was received this day. I will think over and give some data that may be what in part you may desire.

In the early days of Brother Finney's preaching, we did n't have inquiry meetings, but at the evening service, after very plain direct presentation of truth, a decision was called for: those who would now consecrate themselves to God were requested to come forward for prayer, at other times rise upon their feet in the presence of the congregation. At other times all would be requested, who would now renew or make for the first time the consecration God required, to kneel down in their pews as evidence of such consecration; after prayer, Christians near by were in the habit of saying a few words to them by way of inquiry as to their state of mind But above all, my brother, the days were days of *labor*, and of prayer by the brethren, such as I never knew before or since. His first preaching here was attended with decided opposition, by some members of the church, also by a number of the impenitent, many of whom were then and afterwards converted to Christ, and are to-day among the most stable Christians we have. The second time Brother Finney came here was the winter of 1831, when the Word was accompanied with such power of the Spirit of God, that men bowed in their hearts like tall grass before the wind ; many, very many among us were turned to the Lord, and to this day are " living epistles, known and read of all men." Brother Finney's labors in Troy, in 1826 and 1827, of which I know personally, were much like unto his first visit to Auburn, in power and results, the fruits of which are as decidedly visible to-day. Then next in New York and Philadelphia : in the last-named city, my wife was one of the number of converts. Over ninety were added at one time to Rev. Mr. Patterson's church where Mr. Finney preached, also quite a number to other churches in the city, as results of his labors in that city at that time. The power of God in His truth was then and there displayed as decidedly as in any other locality. In New York City, in Prince Street Church, I spent one Sabbath ; and in the evening, after sermon, when called upon for a public manifestation of desire for prayer and consecration, it was thought that from four to five hundred came promptly forward. The central seats of the house and the centre aisle were crowded full of anxious inquirers. Then, too, Rochester. N. Y., is probably more indebted under God for its decided Christian character this day, as a city, to the different evangelical labors of Rev. Mr. Finney than to any other person. I think it was his second visitation there, say about 1836 or '38, when the most part of the lawyers, and many of the most prominent men of the city, were converted. Among the lawyers was Judge Gardner of the Supreme Court, and at one time the Lieut.-Governor of the State; of whom it was once said, he was *a great infidel,* but of whom it can now be said, he is a Christian and an elder in the First Presbyterian church of that city. One of those young lawyers, then converted, left the office, came to Auburn, and studied for and entered the ministry.

Perhaps twenty-five years ago, Mr. Finney again held a protracted meeting at Rochester. I spent a week there, and put up at the Eagle Tavern, where Judge Strong of the Supreme Court was at the time, who told me that he was in the habit of adjourning, so as to permit all to attend the meetings. After sermon, the inquirers were invited to pass into the adjoining rooms. The next morning after, there was held a general prayer-meeting, and oh, my brother, what power was there! The very thought almost braces me up like a clarion trumpet for the battle.

During the later years of Brother Finney, he has held two or three inquiry meetings a week, according to the state of the public mind.

At Buffalo, his preaching was blessed, not however so wonderfully as in some localities; but the fruits thereof have been remarkably permanent. The now Rev. Dr. Lord of that city was then a lawyer there, and prominent as a young man, and very successful in his profession ; but on hearing Mr. F. preach his second sermon, I think, he went forward for prayers, consecrated himself to Christ, left his law office, and after three years' study in the seminary at Auburn went forth to preach the gospel, and has preached in Buffalo over one third of a century. Many other men, Christians, are now what they are, because of the truth through him.

I am glad, my brother, that you are desirous of placing something before the public that will justify the labors of evangelists in the minds of Christians. When and where the Master evidently approves by the witness of his spirit in the conversion of souls, why should any that love Jesus draw back in unbelief, condemning the labors of those who follow the directions of *their* Lord and ours. A prominent lady of the city, upon whom I had been pressing the truth of God, last week said to me, " Oh, sir, I see it, my greatest sin is, *unbelief, unbelief.*"

Oh, that when the heart of Christians riseth up in opposition to the work of evangelists whom God acknowledges they would inquire of the Lord, and see to it, that they were not in the way of his salvation through unbelief.

My heart clings more than ever to the children of God, especially to the older class, who have long been in the war, and " held the fort " when the battle raged.

Yours in Christ,

RICHARD STEELE.

To illustrate the extent to which the opposition to Mr. Finney's revival efforts sometimes rose, we quote, with a few brief extracts, the title of a pamphlet published by the deacon of an unevangelical church at Trenton, N. J.

A

"BUNKER HILL" CONTEST,

A. D. 1826,

BETWEEN THE "HOLY ALLIANCE" FOR THE ESTABLISHMENT OF HIERARCHY AND ECCLESIASTICAL DOMINATION OVER THE HUMAN MIND,

ON THE ONE SIDE,

AND THE ASSERTERS OF FREE INQUIRY, BIBLE RELIGION, CHRISTIAN FREEDOM, AND CIVIL LIBERTY,

ON THE OTHER.

THE REV. CHARLES FINNEY,

" Home Missionary " and High Priest of the Expeditio s of the Alliance in the Interior of New York. Headquarters, County of Oneida.

Among the charges made was that of concerted action, among Presbyterians especially, for a national church, by whose strength " all the opposition of infidelity would be *borne down and overpowered.*"

The description given of inquiry meetings shows the animus of the opposition : —

"The next step in course, in these revivals, is to establish what are termed anxious meetings. They are generally, if not always, held in the night. The room is darkened, so that persons can only see to walk and discover each other ; and the reign of universal silence is interrupted only by now and then a dolorous groan from different parts of the room. The leader or leaders tread softly about, as they proceed, whispering to each individual some question or questions, such as ' Do you love God,' etc."

In another place it is said, " That in a circle of the anxious, Mr. Finney would go round, and, by putting his eyes on each individual for a few seconds, tell the exact state of their mind ; and would congratulate one and another with their new hope, even though they were strangers : and also, that these were in such cases *private reporters.*" The reviewer inquires : Why did not these authors, after describing the darkness of the rooms at these meetings, say that Mr. Finney professed to have such powers of vision that he could see the faces of converts in the dark, as well as "tell the exact state of their minds"? This would have increased the wonder. They have been rather more cautious than usual in this statement. They speak of it only as a report ; but they show their good-will

The committee of the Oneida Presbytery, referring to the published misrepresentations and slanders, add : —

" We close our notice of this pamphlet, with a few observations addressed to our brethren in the ministry and to the members of our churches.

" Brethren, we here see on record that hatred which exists extensively against those revivals of religion with which our churches have from time to time been blessed. We think this pamphlet will do good. While it will gratify and harden some who have advanced far in the broad road, it will lead others less advanced to pause. It will tend to unite the true disciples of Christ, and teach them their duty to come out from the world and be separate. For several years past a spirit of bitterness has been manifesting itself, particularly in this State, against a faithful ministry, and against the benevolent exertions of the church of Christ. This moral poison has been circulating among a considerable portion of the community, in scurrilous newspapers and pamphlets, which have passed unnoticed. Among the unenlightened and irreligious they have had more influence than Christians have generally supposed. This pamphlet has embodied the substance of all this opposition in a more imposing form; and Christians may here see in embryo that gigantic spirit of the world, which, under God, they must meet and conquer by the spirit of Jesus. Those revivals of religion which are here vilified, are indispensable to the fulfilment of those prophecies, which point us to the future prosperity and glory of the church. We are not to be alarmed, therefore, at this opposition. A great cry is raised about the immense sums which are contributed to carry into effect the plans of benevolence. But when tenfold more is expended in the grog-shop, in the theatre, and in gambling-houses, these opposers manifest no uneasiness, and will not unite with Christians to put an end to such shameful waste of time, and money, and health, and life itself."

In a very clear statement of Mr. Finney's position and usefulness, there is a touch of deserved irony in the reference to his accusers. It cannot fail to interest all Christian people of the present day who have not read or have forgotten it.

"As much has been said at home and abroad respecting the character and proceedings of Mr. Finney, it will probably be expected that the committee will not be silent

respecting him. We think it due to him, and to the
cause of Christ, which we believe he loves, to state that
his Christian character, since he made a profession of
religion, has been irreproachable. He was licensed by
the presbytery of St. Lawrence, and is now a member
of the presbytery of Oneida. He possesses a discriminating and well-balanced mind, has a good share of courage
and decision, possesses naturally a good temper, is frank
and magnanimous in his deportment, ardent and persever-
ing in the performance of the duties of his office, exhibits
as much discretion and judgment as those who may think
him deficient in these qualities would do did they possess
his zeal and activity, and, on the whole, is as well calculated to be extensively useful in promoting revivals of
religion as any man of whom we have any knowledge.
To say that he never errs is more than can, with truth,
be said of any man who has ever done much to promote
the temporal or spiritual interests of his fellow-men.

   " We confess we feel no great respect for those who sit
down in ignoble ease in the vineyard of the Lord, and
make their sage remarks upon the imprudence of those
who 'bear the heat and burden of the day.' Wisdom,
judgment, and discretion are important virtues in the soldiers of Christ ; but of all men in the world the professed
minister of the gospel is the most unwise and imprudent,
who dares to incur the displeasure of Almighty God, and
expose the souls of his fellow-men to eternal death, by
his unfaithfulness."

   We have not space nor inclination to review the controversy about Mr. Finney, opened by the good, but mor-
bidly fearful Dr. Nettleton, in his declining years, which
resulted in strange antagonisms even among revival men
like Dr. Beecher, at one time opposing the evangelist
whom he afterwards invited to Boston. Time and death
are clearing away misapprehensions and softening down
all asperities which they once created.

It was related to the writer, in the neighborhood of the occurrence, that, at a revival meeting, where a Baptist minister was with Mr. Finney in the pulpit of the type of character displayed in the "beloved disciple," after handling the law of God in his masterly manner, till Sinai flamed and thundered around the sinner, and the audience were intensely stirred with their hopeless condition under the blackness and lurid flashes of that condemning mount, he stopped, and said to them with subdued tones, "Now, Brother G—— will tell you about his Jesus!" The gentler herald of the gospel then spoke to anxious souls of Calvary, with its crucified substitute, till the fountains of tears were opened. We heard him twenty years or more since, in Syracuse, when his tender exhibition of divine love choked his own utterance, and moved the vast assembly.

Among the great results of the revivals of these years was the free church movement in New York City, in connection with which Mr. Finney was called to the Chatham Street Chapel. Baxter Payne, a layman, was a pioneer in the movement, with "Father Cunningham," an elder in Dr. Gardiner Spring's church. Out of the widening circle of Christian faith, prayer, and activity, grew the "First Free Presbyterian Church," of which Rev. Joel Parker was pastor, sustained by the sympathy and munificence of such men as Lewis Tappan and Dr. Bliss. Rev. E. P. Barrows was called to the Second Free Church, and in March Mr. Finney, to lead a third enterprise. No hall could be found for public services, and finally Chatham Street Theatre was suggested. Mr. Blanchard, the lessee, was waited upon with the proposition to sell his lease. "What for?" was the blunt response. "For a church," was the reply. "A w-h-a-t?"—"A church, sir." With a look of inexpressible surprise, he said, "You mean to make a c-h-u-r-c-h here?" Then with a sudden reaction of feeling filling his eyes with tears, he added : " You may have it, and I will give one thousand dollars towards it !" The bargain was soon completed : and at the morning rehearsal, by pre-arrangement, "The voice of free grace" was sung, and Lewis Tappan announced to the actors that on the following Sunday, and thereafter on every evening, there would be preaching in that place ; the scenery would be removed, the pulpit placed in the centre of the stage, an anxious seat would front the footlights, and all were invited to be present. The pit was covered with a floor, and seats extemporized for three hundred persons, for a five-o'clock morning union prayer-meeting next day. The hour came, and with it *eight hundred people.* The services, conducted by well-known clergymen and laymen, were intensely solemn. The expense of refitting the theatre, $6,000, was raised ; "posters" announced the Sabbath services, and May 6th the "Chatham Street Chapel" was dedicated, the throng filling every part by 10 o'clock. Mr. Finney preached from the text, " Who is on the Lord's side?" Those present at the sacramental observance in the afternoon, and in the evening, when Mr. Finney again preached from, " I call heaven and earth to record this day against you, that I have set before you life and death, blessing and cursing ; therefore choose life, that both thou and thy soul shall live," never forgot the great occasions. Hundreds were unable to get standing-room in the chapel. An attempt at disturbance was quelled by the police, and the solemnity was subduing. For seventy successive nights, Mr. Finney held the throngs by his divine logic and powerful appeals, and witnessed the signal victories of the Holy Ghost.

Of one of the occasions of culminating interest here we have received an account from Mr. Watts, a layman of Pittsburg, then a youthful hearer :

"It was a day of fasting and of prayer. The sermon

was upon the ninth chapter of Ezekiel. The attendance
from other churches was large, and the edifice crowded.
At the close of one of the most searching sermons peculiar to Mr. Finney, he called upon all who intended to
humble themselves before God and consecrate themselves
anew to his service, to leave the pews, and stand in the
middle aisle. One arose and then another, until, with the
exception of probably less than fifty, the whole congregation, of fifteen hundred or two thousand, stood up, and
then all who could knelt, while Mr. Finney reconsecrated
the whole anew to God in solemn prayer. The effect can
never be forgotten by any one who witnessed it; a revival
already in progress increased in interest, and many were
brought into the church.

" So great was the interest in personal religion during
the revival, that reporters took down the reports of many
of Mr. Finney's sermons, and they were published in the
" New York Evangelist." A batch of the papers hung out
daily on the bulletin in front of the office ; and it was dif-
cult to gain access to the paper, so intense was the anxiety
of the people to know the way of salvation. I was but a
lad at the time ; but, failing to get the paper in the crowd
I raised sufficient money to subscribe for it for six months,
and have taken it ever since. Indeed, the " New York
Evangelist," I doubt not, owes its success to its origin in
those revival times. This interest was manifested everywhere ; it was the topic of conversation at the boarding-
house and in the shop. I remember Mr. Lewis Tappan
had been explaining to his class the simplicity of some of
the doctrines of the Bible, when he was met shortly after
on the entrance to the church by an infidel, who accosted
him, and asked him to explain the doctrines of election and
predestination. ' My friend,' said Mr. Tappan, ' you need
not concern yourself about these ; the only doctrine which
immediately concerns you is the doctrine of repentance ' :

and he kindly and urgently pressed upon him the necessity of repentance.'"

Around that centre of spiritual force, all the means of
mercy were in intensely active use; and the first man who
begged for deliverance from sin's captivity in the old bar-
room of the theatre with anguish cried : "O Lord, forgive my sins. The last time I was here Thou knowest I
was a wicked actor on this stage. Oh Lord, have mercy
on me ! "

Mr. Finney continued here about two years, and then
accepted a call to the Broadway Tabernacle. While in
New York he delivered his "Lectures on Revivals," which
were reported, and afterwards published by him, both in
this country and in England, and which have no rival on
that subject, as the president of one of our most popular
theological seminaries recently said to the students under
his care.

Mrs. G. W. Thompson writes of Mr. Finney in Rome,
1825 : "He was tall, straight as a larch, not heavy, but
well built. His complexion was blond, his blue eyes
large, open, and penetrating, outraying with animation
and intelligence, and his face glowing with youthful vigor.
His dress was gray, and he wore a stiff standing collar, and
was close-shaven, as all gentlemen then were.

"Mr. Finney had a high forehead, from which his hair
was combed directly upward and backward. His watch
key and seal hung from a fob in his pantaloons. In his
appearance there was more of the lawyer than of the minister. His all-pervading earnestness made him forget himself, and the man sunk, as it were, behind his grand theme.
Blended with an inborn dignity there was a childlike
frankness that disarmed prejudice and chained the listener.

"But the secret of his striking magnetism, it seems to me,
lay in the elevation of soul consequent upon his constant
recognition of the reality of eternal things, which endued
him with a power that words failed to depict."

CHAPTER X.

Mr. Finney removes to Oberlin. — Origin of the College. — Goes to England. — Success there. — His Vindication at Home. — Death. — Letter from Prof. Mead. — Sources of Mr. Finney's Power. — Illustrative Incidents. — Rev. Daniel Nash. — Co-worker with Mr. Finney. — Life and Labors.

We come now to Mr. Finney's removal to the West, where he was to fight new battles for truth and righteousness, and win victories of quite a different sort, but no less glorious and far-reaching in their influence.

Oberlin College originated in the brain and heart of Rev. J. Shipherd, of Elyria, O., who associated with him Mr. P. P. Stewart, a Cherokee missionary, then residing in his family. The twelve articles of the "Oberlin Covenant" made at that time are unequalled, so far as we know, out of the Scriptures, in their spirit of consecration, and brief summary of consistent Christian living. This institution "was the offspring of the revivals of 1830, '31, and '32."

Ground was broken in the wilderness in 1832, while Mr. Finney was a pastor in New York. In December, 1834, after a protracted discussion, the board of trustees decided to admit students "irrespective of color," and at the same session also appointed Mr. Finney professor of theology. He accepted, and on his way to Oberlin was met with the offer of the chair of pastoral theology, in Western Reserve College; which was repeated by a delegation sent later to the former place. He was chosen President in 1852.

We shall not even name the "heresies" of the suspected

college, which once distressed so many good people in the
land ; it is enough to say that they have ceased to trouble
any branch of Zion, while all truth and its reforms have
a home and broadening outflow at Oberlin. The almost
uninterrupted revival, and extending influence of the institution, are known wherever there are friends of God and
humanity. Mr. Finney resigned the Presidency in 1866.

In reply to an inquiry, Mr. Finney says : —

"After my settlement at Oberlin, I labored half the
time abroad as an evangelist, until 1860, when my strength
no longer permitted such labors. I was in England a
year and a half, at two different times, making three years
there in all. Nine months I occupied Whitefield's old
Tabernacle, was several months in Birmingham, Bolton,
Manchester, and Edinburgh, and three weeks in Worcester."

The volumes on "Systematic Theology," and the published sermons in the "Oberlin Evangelist," for many
years edited by him, are packed with original and practical
religious thought. His intellectual riches were apparently
exhaustless, and his spiritual power certainly so, for it
was supplied from communion with Christ.

Of his pulpit power we find a very satisfactory estimate
by Prof. Henry Fowler in his "American Pulpit," written
when Mr. Finney was in his fulness of strength, but not
at the height of his influence among men ; for this waxes,
nor has it for a moment waned. The Holy Ghost, doubtless, is understood as the real source of power in the statement which we quote. Prof. Fowler wrote in 1856 : —

"Mr. Finney is one of the most remarkable preachers
of America. With strong logical powers, and educated
as a lawyer, he deals much in convincing argument. The
law of God, in its various relations, is his favorite subject.
. . . He has not the grace nor the persuasive appeal
of Mr. Kirk, but for a certain scope of preaching is

unequalled, — that of impressive argument, and such presentation of the relations of religious truth, as in its completeness and clearness works irresistible conviction, and brings sceptic, infidel, and apathist alike into brokenhearted submission to the power of God. . . . His reading of hymns produces a deep impression, particularly those of the class, 'Majestic sweetness sits enthroned,' which is a favorite with him. His sermons are usually an hour and a quarter. Occasionally his flights of imagination are sublime, and his sweep of oratory magnificent. He also has dramatic power."

It was an impressive scene, and the most emphatic verdict possible to the evangelism of Mr. Finney, when at Oberlin, July, 1871, the National Congregational Council, filling the large church, rose in a body upon his entrance, and remained standing, while the veteran evangelist, pastor, and president, with unweakened step and the fire of early manhood in his eye, moved along the aisle to the pulpit.

The more striking and suggestive was this testimony to his past and present greatness and usefulness, when it is recollected that there were some present, we believe, joining in this merited homage, who, in Boston, not many years before, had declined to invite him to labor for the winter months among the churches. It is stated that conversions have been few in the parishes which refused the aid of God's honored servant.

Equally decided was the eloquent tribute spoken later, August 1, 1874, at the dedication of "Council Hall." After impressive introductory exercises, the Rev. T. M. Post, D. D., delivered the address, from whose eloquent sentences we can only briefly quote : —

" I am happy to congratulate the friends of Oberlin upon the domiciliation of their theological seminary in its own house, with its conveniences and facilities for doing more

effective work; that there has been established a permanent armory, whence, from year to year, and I trust I may
say from age to age, your young men may go forth
equipped for the battles of the Lord, in behalf of truth,
humanity, and Christianity throughout the world.

" This enterprise was founded upon the royal principle,
upon which all great enterprises that are to last foreve:
have been founded : upon faith in God, and supreme and
entire consecration to Him for the spread of His kingdom.

"I congratulate you, beloved friends, before whom I
speak to-day as a stranger, with no suspicion of aspiration
to personal honor in the result of your enterprise, on its
grand success. It has grown up in the wilderness like a
thing of God, and now ranks in number amid the very
foremost among the literary institutions of the country.
It has, moreover, vindicated its origin by its type of Christian manhood, of Christian thought and act, and by the
spirit it breathes of liberty and humanity. By its espe-
cial genius of evangelization it has contributed prominently
to the new impulse, to the wider and more popular evangelization that marks the times,—an impulse reminding
one, though of a higher and more spiritual type, of that
imparted to the preaching of the gospel in Europe by the
institution of mendicant preaching orders in the twelfth
century.

"Oberlin may, to-day, stand amid her institutions and
rest her case with her children, the living and the dead;
may point to those now manfully engaged in beneficent
and Christian work the world over, and to the graves of
those fallen for Christ and country, scattered beside the
mission-house in far-off lands, or along the sad streams and
the deep forests of the South, where nature and solitude
and the nightly stars keep watch over their dust, or resting
under yonder monument, under the shadow of the halls

that sent them forth, in the day of our great necessity, for God and liberty.

"Oberlin may rest her case also upon the revival influences that have been born here, and have propagated themselves like successive surges throughout the land. In view of all this, it is not your joy alone that accompanies the dedication of this edifice, but the joy of all that love the appearing and the kingdom of our Lord Jesus Christ.

"That Oberlin has overcome the distrust or oppugnance of men; that the public mind is swaying in an opposite direction, is honorable and auspicious, both for itself and the public. It is significant, with both, that the spirit is triumphing over the letter; that life is felt to be more than dogmas; soul more than symbols; the unity of the spirit more than the unity of formulated dialectics; that earnest Christian living, loving, and doing is coming to outrank, in public thought, the distinctive theological shibboleths that have come hissing down the centuries. Not, we trust, that an era of indifference to Christian doctrine, or of blindness to the relation of belief to life, is approaching, but one when Christianity shall be recognized as a life more than a thesis, and Christian love will grasp hands with all who show the spirit of Christ; when the church shall go forward under the apostolic motto, ' Whereunto we have already attained, let us walk by the same rule ; let us mind the same things; and if in anything ye be otherwise minded, God shall reveal even this unto you.'

"In the path of Christian love lies Christian truth. Only in that way shall we find it. There we shall surely discover it, for that leads up to God.

"In that direction, I believe, the church is moving. To this issue time works — time that modifies, mollifies, and meliorates so many things in the public mind and in the individual soul.

"Time touches many things with change of beauty and

excellency to the higher perfect. If it takes from the
brilliancy of bloom, it brings the ripeness and richness of
fruitage. If it takes from the Boanergic energy of earlier
years, it brings more of the softer air and sweeter light of
the City of Peace. If there is less of the Titanic vigor
which once hurled the glittering and crashing bolts of
Sinai, if there is less of Michael the archangel trans-
piercing and trampling the dragon, there is more of
Christ blessing the little children, and breathing out his
ineffable tenderness and sympathy in the chamber of love.
If it was the locks of the youthful John that lay in the
bosom of Jesus, it was upon the hoary head that the Lord
in his glory laid the hand that wields the sceptre of being,
saying, 'I am the first and the last; I am he that liveth,
and was dead; and, behold, I am alive forevermore, amen;
and have the keys of hell and of death. Fear not.' It was
to the dimmed eye of age that revelations were given of
the future glory of the kingdom of God, of the golden
city, the white-robed ones, the river of life, and the
jasper throne. So to the ear from which the tumult of
mortal life was passing away, it was given to catch the
hallelujahs of the angels and rifts of the everlasting song.
Heaven grants no richer benison to any institution, than
minds which, having reached the solemn confines of two
worlds, stand as mediators between both, in the calm and
solemn light of eternity, look back upon and measure the
things of time with heart-beat still in loving sympathy
with this mortal life, but touched and toned with the
mighty pulses of immortality.

"Methinks, beloved brethren, voices from that world
are calling to us to-day. While we are mingling congrat-
ulations upon the dedication of this noble and commodious
structure to theologic culture, while we joy with these
brethren in the joy and hope of a finished work, we believe
there are others who have wrought to this result, and who

dwell no longer in houses of clay, who blend the gladness of other worlds with yours. To-day marks an epoch in the history of your institution — another and lasting step, I trust, of the success of your enterprise. May the day be long remembered as the inauguration of an armory that shall, from age to age, thoroughly furnish the youths of Oberlin to the great conflict of the kingdom of Christ, of a fountain opened that, through all the future, shall send forth ' streams that shall make glad the city of our God.'"

At the close of Dr. Post's address, the choir sang "Praise now the Lord."

President Fairchild remarked that "it would be interesting to get some report from the seminary during all its years, and as I look about I imagine that a well-directed call will bring forth echoes from all these old quarters. But first we need a few words from President Finney."

The venerable Ex-President Finney then addressed the audience as follows : —

" I have been asked a great many times how I came to be connected with Oberlin Theological Department. I will try to state, in a few words, how this theological department came to exist, and the stress laid upon this department by the men who, under God, sent me here.

" I was pastor of the old Broadway Tabernacle Church in the city of New York. In erecting the building, a room designed for a theological lecture-room had been fitted up, under the orchestra, but no class had been formed. Just at this period the explosion of Lane Seminary occurred, which threw off the young men that formed the first theological class in Oberlin. When Mr. Arthur Tappan heard that those young men had left that seminary, he urged me to come West, and choose such location as I pleased, hire rooms and accommodations for

myself and the whole class, and instruct them in theology
until they were licensed to preach, and he would pay the
whole expense. He wished to do something for this then
wild, uncultivated West. For at that 'time western Ohio
was regarded as the verge of Western civilization, and he
well judged that men who were to labor in the West had
better be educated in the West as far as practicable. Mr.
Lewis Tappan, Mr. William Greene, Rev. Joshua Leavitt,
a Mr. Higgins, and a few others agreed with Mr. Tappan,
and joined in urging me to come West. As my mind was
under the pressure of deciding this question, Revs. J. J.
Shipherd and Asa Mahan arrived from Cincinnati and
urged me to come here. This was the first I had ever
heard of Oberlin. It had not at that time any existence
as a college or theological seminary. A meeting was
called of the friends I have named and referred to, and
they proposed to endow eight professorships, to retain the
principal in their own hands, and pay the interest, I
believe, semi-annually. I did not propose to resign my
pastoral relation in New York, but to spend half of each
year here, and half in New York. My church in New
York were to defray the expenses of my travel with my
family, both ways.

"I imposed two conditions upon the trustees : (1) That
colored people should be received on the same 'condition
as the white; (2) That the trustees should never inter-
fere with the internal regulations of the institution as the
trustees of Lane Seminary had done.

"After the preliminaries were settled, I foresaw that it
would be next to impossible for us to succeed for want
of funds, as everything had yet to be done. We should
be new-school in theology, antislavery in principle and
action, revival, temperance, and aggressive in our work;
we should meet with almost universal resistance, and find
it impossible to secure funds enough to give us success.

I had a long private conversation with Brother Arthur Tappan on this subject, and the solution of this difficulty was as follows: He said, 'You shall not want for money. But let the promise which I now make you be a secret between you and me. Send out your agents, and collect what you can; and do this mostly for the sake of advertising the work that you are about. Stir up your trustees to make what efforts you can to get funds, put up your buildings as fast as possible, and let them be permanent and tasteful structures, collect a library, get your philosophical apparatus and whatever you need to carry on the work, with the least possible delay, and whatever of funds the trustees fail to secure from other sources, I will supply to the full extent of my yearly income, which is, at present, one hundred thousand dollars.' This was satisfactory, as I had the utmost confidence in Mr. Tappan. So far as I know, this promise of Mr. Tappan was known to no person living but myself.

"I came on to the ground in the spring of 1835. The first living thing that I saw in wending my way from the State road through an unbroken forest, with no path, was a hedgehog. He was a symbol of the state of feeling that for some years prevailed in the country towards Oberlin. As he took a defiant attitude and erected his quills in every direction, I seized a club and killed him. I have had to fight a good many hedgehogs since, but never killed anybody. On arriving, I found that the first living thing that was seen when Brothers Shipherd and Stewart arrived on the ground was an old bear, which they treed, on the spot where the Park House now stands. There was no clearing here when I came, except what is now the public square. All around was an immense and unbroken forest, and the deer were so plenty that they seemed to look out from the woods upon us to see what we were about. To escape from the pressure that was

upon my mind, I would frequently take my rifle and go
into the woods, and would seldom go more than forty
rods from the clearing without seeing a deer. Brother
George Clark, who boarded at Mr. Shipherd's where Mr.
Hulburd now lives, shot a deer almost from the door of
the house, that came out of the woods to see what we
were about in Oberlin.

"Where this building now stands was then a forest.
The country around us bristled with opposition. A yeai
or two after I came here, I went out on to the ridge,
towards Elyria, to get some slips of currant bushes. The
man was very cross when he found I was from Oberlin,
and snapped out, 'You 're going to compel the young men
to marry nigger wenches over there, and you 're going to
try to unite church and state.' For years the opposition
was so great that they threatened to tear down our buildings, and force us to abandon the enterprise. In 1837,
the great commercial crash prostrated the business of Mr.
Arthur Tappan and the other brethren who had endowed
the college, and left the faculty without the wherewithal
to purchase our bread. Arthur Tappan had furnished ten
thousand dollars towards building Tappan Hall; and as an
incentive to the trustees to make efforts to raise funds, and
to conceal his promise to me from them, he required them
to give a note, which, on his failure, fell into the hands of
his assignees, and the trustees were obliged to pay it. Mr.
Tappan wrote me, confessing his promise, and saying that
he was never more grieved than by the fact that he was
unable to fulfil the pledge he had made me. The history
of Oberlin has been very romantic. If it were written, it
would prove that 'facts are sometimes stranger than fiction.
I have lived to see more accomplished than I ever expected.
And now, when I walk the streets and see our throngs of
students, and our fine buildings going up, and recall the
dangers overcome, and the obstacles removed, in our early

history, it reminds me of the saying, 'A little one shall chase a thousand,' and I am ready to put my hand upon my mouth, before the Lord, and be still."

From Dr. Budington's speech, 1871, we quote a passage : —

"It seems to me a most auspicious fact, that in inaugurating this first session of the National Council we signalize it by work, that we forever associate this council with the laying of the corner-stone, at Oberlin, of a theological hall, and that this our first work, as it is to be associated with a theological school, so it is to be associated with that inspiring and blessed doctrine, the endowment of the Holy Ghost, to which we have all listened, from the lips of President Finney, with bated breath and swelling hearts. Blessed appointment of the God of our fathers, that we should lay the foundation-stone for a school of the prophets on a doctrine like this, — a doctrine that should underlie all institutions and all work for Christ ; that 'power from on high' is the one necessary and indispensable qualification for Christian ministers and Christian laborers alike."

The president called on Rev. Dr. Peabody, of Harvard University, who spoke as follows : —

"MR. PRESIDENT, — Permit me, with the utmost brevity, to offer a word of hearty greeting from the oldest of our colleges to one which, though by two centuries her junior, can yet vie with her as the prolific mother of colleges. The establishment of Oberlin College marks an era. It was the first seminary of learning expressly designed to be a focus of moral, social, and religious propagandism. Other colleges prepared men for subsequent Christian work; yours trained them to the work by setting them to do it.

"I may personally claim an interest in the special services of this hour, as I, though a stranger, can contribute some precious reminiscences. In times that seem to me almost prehistoric, when I was a student in theology, I

11

listened to a course of sermons by the venerable man whom you honor (and long may he yet remain to bless you) as leader and chief in this great enterprise. His name was not fragrant in my circle, and I became his hearer with strong adverse prejudices. Before he had finished his first sermon my prejudices had vanished; and I heard him through his course with delight and with profit, I trust, both to mind and heart.

"May the spirit of the fathers rest richly upon those who enter into their labors! May all that gave grace and glory to your times of conflict and trial crown the years of culminating prosperity that open before you; and may the love of God and the grace of the Lord Jesus Christ so dwell among you, that they shall flow ever hence to gladden and bless our land and race!"

The audience adjourned to the chapel of Council Hall, where the dedicatory prayer was to be offered by Prof. Finney.

When all were seated, President Fairchild gave out the hymn, —

"All hail the power of Jesus' name,"

Which was sung by the congregation.

Prof. Finney then rose to offer the dedicatory prayer. It was difficult to realize that the man who stood before the assembly, tall and erect as in his youthful days, fresh and animated in all his features, with eye still bright and piercing, and voice yet clear and ringing, was bearing the weight of eighty-two years, and that, as evangelist, pastor, college president, and theological teacher, he had endured labors that long before this would have crushed a more vigorous constitution. It seemed to all a cause of gratitude that the one who had gathered the first class in the seminary, who had gone with the several classes while tabernacling, first, in the leaky Cincinnati Hall, then in

Tappan Hall, then in the college chapel, should be permitted to lead them into this new and commodious building, where the seminary is to have its permanent abode, and that it should be set apart for its sacred use through his words of consecration and petition.

Before beginning his prayer, he said he had felt somewhat embarrassed with regard to performing this part of the service, because the house is not entirely finished. He had several times refused to dedicate a house of worship that was not paid for; but this is neither finished nor paid for, and he had had some hesitation about offering it to God in this state. But he remembered that he had often offered himself to God, and he was not finished yet, and why should he not offer this house? He would do so, relying upon the determination of those having it in charge to finish it as soon as possible. He then offered the prayer of dedication, after which the doxology was sung, and the exercises were concluded with the benediction by President Fairchild.

We must here leave this venerable servant of Christ, active in His service still, at the age of eighty-three. President Finney has been blessed in his domestic relations, having found in the living and the dead co-workers in the cause he loves and will serve, till he falls on the field, to rise among the ransomed thousands saved by his varied ministry, who passed into the heavens before him.

Mr. Finney's transcendent power in wielding the truth, intellectually, lay in his thorough knowledge of the laws of mental and moral activity, and discernment of spiritual conditions. He made no random or experimental efforts. As a skilful physician studies his cases, and follows a remedy, when its work is done, by the next in order, so he dealt with human souls smitten by sin. This was seen wherever he labored. We give a few illustrations. When he was in Rochester he gave his course of lectures on "Moral Government." The first three were outside of direct spiritual application, until the fifty lawyers attending them were committed to the great principles of the divine administration; and, when he reached eternal punishment, before he finished the sermon, Judge Gardiner was so overwhelmed by the pressure of the awful truth, that he left the gallery and stole down to the pulpit, and before Mr. F., who missed him, was aware, he pulled his coat and said, "Mr. Finney, stop and tell the people to pray for me." He went to the front seat; and, when others were invited, the bar was largely represented there, and nearly all were soon among the rejoicing converts.

While Mr. Finney was in Providence, before his first visit to Boston, Rev. Dr. Wisner of the Old South was sent there by his brethren to hear the evangelist and report. He did not make himself known till he had heard three sermons. He then went to Mr. Finney, and said to him, "I came here a heresy-hunter; but here is my hand, and my heart is with you."

When Dr. Wisner returned, and the stage drove to the parsonage, he was met by the pastors, who were expecting him. Quietly laying aside his travelling wardrobe, and directing his attention especially to Dr. Beecher, he said, "When Dr. Beecher preaches, he has prepared himself, and makes a profound impression; but what the next blow will be we cannot tell. Mr. Finney strikes home, and repeats the blow on the same spot, only harder, until the driven wedge splits the log, and there is no help for it."

Mr. Finney came, and after preaching a few months in Park Street was invited to Essex Street, where he remained about six months, till called to the Chatham Street Church, New York. It was estimated that not less than three thousand souls were converted during the time he was in Boston. A friend of Mr. Finney, who has had much to do in securing the publication of his works, speaks of the wonderful scenes in those days at family worship, when the evangelist seemed to be transfigured, so glowing were his intercessions, and so sensibly present was the Holy Spirit.

Among the converts, when Mr. Finney was in London, was Captain Moody, having in charge the English supplies, who brought to this country in a British vessel a company of converted infidels and young clergymen, also, who had found Christ under his preaching, to be educated at Oberlin. Captain Moody once stated that when Mr. Finney was asked in England why it was the people thronged him, for he was not an orator, he replied, " When I load my gun, I do it for the kind of game I am after; and I aim as near the heart as possible, for I find that is the place where it does the best execution."

When the evangelist was in northern New York, a man who lived in a neighborhood which was so abandoned and lawless it was called Sodom, while on account of his own Christian profession he was named Lot, went to an adjoining town to hear a sermon from the famous preacher. Mr. Finney, in his always wonderfully wise adaptation of truth to the state of feeling, on this occasion was dwelling upon the love of God. This suited the hearer from Sodom, whose report upon his return created such a desire there to hear him, that, notwithstanding a formal vote of the community never to allow evangelical preaching there, he was urged to go until he consented, walking several miles to fulfil the appointment. Tired, he sat down near the place to rest, and, as was his rule before preaching, to get by prayer assurance of a blessing. He was not aware of the names referred to, and took for his text the angel's words to Lot in ancient Sodom: " Up, get you out of this place ; for the Lord will destroy it."

As Mr. Finney depicted the guilt and doom of ancient Sodom, the faces around him darkened and grew fierce ; but no one moved. He told them he had heard of their purpose not to have a gospel sermon delivered there, which only deepened the already intense feeling; till, like a bursting reservoir or falling barrier before the swelling stream, the crisis came and the breaking down, some of the people falling, while cries for mercy went out from the crowded room upon the summer air. Mr. Finney was compelled to leave them to attend his evening service; but the meeting continued all night, and the mighty power of God for weeks swept in broadening circles among the people.

A number of years afterwards, a gentleman called on Mr. Finney, at Oberlin, while engaged with a committee, and was so emphatic in his desire to speak with him, that he stepped aside for private conversation. The visitor then reminded Mr. Finney of the meeting at "Sodom," and said he was the first person on the floor in deep distress spoken to by him, with the inquiry if he felt that the fiery storm was gathering over his head. The young man replied he did, and begged for prayer. Mr. Finney pointed him to Christ, and crept along to the next prostrate and anxious one. The application of the sermon, the character of the assembly, and all the circumstances, made it a remarkable and memorable occasion, even in the evangelist's eventful career.

While the pen was tracing these last lines, the telegraph announced the sudden death, on Monday morning, August 16, with heart-disease, of this illustrious leader in our American Zion. Although a careful stewardship of a naturally vigorous constitution prolonged his life to the advanced age of eighty-three, the loss will be felt almost as deeply as though he had departed in the midst of his years. None of us thought of him as a worn-out warrior, with nothing to do but to die. There was certainly no sign of decay in the contributions of his trenchant pen to the religious press. Not long ago we received a letter from him, in which he said : —

"A new course of lectures on Pastoral Theology, which I must prepare and deliver, will use up my time and strength for the summer; and I should not dare to undertake any additional labor. There is plenty of room for a very useful book on the subject upon which you are writing. Nothing like justice has ever been done to it. The methods of labor pursued by evangelists, you are aware, have been very diverse, with equally various results in their outcome. The question of such an order of ministers as a divine gift to the church needs to be thoroughly discussed."

He also refers to a record of the great revivals between 1824–30 which he has made, with an exhaustive discussion of the measures employed, and the opposition to them by brethren in the ministry, which we hope, now he is gone, will erelong be given to the public. For, while he needs no vindication beyond his great life-work and holy example, the calm, clear review of a crisis in the history of the American churches second only to that of Edwards' and Whitefield's time, will be a priceless addition to revival literature.

Mr. Finney, we believe, was the first American evangelist who labored abroad; and also the first to recognize the valuable assistance of woman in revival efforts, in the very effective aid received by him from his gifted wife.

Of Mr. Finney's family, one son is an able lawyer in California, and another a distinguished civil engineer, we believe, West, and an active Christian. Two gifted daughters married well-known public men, — Prof. Monroe, member of Congress, and Gen. Cox, Secretary of the Interior under President Grant and ex-governor of Ohio.

We have just received a letter from Prof. Mead, giving interesting details of his closing hours. Reference is made to his fondness for singing, in which he also excelled, having in early manhood taught "singing-schools," and led the church choir.

OBERLIN, O., Aug. 24, 1875.

DEAR BROTHER,—The death of Mr. Finney came upon us as a sudden shock. He had been in his usual health, though somewhat wearied with the multitude of calls he received during and after the commencement exercises. Almost every day he had taken his customary ride, always inviting some invalid to ride with him. To the last he was just as thoughtful as ever of the sick and afflicted, and made many calls upon them from day to day. Saturday night and Sunday morning, Aug. 15, he was rather more than usually wearied. But in the afternoon he was well as usual again, and spent the time in cheerful conversation with his youngest son and wife, with Mr. and Mrs. Monroe (his daughter), and with Mrs. F. The son and his wife had fortunately come from a distance, just in time for a last visit and for a final benediction. Everything conspired to render this last day of his life peaceful and joyous. It was a beautiful day, and he enjoyed the refreshing air in a short walk towards evening with Mrs. F. He talked as usual of heaven and of its nearness. Yet nothing that he said led Mrs. F. to imagine that his end was near. He was accustomed to speak of the probability of his passing away suddenly. The family gathered in the evening to sing his favorite songs of Zion. He was a singer, and joined with them as usual. The last hymn he sung was "Jesus, lover of my soul." His voice was not as strong as it had been previously. During the night he complained of discomfort from indigestion. This increased, and he was restless and sleepless through the first part of the night. His watchful and careful wife, as usual, met every wish, and ministered to him. He expressed some apprehension that he might die before morning; but this was so common that she was not impressed by it, but told him that she thought he would rally. Among the remarks he made was this: " I have not done much for the Master these past years, but, thank God, I have not apostatized. He asked for water about two or three o'clock, and said, as he took it, "Perhaps this is the thirst of death." After drinking he had increasing distress, and said " it was a mistake," meaning the taking of the water. A little after he said, " I am dying." His eyes immediately rolled back, and in a few moments, without apparent distress, he quietly breathed his last.

Yours, truly,

H. MEAD.

His last sermons were preached a few weeks before his death, in the Second Church, from Isaiah xliii : 9–10, which made a deep impression, especially upon the students, by whom the discourses were the theme of feeling remark in the prayer-meetings.

Prof. Morgan, who has been forty years associated with him, conducted the funeral services. Prof. Fairchild, who gave an outline of Mr. Finney's eventful life, was followed by Prof. Cowles, with a clear presentation of his pulpit power, which he thought largely due to his views of human responsibility, in contrast with the extreme Calvinism of previous years. The remarks of Prof. Morgan, in closing the addresses, had reference to the sweet and loving spirit recognized by those who knew him best. The large procession returned from his burial to see the glory of a cloudless day flood the landscape, on which a new green mound had been made, which shall be a shrine of hallowed thoughts and memories to the church of Christ, till the earth and the sea give up their dead.

In closing this brief sketch, we seem to hear from his lips of benediction, as he stepped into his chariot to join Elijah the prophet, of whom his ministry reminds us, those last gentle words of that fraternal affection he cherished towards all who served his Master, " God bless you, my dear brother ! "

In connection with Mr. Finney's earliest labors, is sacredly and tenderly associated the name of Rev. Daniel Nash, also an evangelist. He was born in Abington, Mass., Nov. 27, 1775, and at the age of thirteen years removed with his father to Cummington, in the same State. His chosen trade, like the Master's whom he served so faithfully, was that of carpenter. He made a profession of religion in 1801 or 1802, and three years later felt called by the Spirit to prepare for the ministry. Having only a common-school education, and no means to spend on further culture, he commenced the study of Greek and theology with Rev. Samuel Whitman. At the end of a year he began to preach, and was settled at Hamilton, where he remained six years. His pastorate was attended with spiritual harvest. Subsequently he was settled in Lebanon, an adjoining town, and also in Mentz, where he buried his wife, leaving seven children, one of whom was for forty-seven years missionary among the Cherokees. In 1816, he went to Lowville, where he was pastor till 1823. Here he commenced his itinerant service.

We have received a letter from Mr. Finney, which goes back to this date, and sheds interesting light on the character and unheralded usefulness of his life.

OBERLIN, July 7, 1875.

DEAR BROTHER,— The first time I ever saw Rev. Daniel Nash was at the meeting of the presbytery which licensed me to preach the gospel. He was, then, rather hyper-Calvinistic in his views, and, as he afterwards told me, formal, dry, and speculative in his preaching. Soon after that, he was confined to his room with disease of his eyes, and was almost entirely blind for about six months. During this period, as he afterwards informed me, he gave himself to much prayer, had a great searching and overhauling in his spiritual life, and, before he could see enough to be abroad, was powerfully baptized with the Holy Ghost. Soon after this he came to me in the midst of a powerful revival of religion at Evans Mills, in the northern part of Jefferson County, N. Y. I could not fail to see that he had been made over, and was quite another man. He was full of the Holy Ghost. He had the strongest faith, and was the mightiest man in prayer that I had at that time ever seen. Afterwards, he labored with me in revivals in Gouverneur and DeKalb in the southern part of St. Lawrence County. In the midst of the great revival in Rome, Oneida Co., he came to me and labored in prayer and conversation with great effect. He followed on to Utica, and afterwards in Troy and New Lebanon, east of the Hudson River. He was a most wonderful man in prayer, one of the most earnest, devout, spiritually-minded, heavenly-minded men I ever saw. After we parted at New Lebanon, I went to Wilmington, Del., and from there to Philadelphia, to which places he did not follow me. He labored about in many places in central and northern New York, and gave himself up to almost constant prayer, literally praying himself to death at last. I have been informed that he was found dead in his room in the attitude of prayer.

While I was laboring in Boston in the winter of 1831 and '32, I wrote asking him to join with me in keeping every Friday as a day of fasting and prayer, for the more general outpouring of the Holy Spirit. He replied that his body was nearly worn out, that the Holy Spirit had laid the world upon his heart and pressed him almost to death. Those that knew him, during the period of which I speak, will never forget his prayers, and the unutterable groanings with which he was exercised by the Holy Spirit. The manifest and instantaneous answer to some of his prayers was so startling as to arrest the attention of everybody about him. He lived but a few years, after I became acquainted with him, but what years were those, and what a life was that! He lived almost in heaven. I have seen him for days in a state of mind so joyful and triumphant that his face literally shone with the joy of his soul.

At those seasons, he would say to me, " Brother Finney, I cannot pray ; my soul is so full of heaven, I can do nothing but praise. I cannot get down to earth and get hold of sinners." But soon he would come down and take the load of unconverted sinners upon his heart, and such agonizing, prevailing prayers I never heard from any other man. Many times in meeting his soul would become so full of anguish that he could not remain and keep silent. He would hastily and as slyly as possible retire from the meeting, and seek a place where he could pour out his soul to God, and for hours would continue to wrestle and agonize, and groan his soul out to God, till his strength was completely exhausted. The spirit of prayer that was upon him was quite a stumbling-block to professors of religion, who had never known the Holy Ghost as the Spirit that maketh intercession for the saints according to the will of God with groanings that cannot be uttered. I should here say, that very much of this type of prayer prevailed in the revivals through central and northern New York at that time. Many laymen and women were exercised in a similar manner, and sometimes would pray all night in their closets with unutterable groanings for the salvation of sinners. It is devoutly to be wished that the Lord would stir up some one who labored in those revivals, and who sympathized with this spirit of prayer, to write out and publish a brief history of the spirit of prayer that prevailed in them, with the many wonderful and manifest answers that occurred from day to day.

C. G. FINNEY.

Mr. Nash's record of this period of united labors, from Governeur, Sept. 2, 1825, gives interesting details of Mr. Finney's efforts, no less than his own. Of his own religious experience he wrote in his journal : —

"For the last two years I have seldom had a serious doubt of my own adoption. The daily leading impression on my mind is — I must live for God. Last autumn, for weeks I wished to die and go home. Oh, how glorious Jesus and heaven appeared ! At present, my heart's desire and prayer to God, by day and by night, is that sinners — lost, sinking, hell-deserving, heaven-daring, God-provoking sinners — may be saved. God, in a measure, satisfies my desire ; for I see many come to the kingdom, and many in answer to special prayer. Blessed be God, I do understand what the prayer of faith is ; and my soul does know what it is to agonize, and travail in birth, for sinners. Last year, God prospered me ; and probably seventy were born again in the places where I labored."

From Western, Oneida Co., Jan. 12, 1826, he writes to his uncle : —

"I mean to communicate to you tidings which make angels rejoice, and the arches of heaven ring with hallelujahs to God and the Lamb. Bro. Finney came here about the first of October ; sickness prevented my coming till within a few days. Previous to this, he tells me between eighty and ninety were hopefully converted in this town. While he was preaching here, some wild fellows from Rome, three miles from this, came out occasionally to see the wonderful work, to take a ride, to be amused. God meant it for good. The Spirit sent some arrows into their hearts. The sacred fire spread rather invisibly, till between two and three weeks ago it burst, and the explosion was very great. Almost the whole village was simultaneously shaken. Judges, lawyers, doctors, merchants, mechanics, rich and poor, old and young, giddy and profane, turned out and came to the meeting of inquiry, asking the way of life. Since that time, though we have not ascertained the exact number of converts, I believe more than two hundred have been born into the kingdom of God. Last week I spent several days there with Bro. Finney, and twenty or more obtained hopes in about as many hours. Three, four, five, six in a day, is common business. Meetings every evening. Sometimes half a dozen are converted at a single meeting for inquiry.

"At the close of the meeting may be seen a cloud of young converts coming forward to speak to their ministers, with heaven beaming in their countenances. Amongst them you may see the child of nine or ten, and the old man of sixty. It is heaven below."

Utica, May 11, 1826. "In Rome, Verona, Whitesborough, New Hartford, and Trenton, the work of God moves forward with power, in some places against dreadful opposition. Mr. Finney and I have both been hanged in effigy. We have frequently been disturbed in our religious meetings. Sometimes the opposers make a noise in the house of God; sometimes they run out; sometimes talk in the midst of worship; sometimes they gather round the house and stone it, and discharge guns. A lad of seventeen bruised a Christian's nose, in a store, because he prayed for him by name, and told him if it were not for the civil law he should not go out of that store alive. Thus the people gather together against the Lord, and against his anointed. 'But he that sitteth in the heavens shall laugh, the Lord shall have them in derision.' 'None of these things move me.' 'My refuge is in God.' Many hundreds have been converted here."

"The revivals in Oneida and in this region are attended with power, and produce a tremendous concussion. There is almost as much writing, intrigue, and lying, and reporting of lies, as there would be if we were on the eve of

a presidential election.   Oh, what a world! How much it
hates truth! How unwilling to be saved! But I think the
work will go on. It is now rising and extending, and the
opposition is strong proof that Satan is afraid the work will
extend.   It is probable that professors of religion, in every
direction, will soon be obliged to take stronger ground
than heretofore, and come out more decidedly and boldly,
or fall into the ranks of the enemy.   God will not always
bear with that temporizing policy, which has been pursued
so long, and which has brought so few into his kingdom.
He will overthrow it.   The spirit of apostolic times must
be revived, or the world never will be converted.   What
is the chaff to the wheat?"

In respect to their plan of labors, he writes : —

"When Mr. Finney and I began our race, we had no
thought of going amongst ministers.   Our highest ambition was to go where there was neither minister nor reformation, and try to look up the lost sheep for whom no
man cared.   We began, and the Lord prospered us.   We
soon became the subjects of much speculation, and were
soon drawn into contact with ministers.   But, at present,
we go into no man's parish, unless called.   Ministers who
do not want us have only to refrain from inviting us into
their parishes, and we shall not trouble them.   We have
room enough to work, and work enough to do.

"I have many trials, but none that lead me to doubt
my adoption.   Few days pass, perhaps, when I do not tell
my Saviour as Peter did, 'Thou knowest that I love thee,'
and sometimes he helps me to climb up by faith, till I can
see the foundations of the upper temple ; and sometimes I
think I reach the topmost throne.   At any rate I speak
into the ear of him who sits upon the throne, and rest my
weary soul awhile in the bosom of his love."

Mr. Nash rode twelve miles on the 20th November,
1831, and preached.   Upon his return he retired to his

room, and lifted up his prayer to Him whom his soul
loved ; and then his triumphant spirit suddenly passed into
the glory always to him a near reality.   Upon his tomb-
stone might be appropriately inscribed, —

THE MAN OF PRAYER.

That many laymen exalted the human agency in these
great revivals, and treated unjustly pastors whose labors
had not been attended with large harvests is true, and no
one deplored it more than Mr. Finney and Mr. Nash ; and
there was still another evil: "A man of Mr. Finney's
name and fame and aggressive force could not fail of a
numerous following. Besides the truly good and wise
men, on both sides of the ocean, who, recognizing his
deep spiritual character, were inspired by his example to
greater diligence for the Master, there were unavoidably
not a few persons of weak minds and immature judgment
and impulsive natures who aspired to stand in his shoes,
do as he did, and preach as he preached, and, it is to be
feared, some of them hoped to share his fame. Being destitute of his good sense and discernment, his intimate
knowledge of human nature and his familiarity with the
Scriptures, what marvel if some rushed in where angels
feared to tread?   In the early years of his ministry Mr.
Finney suffered much, in spirit and in name, from this class
of followers."

But these weak imitations were clearly those incidental
evils which are unseparable from great moral revolutions.

CHAPTER XI.

WHILE Mr. Finney was near the zenith of his power in
central New York, and had just gone to Pennsylvania and
Delaware, a youthful preacher, of remarkable gifts and
spiritual force, suddenly appeared at the capital of the
State. Albany had not been visibly reached by the revival
influence, sweeping westward; but the churches on the
whole occupied a position hostile to it. The fascinating yet
fearless herald of God's truth startled the staid inhabitants,
around whose city congregations lay a region of equally
quiet parishes, like a new orb of light flinging its splendor
upon the evening sky. He was a temporary supply during
the illness of an able and highly esteemed pastor. From
spring-time to autumn he labored with intense energy and
contagious enthusiasm, kindling zeal in devout hearts, and
awaking the impenitent. So marked was his success, and
rapidly rising his popularity, that the church fathers were
alarmed lest the harmony of the old pastoral relation,
and the tranquillity of the parish, should be disturbed.
It was too late. The closing of the connection did not

make the people willing to part with the devoted servant of the Most High. A colony from his brief charge rallied around him, and besought him to lead them to a field of their own, where together they might enter into God's harvest. He listened to the divine call, and remained.

Before we follow him from this justly popular entrance upon a ministry rarely equalled in usefulness, we will glance over the providential ordering of his life, and preparation for the glorious work opening before him.

In the latter part of the eighteenth century, at Kirkcudbrightshire, in the south of Scotland, near Solway Firth, a plain, devout man turned his face towards the shores of the new world. The farewells were tenderly spoken, and then the good ship bore him away. Landing in New York, he commenced in a small way the business of a grocer. Here, on the fourteenth day of August, 1802, was born Edward N. Kirk, an only son, under whose roof, a third of a century afterwards, the excellent father fell asleep "in the full assurance of faith."

Edward had three sisters. The boy was ardent, bright, and fond of excitement. He belonged to the class of lads especially exposed to the seductions of sin in a great city, nor were they lost upon him. With ripening youth came the prodigal's choice of pleasure. Prepossessing in appearance and manners, he was a favorite in circles of dissipation; and, with a growing aversion to religious restraints, he entered in 1817 the sophomore class of Princeton College, having no higher aim in life than that of his previous years of reckless folly. His honors at graduation were only those of the boxer, the athlete, the skater, the dashing, generous, jovial fellow and faithful friend. From college he went to the law office of Messrs. Radcliffe and Mason, prominent members of the New York bar. He was now in his twentieth year, with his habits of sinful indulgence strengthening upon him. But the

prayer of faith was not forgotten by the God of his
fathers; an upbraiding conscience brought intervals of
sober reflection. Rev. Dr. Waterbury, formerly of Boston, gave an interesting account of those decisive convictions of sin, which at length drove him to the seclusion of
his own room for four days, from whose anguish and cries
for mercy he emerged a new creature in Christ Jesus. In
the narrative, the divine links connecting crises and destinies appear with remarkable and impressive distinctness :

"After a long residence in India, Dr. Scudder sent his
sons to America to be educated. Henry was a wild and
wicked boy, and gave his friends great disquietude; but
his father and mother never lost their confidence in God.
Their fervent prayers for him were incessant. Now, mark
how God answers prayer, and how he rewards, after long
years and heavy trials, the faithful labors of his servant.
I had been brought to know and love the Saviour through
the influence of Mr. Scudder, when living in my father's
family. In the spring of 1822 I went to New York to
spend a college vacation. While there, I addressed an
audience of young men. At the close of the meeting one
of them followed me up Greenwich Street, and at length
accosted me. His question was direct : " What must I do
to be saved?" I gave him Paul's answer to the same
question ; and it was not long before he fulfilled it happily
in his own experience, and in a few years after entered
the ministry.

"In 1840 this young man, now grown to be that eloquent champion of the truth, the Rev. E. N. Kirk, was
preaching in Dr. Skinner's church in New York, and a
son of Dr. Skinner became a Christian through his influence. He was an intimate friend of young Scudder, and
urged him to come and hear the preacher who had so
wrought upon his own heart. Scudder went, and by the
sermon he then heard was brought to receive the truth as

it is in Jesus, and is now laboring with his father a missionary in India."

The youthful lawyer decided to exchange his chosen profession for the ministry, and, in the autumn of 1822, entered the Theological Seminary at Princeton. The wasted past made him feel the necessity of the severest discipline of study, and accept it with all the enthusiasm of his ardent nature, while he turned to the best account the lessons of regretted dissipation. The stage, which had nourished evil passions, was redeemed from only painful memories, by the aid his memory gleaned from actors, in the culture of his fine oratorical powers. Associated with him in a debating club were young men whose future was no less brilliant than his own. In that circle were James W. Alexander, D. D., Dr. Bethune, Dr. Christmass, and other distinguished men. Four years Mr. Kirk trained himself for his life-work at Princeton, often speaking with power to congregations in the neighborhood; at one time having in charge a parish of colored people. Before leaving the seminary, he was requested by the American Board of Commissioners for Foreign Missions, to represent their noble cause before the churches. He accepted the invitation, prepared his agency sermon; but, somehow, the expected effect did not attend its delivery. There were then, even among Christians, grave objections to the expenditure of men and money, upon distant, dark, and perilous realms. The discourse failed to silence them, and break up the prevailing indifference. One Sabbath, when entering a church to repeat it, a physician met him with very emphatic arguments against the work of the Board. With his mind and heart stirred and stimulated for the occasion by the attack, Mr. Kirk laid aside his sermon, and for two hours held the audience spell-bound, while he swept before the torrent of his eloquence all the objections he had heard since he entered upon his advocacy of the hallowed cause.

The contributions poured in at the close of the appeal. It was the last of that elaborate essay, upon which so many hours had been spent, and the beginning of his unrivalled extempore preaching. After nearly two years of service for the American Board, in the spring of 1828, while travelling with Rev. James W. Alexander, who was out of health, between whom and himself an intimate friendship grew up at Princeton, and whose conversion, a year before Mr. Kirk's, had great influence upon his own religious thought, he preached at Albany in the pulpit of Dr. Chester. This excellent pastor was laid aside, by ill-health, from pastoral duties. At the expiration of the time for which Mr. Kirk was engaged, he was not invited to remain longer. His attractive, faithful, successful ministry as stated, created uneasiness among the friends of the pastor; and they feared to retain him, indulging to some extent the entirely unjust suspicion, that the youthful pulpit orator hoped to supplant the good man whose place he occupied. In addition to this element was the restlessness of inactive professors and worldly people, under his searching exhibitions of truth, which feeling was intensified by the conflict, created by Mr. Finney's remarkable labors, between " old-measure men " and " new-measure men," as the parties in the churches arrayed with and against him were called.

A new church became a necessity, for which the religious interest of several months, then increasing, had furnished both men and means. Mr. Kirk saw the hand of God in the crisis, and acted with his characteristic decision, and with wisdom which left no occasion to retrace any step he had taken.

The Fourth Presbyterian Church, of Albany, was organized, and Mr. Kirk was settled over it, — a timely and providential enterprise, giving to the city at different centres of usefulness, equally important, two flourishing branches of the same communion. Eight years of revival

interest in his parish, of greater or less power, followed
the installation of Mr. Kirk, adding over one thousand
to the number of communicants. His voice was heard in
other churches, and his influence widely felt. Indeed, it
is doubtful whether for many years, but for him, revival
efforts would have been permitted to disturb the conservatism of the Albany churches, from which even Dr. Nettleton received only a feeble co-operation.

Nowhere, perhaps, outside of Albany, during his eight
years' ministry there, was his power greater and richer in
fruitage than in his native city, as a prominent actor in the
"Free Presbyterian Church" enterprise, which has been
already noticed in the narrative of Mr. Finney's connection
with the same grand advance into the strongholds of the
kingdom of darkness.

While the latter "magnified the law," and made Sinai
thunder over "all ungodliness and every worldly lust,"
and Calvary, with its atoning blood, was not forgotten,
the former lifted his silver trumpet with no uncertain
sound, but with mellower and more winning tones. In
this special service for the metropolis, they admirably, as
elsewhere, supplemented each other.

A few extracts from the pastor's farewell sermon, when
his health demanded the reluctant release from his prosperous charge, will reveal the heart and soul of the man,
and also his style of his faithful preaching, along with the
opposition, which has met every faithful, uncompromising herald of salvation. It would be quite impossible
to draw a more complete portrait of the faithful consecrated preacher than that given in the unreserved utterances of this great occasion, when his sobbing people, and
tearful hundreds besides, hung upon his fervid, tremulous
lips. Listen to his glowing words : —

"It is usual on such occasions for the pastor to speak
of his own labors. I cannot do it. If I tell all that is in

my heart, I shall fall upon my knees and cry, 'Deliver me
from blood-guiltiness.' I shall supplicate forgiveness of
the church. I shall weep at the feet of sinners, and ask
them to forgive my selfishness, and my unfaithfulness and
cruelty to their souls.

"But to illustrate God's goodness, let us place the beginning and the end of the period of eight years together.
On the 16th of November, 1828, I preached the first
sermon to a company collected in the consistory room,
kindly offered to us by the officers of the North Dutch
Church, who have thus imposed a debt, which we would
cheerfully repay in the same currency if an opportunity
occurred, as we have endeavored to repay it in thankfulness and benedictions.

"There were then two views taken of the enterprise. On
the one side, both the friends and the enemies of God said
it was unwise and uncalled for. I was charged with fanaticism and boyish indiscretion. It was said by the sagacious,
'What do these men build? behold, if a fox go up their
walls, they will fall down!' When this building was commenced, some ridiculed : obstructions met us in the usual
financial arrangements ; suspicions were set afloat concerning the safety of crediting any one connected, even indirectly, with the enterprise. When the first indications of
the special presence of God's spirit were experienced, we
were branded with the severest epithets, and the ears of
God's children were open to the falsehoods of the wicked.

"Now, God forbid that I should refer to the past in a
spirit of revenge or of boasting. I should loathe myself if
I could ever indulge such feelings, but especially on such
an occasion. God knows my heart towards this whole
community, and towards those who were once my bitter-
est enemies. I do not boast; but I say that on the one
side were these views, and feelings, and predictions; on
the other, with much human imperfection, we certainly

had for our leading principles and feelings a determination to sustain the plain, honest exhibition of the truths of
the gospel, without consulting unconverted men, whether
they were pleased or displeased, and an unwavering confidence that God would bless us if we served him.

"There were many considerations which induced me to
remain here. Low and selfish motives were attributed.
My friends (I say it to the glory of God), I had as much
confidence, when I met in the first prayer-meeting with
twenty persons, that God would greatly bless us, as I have
now that he has blessed us. Do not call it presumption,
for I knew that I was surrounded by a praying band.
Among many other considerations which induced me to
remain and bear the peltings of the pitiless storm, was the
fact, as stated then to me, that a number of Christians
were engaged in prayer from sunset to sunrise, that I might
not be permitted to leave the city. That turned the scale :
I could not desert' such spirits, and I knew God would
bless them. I saw it, I felt it ; and I feel now as if I could
go gladly to attack the spirits in the pit, if God sent me,
surrounded by such hearts. And, more than this, this
enterprise and my unworthy name were on the lips of
hundreds of God's praying people, from this city to Buffalo. An eminent saint, who preached over a wide circuit, was in the habit of encouraging the churches to bear
our cause to the mercy-seat continually.

"I consider this church as a monument, inscribed with
the evidences of the power of prayer, and the faithfulness
of Jacob's God. The enemy said, 'By whom shall Jacob
arise, for he is small?' We replied, 'In God is our trust,
we will make our boast in the Lord.'

"Now let us see how the Lord hath dealt with us.
Truly he hath encouraged the hearts of them that believed,
and he hath silenced the enemy and avenger. I preached
from November, 1828, to February, 1829, at which time

the church was organized. And it seemed as if the Lord
would try our faith by suspending the manifestation of His
favor, until, as a distinct, organized, and consecrated church,
we sat down for the first time to celebrate the death of
Christ. I shall never forget that day. After its toils
were over, I was sent for, late at night, to see a trembling
soul who had that day been brought to see her guilt and
danger. That was the first fruit of a glorious harvest.
An inquiry meeting was appointed, and, to my surprise,
upwards of sixty were present. From that day to this,
we have not passed the year without some special outpouring of the spirit of God.

"It would animate the hearts of other Christians to hear
a description of the exercises of many who have been converted. Never can I forget that beloved apartment of
this building, where I have met the inquirers, and where
I have seen them consecrate themselves to God and the
Lamb. Oh, what change in individual character, in
families, nay, in neighborhoods, hath God's blessed spirit
wrought! Within this period there have been united to
this church, by letter and on confession, one thousand and
twelve members, making an average of one hundred and
twenty-five each year. The Sabbath school has contained
one thousand five hundred pupils.

"The foundation-stone of this enterprise was laid
emphatically in prayer. The duty of prayer has been
enjoined and urged incessantly. Meetings for prayer
have been multiplied to a degree, in the estimation of
many, extravagant. We have assembled in the early
morning for months. We have met for long periods at
ten o'clock every morning to pray directly for the conversion of the impenitent. We have believed in the
transcendent importance of the conversion of men. We
have prayed for it. We have witnessed it in hundreds
of joyful instances. All our history is such a demon-

stration of the efficacy of prayer, that, if I had never had any other proof, I should feel an overwhelming sense of obligation to pray without ceasing.

" We have met, as before remarked, with the sentiment, in various forms, that the Church and her ministers must not go in advance of public sentiment."

Mr. Kirk then, in ringing sentences, proceeds to state and defend the aggressive position of his people on the great reforms of temperance, Sabbath-keeping, purity, and American slavery.

Returning to directly gospel ministrations, he adds: " When I preached to another congregation, they turned me from them because I preached too directly and pungently. I could never hear any other objection on the most careful inquiry. On that point I was entreated to change. But on that point this church took its stand from the commencement, and determined to welcome the most direct and pungent preaching that was according to the word of God. Now, for the importance of it: it is to us most manifest that God has connected the conversion of hundreds with that as an indispensable means. As to the policy of it, it was said, ' Why, men will desert your churches.' God has shown us that it is not so. And, more than that, I am the living witness to the fact that the churches in this city will now bear a degree of directness and pungency that would once have been thought intolerable. I am told that I have altered. I say that public sentiment has altered. One of the most convincing proofs of it to me is, that I am ashamed now to preach those very sermons which made the disturbance, because they are too tame and pointless.

" And now, dear friends, having shown what God hath wrought for and by this society, you will permit me to speak more directly of God's mercies to me as your pastor. No man can tell what I have passed through in this city. My entrance here was flattering; my reception everything I could ask as a man and a minister. So long as foreign missions was my topic, all went well; but when I turned to show the amiable and moral and respected of this community that they were more guilty than the heathen, and were going to a deeper condemnation, they rose in might against me. I had never known an enemy before since my conversion: I had never been slandered. But now a new scene awaited me in this goodly city: I was reviled, my sermons and sentiments were misrepresented, friends grew cold and enemies multiplied. For a stripling this was new, and, you may be sure, wellnigh overwhelming. My heart overflowed with love to all: I could not see why any should persecute me. But, oh! it was a blessed school: I would not part with the lessons there learned for all the enjoyments of an undisturbed prosperity. Yet for three years I walked the streets of this city, feeling as if, by God's command, I was an intruder here. I have felt as if the very houses frowned upon me. Cheerfully would I have fled and hid myself, like Elijah in a cave, but the very style of the opposition showed clearly that the controversy was with God and his word, not with the lips of clay which uttered it.

"But I turn from that to speak of the hearts which cherished and the hands which upheld me in those trying days. Brethren, sisters, I thus publicly thank you. You gave not only a cup of cold water to a disciple when it was a reproach to you: you shared his sorrows, you shielded his reputation with your own, you would have shared the last earthly comfort with him, you would have died with him for Christ. You wept for me, you carried my burdens, you prayed for me. I know it: and my heart thanks you; my soul clings to you. But chiefly I recognize the goodness of God in it, in whose hands are all hearts. I thank the members of the church for their forbearance and sympathy and respect, and the many proofs of their love. Since commencing to form this church, I have preached to you about one thousand sermons. I have assisted other churches in sustaining more than thirty protracted meetings. I have delivered ninety addresses on temperance; more than a hundred addresses on foreign missions; many on slavery; many for objects in our city, for the tract, Bible, education, and other societies; attended and addressed the various societies in three anniversaries at New York, one at Cincinnati, one at Lexington, Ky., one at Boston, one at Troy. I have performed a tour through many principal cities in this State and into Canada, on the subject of common-school education.

" With the fullest sense of my unworthiness to labor in so glorious a cause, do I, this night, render thanks to God for bestowing upon me the ability and disposition to perform these labors. Brethren, I have become a fool in glorying; but God is my witness, I do it for his glory. David could not hold his tongue from uttering the mercies of God after his great deliverances. And now, brethren, I am about to say farewell. I leave you, not because I do not love you; my heart grows closer to you every day. This church appears to me more interesting and more important than ever. I go because I believe I ought to go. Whatever I am now, or may be hereafter, is my country's and my God's. I consecrate it to the church of Christ and to the human race. Brethren, what mean ye to weep and break my heart? Oh, it is with a heavy heart that I say to such friends farewell! Deeply shall your names, your countenances, be engraven on this memory. I shall carry a catalogue of them with me, and spread it before that mercy-seat at which we have so often met. My children! my brothers! my fathers! walk in the truth. God has been with you, is with you, has promised still to be with you. Look at all the way in which he has led you.

Ebenezers line the path of your history. Each one speaks to your heart, — 'Be of good courage, for our God is an unchanging God.'

"Citizens of Albany, farewell! Have I wronged you, have I misled, or have I been as a prophet of the Lord in the midst of you? Speak, for I am now sealing the first section of my ministry, perhaps the last among you. I have stood on yon heights, and looked over your dwellings, and my anxious thoughts have dwelt upon your spiritual interests; my fervent prayers have arisen for you and for your children. I have been willing to labor for the general good, just as much as for this individual association. If any have injured me, I would that they knew how fully they are forgiven. If I have injured any, I would that they knew how sincerely I implore forgiveness. Many of you have kindly appreciated my desires for your welfare, whatever you have thought of the imperfect manner employed to promote it. You are kind, and your kindness will be remembered.

"Members of sister churches! God bless you, and make you grow in grace and in the knowledge of our Lord Jesus Christ. Remember your absent brother.

"Unconverted fellow-citizens, hear the last words of a parting friend. Make Christ your Saviour, and heaven your prize. 'Ye must be born again.' Turn, then, quickly to the Lord, and your souls shall live.

"Again, dear friends, *farewell*, FAREWELL!"

Mr. Kirk sailed for Europe in April, 1837. Changing his plan of going directly to Germany, he went to Paris. Here he held a series of religious services, associated with Dr. Baird, and subsequently conducted meetings in English in Rue Saint Aime, creating a deep and general interest. He visited London, and preached in Surrey Chapel, — Rowland Hill's old church, — and a hundred or more conversions were among the immediate fruits. A

repetition of such scenes was had in Lady Huntington
Spafield's Chapel. He declined urgent invitations to
settle in London, and accepted the appointment of Secretary of the Foreign Evangelical Society, with special
reference to communicating information to the American
churches, and creating interest in its operations.

This led him back to his native land in September,
1839, to perform the duties assigned him. Upon his
arrival, he found the country under the cloud of financial
adversity, disposing the public mind to thoughtfulness
upon the soul's need of imperishable riches in Christ, —
a condition of feeling fresh in the recollection of the
present generation, nearly twenty years later, followed
by a general awakening throughout the land.

The peculiar adaptation of Mr. Kirk to the field white
for harvest, as an evangelist, was apparent to the churches.
He seemed to have come home, and so it evidently was in
the divine plan, for this very purpose. He yielded to the
judgment of his brethren, on the single condition that the
churches should contribute enough to the society he represented to satisfy it for the withdrawal for the time of his
services.

This arrangement was of God, who not only supplied
the treasury by opening the hearts of his stewards, but
sent his ambassador forth to do a work which he alone,
at that crisis of religious feeling, could achieve. He was
the finished orator among evangelists, and next to Dr.
Nettleton, though widely different, was welcomed into the
pulpits, which were not open to the "sons of thunder,"
who, no more faithful, had about them more distinctively
the "new-measure" odium. He commenced his evangelistic tour among the churches at Baltimore, not long after
Elder Knapp had fought his battle for truth and purity.
He held a series of meetings successively in Philadelphia,
New York, Boston, Hartford, New Haven, and other places.

At Philadelphia, there had been nothing like the scenes which attended his preaching there since Summerfield's visit; nor was the " effect so great now in the way of eloquence, but greater in the way of religious impression and permanence." The whole city appeared to be profoundly moved. Such throngs in and often around the churches ! Such inquiry meetings, when, like an inspired prophet, Mr. Kirk, in the ripeness of early manhood but with self-forgetful love of souls, spoke briefly to the tearful hundreds of sin and the great salvation ! Prof. Fowler said of those scenes : —

" Those meetings are an exponent of a noteworthy religious movement in America, the revival movement. They are the fairest representatives of revival meetings. They constitute a marked feature of the American church. The leading idea of those who sustained them was to arouse attention to religious concerns by special religious meetings, and then by their daily repetition hold the attention till it became rooted in religious conviction, and bore the fruit of an abiding Christian character. They were sometimes continued for weeks, and one, two, three, and even four meetings were held each day. Some were prayer-meetings ; some were allotted to lay exhortation ; some to personal conversation ; some to preaching. They were held at all hours : the rising sun looked in upon a company of suppliants ; the man of business laid down his employment in its midst, and went to the sanctuary ; and at evening, especially, gathered men and women, the old and the young, either to hear or to exhort, or to pray, or to scoff. For the time, all other gatherings were set aside. The social party and the literary lecture were made secondary. Even useful and necessary avocations were more or less neglected. Eternal verities asserted a controlling sway over the mind. And these meetings were continued week after week; hence they were called 'protracted meetings.' And they did not occupy the minds of a moiety only of the community : they were a living presence among the people, and a pressure upon the public attention. When they did not kindle enthusiasm, they at least aroused opposition. Few were able to disregard, and fewer to despise. They were either loved or hated.

"It was in such seasons that Mr. Kirk was most effective. Here all his fine powers were brought into the fullest exercise. His tender sympathies embraced the crowded audiences; his modulated tones stole into their hearts ; his passionate appeals stirred the deep fountains of emotion; his earnestness was electrical; his eloquence irresistible. He gave himself up to the work. There is no enumeration of the number of times he spoke ; neither is there any possible reckoning of the results. But those were times remembered by many, and recalled as life eras.

"We have distinguished Mr. Kirk as the 'evangelist preacher,' because it was in these revival meetings that he came most prominently before the public, and because he is in the minds of most men distinctively associated with them. Moreover, his peculiar gifts are best manifested in the style of mingled argument, pathos, and appeal which characterize revival meetings. So strikingly was this the case that many doubted the propriety of his establishment in one place, regarding him as belonging to the church universal, and not to be appropriated by one community."

Dr. Kirk had a very humble and yet an efficient co-worker in some of his fields of spiritual harvest, who was doubtless drawn to him by his antislavery position : we refer to Aunt Dinah, who had been a slave in Duchess County, N. Y., but who had purchased her own freedom. She was converted in a Methodist revival, and learned to read the Bible after being taught the alphabet by her master's little daughter. She became familiar with standard theological works, of which those of Dr. Jonathan Edwards were her favorites. She joined Dr. Kirk at Albany, and identified herself with him in his revival labors, and was thoroughly appreciated by his large and noble heart. Aunt Dinah followed him to a number of places, even to New York City, where she did excellent service for her new master. The tidings of the Spirit's presence was the welcome call to her; and distance, inclement weather, and pilgrim-travel were no hindrance to the loving disciple. Nor was Aunt Dinah intellectually an ordinary woman. She had a clear, discriminating mind, intuitive knowledge of character, rare discernment in respect to preaching, and by a thorough study of the Bible possessed an amount of theological lore which often surpassed the skill of doctors in divinity. "But most of all was she distinguished for her humble, genuine, and glowing piety, for her love towards all God's creatures, and for her absorbing interest in the redemption of sinners. Her person was not attractive. She was much bent, not by years, but by an injury to her back, caused by a blow from her master; her features were strongly marked, her color that of the full-blooded African, strikingly contrasting with the snow-white head-dress she usually wore, and her manner heartily affectionate, blunt, earnest, and decided. Her conversations on religious subjects, and she talked of little else, were prized by all. Her expositions of Scripture were discriminating, with the peculiar unction which comes from a living experience; her personal appeals pungent and effective, as well as pathetic; and her frequent talks in female prayer-meetings, Sabbath schools, and occasionally in religious gatherings of both sexes, were never amiss. She inspired strong affection in those who knew her; and her circle of friends was not only large, but included some of the prominent citizens, at whose houses she was always welcome. The anecdotes about her are numberless, but our limit forbids their mention. For the last few years of her life she occupied a room in the basement of one of the New York churches, making occasional visits to her old friends. She died March 20, 1846, aged seventy-four years.

" At this time there was stopping at the Astor House the brother of an English officer, who preferred the request that Aunt Dinah should be buried in Greenwood Cemetery by the side of his brother, in accordance with his dying request. It seems this officer was taken sick at a New York hotel, and Aunt Dinah, happening to hear of it, sought his room, ministered to his wants, and began in her usual way to talk with him about his soul-interests. He encouraged the poor negro's remarks, for they afforded him relief from the tedium of confinement; but, as they were continued and repeated, he began to awake to a higher interest, and finally became a penitent and believing Christian. His wish was complied with. Twenty-six dollars were found in her room, laid by for her funeral expenses. To this more was added. A procession of carriages followed her remains to their resting-place in Greenwood, and a slab of Italian marble was erected above it, which bears an appropriate inscription."

In 1842, Mr. Kirk was invited to establish a church in Boston, and accepted the call. June 1st he was installed pastor of the " Mount Vernon Church." We suspect he sometimes feared it was the mistake of his ministerial life; for, although he became one of the most useful pastors, and his influence was felt, and will continue to be, not alone in Boston, but all over New England and throughout the Christian world, his harvest-work was largely done before he exchanged the extempore discourse for the written sermon, and the broad field of service to which he was preeminently adapted for the warmer circle of parish duties. But God makes no mistakes; and we must believe that

13

Dr Kirk was guided by Him in all his consecrated life, whose view takes in all results for two worlds.

The vital connection of Dr. Kirk with the Boston Tract Society, which took its separate position on the question of slavery; his influence everywhere, in behalf of a spiritual Christianity, and revivals; his public addresses, and his sermons on special occasions, many of them published; his excellent "Lectures on Revivals," recently issued in a neat volume; all suggest the unlimited and mighty influence for God and humanity he exerted during his long pastorate in Boston. Dr. Kirk was never married; and yet men have rarely had, and showed on proper occasions, a more domestic, social, and genial nature. Reasons which were peculiar, and to him sufficient, deprived him of a home, except that which was ever pleasant to him, and to all who entered its warm enclosure, in which his sisters presided. He was fond of music; and had in his parlor an instrument of glass cups, played by the fingers, on their margins, of Æolian sweetness, — the only one of the kind, probably, in the country. For several years before his death, his sight gradually failed until he became quite blind. He was fortunate in having a sympathizing, congenial colleague, in the present pastor of Mount Vernon Church, Rev. Mr. Herrick. It was touching and beautiful to see him led to his seat in the pulpit by his younger brother in the ministry, and listening, with unaffected interest, to the excellent sermons of his very worthy successor.

Dr. Kirk, while preparing an essay on revivals for the "Ministers' Meeting," suddenly dropped the pen, and went into the sleep of apoplexy, to awaken no more on earth. He quietly passed to glory, March 27, 1874, at his residence in Staniford Street, Boston. A more fragrant memory, and a purer example, few men in the world's history have left for its succeeding generations.

CHAPTER XII.

THE WHITEFIELD OF THE SOUTH. — REV. DANIEL BAKER, D. D. — CONTEMPORARY WITH EVANGELISTS AT THE NORTH. — EARLY LIFE. — CONVERSION. — LONGING FOR THE MINISTRY. — PREPARATION FOR IT. — COLLEGE EXPERIENCES. — GOES TO PRINCETON — PASTOR AND EVANGELIST. — REMARKABLE SCENES AT BEAUFORT, N.C. — LABORS. — AGENT AND PRESIDENT OF AUSTIN COLLEGE. — AN AUTHOR. — CHARACTERISTICS AND POWER. — GREAT USEFULNESS. — HAPPY DEATH. — REV. JAMES GALLAHER. — WORK AS EVANGELIST. — LITERARY EFFORTS. — HIS DEATH.

IT is a singular coincidence that nearly all of the prominent evangelists of the early part of the nineteenth century should have been born within a few years of each other, or between 1790 and 1800.

Rev. Daniel Baker, D. D., contemporary with Mr. Finney and others at the North, was the distinguished evangelist of the South. In spiritual harvest, he was the Whitefield of that section of our land to which that English orator first came; the latter founding there an orphan asylum, and Mr. Baker a college. Our evangelist was comparatively little known in New England, because he lived, labored, and died in the Southern States. He was born at Midway, Liberty County, Ga., August 17, 1791. His ancestors emigrated from Dorchester, Mass., in 1752, having originally come to that colony from Plymouth, England, fugitives from the persecuting power of Laud. They were practical, patriotic, and godly men. Daniel, whose father was a deacon, was the seventh and youngest child by the first wife and mother. When a boy eight years old, he was called from his pastime " under the

shade of an oak on Colonel's Island, the summer residence of the family, to see his father die," a scene which
left an abiding shadow upon his young spirit. His mother
died several years before. One night he dreamed he was
in heaven, and rushed by the angels to find his sainted
mother : but as he bounded to her side with delight, she
rose in the air with them, an angel, too ; and, singing,
they faded from sight, and the sweet music was lost in the
glorious skies. He said that never to his recollection had
he heard the tune before, nor did he hear it afterwards,
until twelve years later, when at family worship with Rev.
Dr. Moses Hoge. This singular dream made a deep and
lasting impression. Soon after, he read one day in the
Shorter Catechism, the " Dialogue between Christ, Youth,
and the Devil," which awakened in him unusual anxiety in
regard to his religious state, and was followed by another
equally striking, but entirely different, and to him no
less affecting dream. He thought he was dead, and among
the lost, conscious that his day of grace was over, and
longing to return to earth, and enjoy one more hour of
mercy. Upon awaking, he was glad that he was alive,
and was also depressed with the fear that there was no
hope for him. He wished himself a bird or even an insect,
to escape the judgment-day. While thus unhappy, he
was terrified by an awful thunder-storm. His convictions
were deepened, by noticing his brother's habit of retiring
daily at sunset, for secret prayer. Opening a hymn-book,
he read, —

> "Come, humble sinner, in whose breast,"

And resolved to repair to the grove also and cast himself on
Christ, and, if he " must perish, perish there." The burden
of his guilt and fears rolled away, and joy filled his heart.
With the dawn of eternal life, came the exclamation, "Oh,
if I could only be a preacher !" The very desire seemed to

be a day dream, and was soon for a while dismissed; but his youthful hope, fondly cherished from childhood, of visiting Savannah, thirty-five miles distant, to see the wonders of a city, was to be now realized, and to change thenceforth the quiet current of his life. Mounted on a bale of cotton laid upon a cart, his brother on horseback, and by his side a servant on foot, he went to the metropolis of the State. A situation was obtained in a store for the bewildered boy. The merchant who employed him was a man of the world, and a neglecter of the means of grace. Daniel erelong began to take Sabbath walks, and tried to swear, but the " oath died unuttered on his tongue, and he never attempted it any more." Exposure to death while hunting, and again when bathing on Sunday, along with the sudden death of a wicked companion, sent him to his Bible, and also to his knees, begging for reclaiming grace.

With the restored joy of God's salvation, his desires to preach the gospel were once more awakened with greater intensity than before. He was now in his nineteenth year, and the necessity of a decision of the question of his life-work was keenly felt. His brother visited him at this critical moment, and incidentally remarked that a letter had been received at Midway from an old pastor, stating that President Hoge, of Hampton Sidney College, would receive there, in behalf of the institution, a young man of piety, to be educated for the ministry. This was God's timely providence; and, obtaining release from his business engagements, he started for that seat of learning. With the difficulties he encountered in classical studies, came despondency, relieved only by the thought that he might at least preach to the negroes.

After a searching review of past experiences, and a new consecration, expressed in resolutions to avoid undue levity to which he was tempted, not to overestimate oratory which he much admired, and to be more in prayer, he united with the Presbyterian Church, April 19, 1812. His journal for the succeeding months and years reveals a spiritual life, occasionally overshadowed with doubts and depression, but revealing to all who knew him the prevailing peace of a victorious faith in Jesus, often attended with holy raptures. He records July 31, 1813 : "Dry logical sermons, with rounded periods, delivered in a cold, formal, and heartless manner, I can never relish, however beautified by the superficial elegances of composition; and I question if the good effects which flow from such preaching will be sufficient to compensate the minister for all his care, labor, and refinement. I love warm, animating, lively, *evangelical* preaching, full of fire, breathing love and compassion. Oh, may I never become a cold, lifeless, sentimental preacher, but may I imitate the zeal of a Whitefield, the tenderness of a Hervey, the affection of a Baxter, and blend all with the pure, sound, evangelical principles of a Doddridge ! "

In 1813, he entered the junior class at Princeton College, New Jersey. Here he repeated his loyalty to his King, in special prayer and efforts for students, associating with himself three others, who were called in contempt the "Religiosi," reminding us of the "Holy Club" in Cambridge University, England, three quarters of a century before. But the "praying band" fainted not, till a precious work of grace went through the college. At the commencement of 1815, he graduated with honor, intending to return, after vacation, to the seminary. But circumstances pointed to private theological instruction, under Rev. William Hill, of Winchester. Here he began to address religious meetings ; and his first theme was 2 Kings v, 1. Although "religion was at a low ebb," he commenced visitation of the people to awaken, if possible, serious interest. A· portion of his time was occupied in teaching in the female academy, among whose students conversions occurred. March 28, 1816, he was married. One of his neighboring fields of spiritual culture was Jarratt's Town. During a walk thither, an old negro who met him on the road, said, "Why, massa, you *russelled* de people when you was here before." Mr. Baker replied, "*Russelled the people*, what is that?" The negro answered, "Yes, massa, you russelled de people, you come too close on 'em, you say de best way to try if de tree be sound is to take a stick and knock 'em." By way of illustration with his plain staff he struck soundly a tree beside him.

With much fasting and prayer, Mr. Baker was devoted to the preparation to "do his master's will." In the autumn of 1816, he was licensed by the presbytery of Winchester, after considerable debate and delay, because he was not familiar with "systematic theology." One of the members in favor of his licensure remarked, "*The Lord has licensed him!*"

We next find our evangelist in Dr. Muir's church, Alexandria, in the midst of a "remarkable awakening." He received a call to Harrisonburg, and also to become seaman's preacher in the city of New York, but accepted the former, and to increase his small salary also taught a private school. Of his pupils, two became distinguished college professors. Meanwhile, having preached in Savannah, he was called to the Independent Presbyterian Church there, and at the same time to the Second Presbyterian Church of Washington City. Although financially the inducement was less, he felt it his duty to go to Washington, and aid an important though struggling enterprise.

The welcome to this new field was very cordial; and his popularity soon opened a providential source of additional income, by an offer from Commissioner Meigs of a clerkship in the Land Office. Among his hearers were John Quincy Adams and Andrew Jackson. Mr. Adams, who was then Secretary of State, greatly embarrassed the yet youthful preacher, when upon his first attendance he walked up the aisle just as the text was announced: "Ephraim is a cake not turned." His friendship for the pastor was valuable and practical. He advanced twelve hundred dollars to purchase a home for him, and lent freely sums of money when needed. The Secretary of State also became a trustee of the society. While residing at the capital, Mr. Baker published a very able work entitled "A Scriptural View of Baptism." After two years of devoted ministry, and activity in every good work, and receiving more than a hundred members into the communion, he accepted, in 1828, a second call to the church in Savannah. August 10, 1830, having become deeply dissatisfied with himself, and the lack of saving interest in the gospel among his people, he says: " I took 'Payson's Memoirs' in my hand, and, going out early that morning, I spent nearly the whole day in a distant graveyard, engaged in reading and fasting and prayer. That day marks a memorable era in the history of my life. Returning to my dwelling that evening, about the setting of the sun, I resolved to turn over a new leaf, and, in preaching and invitations, to be more faithful and diligent than I had ever been." In his journal, he refers again more in detail to the " Bethel indeed he had in a brick tomb under a shade, in the burial-ground for colored people." He evidently came into a baptism of the Spirit which threw into shadow his previous experience. Special meetings were appointed, a rising concern was soon visible, and conversions multiplied. When a lady complained respecting a church-meeting that it was exclusive "for his dear members alone, while the poor sinners were neglected," he immediately proposed, if she would attend, to have a meeting for those among whom she classed herself, where no others should be invited to attend. The following Sabbath he made an interesting statement upon the condition of religious feeling, and "respectfully invited all who had the candor to admit that they were not converted to be present, and none but such. Having spent the day in fasting and prayer, I went to the lecture-room and found it crowded. What an opportunity, and how great the vantage-ground which I occupied! It was a solemn and melting time."

And now came the too common trial of the fearless, faithful servant of Jesus, *opposition in the church.* One of the elders said to him, "None of the young people will join our church, if you continue to preach in this way." Mr. Baker replied, "I do not wish them to join unless they are converted." The elder added, "But the pew-holders will give up their pews." Mr. Baker's "mind was made up," and he proposed a four days' meeting.

Two of the elders did n't relish the aggressive movement; and one of them, a man of high standing, sent in a written protest. With great wisdom and tact Mr. Baker suggested a postponement of the further consideration of the matter, and that "perhaps the respected brother would withdraw his protest," which he did, and yielded to the majority. The failure to obtain anticipated aid from ministers was followed by discouragement; then came the glad arrival of Rev. Mr. Joyce, a successful laborer in similar meetings, and glorious displays of the divine power. There were hundreds of hopeful conversions. Mr. Baker now received a call to his former charge at Washington, urged by John Quincy Adams and Andrew Jackson, which he declined, to give himself wholly to the work of an evangelist.

The tidings of the remarkable revival in connection with a protracted meeting went abroad, and invitations to hold similar meetings reached him from various places. Wherever he went rich blessings attended his labors. He, however, regarded the work in Beaufort, S. C., as the most extraordinary in its power.

The Episcopal pastor, Rev. Mr. Walker, opened his pulpit to the evangelist, who modestly proposed to "stand below"; but no, he must go into the pulpit. Mr. Baker wrote, "Oh, what blessed meetings we had! Three times each day did I preach, and night and day to full houses. Besides, it was usual to have what was called a 'concert of prayer' at the going down of the sun. A few would afterwards meet at the house of a neighbor, and after singing 'Blow ye the trumpet, blow,' would unite in prayer." Among the converts was Col. Stevens at eighty-six, who had "followed Whitefield, and heard him preach many sermons with no saving effect." Rev. Mr. Elliott, Bishop of Georgia at a later period, was another subject of the work. As this was a good example of his evangelistic successes, we will add extracts from the pen of Mr. Grayson, a distinguished member of Congress, then editor of the "Beaufort Gazette." Of the immediate effect of Mr. Baker's "apostolic, untiring zeal, which no one can conceive who was not present," he wrote: —

"Politics were forgotten; business stood still; the shops and stores were shut, the schools closed; one subject only appeared to occupy all minds and engross all hearts. The church was filled to overflowing; seats, galleries, aisles, exhibited a dense mass of human beings, from hoary age to childhood; and, when crowds moved forward and fell prostrate at the foot of the altar, and the rich music of hundreds of voices, and the solemn accents of prayer, rose over the kneeling multitude, it was not in human hearts to resist the influence that awoke its sympathies, and spoke its purest and most elevated feeling.

"The union of sects produced on the occasion was not the least striking feature of the event. Distinctions were laid aside. Our community seemed like one great family;

and it was impossible not to exclaim, 'What a beautiful thing is this religion!'"

In regard to this remarkable revival, an Episcopal minister, well acquainted with the circumstances, thus writes : —

"The duellist threw away his pistols ; the infidel believed in Christ ; political feuds were forgotten, and the power of the gospel confessed.

"The notice of his visit, and of the proposed religious services, was sent from house to house. In one instance it was received at a whist club, during their weekly meeting, and read aloud by one of the party, amidst shouts of merriment. The intended meeting, its originators, objects, and agents, all afforded ample scope for ridicule. Some advised abstaining from the services, by way of frowning down such folly ; but, confident of their ability to withstand all the preacher's snares, they determined to attend, and prove the strength of their own armor.

"Not many days after, eight of this party of eleven were found 'sitting at the feet of Jesus,' and testifying to the power of his grace. One of the number is now a bishop, and another an esteemed presbyter of the Episcopal Church.

"The services were held twice or thrice a day, alternately in the Episcopal and Baptist churches, — the only two places of worship in the town, — the use of the Episcopal church being tendered by the vestry for that purpose.

"A holy atmosphere pervaded the town, and affected the entire population to a degree unparalleled, save in the revival described by President Edwards, at Northampton, in 1735.

"Once, at the close of an evening service, the minister invited those who desired the prayers of the brethren to kneel around the chancel. There was a momentary pause in the church, when, simultaneously, every pew door appeared to fly open ; and not the chancel only, but the aisles also, were thronged with a kneeling multitude, in solemn silence 'waiting for the moving of the waters.' God was manifestly present 'in the assemblies of his saints.'

"It is a singular fact, attesting the disinterestedness of the preacher, that out of two or three hundred conversions in Beaufort, under Mr. Baker's ministry, not one became a Presbyterian. The Episcopalians and Baptists reaped the fruit of his labors. He seemed intent upon the conversion of souls. But two have, drawn back from their profession, one of whom had been intemperate for many years. Six months after the events described, the writer was present at their communion, and saw, what he has never seen elsewhere, the entire congregation, with two exceptions, remain for the sacrament. Eight men went from this one congregation to preach the gospel of Christ. The leaven has infused a new life into Episcopacy."

Such was the unselfish devotion of the evangelist ; nor less noteworthy was the aggressive freedom and spirituality of the Episcopal Church and clergy.

Mr. Baker, after graphically describing the marvellous effect of the revival upon the intensely bitter and growing political strife, making friends of those who went armed for deadly conflict, alludes feelingly to his ride back to Savannah in a row-boat, through the kindness of a Christian brother ; and then relates, with unaffected modesty, the overwhelming surprise with which he found "a most courteous and beautiful letter" there from the "citizens of Beaufort," apprising him that they had deposited to his "credit in the Bank of the United States the sum of nine hundred and sixty-one dollars and fifty cents." He regarded this gift as a special providence, when just relinquishing a salary of two thousand dollars for a few hundreds in the service of a missionary society of Georgia, that he might prosecute his evangelistic work.

For the three succeeding years he held protracted meetings in Georgia and Alabama principally, but also in the Carolinas. His attention was now turned to Ohio. "We started," he says, "with one gig and a barouche, containing my family and baggage, my two sons riding, in turn, a little pony." At Charlotte Court-House, Va., his horse fell and broke a shaft, which detaining him, he was desired to preach. The result was a season of refreshing there, at Prince Edward, and other towns. In the summer of 1834, he reached Ohio, intending to make Springfield his radiating point. After holding several successful meetings, he decided to return to the South, having received an invitation to labor in Kentucky. The principal reason for this change of plan was the antislavery excitement around him, respecting which he frankly says : —

"Although I was myself no slaveholder, yet I was no abolitionist. I verily believed that the relation of master and slave was recognized in the Bible, and that ecclesiastical bodies have no right to legislate upon the subject. Pained by the harsh remarks which poured into my ear from day to day, I became very restless, and wished to return South again."

Conscientiously occupying this ground, he remained with the Southern branch of the General Assembly when the excision rent asunder that powerful body.

Mr. Baker never intruded his views upon any, but kept steadily at his chosen employment — of saving souls. Equal wisdom in Ohio, when forcing the subject upon his attention could do no good, would have retained him there, with spiritual results which God alone can know. A few months later he is in Frankfort, Ky., a settled pastor, itinerating, at request of presbytery, among the churches within their bounds, and holding protracted meetings. In the penitentiary he had a revival, receiving within its walls a dozen or more into the church — "a rare and solemn occasion."

He also labored among the colored people. In Alabama, where he had harvest seasons, he met Rev. John Breckinridge, who was deeply interested in the religious condition of Texas, then the "Lone Star," and turned his attention to this new field for missionary activity. Late in the autumn of 1839, he started for that wild region, passing through several of the principal towns in Tennessee, and holding meetings under appointment of the Assembly's board.

We have not space to follow this heroic, devout, happy servant of Jesus through his perilous wanderings in his Lord's service through Texas; his tours eastward; his agency for and his presidency of Austin College, at Huntsville; nor to glance at the revivals in which he always lived. Few families have had a more romantic, trying, and precious history than his own. Two of his sons entered the ministry: one of them, the Rev. Wm. M. Baker, his biographer, was at the time pastor of the Presbyterian Church of Austin, and is now settled in South Boston, Mass. He is also the author of several works, one of which, "Inside: a Chronicle of Secession," was first published in "Harper's Monthly," and its manuscript hidden in Texan earth, to prevent possible detection while going through the press. Dr. Baker died at the house of his son, at Austin, Dec. 10, 1857. When lying at the gate of glory which flooded his soul, he said to his son, "William, I want this epitaph carved on my tomb — 'Here lies Daniel Baker, preacher of the gospel. A sinner saved by grace.' Remember, '*A sinner saved by grace.*'" With heaven's serenity on his face, his eyes looking upward, he murmured, "Lord Jesus, into thy hands I commend my spirit;" and, closing the lids over their fading light, he "fell asleep in Jesus."

When the news of his death reached the legislature in session, both branches adjourned immediately, to pass, upon their return to the capitol, resolutions, and pronounce eulogies, rarely bestowed upon even a departed statesman. He was a public benefactor in the founding of the college, and in all public enterprises where his influence could be felt; pre-eminently so, as a spiritual force of the highest order among the churches.

In preaching, his style was colloquial, clear, tender, often eloquent, and intensely earnest. Sometimes he carried notes into the pulpit, but oftener had none at all. His physique was commanding, and the simplicity of his character apparent in every feature and lineament of his face, and in every action. The means employed, besides ordinary services, were the inquiry meeting, kneeling before the public altar, and circles of prayer in the dwellings. But his real sources of power were the same as those of every true evangelist and pastor, the oracles of God, the closet of intimate fellowship with Christ, and that endowment of the Holy Spirit which descends in answer to much believing prayer.

His work South was similar in character and fruits to that of Northern and contemporary evangelists in the Middle States and New England. There may be wonder expressed by some that he could be so blessed in a land of slavery. They forget how recently dates our temperance reform, and how much education may blind the mind in certain directions of reform. God, with patient mercy, bears with man's ignorance and sin, and bestows spiritual blessings upon his erring yet praying people.

Daniel Baker was wonderfully owned of God, and has gone to those rewards into which our always antislavery evangelist, pastor, and reformer, Dr. E. N. Kirk, followed him.

Dr. Baker was a Southerner in his views; but he liberated his inherited slaves, and when he saw the rising storm of civil conflict, which over his grave became a fratricidal war, he lifted his voice for the Union. Through the press he made an eloquent and tender appeal to the South. He besought the people to remember that our common country should rise above all sectional differences in this regard; that in Northern and Southern veins ran the same blood; and warned them against rash and suicidal action. It was well that he passed away before the clash of arms echoed through the States in which he had carried the banner of the cross; for the sound would have broken his great, loving, and true heart. There is another interesting fact: Dr. Baker's revival sermons have been scattered by Mr. Moody among the thousands of people abroad whom he has addressed. The attention of our lay evangelist was directed to them as the best of the kind for his purpose, and a few of them were reprinted for general circulation. Thus not only does the departed ambassador yet speak for his King, but in this association of the dead with the living we have another of the divine links in the world-embracing system of evangelistic agencies. Dr. Baker, while preaching in the proslavery South of his day, besides the ingathering of a multitude soon to fall in death on plains of fiercest battle, was also preparing weapons to be used in a grand and victorious spiritual campaign beyond the sea.

Rev. James Gallaher, a Presbyterian clergyman, South, born in 1792, one of ten children, three of whom were ministers, was many years a successful evangelist, principally in Missouri, supplementing, to some extent, Mr. Baker's labors elsewhere. He graduated at Washington College in 1815, studied theology under private instruction, and upon receiving license was called to the churches of New Providence and Rogersville, in Hawkins County, Tenn., and installed over them June 10, 1816. In 1830, he took charge of the Third Presbyterian Church of Cincinnati. In 1835, he was called to the theological department of Marion College, Mo. While here, he was almost continually engaged in evangelistic work, and with marked success. His personal presence was striking, his manner earnest, his dress careless, and his temperament nervously restless. Rev. Dr. Ross, of Huntsville, Ala., and Prof. Robert C. Breckinridge, warmly commended him. Mr. Gallaher itinerated through the region in which prevailed the great revivals of 1800, and saw on every hand evidences, clear and abundant, that God then made bare His arm with singular power and majesty, to scatter the Egyptian darkness of French infidelity, deepening into starless night over all the West. The "falling down" in those wonderful meetings of hundreds in a single day was in his view the work of the Holy Spirit, "reproving of sin, of righteousness, and of judgment to come."

In 1838 Mr. Gallaher held meetings with brethren in Mississippi; and in 1845 was among the canebrakes and threading paths beneath the cottonwood-trees of the Red River country, seeking the scattered Presbyterian flocks, reviving declining churches and organizing new ones. He conducted camp-meetings which had some of the old glory of the days when he was a boy. We will give his account of them, which suggested protracted meetings, and a single illustration of his skill in the management of those out-door gatherings of people who were really hungry for the gospel : —

"The origin of camp-meetings in the United States was among the members of the Presbyterian Church. They were first held in Logan County, Kentucky, during the revival of 1800. The multitudes which came together were so great that accommodations could not be found in the neighborhood of the place of worship. Many of these people had recently removed to the West from Virginia, North Carolina, or Pennsylvania. On the road, while they were removing, they had camped out, and cooked

14

their own provisions and provided their own lodgings. The idea originated among them, during the great revival, that they could camp out near the place of worship and take care of themselves, as well as they had done on the road while on their journey. The experiment succeeded admirably. The country being new, this mode of holding large meetings seemed peculiarly adapted to their circumstances. Indeed, it was believed to possess a striking resemblance to the 'Feast of Tabernacles' in the Old Testament church. Moreover, these meetings were crowned with precious divine blessings. Among the Presbyterians of the West and South, also the Methodists, the Baptists, the Cumberland Presbyterians, and other denominations, such meetings have been held with great and good results. In many parts of the West and South they have now worshipped in this manner, occasionally, for the space of fifty years. During that extensive and powerful revival in the State of Ohio, from 1828 till 1831, quite a number of camp-meetings were held, at which many thousands assembled to worship God. The everlasting gospel was preached, the blessing of God sent down, sinners converted, the church made glad, and heaven filled with rejoicing."

"I had been called by the brethren to preside over the camp-meeting at Sharon, in 1831. It had been in progress from Thursday noon until Saturday night. The whole scene had been solemn and delightful. The preaching was enlightened, captivating, and powerful; the seasons of prayer and praise were edifying and precious. The Holy Spirit brooded over the assembly. The awakened sinner exclaimed, 'Surely God is in this place, and I knew it not!' and the young convert answered, 'This is none other but the house of God, and this is the gate of heaven.'

"Saturday night had come. The lamps were lighted,

and suspended to the trees that stood here and there through the camp-ground, and the seats before the pulpit were occupied by perhaps about two thousand people. During the preliminary services, a number of young men clustered around a tall sugar-tree that stood some twenty steps from the pulpit, and commenced a low-toned conversation. I wished, if possible, to get them seated and silenced without the necessity of a public rebuke. Rev. Mr. Stafford, of North Carolina, was there. I requested him to make an address to the assembly, of about ten minutes' length ; for the people were still collecting, and the hour for the sermon had not yet come. Mr. Stafford's address was appropriate and powerful. The congregation were interested, but not a man in the circle round that tree moved or sat down, and the vexatious hum evidently increased. A hymn was sung, and during the singing I left the pulpit and took a seat in the crowd, half-way from the pulpit to the circle around the tree. At the close of the hymn I arose and said, 'I have long endeavored to avoid giving any public rebuke for the improper conduct of an individual at a place of public worship. I believe the practice generally does more harm than good, and therefore I have shunned it. But now I am about to depart, for once, from my long-established practice. There was an individual here this morning that came for no good. Indeed, I understand that he came with the preconcerted design to do mischief and make all the trouble he could. He was on the ground this afternoon. He is a very bad character, and I learn that he is here to-night. I am not speaking at random. I have documents in my possession to establish every word that I say. And as this matter of exposing an individual is somewhat trying, I mean to make thorough work now, as I have undertaken it, and I will tell you his name before I have done. Now, I wish you all to sit down,' waving my hand to those around the tree. Instantly the tree was deserted; every man was seated and profoundly silent. During a pause here of some seconds, the interest was intense. I then proceeded : —

"'The individual to whom I allude is a liar, a most notorious liar, and I am able to prove it on him by testimony that none of you will dispute : further, he is a thief.'

"'Oh! oh! oh!' said low voices in the crowd.

"'Yes, he is a thief; and more than all this, he is a murderer.'

"'Oh, that is too bad!' said low voices in the crowd.

"'No, it's not too bad. I tell you he is a murderer. I have the proof at hand. He is a murderer from the beginning. The proof to which I refer you is contained in the New Testament, and the name of this disorderly and troublesome individual is the devil.'

"Rarely has the name of the devil brought relief to so many anxious minds as on this occasion. The deep, long respiration, denoting that the burden was gone, could be distinctly heard from the pulpit, and from many in the crowd. I then, in a few words, told them that the Scriptures warned them to beware of their adversary, the devil. This address was speedily wound up; and then we had a sermon from another minister, to a very silent and attentive congregation, all seated in the most orderly manner.

"I had almost forgotten the above incident, and perhaps it would have faded entirely from the pages of memory, but some eight or nine years afterward, Dr. McKinney, now of southern Missouri, came to my house at St. Charles. 'Do you remember,' said he, 'the company of men at the Sharon camp-meeting, in Ohio, who gathered around the sugar-tree, and kept talking after the commencement of worship, and refused to sit down when requested?'

"'You remind me of the circumstance,' said I.

" ' Well,' said the doctor, 'I was one of that company. I was not then a professor of religion; indeed, I was very far from it. A number of us had come down from Oxford. Gay, thoughtless young men, we had high notions of our consequence and independence, and thought we were entitled to do very much as we pleased. When you commenced speaking of the individual that had come there for no good, but with the purpose of being troublesome, I began strongly to suspect that the reference was to me. The further the description advanced, the more exactly it appeared to fit my case. I became greatly alarmed, insomuch that even when those severe charges were made, 'the liar,' 'the thief,' 'the murderer,' conscience told me I was guilty of all. I had been false to God; I had vowed, and basely broken my vows. As a sinner I had robbed God, and I deserved the charge. I had indulged hatred against my brother, — and God calls such a murderer in the heart. I was awfully agitated, and when you said that you would tell the name of the offender, I fully calculated that my name would presently be called out before the whole assembly. When you requested the company to be seated, I was down in a moment; and never was I more relieved than when told that the offender was the devil; and never was I better pleased than when I found nothing more required of me than to keep my seat, and keep quiet, and listen to a good sermon.'

"Such was the narrative of Dr. McKinney; and the reader should know that he became a Christian minister, preaching 'that faith which once he destroyed.' "

Mr. Gallaher gives very forcibly and suggestively his ideas of new measures, with a telling illustration: —

"To us, short-sighted mortals, it seems matter of regret that a controversy about revival measures should ever have sprung up in the Christian church. As this world perishes by neglecting the great salvation, it is impossible

for one man to legislate for another how he may most
successfully, in all cases, call up public attention to the
great truths of the gospel. Let the right thing be
attempted at the right time, in the right spirit, and by the
right man, with judgment and good taste, and the results
will be admirable; but let the ass attempt to put on the
lion's hide, or the crow undertake to emulate the eagle,
and you will have a dolorous account of the indiscreetness
and the unhappy character of the measure. The agitation
of this subject has often reminded me of the notable lines
of Pope, —

> " ' For forms of government let fools contest:
> That which is best administered is best.'

"Dr. Anderson, of Maryville, Tennessee, came forward
during a sacramental meeting to receive into the communion of the church a large company of young converts.
The assembly was crowded, the solemnity intense, and
the stillness awful, while every eye was fixed on the affecting scene. In that congregation were a number of professed infidels. Some of them avowed Deism, some
Atheism; but they were men of genteel manners, who, in
a Christian assembly, would deport themselves with the
utmost propriety.

"The solemn profession of the religion of Jesus Christ
was now made, the young converts took the vows of God
upon them. At the close of this deeply interesting service, Dr. Anderson made a brief address to the young
converts, exhorting them to ' walk worthy' of the high
and holy ' vocation wherewith they were called.'

"He then said, ' And now I turn to the ungodly part
of this assembly. Ye candidates for the second death!
I turn to you. You have witnessed this solemn trans-
action; you have witnessed the consecration of these
immortal souls to God; you have heard their vows of

eternal allegiance to King Jesus. Now, though you have rejected the gospel for your own souls, though you have judged yourselves unworthy of eternal life, yet, in behalf of these who have named the name of the Lord Jesus, I appeal to you. Will not you pledge yourselves to-day, that you will throw no stumbling-blocks in the way of these souls? that you will not attempt to entangle them in the net of perdition, and drag them down with you to the agonies and the darkness of hell? And now let every man that, before earth and heaven, is willing to enter into this solemn pledge, signify it by holding up his right hand.' The solemnity was overwhelming. The burning zeal of the minister kindled a flame through the entire audience; right hands arose, and were held up over the whole congregation. The sinner's heart trembled because of the presence of the God of the whole earth; the Christian bowed his head and worshipped, saying, with the venerable patriarch of old, 'This is the gate of heaven.' The first right hand that was lifted up, in this memorable scene, was that of Dr. McGee. He had professed, for many years, to be a confirmed atheist. He was a scholar, a gentleman, and possessed many amiable endowments, but had long been settled down in absolute atheism. The doctor soon became a preacher of that faith which once he destroyed, and lived many years to adorn the gospel profession by a holy life, and proclaim the riches of a Saviour's love to dying men.

"Such is a brief history of one of the boldest, strongest, and newest measures that I ever saw attempted in a revival of religion; and yet, perhaps not one of the vast assembly present ever dreamed of calling in question its propriety or its usefulness. Why? Because it was done with judgment and good taste; it was done in the right spirit, at the right time, in the right circumstances, and by the right man. But now let the wrong man, without judgment or good taste, attempt such a measure, and he will soon be in a condition to deliver lectures or publish letters on the ' evils of revivals.' "

We close this sketch of Mr. Gallaher with a passage from his pen which is a good illustration of the descriptive powers of the evangelist, and of which a part has been widely circulated without the author's name : —

" I stood on the bank of Red River, by the side of a dear brother whose ' heart trembled for the ark of God.' Said he, ' We are glad that you have come to preach to us, and that you have stayed so long.   But now that you must leave us, what can we do?   You see the condition of our country.   A little labor, seasonably bestowed on this field, would secure great results.   What shall we do?   Cannot some of the middle-aged ministers up in your country be persuaded to make us a visit and continue with us a few months?   There is scarcely a man of any note, who has been preaching fifteen or twenty years in Missouri, Illinois, Kentucky, Ohio, or the States farther east, but would find, on visiting this country, many of his former hearers and acquaintances.   The whole country should be explored, as speedily as practicable, by men of experience and judgment, that the religious population already on the ground may be embodied and organized.   An organization, even though it be small, will hold together and subsist for years, when the same materials, left in an unorganized state, would be dissipated and scattered to the four winds.'

" Said I to this friend, ' What is the extent of the country west of Red River which is already settled ? '

" ' I would say that it is six hundred miles in length by four hundred in breadth.'

" ' Well, you know that when our divine Saviour sent out his disciples to preach, he sent them ' two and two.'   The promise to Israel by Moses was that ' one should chase a

thousand, and two should put ten thousand to flight';
that is, two of God's Israel, when acting together, can do
tenfold more than one would be able to accomplish alone.
When Paul and Barnabas, and Paul and Silas, went
together, according to Christ's original plan, what mighty
results followed that ministry! Now, could the condition
of this country and the importance of the present crisis
be laid before our brethren in the better-supplied portions of our church, peradventure ten or twelve ministers might be found who would be willing to come and
explore this broad land, two and two, travelling together
according to the Saviour's plan. Could not much be
accomplished in one campaign of five or six months, by
ten or twelve enterprising and self-denying ministers?'

"The countenance of my friend kindled up at the
suggestion. His eye sparkled, his features glowed with
ardent anticipation, as he exclaimed, 'It would be as "life
from the dead" to the cause of religion throughout all
this region. The fact that the church cared so much for
her scattered and destitute children, expressed in that
unequivocal and affectionate form, would be of great
importance and value. The labors of such self-denying
ambassadors of Christ would doubtless be accompanied
with the happiest results. A good impression would thus
be made on the whole population, that would be remembered while the present generation remains alive. An
impetus would be given to the cause of religion in this
land that might go down to the end of time.'

"Such was the substance of my last conversation with
that pious friend, as we stood together on the bank of
Red River. I returned to the country up the Mississippi.
I brought the subject of this great missionary enterprise
before many of our ministers and people. They saw at
once its importance and its feasibility. But such an
undertaking requires time; and before the suitable men

could be found and the necessary arrangements completed we were startled by the thunders of the Mexican war. The smoke arose, and darkened all the land, and multitudes of armed men were called to muster on the very field of our contemplated mission.

"I hope that our church will wake up to that great enterprise, — an early occupancy of the frontier settlements by missionaries of talent and experience. Much, very much, has been lost irrecoverably by the neglect of this momentous work during the last thirty years. 'Oh that my head were waters, and mine eyes a fountain of tears, that I might weep day and night for the slain of the daughter of my people!'

"Only those who have traversed the mighty West in its length and in its breadth can properly appreciate the importance of its moral culture to the church, to our country, and to the world. I stood on the bank of the Mississippi, opposite the mouth of the Missouri River, where, after its long career from the Rocky Mountains, the wild and turbid Missouri unites with the clear and tranquil wave of the 'Father of Waters.' I was meditating on the connection of this great country with the kingdom of Christ. I looked south, and thought of the twelve hundred miles from the point where I then stood to the Gulf of Mexico. I looked north, and thought of the sixteen hundred miles to the head of the Mississippi. I looked east, and thought of the thirteen hundred miles to the head of the Ohio Valley. I looked west, and thought of the three thousand miles to the head of the Missouri. I thought of the immense capacity of this land to sustain human life, I thought of the teeming millions who will presently be here, I seemed almost to hear the tread of coming generations; and I lifted my hand to heaven, and said, 'Lord Jesus, this land shall be thine! We will preach and pray; we will hold up the banner of thy dying love, and call for help from on high, till waves of redeeming mercy shall roll over these wide plains and along the shores of these mighty rivers. And among the multitudes of people that shall dwell here, every knee shall bow and every tongue confess to the Lamb that was slain.'"

Mr. Gallaher was chaplain to the House of Representatives in 1852–3. His death occurred at St. Charles, Mo., to which retreat he removed in 1840, and was a peaceful transition to his eternal rest. He published two books of considerable popular interest,—"Adam and David," which Rev. Dr. Kirk of Boston once remarked to the writer is a "remarkable volume," and the "Western Sketch-Book," which is an intensely interesting series of pictures of life at the West. He was not a representative man in respect to a great crisis of religious activity, nor in wide-spread, moulding power, but an original, devoted, and very useful evangelist where he was greatly needed.

CHAPTER XIII.

THE PIONEER BAPTIST EVANGELIST. — HOW HE BECAME SO. — EARLY
LIFE. — CONVERSION. — ENTERS THE MINISTRY. — THE CONDITION OF
BAPTIST CHURCHES. — GIVES UP THE ATTEMPT TO HAVE UNION MEET-
INGS. — PRINCIPAL FIELDS AND SCENES OF HIS LABORS. — HIS
DEATH. — RESULTS. — CHARACTERISTICS.

IN an old-fashioned sanctuary of moderate dimensions,
at North Rutland, New York, one of the earliest "protracted meetings" in that part of the State was held during the autumn of 1832. Among the neighboring ministers
present was one comparatively youthful, deeply affected,
while he listened for the first time to that sacred song,
"The Power of Prayer," one stanza of which so impressed him that he desired its repetition. It was the
following : —

> " To leave my dear friends, and with neighbors to part,
> And go from my home, it affects not my heart
> Like the thought of absenting myself for a day
> From that blessed retreat where I 've chosen to pray."

Snugly settled upon a farm near Watertown, New
York, with a parish in the village, he was hesitating
about leaving both for the uncertain support and wandering life of an evangelist, to which he felt he was
called. The appropriate words of the melody "melted
him into tenderness, and at the same time exalted him
into the ecstacy of a precious and entire acquiescence
in the will of God."

The pastors went home at the end of a week without

visible results among the impenitent; but Christians continued in prayer and went on with the meetings. The Watertown minister returned and entered into a powerful work of grace. Here occurred his first experience of those physical phenomena which were seen in the "Great Awakening," nearly a century before, and at other periods of deep religious feeling. We give in his own words the remarkable scenes : —

"Deacon Spencer Woodward, of Bellville, a man of strong faith and 'full of the Holy Spirit,' fell in with a company of hardened scoffers, as they were standing on the village green, mocking the saints of the Most High. One of them had a cane, the head of which consisted of a piece of deer's horn, and as the deacon was passing, in order to cast derision on the services of religion, he was asking his young companions, to whom he was extending his cane, to come forward and lay hold on 'the horns of the altar.'

"Father Woodward stopped, and turning to them, remarked, 'Young men, if you knew what you were about, I should think your damnation sealed, and should not think it worth while to waste my breath on your account; but you are ignorant of the things of the kingdom of God. On this evening you will be made to see the power of the Almighty.'

"He induced them to enter the meeting-house, though it was some time before sundown and there was no service as yet, and leading them to a pew and shutting the door (it was an old-fashioned pew with a straight back and a high door) told them that nobody would disturb them. 'Now,' said he, 'brace yourselves, for God is about to come down in great power.' He then knelt in prayer in the aisle at the pew-door. He got hold truly of 'the horns of the altar,' and the 'Holy One came down from Teram.' The young men trembled like Belshazzar when

he saw the handwriting on the wall. Some of them got
down on the floor, and their knees knocked against
each other and against the sides of the pew. Soon one of
them sank down to the floor utterly helpless. One of his
companions reached over and whispered to Father Wood
ward, 'Uncle Spencer, he is dying.' — 'Get some water,'
said Father Woodward, 'and fetch him to. Don't let him
die.' One of them ran for water, but his hands trembled
so that he spilt half of it out of the pail before he reached
the prostrate man. The deacon told them to lift him up,
adding, 'I told you that God was coming down : now prepare to meet Him.' Two of the stoutest of the young
men took hold of him but could not lift him; their
strength failed them. The deacon raised the young man
up, his consciousness soon returned, and very shortly
afterwards he was converted. Some of the others, also,
were led by this event to seek and find salvation. Another,
by the name of Coburn, was smitten down during the
meeting that evening, and carried to a house, where he
remained until midnight, insensible."

The months following matured Mr. Knapp's purpose,
and in September, 1833, he preached his farewell sermon
to his charge, that he might devote himself wholly to his
chosen calling. He was advised by Rev. Nathaniel Ken-
drick, D. D., principal of Hamilton Literary and Theological Institute, to ask an appointment from the Board of
the Baptist Missionary Convention of the State of New
York, to labor in Jefferson and Oswego Counties. But
such was the opposition to unusual methods of Christian
activity that he was rejected notwithstanding his high
endorsement. Such was God's humbling discipline, and
proved to be his best preparation for the service before
him. He writes of it : —

"In my distress I cast my burdens on the Lord. I
sought to know the will of God. I cried unto the Lord,

and blessed be His name, very soon He made known His ways, and lifted upon me the light of His countenance. After spending one whole day in fasting and prayer, and continuing my fast till midnight, the place where I was staying was filled with the manifested glory of God. His presence appeared to me, not exactly in visible form, but as really to my recognition as though he had come in person, and a voice seemed to say to me, 'Hast thou ever lacked a field in which to labor?' I answered, 'Not a day.' — 'Have I not sustained thee, and blessed thy labors?' I answered, 'Yea, Lord.' — 'Then learn that henceforth thou art not dependent on thy brethren, but on me. Have no concern but to go on in thy work. My grace shall be sufficient for thee.'

"From that night I felt willing to sacrifice the good opinion of my brethren, as I had previously sacrificed the favor of the world, and swing off from all dependences but God. Up to this time I had concerned myself too much about the opinions of other and older brethren, distrusting my youth and inexperience. But the Lord taught me that He was my only infallible guide. I joyously acquiesced in His will; and from that day to this have rested in this divine manifestation. Ah! how reluctant we are to cleave to the Lord! How prone to cling to creature dependences! Since I have endeavored to seek divine direction as to all my fields of labor, I have learned that it is possible for me, generally, to gain as clear impressions of the will of God concerning my duty as though it was announced in audible tones."

This was the entrance of Elder Jacob Knapp, the pioneer Baptist evangelist, upon his long and successful career. He was born on a farm near Masonville, Delaware County, New York, December 17, 1799. His parents were members of the Episcopal Church, and he records

that he was "early taught the Creed and Catechism," and
often had "seasons of secret prayer, and of deep anxiety
about the future welfare of his soul." Upon the death of
a revered mother, when in his seventeenth year, he was led
to feel the "need of a comforter and friend this world
could not afford, and to see the emptiness and vanity of
all terrestrial enjoyments." His anxiety impaired his
health, awaking paternal anxiety; but he kept the cause
of it a secret, often spending midnight hours in the barn
crying to God for mercy. One Sabbath morning, with a
Bible and hymn-book, he went to the woods, resolved not
to return till he found relief. He read and prayed, with
only deepening distress, till in despair he closed his eyes
"expecting to open them in hell." Instead of that dreaded
doom, his burden was suddenly gone; and rising, to his
uplifted eyes, Jesus seemed "descending with his arms
extended for his reception." Joy burst forth in songs,
and he soon re-entered his home, a new creature in Christ
Jesus.

A revival in the Baptist Church near was so in contrast with the forms and services of his own that he
desired to join it. Opposition from his friends prevented,
and he sadly fell into sin, joining ungodly companions in
trifling with sacred things; sometimes preaching mock
sermons for their amusement. But the devil carried his
impious demands too far; an invitation to preach the
funeral sermon of a horse shocked and alarmed him. He
had not wholly ceased to pray in solitary moments, and
now he became more thoughtful and careful in his conduct.

These experiences were mainly during a few months'
residence in another county. Upon his return to old
associations, he was met by an invitation to attend a New
Year's ball, which he accepted. Learning that a prayer-
meeting was appointed the same evening, his conscience

awoke with strange power, and thrust on his inward ear
the words, "He that is not for me is against me." He
turned his steps to the house of prayer, and while the music
of the dance came into its quiet air, his heart was beating
wildly with a tempest which only one voice could still.
He rose, unburdened his anxious heart, begged for prayers,
then all present fell on their knees. The cries of supplication reached the ball-room, smiting nine of the gay
company with deep conviction of sin.

The reclaimed youth of nineteen now united with the
church and felt intense yearning for the gospel ministry.
A few months later his father proposed to establish him
on a farm, with flattering prospects, as he had done his
brothers. But what to him was worldly success compared with the privilege of entire devotion to the service of his Lord! With five dollars and his "pack," containing his scanty wardrobe, he started afoot for his old
home, two hundred miles away, where he felt that God
would give him helping friends. With frequent changes
in the place of his abode, often penniless, April, 1821, he
directed his steps to Gilbertsville, where, he had learned,
there was an academy.

The principal became interested in the wanderer seeking
knowledge, and took him into his family. In a small
Baptist church in the neighborhood he began his ministry
by taking charge of the meetings, and soon was in the
midst of a precious revival. He then went to teach at
New Lisbon, and was made a rich blessing to the pupils
there. His heart, meanwhile, was bowed under the pressure of the unsettled question of his life,—whether, in the
face of formidable difficulties, he should push his way into
the ministry. After spending a whole night in prayer at
the school-room, the next day a letter came from Hamilton
Literary and Theological Institute inviting him to enter it
and finish preparation for the pulpit. He went, and from

it was called to the pastorate of a church in Springfield,
New York. There, he says, he fell into the devil's snare
of seeking popularity at the expense of fearless fidelity,
over which he soon afterwards mourned, and consecrated
his life entirely to the work of saving souls.

In the fall of 1830 he accepted a call to Watertown,
where he made the mistake, as he felt it to be a few years
later, of purchasing a farm. It was during the two following years that the work of an evangelist grew in
interest to his thought, till we find him subdued under
the influence of a simple melody, in the plain old meeting-
house of North Rutland. Amid strong opposition from his
own denomination, from that hour he became the pioneer
evangelist of his ecclesiastical order in this country. And
here we pause again to look out upon the spiritual condition of the churches in the region which was to be the
principal field of his subsequent labors.

No Sabbath Schools were then in existence among the
Baptists, and the missionary cause had scarcely stirred the
heart of this branch of Zion. They had only two institutions of learning, and those of comparatively humble
pretensions. Christian stewardship for money was little
felt, and the spirit of benevolence not widely diffused.
Indeed, the sect was oftener evil-spoken of than honored. The most depressing influence of all was Antinomianism, entrenched in the bosom of the churches.
Apathy and selfishness found refuge in the sovereignty
of God; decrees were the spiritual burden-bearers; and
the membership could look with quiet indifference upon
the unsaved multitude, among which were their own
children "treasuring up wrath against the day of wrath."
The saints would be saved and all the elect gathered into
the kingdom, because eternal foreordination had fixed the
result without the necessity of human anxiety or effort.

God clearly called Jacob Knapp to wield his sledge-hammer, even though with eccentric and, to critical eyes, grotesque movements upon the incrustations above all warm spiritual life, and break it in pieces, amid the old cries of "Enthusiasm!" "New measures!" and "Man-made converts!" Intensely denominational in his convictions, he soon abandoned the attempt to hold "union meetings," like Nettleton confining his labors to his own denomination, but inviting Christian co-operation, with the distinct understanding that immersion followed closely, in his views of duty, upon conversion. Besides, he saw a difficulty very naturally attendant upon union efforts in villages, where each denomination was weak and anxious to gain strength by accessions from the converts; this was unholy strife over the "division of the spoils," amid the scorn of the ungodly. It is quite evident, therefore, that his special work was directly within the boundaries of his own people.

Elder Knapp now moved upon "Satan's Seat," the name given to Turin, Jefferson County, on account of the prevalence there of infidelity. The opposition was bitter; and he was threatened with prosecution for slander because he used, in illustration of Universalism, an occurrence in that village. The arrest was suspended to give him time to make an apology the next evening, when his enemies had notified him they would be present to hear it. The church was thronged and the excitement intense, some cursing aloud while Christians prayed. The text was Prov. v, 11, 12, and the sermon such an one as a man could preach only in the peculiar circumstances, when the powers of darkness met in a death-struggle the Spirit of God among the people. Strong men under conviction sank helpless to the floor, and were borne to their homes by those who could both watch and pray over them. From that night the revival swept over the town. At Constableville, Loraine, Hannibal, and Oswego, the most important village in the county, now a flourishing city, similar scenes were repeated.

One incident illustrates the illuminating power of the Spirit in an atmosphere of believing prayer. A lady who was a member of the Congregational Church became convinced that she was unconverted, and, upon seeking counsel, was told to "go to God and cry for help." A few hours afterwards a friend came to Mr. Knapp under great excitement, saying she feared the woman was dying. He found her in her room, kneeling, pleading, and unable to speak above a whisper. Dreading the effect of her death upon him and his work, he says he was "on the point of requesting her to cease her supplications, but this text broke upon my ears as in peals of thunder, 'The bruised reed he will not break and the smoking flax He will not quench, till He send forth judgment unto victory.' I then said, 'God will not break the bruised reed, and God forbid that I should quench the smoking flax. Let judgment come forth to victory!' In a few moments her countenance changed, a heavenly smile came over it, and she began to whisper, 'Blessed Saviour! Sweet Jesus! All is well!'" Her subsequent experience verified the promise of that hour; it was her translation from darkness into light eternal.

At Auburn, Ithaca, and New York City he successively labored, sometimes amidst fierce opposition, but with great success. He removed his permanent residence, in 1835, to Hamilton, for which he gives two principal reasons: that he might be of service indirectly to the students in the Theological Department of the Baptist Institution there, by leading them to an advanced position on the subject of revivals; and also, at that important centre of influence in the denomination, disarm the prejudice against him which necessarily interfered with his usefulness. In both respects his success was quite equal to his expectations. A revival of great power was soon in progress, including the institution in its sweep, and pervading the whole town. Prayer-meetings were sometimes continued all night. At Bennington, Vt., Waterville, Bridgewater, Penn Yan, Utica, Schenectady, Seneca Falls, Brooklyn, and Rochester, N. Y., his labors were attended with similar fruits, sometimes meeting with opposition like that in apostolic days.

We quote his own account of scenes in each of the two last mentioned cities, as illustrative of his peculiarities, and his own criticism of them. Of Brooklyn he writes : —

" I remember a striking instance of the power of God in the conversion of an avowed atheist. He came to the meeting to hear me preach on atheism. In the course of my sermon, I remarked that ' atheism was the little end of nothing whittled to a point. Since the atheist denied everything and admitted nothing, it was itself the little end of nothing.' This remark arrested his attention and mortified his pride. So, in order to be revenged, he requested a Christian neighbor to ask prayers for the little end of nothing. The request was complied with ; nor was it overlooked amid the multiplicity of claims upon our prayers.

" On the evening of the third day, as we repaired to the lecture-room for the purpose of spending a season in prayer, who should rise up but this infidel? Pale and haggard, not having slept for three nights and borne down by deep despair, he broke the silence of the spell-bound congregation by saying, ' My fellow-citizens, you see before you the greatest sinner whom God ever suffered to live. I have denied the existence of my Creator. I have ridiculed his Son Jesus Christ. I have studied the Word of God in order to pick flaws and make out contradictions. I have cursed my Maker more times than there are hairs on my head ; and as for you Christians, there has been nothing

too bad for me to say about you; and all I ask in return
is, that you will not treat me as I have treated you.' He
took his seat. I said to him, 'My dear sir, do you not
wish the prayers of God's people?' He answered, 'No.
Prayer can do me no good; I must be lost.' I told him,
' God is merciful; Christ has died to save the chief of sinners.' He replied, 'I know that; and this knowledge will
be the keenest part of my sufferings I have sinned against
infinite goodness and unparalleled mercy. *I deserve to be
damned and I must be damned.* All directions to Christ
as a Saviour avail nothing. I have not made the first
attempt at prayer, under the full conviction that prayer
will do no good.

"He passed another sleepless night, walking his floor
and contemplating his fearful doom. To him it was a
night of terrors. But just as the gray of the morning began
to dawn, some mysterious agency whispered in his ear,
' Whosoever *will*, let him come and take of the waters of
life freely.' For the first time in his life he dropped on
his knees, and pleaded for mercy through Jesus Christ.
In a few moments his load was gone, and his soul felt the
peace of believing, and unspeakable joy beamed in his face.
He rose from his knees, clapped his hands, and shouted,
' Glory, glory to God!' and but for the fear of making his
neighbors think he was crazy, he said he should have sung
out at the top of his voice.

"Much complaint in those days was made because I
ventured to cross the ancient landmarks and got betimes
out of the old ruts. I sometimes made remarks which did
not always accord with every person's notions of propriety.
Such expressions as the one just named, which arrested the
attention of the atheist, were deemed highly objectionable.
But objectors have acknowledged that the very things to
which they took exceptions had ' fallen out for the further-
ance of the gospel, ' and that they would not undertake to

dictate to a minister who was zealously and successfully laboring for souls."

In January, 1839, he was in Rochester, N. Y., where Christians of all denominations were awakening at the Spirit's call to harvest-work. In the midst of a wide-spread and deepening revival, he levelled his batteries against a notorious gambling club, whose destructive influence was felt throughout the city. Then followed scenes perhaps unparalleled in his own experiences among the enemies of his ministry. Having learned, from some of the number hopefully converted, the dark secrets of their midnight orgies, he gave notice that he should expose them. The hour came, and thousands were unable to find standing-place in the church. After being interrupted in his fearless warnings and earnest appeals, he closed, with a strange awe resting upon the audience. But the next day a meeting of the citizens was called, in front of the sanctuary, with the evident design of creating a riot We quote his account of what follows : —

" No arrangements were made by the children of God to prevent it, beyond the appointment of prayer-meetings in various places. The evening arrived; the meeting-house was crowded to suffocation. From the basement earnest prayers were offered unto God, and from the pulpit His Word was preached to a solemn and deeply-affected congregation.

" In the mean time, a crowd of about a thousand men had gathered around the building in separate groups. One company was stationed in a back yard, armed with stones. At three minutes before eight o'clock a stone came whizzing through the window towards the pulpit. Simultaneous with its passage came a flash of lightning, followed by a peal of thunder (this was in the month of February, and snow was on the ground). In about a minute afterwards another stone came through the window, accompanied by another flash of lightning, and followed by a still louder clap of thunder. Scarcely had another minute elapsed before another stone entered the building, when instantly the heavens pealed out their thunder more terribly than before. The house where the people were assembled was shaken, and the earth trembled beneath their feet. Fear seized hold on the ungodly crew, and dropping their missiles they hastened from the spot, as if they would hide themselves from the presence of God, lest He should ' cut them off with a stroke.'

"Shortly after I had retired for the night the house of Deacon Sage, where I lodged, was assailed, and several of the windows were broken, but no one was injured. The work of the Lord went on with increasing power; and though the ungodly raged, their counsels came to naught."

The meeting closed, when the defeated ranks of the wicked rallied for a final attempt to silence or disgrace the evangelist. He was stopped upon his departure by a crowd of excited men, and arrested by the sheriff for slanderous charges against the gamesters. He gave bail, and finally was released from the angry mob, who desired his death. The suit, months later, went by default.

At Baltimore, his rebuke of rum-selling, it seems, originated the Washingtonian Society, which had its day of extensive activity and great popularity. We give his own account of this once wide-spread organization: —

"A very peculiar providence of God occurred during this meeting, illustrating the way in which God can make the wrath of man to praise him. During the progress of the revival several well-known drunkards had been converted. This fact had enraged the rum-sellers. On the evening in which I preached on temperance, two men, named Mitchel and Hawkins, together with other hard drinkers, were present. From the church they went to a grog-shop, whose proprietor began to indulge in out-bursts of rage and cursing against me and my preaching. After a while Mitchel got up, and declared that he would not hear Mr. Knapp abused any longer; that he believed he was doing a great deal of good in the city; and turn-ing towards the rum-seller, he remarked, ' If you keep up this abuse any longer, I will never drink another drop in your house, nor anywhere else, as long as my name is Mitchel.' But the enraged proprietor continued to deal out his anathemas; whereupon Mitchel, true to his word, then and there solemnly pledged himself to absolute and total abstinence thenceforth through life. Hawkins and others joined with him in the pledge. This was the origin of the Washingtonian temperance movement, which swept over the country with such wonderful power, and by which tens of thousands of drunkards were reformed, and thou-sands of families were made happy for this life and the life to come. To God be all the glory ! "

Here, too, he preached against slavery to the conster-nation of his brethren, and amid threats by the throng encircling the house of God, who, in a short time, under his untrembling utterances of truth, dropped their missiles and went quietly away. His success in Albany was equally great.

At New York City his experience was similar, — a leading daily paper headed the opposition, and to the evangelist's entire satisfaction, because this advertising of the meetings drew all classes to hear him, many of whom were subjects of the revival. Here he was called to the pastorate of the Tabernacle Baptist Church, and accepted the unanimous invitation of the people only to find, before a year had expired, that he was out of place, and must return to the work of an evangelist.

December, 1840, he held a series of meetings in Hart-ford, Connecticut, where the scenes of religious awakening,

and of wonderful defeat of the counsels and deeds of the
ungodly, were renewed. Thence he went to New Haven.
There were events of special interest in connection with
the college.

He wrote in his journal : —

"The Lord owned and blessed his truth during this
effort, and made the gospel the power of God unto the
salvation of very many. Christians of all denominations
came in, and took a deep interest in the progress of the
work. Dr. Taylor, professor of theology, attended, and
was heard to say, that he 'thanked God that the gospel
was being preached so faithfully.' The students of Yale
College were quite constant in their attendance ; of these,
seventy-one were converted. At the close of the meeting
they sent me a letter containing all their names, and one
hundred and twenty dollars as a personal testimonial.

"At first some thought that the interests of the cause
would be better promoted by holding an additional meeting in connection with, and for the sake of, the students.
Accordingly, the services of Dr. Kirk were obtained. But
he had scarcely reached the ground before he recognized
the importance of maintaining an undivided interest. He,
therefore, together with nearly all the professors, came to
my meeting, and rendered hearty co-operation in conducting it. And I am bound to say, that seldom, if ever, have
I found a more noble, unsectarian class of Christians than
were the Congregationalists of New Haven. Their piety,
liberal-mindedness, and intelligence won my highest admiration and affection.

"In this city there was a noted gambling-house, to which,
as I learned, many of the ungodly students resorted, especially the high bloods from the South. I regarded it my
duty to expose this den of iniquity, and warn all against
it. This exposure brought out several of the students,
and all the hard characters of the city. Thirty-eight of

the students entered into a solemn covenant that they would break up the meeting at the risk of their lives.

"Arming themselves with clubs, bowie-knives, and other instruments of death, they came into the church, and stationed themselves in different parts of the house, — some in the gallery and some below. As soon as the congregation was dismissed, they undertook to keep the people from going out. They blocked up the aisles, and refused to give way, resisting the pressure by a display of clubs and threats of assault.

"I requested them to stand aside and let the people pass; but they stood their ground, and brandished their weapons. I then called for the tithing-men (as the law of the State required). As soon as these officers began to appear, the students cried out, '*Yale! Yale!*' (the sign-word agreed upon), when instantly those in the galleries threw themselves over its breastworks, and slid down the pillars into the crowd below. A sharp scuffle ensued, and very shortly law and order prevailed. Some of the mob were carried off to the watch-house, were tried the next day, and fined.

"After this, for four or five nights in succession, a mob would form on the college-green, and come down to the church about the time of dismissing the congregation. They avowed their purpose to kill me, and on several occasions I went to my lodgings surrounded by a body-guard. On one evening I exchanged cloaks with a brother, and passed out before many of the congregation had left the church. On my way home alone, I met several hundreds of the mob. Those in advance asked me if the meeting was out. I replied, 'Yes; and unless you look sharp, Knapp will be gone.' They started on the run, and I went quietly to my room.

"The mob was finally broken up by the following remarkable providence. One of them had sent me an

abusive letter, threatening my life if I did not leave the
city. On the evening of the day in which I received it, a
number of the desperadoes came into the sanctuary, and
seated themselves in the gallery. Shortly after I had
commenced preaching, a rifle-ball was thrown at me ; but
hitting the shade of the lamp, it was turned out of its
course. Some thought that it had been shot from an air-
gun, but the possibility is that it was thrown by hand.
Brother Teasdale immediately arose, and read to the congregation the letter referred to. This letter called me
'the prince of liars,' because I had related publicly how
God had broken up the mob in Rochester by sending
thunder and lightning, and challenged a repetition of the
scene. Deacon Sage, of Rochester, who was providentially
present, rose and corroborated my statement. No sooner
had silence been regained than a flash of terrific lightning
blazed through the house, followed by awful peals of
thunder and torrents of rain. This marvellous coincidence
effectually dispersed the mob.

"Nevertheless, the thirty-eight, who had banded themselves together to break up the meeting, did not abandon
their purpose. They changed their tactics. They arranged
to gain access to my lodgings, and, disguised, to seize me,
gag me, and putting me into a carriage, to carry me into
the woods, and there deliberate as to what further course
should be pursued. But one of their number was seized
with convictions, which led him to reveal to me the plot.
Several of the brethren resolved to stand guard each night.
The desperadoes, learning that the house was well protected, resorted to stratagem. One night, after I had
retired, the footsteps of a man were heard clamping on the
sidewalk. In a moment the door-bell was pulled with great
violence. Occupying a front room, I opened the window,
and asked what was wanted. A man at the door replied
that he wanted to see Mr. Knapp. I said, 'I am the

man.' He remarked that 'a person, some little distance off, was under deep conviction, and wanted Mr. Knapp to come right away and pray for him.' I told him to 'tell the man that he must pray for himself, or he would go right down to hell.' I understood the plot at an instant, and learned, on the day following, that a carriage was in readiness, and a company of men, to carry me away, and that this man had been paid one dollar to decoy me out of the house.

"After this, two of the gang were converted, and one of them told me that ' it seemed to him that he could not be happy even in heaven, in view of the many souls he had already sent to hell.' He had kept a depository for the sale of infidel books, and had engaged actively in every effort to disseminate the poison of error."

In New Bedford, Providence, and finally in Boston, his career was not dissimilar in general character and results. The fearlessness of his assaults upon the popular theology, and the traffic in ardent spirits, rallied opposition in the form of a large mob in Bowdoin Square, whose dispersion Mr. Knapp thus explains : —

"This movement had been anticipated, for it was publicly announced. Some well-meaning, but cowardly, people withdrew from the meetings, but the faithful held on in prayer. For a short time it seemed uncertain which way the scale would turn ; but the prayers of that eventful night — a night never to be forgotten — brought the victory. The brother with whom I was boarding, unable to sleep, came into his parlor about midnight, and not knowing that I was there, knelt down, and in doing so placed his knees on my prostrate form, as I lay on the floor in the agony of supplication to God. I afterwards ascertained that very many others had been passing that night in sleeplessness and in prayer."

Succeeding this season of remarkable excitement, was a

reaction unusual in extent after his efforts in a community.
We will let him and his brethren speak on the subject.
He says : —

"In this instance the opposition to my ministry arose,
not from without, but from within. Jesus was 'wounded
in the house of his friends.' It did not culminate while I
was on the ground, but broke out after I had gone to
another field. The very men who had given me their
countenance while laboring to give strength to their
churches, enlisted their sympathies against me, as an
apology for their want of success in taking care of the
increased flocks committed to their charge.

"The assault that was made against me was of a twofold character. In the first place, the value of the work
itself was disparaged. It was alleged that the converts
brought in under my ministry did not hold out. Now I
know full well that it is in the order of God's kingdom
that the chaff shall grow with the wheat, and I doubt not
that many who have been brought into the church under
my labors will not be admitted into the church in heaven.
But in this respect I believe that a careful and statistical
investigation would show that the proportion of apostates
and worthless professors has been no greater under my
preaching than it has been under the labors of stated
pastors. And it should be borne in mind that very many
of those who had been brought in during the protracted
meetings, had never received any previous religious culture, and found themselves embarrassed when brought into
the atmosphere of refinement and culture. These persons
needed, of the pastors and the older church-members,
solicitous watch-care ; but, alas ! in too many instances they
were neglected, and made to feel the chilling repulsions
with which aristocratic bearing and suspicious reserve met
them as they crossed the threshold of the Christian church.
If there is one thing which pains me more than another,

that awakens in my heart anxiety as to the future of Zion, it is the growing desire of ministers and churches to gather their converts from the ranks of the wealthy and the intelligent. The church of Christ is no place for caste. There, if anywhere, the rich and poor should meet together; and there, if anywhere, if any discrimination exists, it should be an intenser anxiety to gather into the fold of Christ those who, by reason of poverty, neglect, and vice, are tempted to exclaim, 'No man cares for our souls!'

"But instead of a redoubling of diligences lest any of these lambs should 'fail of the grace of God,' measures were immediately inaugurated which practically left them to perish. Two of the pastors went off to Europe, and were gone several months. One church was closed during most of one season, for enlargement and repairs."

Wrote the pastor of Tremont Temple : —

"This was a most wonderful period in denominational history. The laity that upheld the hands of the ministry were unsurpassed in character, in talent, and in devotion. Every church was strong, because each church might, like the sultan of the East, point to her stalwart men as the walls of her defence and the implements of conquest. It was at this period Daniel Safford introduced Rev. E. N. Kirk, D. D., to Boston. It was a remarkable happen-so, even if it were a happen-so, that Mr. Kirk followed Mr. Knapp so frequently. One was the John the Baptist, preaching repentance, and the other was the reaper. One was the blacksmith, the other the silversmith. Said Dr. Kirk, 'I delighted to follow Mr. Knapp, because he stirred the conscience, and made a great number ready to listen to the truth, presented in a milder form. They were too mad to hear him, they were under too deep conviction to rest content; so, many gladly came to listen to me who might have gone, unmoved, to perdition, had it not been for the sledge-hammer style of Mr. Knapp.' For this reason he followed him, in Baltimore, in New Haven, and in Boston."

A. Wilbur, Esq., a prominent layman, went into statistics, and in his summary states : —

"Mr. Knapp commenced his labors in Massachusetts with the Baptist church in New Bedford, in the Taunton Association, in the summer of 1841. That church, during the four consecutive years, baptized 262, and excommunicated in the same time 28, or about 10½ per cent on her baptisms. All the other churches in that association, taken together, in the same four years, baptized 488, and excommunicated 105, or nearly 22 per cent on their baptisms.

" At the end of the four years, the church in New Bedford had gained in numerical strength 205, or 80⅓ per cent on her former number. All the other churches in the association had gained in the same time 284, or 18½ per cent on their former number.

" The church in New Bedford, separately, and the other churches, collectively, have excluded *annually* about an equal proportion, compared with their numbers, viz. averaging about 1½ per cent on their whole number.

" His next labors in the State were in the Boston Association. Here they were mostly confined to five churches in the city of Boston. Two of the city churches did not invite him into their pulpits. One of these, with its pastor, was decidedly unfriendly to the whole movement, from beginning to end.

" Those five churches, where **Mr. Knapp** labored, baptized, during the four years, 1,054 persons, and excommunicated 158, or 15 per cent on their baptisms.

" All the other churches in the Boston Association, taken together, baptized in the same time 1,775, and excluded 336, or nearly 19 per cent on their baptisms.

"The two churches in the city, where. Mr. Knapp did not labor, baptized 122, and excluded 36, or 29 per cent on their baptisms.

"The church that was unfavorable, and took no interest in the movement, baptized 22, excluded 12, or 54½ per cent on her baptisms."

Lowell, Concord, Salem, Marblehead, and other New England cities invited him to labor, and he did so with marked effect. In 1843 he was in Washington, and with his usual courage confronted slavery, coming out of the conflict the victor.

At Oswego and Erie the people were deeply moved; and at Chicago he accepted the invitation to attend a ball, prayed with the triflers, and broke up the gay assembly. He visited St. Louis in 1858, was in Boston again in 1860, and five years later was several weeks in Philadelphia, where many conversions were reported. But the power of his former years of vigorous manhood was evidently waning. He revisited Newark, N. J., Trenton, and New York. His last visit to New York was of affecting interest. In his own words : —

"My return to the city, after an absence of more than twenty years, was very cordial. Fifteen ministers came to hear me preach on the first afternoon, and to bid me welcome. Several of them had been converted under my ministry, and three of them had been baptized by me. During my stay here, I was called upon daily by very many Christians from all parts of the city and State, who ascribed their conversions, under God, to my labors.

"My heart was very much affected by these soul-stirring interviews. The goodness of God shone before me with a new lustre. I remembered the time when I first came to the city, and the distrust with which my labors were regarded, and the purposed neglect with which I was treated ; and, as I felt the contrast, my heart was melted

16

in gratitude to God for the change, and that he had permitted me to live to see it. The entire order of things is changed. Nearly all the ministers who now occupy the pulpits of the city, and, in fact, of the denomination throughout the country, were converted in protracted meetings, or in connection with revival measures. If all things in the churches had continued as they were in 1834 I wonder where the supply of ministers would have come from. Rather, I may ask, would there have been churches enough to have engaged the few ministers that would have remained to us? I do not claim that the change is owing to my labors, but I do say that the very measures which I introduced, and on account of which I suffered persecution, are now almost universally adopted and relied upon as those on which the blessing of God is most likely to rest. As these thoughts were revived in my mind by these kind assurances, I felt like appropriating the prayer of good old Simeon, ' Lord, now lettest thou thy servant depart in peace.' "

He also answers the question of the pecuniary reward of his ministry : —

During the first seven years of my labors as an Evangelist
my salary averaged $300 per annum $2,100
From 1839 to 1843 (four years) it averaged $2,000 per
annum 8,000
During sixteen years of labor in the West it averaged $380
per annum 6,080
During the remaining ten years it averaged $500 per
annum 5,000
In all, during thirty-six years, it has amounted to . . 21,180

Divide this amount ($21,180) by thirty-six years, and my
annual compensation has averaged $588.31
Deduct, for annual travelling expenses, say . . . 88.31

and I have realized per annum $500.00

In justice to Mr. Knapp, we quote the substance of his article on "How to Get up a Reformation ": —

"I use this phraseology, because it is the very language of those who are novices concerning this subject, and make so many complaints against special measures.

"God works by means, and by appointed and established means. His Spirit is hovering over all of our cities, towns, and country places, ready to respond to a faithful use of the means at all times. 'The set time' in which to favor Zion is always when 'her sons take pleasure in her stones, and favor the dust thereof.'

"Is it not proper to excite an enthusiasm on the subject of foreign or home missions? And would not God be pleased to have us get up a revival in the interest of education or of temperance? Why, then, is it not equally proper to put forth special efforts to promote the salvation of souls?

"But how shall a revival be brought about? Not, as some would imagine, by a resort to eccentricities and sensational appeals. It is probable that some such agencies may conduce to bring people to listen to the truth of God, but of themselves they are powerless and hurtful.

"The great necessity in promoting a revival is the outpouring of the Spirit of God. Until the Spirit be poured out from on high, the most pungent truths, the most tender appeals, and the most attractive manner, are in vain. Everything will remain as hard and as dead as a stone wall (and sinners are dead), until infused by the quickening influence of the Spirit's power.

"Consequently, our first work is prayer. Earnest, importunate, believing prayer must be made.

"An essential element of ministerial power is the spirit of love. No amount of learning, no degree of genius, nor measure of eloquence, will atone for the lack of that genuine spirit of sympathy which has its origin in love. A people will bear plain-dealing from one who can rebuke with much long-suffering and kindness. They will overlook many defects in execution on the part of one of whose sincere affection for them they feel assured. There is eloquence in love: it lights up the face with its radiant beams, and transmutes the glistening tear into a precious pearl. It magnetizes, enkindles, and subdues.

"The preacher that would have power with men must have power with God. He must be filled with the Spirit; and so greatly filled, that all other rivals for the control of his being shall be expelled. Much is said in the New Testament of 'being full of the Holy Spirit.' The apostles gave thanks to God, who always made them to triumph. Luther was powerful only as God was with him and in him. Wesley and Whitefield were eloquent and powerful because they were crucified to the world, and because 'Christ lived in them.' I know of no reason, in the divine economy, why, if there be an equal degree of seeking for it, there should not be marked and numerous evidences of divine effectiveness in ministers now as in former times. God is as willing to give the Holy Spirit to them that ask him now as he was formerly. And the promise still holds good, 'If any man will do His will, I and my Father will come to him, and make our abode with him.'

"When the Holy Spirit comes down in power, it visits the hearts of the community, and they are inclined to come in and hear the preached word. It was not the preaching of Peter which brought together the crowds, but the Holy Spirit, which came down in answer to prayers, continuously and unitedly offered by the waiting disciples.

"The Holy Spirit likewise indites the prayers and sermons. When God's ministers are filled with the Spirit, there is a kind of inspiration about their sermons, which makes them 'mighty to the pulling-down of the strongholds,'—a sort of inspiration in the conception and expression of their thoughts, and in the method of their delivery. Those who have imagined that I have depended for effect on eccentricities of speech, or tactics of management, have utterly misapprehended me, and done me great injustice. My reliance has been upon the power of God's truth, made effectual by his own Spirit, and the hearty co-operation of the church, as 'workers together with him.'

"I can conceive of a difference between a revival and a reformation, and desire only the former. But in all my efforts I have labored assiduously to bring about a *reformation*. I have sought to do a work which should abide, — a permanent element of power and blessing after I had passed on to other places. In laboring for reformation, it has been my custom to expose all the sins of God's people. He says, 'Lift up thy voice like a trumpet; cry aloud; spare not. Show unto my people their sins, and the house of Israel their transgressions.'

"If the work drags, I preach on some subjects which are applicable to both saints and sinners; appoint a fast, requiring all who join in it to abstain from all business and all food during the twenty-four hours. Sometimes we have held three or four such seasons in one meeting. Thus, by prayer and fasting, by preaching and exhortation, by humiliations and confessions, we have sought the Lord, until He has 'come and rained righteousness upon us.'

"When the church is aroused and consecrated, and the presence of the Spirit realized, then pour on God's truth, *hand over hand;* now thundering out the terrors of the law, until the mountain is covered with fire and smoke, and the people tremble; then ascend Calvary's bloody summit; bid the smitten people 'Behold the Lamb of God, who taketh away the sin of the world.' Preach Christ crucified; knock out every prop on which sinners lean. Sometimes the prop is one thing, sometimes it is another. It may be Universalism, or Unitarianism, or morality. No matter what it is, let not one remain; and see to it that the soul build on no other foundation than that which is already laid, which is Christ Jesus.

"Men in all ages are liable to go to extremes: and though the present generation of ministers have made many improvements on the past, yet I think the tendency now is to make the gospel pleasing to the tastes of unconverted men; and, as the result of this desire is to give 'none offence,' the doctrines of human depravity, of the enmity of the carnal mind against God, the necessity of the new birth, and the certainty of eternal punishment to the finally impenitent, are not made as prominent, or dwelt upon as much as formerly. But the truths of the Bible are adapted to the condition of man in all ages and circumstances, and any deviation from this standard is dangerous.

"There are two methods of carrying on a successful revival of religion. One is by calling in the aid of an evangelist, and making a special effort to enlist and arouse the entire community.

"But when this plan is not practicable, let the pastor of a church, in connection with his most spiritually-minded brethren, seek in prayer the outpouring of the Spirit. Then let them seek out the most seriously-disposed persons in the congregation; when one person is converted set him to work to win others, and endeavor to give every member of the church something to do.

"Formalists and hypocrites may say what they please against excitement, but from the earliest days of God's communication with men there have been seasons of religious refreshing and declension. There was a declension before the flood, and a revival under Abraham; a declension in Egypt, and a revival under Moses; a declension before the days of John the Baptist, and a revival shortly after Christ. And so it has been from that day to this;

and so it will continue to be, so long as man is what he is, the devil is what he is, and God does not change.

" The history of the Apostles is a history of excitement; deeper, stronger, and more lasting than we have ever had since. The history of the church is the history of strong and purifying excitements."

Towards the close of life, he thus alludes retrospectively to himself and the results of his ministry : —

" I am now an old man. I have outlived the generation of my early associates. Multitudes of those who have professed conversion under my labors have gone to the judgment before me, and the influence of my labors will be projected into the future after I shall have gone to my account. I realize that my life has been burdened with fearful responsibilities. The destinies of multitudes dead, living, and yet unborn, are linked with the influences I have exerted.

" As I have commended others to the mercy of God through Christ, so I look to the same source for the pardon of my sins, and the overruling of all my mistakes. And though deeply conscious of my failings and errors, I am, nevertheless, sustained with the conviction that God has made me the agent for the accomplishment of great good ; and I trustfully look forward to the gracious recognition of my Saviour when the results of my life-work shall be summed up."

In reply to inquiries respecting his life-work, he stated that he had held a hundred and fifty meetings, and preached nearly fifteen hundred sermons. He ceased to keep any account of the number of hopeful conversions after a hundred thousand names had been recorded, because it was not only difficult to be accurate, but on account of his doubts respecting the right to do so ; and, touching the number of them who became clergymen, he adds : —

" A student in Union College told me that he knew the

names of twelve young men, converted in my meetings in Schenectady, who had entered the ministry. I have been informed that about this number of converts in Yale College, during my meetings in New Haven, became ministers. There were five young men converted in the Utica meeting who became ministers.

"I can speak of about forty, converted in five meetings, who entered the ministry: in Schenectady, twelve; New Haven, twelve; Tabernacle Church, New York, six; Utica, five; Baltimore, five. Total, forty."

He defends the use of the "anxious seat" on the ground that it serves as a test of character, is a public committal, is a convenient way of making a public acknowledgment of the need of Christ, is an encouragement to other convicted souls and to Christians, and adds:—

"It may be asked, however, 'What authority have we in the teachings or examples of the Bible for anxious seats?' Answer: I have shown that the principle of publicly avowing our desire for salvation is recognized by Christ. I am not tenacious about the way of carrying out the principle, whether an inquirer rise on his feet and speak, or whether he take a seat assigned for those in his condition. I prefer the latter course on several accounts. Some persons are timid (especially ladies), and shrink from speaking for the first time before a large and promiscuous assembly. They can quietly walk forward to an assigned seat much more readily. Again, the interest of the meeting is ascertained and concentrated. Scores may rise from their seats and sit down again, and be unnoticed, and the church fail to appreciate the extent of the feeling. Besides, the anxious become more accessible to the acquaintance, sympathy, and instruction of the minister and brethren. In many cases the mere act of coming forward has brought no relief; but, once forward, the anxious soul comes in contact with some one who takes an immediate interest in his case, prays for him, converses with him, follows him up, and thus he is saved.

"It should be borne in mind that while the means of grace are divinely appointed, such as the preaching of the gospel, prayer, singing, baptism, and the Lord's supper, the measures in detail which are to be adopted in applying these agencies are left to be determined by the varying circumstances and exigencies of the time, and place and people."

Mr. Knapp was most emphatically opposed to honorary titles as unscriptural and therefore evil in tendency. He believed in speedy admissions to the church to be of apostolic authority, and no more likely to be attended with premature profession of faith than the delay common in some churches.

Elder Jacob Knapp died at Rockport, Ill., March, 1874, where he had for some time resided.

We think that the impartial judgment of the reader will be, that Elder Knapp was an original, able, earnest, somewhat eccentric, sometimes injudicious, but a very fearless, successful, and useful evangelist, whom God greatly honored, whatever points of criticism may be apparent to any in his measures and manner. As stated before, his was a pioneer work in revival interest, especially so in his own denomination; and he swung a strong arm, laying heavy blows upon the Antinomianism and lukewarmness of the churches, while he did not spare the most popular impenitence or gigantic public evil. It was this peculiar, divinely appointed service which was so nobly recognized by Dr. E. N. Kirk.

CHAPTER XIV.

In the comfortable home of a snug farmer, who also had learned the trade of shoemaker, was born at Stonington, Conn., Jabez S. Swan, February 23, 1800, two months after the birth of Jacob Knapp in New York. He was the fourth of seven children. He was fourteen years of age when the British attacked Stonington; and he offered his services, at the risk of his life, to carry powder to the defenders of his native town. He was compelled to meet the question of preparation for death. He decided against himself that he should be lost if killed; but present duty was clear, and his heart was not ready to yield to the claims and love of Christ.

When he was sixteen, the family removed to Lyme, Conn., where he attended the Congregational Church, there being no Baptist sanctuary within two miles; and became again interested in the subject of his own personal salvation. His impressions wore off, till he was a young man near his majority, when his faithful mother, and a Christian lady visiting her, seized the opportunity to press upon him the peril of delay, and need of Christ, extorting at length a promise to seek the Lord. A week later, he conveyed that saintly woman to her home, and in his apartment under her roof, with a terrific thunder-storm flashing and echoing around it, he bowed in prayer and submission, and rose with the peace and joy of pardon. When on his homeward way, he stopped to tell an aged deacon of the Congregational Church who had counselled him to repent, and believe in Jesus, of the change. The delighted man of God gave, in a single sentence, the secret of ministerial success in the subsequent experience of that convert not only, but of all ministerial harvest-work : " My child, keep with God !" He soon after united with the Baptist Church, and felt himself called to prepare to preach the gospel of salvation. After a struggle over the great question, he consecrated joyfully his life to this service for Christ. He at once entered upon it, with first a verbal, then a written, license from the church, in the spring of 1822.

According to the " Baptist tradition," he felt it necessary to follow some worldly avocation for support, salaries then being few and small. He therefore married, bought a house, and settled himself in the ministry. It was soon apparent that the occupation of time in earning a livelihood, along with his limited education, seriously embarrassed ministerial usefulness. He soon sold his real estate, and determined to seek aid from the Connecticut Education Society, and enter the Hamilton Theological and Literary Institute for further preparation. Disappointed in his efforts to secure assistance, he started off with his wife, trusting to God for success in his endeavor to obtain the mental discipline he desired. He reached Hamilton, supplied a church twelve miles out for one dollar a Sabbath, worked three hours daily, in the fields near his humble home, " for thirty-seven and a half cents," while his wife plied her needle for the students. He bought his firewood standing in the forest, cut and " hauled it home " himself, sometimes in the winter nearly freezing his feet.

The Bible became his principal study, the source, with much believing prayer, it is very evident, with all highly

honored servants of Christ, of their power in winning souls
to Him. Some theological questions troubled him, especially " limited atonement "; but his mind worked clear on
God's provision for all who will accept it by faith.

Mr. Swan left Hamilton, June, 1827, and accepted a
call to the pastorate of the Baptist Church, in Stonington
Borough, Conn., on a salary of two hundred and fifty
dollars. Our youthful preacher was now a pastor in the
place of his birth; and, where he was a powder-boy for
its defence, he planted the artillery of the gospel for the
conquest of souls by Immanuel. He learned in experience, that "a prophet is not without honor, save in his
own country"; and he began to "look for some spot
beyond his own society where he might strike for God
and His salvation with some promise of success." He
went to Milltown, several miles distant, where he soon
rallied the few who loved the Lord to his help; conversions followed till a church was organized. With
scanty clothing, he went to and returned from his field,
through storms and cold, often late at night, sustained by
his faith and its great reward. This, his first revival,
suggested his future work; "it was a kind of miniature
view of what God would do in a wider sphere of action."
Although all denominations in Stonington were anxious
to have him remain, and his salary was raised to six hundred dollars, he accepted an invitation to remove to Norwich at the salary he had received, because he felt that the
field was white to the harvest, and on that account had
committed himself to the people there. In April, 1830,
he commenced his labors, and opened a meeting every
Thursday evening for prayer, with three brethren. When
a sister remarked it was a mistake in brother Swan to
"set up the meeting, for it would run down," he replied
"they were out of danger from that quarter, for they had
not far to run, as only three attended now, and if there

was any run to it, it *would run up.*" He paid the expenses of the weekly gathering, which increased in interest and saving results. The intelligence now reached him of a glorious season of refreshing in Stonington. This led him to the searching inquiry, why he failed of a similar blessing. He was deeply humbled, and the temptation came to him with fearful power to leave the ministry; but he dared not break his vows, and betray his trust. His preaching grew more spiritual and impressive. "Yet," he says, "lying like a canker upon my heart, was my want of success. My house was crowded with hearers, and they gave the best attention, but no break in the ranks was realized."

Several months later, he learned there was a "four-days' meeting" in a town twenty miles distant, and he immediately went to it, to see what it was, and receive any suggestions which might increase his own usefulness. From the sanctuary, filled with the Spirit's presence, he went to a dense forest to pray over his own failure to save men.

He writes: "Anxious seats were employed, and several things which were new to me; yet the *part which God took in the meeting* so overwhelmed me, that the ways and means had no effect to excite my prejudice. It was a day of wonderful speculation among high-geared Calvinists and Antinomians. The ungodly reviled and mocked the whole thing; but God rolled in a tide of divine influence, like the ground-swell of the Atlantic, which no earthly power could resist."

Mr. Swan returned to his charge a more consecrated, self-forgetful minister than he had ever been before, and recounted to the people in the usual evening service the wonderful works of God which he had seen. On the Sabbath, he continued the stirring narrative, and poured out with tearful tenderness his confessions of unfaithfulness, asking the forgiveness of the congregation. The effect was subduing, and the tidings of the strange scenes soon spread through the town. Opposition was organized; but the ambassador of Christ was "walking at liberty," his "views of God, working through his gospel, wonderfully enlarged, and his whole soul girded with inward strength, while his anxieties for the salvation of souls were overwhelming." A protracted meeting followed, with which commenced a wide-spread work of grace, that brought upon the principal actor a fierce and unscrupulous opposition.

Mr. Swan, although a pastor, was now fairly enlisted in the work of the evangelist. He gives his general order of service in prosecuting it among the churches: "It was to commence at nine o'clock with prayer-meeting; at half-past ten, preaching; again, prayer-meeting at half-past one o'clock, and preaching at half-past two. In the evening, prayer-meeting at six, and sermon at half-past seven." Before each sermon, two brethren in succession prayed, and sometimes burdened Christians would drop on their knees, and continue pleading silently with God during the discourse. At the close came importunate supplication, and appeals to the unconverted, requesting them to come forward for prayer. Mr. Swan says, "Under this order of things, I have seen the most astonishing displays of God's power. Once it was so great, that about all in the galleries came down, while others below moved forward, until the hosts were prostrated before God, crying for mercy." If any one objects to such excitement, he points, with unanswerable defence, to similar and yet greater exhibitions of Jehovah's majesty on the day of Pentecost.

He soon ventures upon Hamilton, the stronghold of the denomination, the seat of the principal Baptist institution of learning in the State. The "new measures" were objected to, but Mr. Swan must work in his own way, or not at all. This point was yielded, and there was soon a pervading interest, deepening into a harvest which included in its rich results the college, and enlisted the professors in a movement which was too clearly of God to be opposed. So mighty was the power of prayer that a pious woman, who for two years had been unable to walk, desired to be carried to the sanctuary for the petition that she might be healed, having faith that a cure would be wrought. Mr. Swan records that he could not doubt it, and prayed with her. She was borne away, and he heard nothing for years, when he met her, and she told him that in a few days after the visit to the temple she was perfectly well, and had been so ever since. The elder makes no other comment than to leave the fact to those who care to discuss its meaning.

For eight years, he thus "ranged the churches up and down the valley of Chenango County, spread the gospel net, and many were converted to God." In 1837, he was impressed with the duty to leave Norwich, and go to Preston, where there was not even a sanctuary, leaving a pleasanter charge and larger salary, to build for his Master amid spiritual desolations. In February, 1838, a new, plain church was opened for services, and at the end of two years the communion numbered two hundred members.

Meanwhile, he conducted revival meetings of marked power in Owego, the principal town of Tioga County, N. Y. In 1839, he removed to Oxford, became pastor of the church there, and had an extensive work of grace. At Cooperstown and in Niagara County he witnessed similar "times of refreshing," in which there was occasionally the physical prostration connected with some of the most remarkable revivals in this and the old country. Again, in Stonington, Mystic, New London, Albany, N. Y., Charlestown, Mass., Jewett City, Waterford, Norwich repeatedly,

Lyme, Owego, and Hamilton, also in Willimantic, Mer-
iden, and other places, his labors and successes, varied
with different forms of opposition, signal cases of conversions, and thrilling scenes of interest, sometimes extending
through the night, were abundant and exhausting, yet
continued with cheerful humility and fearless loyalty to
Christ.

Of the second series of meetings in Hamilton, Mr. Swan
writes : —

"When some two weeks had passed, the church began
to strike the revival current, and daylight began to break
over us. Those who had been in polar circles began to
come up under the sun.

"We have, as a denomination, been acquainted with the
variety of evils which contribute to backsliding; but of
late a sort of dancing devil has got in among our churches,
of such strange character that it takes a long series of
revival meetings, attended with the power of God, to
cast him out. Yet God triumphs, notwithstanding human
frailty. Dancers among Baptists are generally cured, when
they come to themselves. It has proved a costly thing to
chant to the sound of the viol in the kick-ups of the Devil,
falsely called 'hops.' Among the wanderers from the
church were some who had chosen dancing scenes before
the prayer-meeting, and yet not gone beyond the sound
of the voice of the Great Shepherd.

"When the work of the Lord began to move with power,
it reached our institution on the adjacent hill. The professors in the institution, including President Ebenezer
Dodge, came in with all their heart and took hold of the
work of the Lord. God also appeared in the schools of
the village, and converts were multiplied in those seats
of learning.

"The custom has long prevailed in Hamilton, when a
general effort is made to save souls, to visit not only the

village, but the whole region round about. This was carried out as I never saw it before. As we might expect,
the inhabitants flowed in from all quarters, and from the
host God gathered jewels. I never saw a more excellent
company of youth than the Lord redeemed in the course
of the meetings."

In 1860 he resigned the pastorate of the Second Church
in Stonington, to add to the service of an evangelist that of
domestic missionary, itinerating over the "waste places"
of Zion. He is still living at New London, Connecticut.
With this outline of a "busy life" in its highest activity,
which fills a handsome volume, we will only notice further
the characteristics, manner, preaching, and providential
work of Mr. Swan. He is a very remarkable man, comparatively little known as an evangelist beyond his own
denomination, because his labours were confined mainly to
his own branch of Zion; and yet, he was not illiberal and
narrowly sectarian, but quite the opposite. Clear and
settled in his convictions, his great warm heart was in
sympathy with all true disciples of Christ. He united
womanly tenderness with the boldness and fearlessness of
the lion. When fidelity to souls required it, like the surgeon of gentlest nature, who can sink the blade through
the quivering flesh of the agonized patient with a firm,
untrembling hand, he would search the conscience and the
heart with unsparing, prayerful severity; and as soon as
the disease was revealed and removed, apply the "balm of
Gilead" with the tenderness of the Great Physician. A
more devoted husband and father no family ever had, and
no minister a truer, nobler wife to help him in his work of
trials and triumphs. He was naturally quaint, witty, and
humorous, but always the faithful, devoted minister,
seeking through all his varied manner and expressions
the consecration and comfort of God's people, and the
salvation of the impenitent. His paraphrases of the sacred

narrative were often very striking, sometimes exciting a laugh, yet having a practical point never forgotten by the hearers.

By this marvellous skill in applying Bible incidents to point an appeal, we think he saved from abandonment, when at its lowest condition of discouragement, the Telagoo Mission, citing the case of Paul and Silas, who on their "way to Europe" to establish a mission were thrown in prison, and tempted to give up the enterprise. Then followed the prayer-meeting and praise, and the victory. The speech was electric in its effect. All his preaching was thoroughly evangelical in the demonstration of the Spirit and with power. Evidently, he knew that "unction of the Holy One," which is the apostolic consecration to soul-saving, and makes it the more singular that he should have misapprehended the real nature of the so-called "Higher Christian Life," in his criticism upon this self-surrendering, working faith, as held by Dr. Edwards, President Finney, A. B. Earle, and a host in the Zion of God. We refer not to the affectation of sanctity, nor high claims to absolute perfection, but the vital union by faith with Jesus, which makes *experimental*, and joyfully so, the testimony of the Word: "Christ *is become to us*, wisdom, righteousness, sanctification, and redemption,"— the starting-point of true growth; the life practically, and not theologically merely, "hid with Christ in God."

Providentially, with his peculiar and, in certain respects, more popular address, public and private, he was contemporary with Jacob Knapp in waking up a denomination, slumbering to a great extent over all the precious interests committed to the church, gathering a multitude of souls to the cross. Who can estimate the results of the repeated revivals at Hamilton, Owego, Norwich, Stonington, and many other towns in New England, and in the State of New York? The ministry, missions, and all the walks of usefulness have their unwritten and endless history,which the judgment only can reveal.

We have not yet found any serious discount made by Christians of his own or other denominations upon Rev. Jabez Swan's long career as an evangelist ; for, when settled, his pastorate was scarcely more than headquarters for his special and constant service. The testimony of the fathers in the Baptist Israel, including such men as Drs. Ives and Neal, is very emphatic to his uniform success. The experience of Luther and Melanchthon is not an uncommon arrangement in God's gracious providence, supplementing mutually labors in carrying forward his sovereign plan of redeeming love in the world.

We think no impartial reader can doubt that he was called of the Lord to a crisis in his kingdom, which he met with heroic faith and untiring zeal, and gave an impulse to whose importance no human wisdom can measure.

CHAPTER XV.

NEARLY contemporary with Jacob Knapp, that chieftain in the Baptist Israel who was reaching the masses, in the wilderness of Chemung County, New York, a humble yet remarkable minister was striking heavy blows upon the reigning ungodliness in the settlements scattered over the clearings of an extensive territory, and planting churches there; and at length goes into border towns and villages of greater population and culture, with a singular power of awakening the people.

Thomas S. Sheardown was this faithful servant of Christ. He was born November 4, 1791, in the parish of Little Coots, in Lincoln County, England, and nurtured in the established church. He says of the effect of parental example, "Hearing my father ask God in his prayers for so many things that he needed, I was led to do the same; and in little matters, when denied by my parents, I would ask God to give them to me. I remember when I was so small that I played with a bow and arrow, as I often lost my arrow I would hide myself in the grass, and ask God to tell me where it was; and, as I frequently found it soon after, that gave me encouragement always to go to Him for anything I was troubled about." This early exercise of faith was the foreshadowing of its maturer but no more simple and scriptural exer-

cise. Of his true mother he writes : "I loved her, and
to this day there is no word in the English language,
except Jesus, so dear to me as mother." When eleven
years old, she sewed inside his vest seventy-five guineas,
with which he went to London, and "launched out upon
the world for himself," and of which he was robbed upon
his arrival in the great metropolis. He resolved to be
honest, pure, and Sabbath-keeping ; but he was "light,
vain, and fond of amusements, and had a passionate love
for the theatre." Of this he was cured by the following
incident : " A gentleman was performing his part in 'the
Castle Spectre,' and when he called upon God to strike
him dead if he was not telling the truth, he fell lifeless to
the floor." The impressive event broke for him the fascination of the stage. His employer, a linen-draper, sent
him to open a branch business in Hull. On the way
thither the vessel anchored at the mouth of the Humber,
near his widowed mother's home. It was nine o'clock in
the evening when he entered the dwelling and found her
reading the family Bible, which, after an affectionate welcome, he took, and, to gratify her, read several chapters
aloud. It was God's night of mercy for him. After retiring, she knelt by his bed and prayed for his salvation.
Touchingly he relates the change which followed.

"I never had such feelings before ; I thought I must
pray, but had no hope that God would hear me. I
thought, if I could only remember some portions of my
father's prayers, I might be heard. Then I tried to pray
in my own way. I felt that it did not become me to lie in
bed, and I got upon my knees. All my trouble appeared
to be removed. I fell into a sweet sleep. Awakening, I
bade farewell to my mother." But no one cared for his
soul, and the "blessed state of mind wore away." A few
years later, living with a Baptist, and brought under more
decided religious influences, he united with the church.

He was an active Christian among others equally so. An aged brother noticing his "gifts," requested him to hold religious services in Skilby, seven miles from Hull. This was a new crisis in his career, the beginning of his useful evangelistic life. The venerable saint said to Mr. Sheardown, "Now, sir, I want you to hold a meeting next Sabbath, where but three or four may be called experimental Christians." Mr. Sheardown demurred, pleading the lack of gifts, and of a call to such a work. But there was no escape from the tender importunity, whose last appeal was, "Now, go this time, and I will tell you where to call. Inquire for Mr. William Wilberforce; he is a Dissenter, and he and his wife are very pious people. You need not fear; the house in which he lives is licensed by the bishop of the diocese for Dissenting ministers to hold meetings." Mr. Sheardown went and found a crowd awaiting his arrival. He was so embarrassed that he resolved not to repeat the visit. The church of which he was a member called him to order for irregularity. At this juncture, he writes : "There was a young brother who wished to preach. He appeared to have the 'preach fever.' Not so with me — mine was the chill, without the fever. He went to Skilby, and took for his text, Isaiah vii, 25 : 'And all hills that shall be digged with the mattock,' etc. He was greatly embarrassed, and talked pretty much all the time about digging with a mattock. It evidently made an impression on the children, for the next time he went they ran into the streets and shouted : 'There comes the mattock man, there comes the mattock man!' I do not recollect that he attempted to preach much afterwards." Mr. Sheardown yielded to repeated urgency, and continued to proclaim the gospel message with success at Skilby. The great question now, of duty to enter formally the ministry, pressed upon his spirit, till his health was seriously impaired. His good wife became anxious for his life.

One Sabbath morning, on the way to church, all doubt and heaviness of heart passed like a drifting cloud from his spiritual sky, before the words of God to Peter : " But the Lord said unto him, Go thy way ; for he is a chosen vessel unto me, to bear my name before the Gentiles and kings and the children of Israel."

The effect was like a second conversion. Gladness unearthly filled his being, and the path into the future glowed with light from Immanuel's throne. After preaching to the poor, and making a business excursion to France, he sailed with his wife, in 1820, for the new world, landing a few weeks later in New York. With no definite plan or purpose, he went on board a sloop, bound for Newburgh, where he met men from the "Lake Country," who urged him to return with them to their homes between Seneca and Cayuga Lakes. He went with them, and in October, 1820, took up his abode at Covert, Seneca County, and in his own words " became a citizen of York State." He knew nothing of backwoods life, but went to work heroically to learn the rough employments of the pioneer farmer, making many ludicrous blunders in his new apprenticeship. In the spring his family joined him after nearly a year's separation since he left them in fatherland. Mr. Sheardown, not long afterwards, was surprised and greatly cheered by receiving a letter from Mr. Wilberforce and others in Skilby, informing him that, as the fruit of his first evangelistic " service for Jesus," there was a church of one hundred members, with a commodious brick chapel and a settled pastor." Temptation to keep secret his lay preaching and even his profession, having no letter from the church to which he belonged, made him a backslider, and darkness settled upon his soul. The Spirit led him to declare his faith, while the discipline of a severe sickness was made a wonderful blessing. His experience was of that almost miraculous character, which

opened to the vision of faith the deep things of God and
eternity, and cast all terrestrial scenes into shadow. While
friends thought him dying, he was clearly conscious,
expecting to live, and filled with the glorious peace of
Immanuel. Upon his recovery, his impression was irresistible that he must remove to some other field of temporal and spiritual activity. The spring of 1826 found
him in the woods of Catlin, Chemung County, domiciled
in a log house, which he had built without a door' or windows. With incredible physical exertions and privations
to exhaust his energies, he now began in earnest the
work of an evangelist, to continue in them till worn out
in the toil. Every school-house, and where this did not
stand, the dwelling, became a sanctuary for faithful labor
and believing prayer.

The organization of a church at Catlin followed, while
conversions, some of them of very remarkable character,
attended his ministry wherever he made his fervent appeals.
Afoot and on horseback he threaded the forests, and continually enlarged the territory of an intense activity, which
would have broken down any other than a man of his
herculean strength and unflagging zeal. He extended his
circuit into Pennsylvania, where he was blessed no less
than in his adopted State.

In one place an attempt was made to blow up the church,
by charging a log of firewood for the stove with powder,
which Elder Sheardown discovered just in time to prevent
the disaster, and use the fiendish plot with tremendous
effect in his sermon. Monuments to his fidelity were left
in Steuben and Schuyler Counties. We have not space to
quote from his autobiography,—very interesting and suggestive pages,—but must close the sketch with illustrative
notices of his preaching methods and sound views on
revivals.

Mr. A. C. Mallory, of Benton, N. Y., records of Mr.

Sheardown : "As a deacon in the First Church, of which Elder Sheardown was pastor, I was permitted to know him in all the intimacy which ever ought to exist between a pastor and the other officers of a church, and most cheerfully do I testify to his prudence and wisdom as a counsellor, and to his fidelity as a laborer in the work of the ministry. As an ordained minister, he commenced his career with a church gathered, by the divine blessing upon his efforts, amid the privations of a new country, where he wrought with his own hands in clearing away the forest and providing for his rising family. Often did he preach three times on the Sabbath, requiring a walk of twenty miles home the same day. He very seldom failed to meet his engagements, and was usually on the spot before the time of meeting. When asked if he never stopped on account of the weather he would say, 'Not often. I make the appointments, and not the weather. It is my business to fill the appointments, and the Lord will take care of me and the weather ' In estimating the value of the labors of our brother in the ministry, it is well to take into consideration the difficulties he overcame."

Another, referring to the suspicion and criticisms which he encountered on account of his foreign origin and his lay preaching, wrote of him : "He was thwarted and hindered, instead of being aided and encouraged, and had reached thirty-eight years before he was ordained. Those who have heard him preach, and who know the measure of grace and gifts given him, can never cease to lament that a dozen or fifteen of the best years of his life were comparatively wasted before he entered fully upon the joyful and all-important work for which he was so peculiarly fitted, and in which he has been so much blessed.

"Yet, amidst all this, he 'abated not a jot of heart or hope.' Always serene, cheerful, and ready to benefit

others he pursued the plan which he had marked out
with the same unruffled calmness as though every one
cheered and encouraged him. The secret of his success
resided in the constraining love of Christ, in energy of
will, in unconquerable resolution, and in indomitable perseverance."

The following outlines of discourses were taken down,
nearly thirty years ago, by a brother, who says in relation
to them, "These sketches may convey some idea of Elder
Sheardown's mode of treating a text, but I never knew
him to take any written plan into the pulpit or use one on
any occasion. I do not believe he ever wrote one. He
was among the most difficult men to follow after, to make
a report. I have many times taken pencil and paper at
the commencement of his sermon, and after getting down,
perhaps, two or three ideas, would become perfectly obliv-
ious to all thoughts of writing, and find myself, at or near
the close of service, with mouth half open and tears running profusely.

"'Text. — Isaiah 50 : 11 ; "Behold, all ye that kindle a
fire, that compass yourselves about with sparks ; walk in
the light of your fire, and in the sparks that ye have kindled. This shall ye have of mine hand, ye shall lie down
in sorrow."

"'Introduction. — The Christian has the promise of
heaven and happiness ; but these are not for the sinner.
The word of God is compared to fire, and its effects to a
furnace. Those characters kindle a fire of their own —
one which God has not kindled. But their fire has neither
light nor heat. It is counterfeit, and counterfeiters grow
more skilful. Hence, ungodly men all have some creed.
There are about seventeen hundred different systems of
religious belief. We notice, —

"'I.   Some of the fires which men kindle.

"'1st, To blunt conscience, some kindle the fire of

atheism. 2d, Others, for the same purpose, deny such parts of the Bible as they cannot comprehend; yet they cannot tell which part is revealed and which is not. 3d, Others deny the immortality of the soul. 4th, Some embrace Universalism. 5th, Some trust in their morality. 6th, Others expect to reach heaven because their pious parents had them sprinkled in infancy. 7th, Some trust in church-membership, like Nicodemus, the High Churchman. But Jesus said, "Ye must be born again." Members of other churches satisfy themselves with the mere forms of religion. They enlist, but do not fight. 8th, Some try to live religion alone — make no profession, etc.

"'II. THE CONSEQUENCES OF SO DOING.

"'"Ye shall lie down in sorrow." This term, "lie down," has reference to the end of a journey. Oh, the sorrow of that soul that has expected heaven and lies down in hell! "They shall have it at God's hand" — no escape. Be not deceived!!'

"His manner during pulpit ministrations was peculiar to himself, and no attempt at imitation could be made without spoiling the picture. Before service, he would walk the aisles singing, and shaking hands with each one who came in. In prayer he left the impression upon his hearers that he walked and talked with God. In reading hymns and preaching, he gestured much. After reading his text he usually laid the Bible upon the seat behind him, and, as he warmed in the work, would sometimes lay off his coat, then his cravat and collar, and for about an hour would pour forth, in a manner indescribably attractive and impressive, thoughts that were a 'wonder to many.'"

Rev. G. P. Watrous, missionary to Burmah, gives pleasant testimony to his power of illustration.

"His familiarity with the Bible, his profound knowledge of human nature, reasoning powers, glowing imagination, good voice, ease and grace of expression, coupled

with strong faith, devotion to his Master, and a yearning love for souls, render him prince of preachers.

"His memory is a treasury of illustrations. On one occasion, wishing to show that plainness in preaching, though
apparent severity, was real kindness, he spoke of an English
ship that was almost wrecked, a short distance from a
certain fort. As the ship's crew were about to give up in
despair, the guns of the fort opened upon them. 'Alas!'
cried those on board, 'the howling storm and hungry waves
have almost destroyed us, and now our friends on the
shore are about to complete our misery and destruction by
firing upon us!' But those were friendly shots; for, as
they flew harmlessly over the ship, they conveyed to it
the rope by which the sailors were all brought safely to
the shore. The ministers of Christ are like those friendly
guns, startling and terrifying in their denunciations of sin,
but aiming at the highest welfare of hearers in their eternal salvation.

"On another occasion, at a covenant meeting, a number
of candidates were received for baptism. A note of discord was sounded, which threatened to mar the harmony
and destroy in a measure the good effect of the meeting, if
it did not lead to subsequent bitterness. 'Stop, brethren,'
said Elder Sheardown, 'we must be careful what we do
and say in the presence of these converts. Two old sheep
were quarrelling; and, as they rushed to butt their foolish
heads, a lamb, in its innocent gambolling, ran between them
and was instantly killed.' The influence of this little
story was most happy: the objectionable matter was
dropped, and harmony was restored to us."

Mr. Sheardown, for an itinerant rising from the common
people to prominence, without culture in the "schools,"
was singularly sound and free from extravagance. He
writes respecting revivals, "To make extra efforts result
in the salvation of souls, the truth as it is in Jesus must

be proclaimed, attended by the demonstration of the Holy Ghost. Sometimes a church will send for an evangelist, in order that they may have what they call a good time. It is necessary, in the very first place, to take away from the church all human dependence, just as much as it is to take away a sinner's dependence on that in which he trusts. Whenever a church is brought down at the feet of sovereign mercy, and led to cry out as did Rachel of old, 'Give me children or I die,' sinners have been converted to God, and Zion has been increased by the addition of living members."

His wisdom in the adaptation of singing to the state of feeling was in harmony with more recent and widely popular use of sacred song. In the inquiry meeting, and alone with the anxious, immediate submission to God was the end he sought.

Mr. Sheardown illustrates the impartial grace of God in the selection of his instruments for carrying forward his own work, disregarding human pride and judgment. In this, "The Lord's ways are not our ways, nor His thoughts our thoughts." Mr. Sheardown continued measurably strong to labor; until his death in Troy, Bradford County, Pennsylvania, Thursday, July 30, 1874, in his eighty-fourth year, after two days' illness. Was buried by the side of his first wife, near Havana, N. Y. He preached Sunday before his death from the text, "What shalt thou say when He shall punish thee?"

CHAPTER XVI.

Other Evangelists of the Middle and Eastern States, whose Work supplemented and extended Previous Labors.— Rev. S. G. Orton — His Life. — Passion for Souls. — Harvest Seasons. — Death. — Rev. Jedediah Burchard. — Life at Albany. — Conversion and Preparation for the Ministry.— Labors.— Testimony to his Usefulness. — Peculiarities. — His Death — Rev. O. Parker. — Boyhood.— Saved from Error —A Successful Evangelist.—Judicious Management of Meetings.— Still in the Field.— Rev. Mr. Avery.

Rev. Samuel G. Orton was born June, 1797, at South Farms, in Litchfield, Conn. Here, when a youth of eighteen years, he was converted in the revival under Mr. Nettleton, catching the spirit of that devoted, self-denying, and faithful evangelist, which distinguished his own remarkable life. An intimate friend and co-worker, Dr. Gregory, to whom we are indebted for an outline of Mr. Orton's career, records of him : —

"His desire to preach the gospel began with his hope in Christ. As a young convert his voice rang out vigorously, and in earnest persuasion he found himself successful in drawing youth to the cross. He was fitted for Yale College ; but poverty staring him in the face, and resolving to depend on his own exertions in teaching to prepare for the ministry, he deemed it wise to join Hamilton College, where he spent four years. While ambitious young men were taxing their brains for college honors, he was found gathering the people into school-houses and private houses, pleading with them to come to Christ, and pouring out his ardent prayers for their salvation. A college officer taunted him for his pious zeal, and rebuked him for the haste with which he had prepared his composition. He said subsequently of him, 'Had it been before my conversion, I should have knocked him down.'

" While a junior in college, in the summer of 1821, he taught a select school of fifty scholars, at Deposit, Delaware County, N. Y. At once his voice was heard in the prayer-room, and all felt that a holy man of thought and action was there. Soon after, a deacon stepped quietly into his school-room as his scholars left. A thunder-storm came suddenly up. While it raged for more than an hour they prayed, and continued alternating and pleading until the storm was over; and they parted with the assurance that God had then and there begun a revival in each of their minds, and that his salvation would surely come. He sent a note to the female prayer-meeting, saying, 'Pray for my scholars!' Two weeks later a Sabbath-morning prayer-meeting at sunrise was commenced, it is supposed, at his suggestion. It opened with that hymn of Dr. Dwight's: —

" ' This morning most sweetly the gales were all blowing
    Directly the breezes from Mount Calvary ;
  The sepulchre 's opened, the odors are flowing,
    Breathe gently, sweet odors, breathe gently on me ! '

" At length it became a daily sunrise prayer-meeting. He was present at all meetings. His colorless face, bespeaking a mind exhausted with study and fasting, and talking with Christ, yet glowing with a faith that surmounts all difficulties, and with arguments fresh from the armory of God and illustrations all new, carried conviction to all minds that he was anointed of the Holy One. All were eager to hear him. At the fitting time he addressed well-chosen words to his school. The harvest was ripe for the sickle. Those fifty scholars came to Christ, and a much larger number outside of his school embraced the cross. In that revival, six young men, at least, turned their attention to the ministry; five of them are still preaching, while one has entered into his rest."

Mr. Orton, at the end of his senior year at college, by Dr. Beecher's advice, went into the theological school, under Dr. Taylor. Health becoming impaired by adding to his studies untiring efforts to save souls, he returned to Delaware County, and took charge of the Presbyterian Church at Sydney Plains. Successful there in his pastoral work, he was also intensely studious in the preparation for future usefulness. Overwork compelled him to leave his parish.

He then became principal of a school in Deposit, where he entered at once into revival efforts. These were crowned with a great blessing, the tide of divine influence sweeping with power up and down the valley of the Delaware. At Colchester, he had a glorious harvest. By request of presbytery, he went to Delhi, the county-seat, a stronghold of infidelity. The first sight that met his view upon entering the village was a shooting-match of two hundred roughs; the next man was a deacon, who grasped his hand, and exclaimed, "God has sent you here!" Mr. Orton's opening sermon was in the court-house, where he noticed a serious expression on the face of a lawyer. The following day he sought his office. The conversation which followed was characteristic of the earnest preacher: "Will you allow me to propound a question?" The lawyer replied, "Most gladly." Mr. Orton then said, with solemn tenderness, "Have you ever given the subject of eternal life your close attention for one hour?" After a pause of reflection, he answered, with evident feeling, "I confess I never have." The faithful visitor added, "Will you do it?" The prompt response was, "I will." And he did; and the religious interest from that time bore down all opposition, until more than a hundred persons, including twenty-six heads of families, were hopefully converted.

In 1830, he went west to join his friend, Rev. D. D. Gregory, also a devoted minister, according to a promise given several years before. At Ripley, "The song of the reapers, as they shouted the harvest-home, awoke the dull ears of thoughtless worldlings. Prayers were sought for the conversion of men, and answers came that awed both saints and sinners."

In 1831, and again in 1858, he gathered from many fields the golden grain of the great Husbandman. At Erie, as in Beaufort, under the ministrations of Mr. Baker, "Episcopalians crowded into his inquiry meetings," and the mighty power of God fell upon all classes. During a single sermon upon the prodigal son, twenty-four persons found peace in believing. In 1832, he accepted a call to Delhi, N. Y., only to remove the following year to Westfield, that he might again go into the field to do the undivided work of an evangelist. He was so feeble that at "Mayville he was lifted into the pulpit." At Silver Creek, Jamestown, and elsewhere, the Holy Ghost wrought mightily through him In Chautauqua County, by the desire of the pastors along the Alleghany River, and in the bounds of the Genesee Synod, the converting, weeping, yet rejoicing messenger of mercy went forth bearing the precious seed, and returned bringing his sheaves with him.

It was only a repetition of such rich harvest, with the differences of local and personal circumstances attending, which were often deeply moving, in Penn Yan and Auburn, N. Y. Dr. R. S. Steele said of him, "His great reliance was upon the Holy Ghost"; and referring to the remark of his own pastor, Dr. Hopkins, that he never had a man in his house who prayed so much, added, "Here, then, I think and feel we have the secret of his power, — prayer, *prayer*, PRAYER!" Dr. Hay of Geneva, and Dr. Gregory of Binghamton, with both of whom he labored, bore no less emphatic testimony. In 1838, he became pastor in

Ripley, O., with the understanding that he should not
withdraw from his favorite employment.   Dr. Gregory
says :

"During twenty-eight years of his ministerial life, he
had the pastoral care of churches, yet leaving his flock to
labor in revivals; while his labors as an evangelist were
of fifty years' continuance.   From a careful survey of the
different localities visited by the outpouring of the divine
Spirit under his preaching, and which were reported at the
time, we find more than ten thousand souls hopefully converted; and the number of young men led by him to
Christ, and who became ministers of the gospel, is very
large.

"We have now before us a successful ministry.   One
entered upon in weakness and fear and much trembling,
but becoming at length mighty through God.   A ministry
which we shall venture to call Pauline in its beginning and
progress and ending; attended with severe and prolonged
bodily sufferings, but imparting the highest measures of
happiness to the spirit; one that exalted Christ, and magnified the power of the gospel, while the subject of it was
lying prostrate in the lowest depths of humility, concealed
behind the cross."

We come at last to the brief statement in Bible necrol-
ogy, which must be true at some time of us all, "And he
died."

"His last physician said he had a constitution to carry
him a hundred years, but for the diseased condition of
one lobe of the lungs.   This pulmonary difficulty was
induced by extreme labor in securing his education for the
ministry, and by blowing the gospel trumpet so long.
This vigorous constitution accounts for his painful death,
of which his daughter, at whose house he died, said, 'It
seemed to us that father died five times.'   During the utter
exhaustion, he rallied, and said gently, 'Lord, Oh, gently

lead me!' His son, President Orton, said, 'His sufferings were extremely harrowing to us as we looked on. Yet, like his blessed Master, he uttered no complaint, but bowed his soul in sweet submission, and at last fell asleep in Jesus.'"

The elements of power in him, were Bible-study, much prayer, self-forgetful zeal, intense earnestness, unwavering faith in the Lord, wisdom direct from the Fountain, and an eye single to the glory of God. His manner was fearless and persuasive. He dispensed with notes early in his ministry. Illustrations were frequent and forcible. We quote a single instance in answering the charge of excitement : —

"Men can be excited upon the affairs of this life. Why should they not be upon the interests of an endless life? The Bank of England, on a certain occasion, was thought to be in danger of bankruptcy. The directors were closeted in their room for a fortnight. At length they saw that all was safe. One of them walked out and met a friend. 'How is it?' said he. '*It's safe.*' — 'How is your family?' — '*My family!* I did not know that I had one!'"

To the last moment of consciousness, "he believed that Zion was soon to put on her beautiful garments, and the days of refreshing would surely come. He wished his clerical brethren would labor harder to save men; yet his charitable heart would not chide or rebuke them."

Without seeking fame on earth, he lived with his eye on "things unseen and eternal"; and in departing with victorious joy he gave an imperishable fragrance to the name he loved above all others, save that of *Christian*, EVANGELIST.

Rev. Jedediah Burchard was an evangelist whose marked peculiarities, some of which were eccentricities, made him the object of more severe criticism than ordinarily falls to the lot of even an evangelist.

He commenced business in a large mercantile house at Albany, the capital of his native State, and put himself within the fascinating circle of gay and fashionable society. With several young men of the same age, among them Martin Van Buren, afterwards president, he was accustomed on the Sabbath to frequent a grove at Greenbush for social enjoyment and literary reading. But his pleasures were interrupted by the memory of a pious widowed mother, and her holy counsels haunted the air of the desecrated day. To his arrested thought, her lifted finger often pointed to the neglected house of God ; and at length he resolved to go. The following Sunday he sought the sanctuary, which was full ; and he was shown into a pew with three elderly ladies. One of these "had an eye like a diamond," was almost a centenarian, and a convert of Whitefield. Young Burchard attracted her attention ; and, at the close of service the next Sabbath, she said to him when leaving the pew, "God bless you, my son !" His pride was wounded, for he feared that others would think her to be his mother ; and he hurried away to his boarding-house. While at the table he suddenly burst into tears ; and, leaving his astonished companions, he went to his room, and there bowed in prayer. Peace followed a bitter struggle. That aged mother, who was deeply taught in spiritual verities, became his cherished friend and counsellor.

His thoughtless companions now awakened anxiety, and he invited them to meet him in a social religious service. Shrinking from the responsibility of the occasion as the hour approached, he committed to memory what he desired to say to them ; but when he rose before them his address was gone from him, and, casting himself upon God, he made his appeal with visible effect. Although active in the Sabbath School, to no part of his usefulness then did he afterwards refer with more interest than little circles for prayer and religious inquiry held for colored servants, in the kitchens of wealthy citizens who not only approved, but desired, these efforts of the zealous young disciple.

Mr. Burchard often related an incident in the experience of the venerable woman to whom allusion has been made. She became deaf, but had unbounded faith that God would cure her. During a Sabbath service, she suddenly startled the worshippers and their pastor by an exclamation apparently of pain. Assuring them that nothing serious had occurred, she found that her hearing was restored. The momentary outcry was caused by a strange and thrilling sensation in her head, and her explanation of the singular occurrence was that "her faith had made her whole."

Mr. Burchard felt called to the ministry, and commenced the preparation for it by private study, removing in 1820 to Sackett's Harbor to continue this course in the home of a sister residing there. Rev. Mr. Snowdon, his pastor, invited him to take charge of his weekly evening meeting.

There was soon a rising interest, especially among Christians. Mr. Burchard suggested that they make requests for supplication in behalf of impenitent friends, to increase their mutual sympathy and spirit of prayer. This was the earliest resort on record to any of those unusual methods for promoting a revival, which, at a later date, were called "new measures." The deacons of the church, and "black Jonah," united with Mr. Burchard in observing an appointed hour in prayer for the descent of the Spirit with saving power. The work of conversion went forward, including, in its sweep, the families of the naval officers stationed there.

Mr. Burchard went into neighborhoods near, and held evening meetings, which were attended with conversions. Rev. Mr. Gale, pastor at Adams, not many miles distant, invited him to supply while he was absent, and, as Mr. Burchard was not licensed, to read on the Sabbath Burder's sermons. This he did, with his own remarks and earnest appeals at the close. When the pastor returned, a revival had commenced, during the progress of which Charles G. Finney, then a law student, was converted. Not long afterwards Mr. Burchard was licensed by the "Black River Association." Rev. Dr. Aiken, pastor of the First Presbyterian Church, Utica, invited him there to assist in evening services for conference and prayer. The evangelist very soon entered fully on his work, and his labors extended widely through New York and into some of the New England States. It is rarely, indeed, that a man has more unsparing enemies in and out of the church; but, having traced his experience till before the public as an evangelist, we shall add, on the other hand, extracts from narratives published not only in local papers, but in the "New York Evangelist," and other well-known periodicals, as the best possible testimony to the general character and results of his evangelistic career. These communications, which have come into our hands, would make no mean volume. We quote from a letter to the "Evangelist," of two columns, from Rev. Dr. Hopkins, Auburn, N. Y., under date of March 10, 1833 : —

"Dear Brother Leavitt, — We have just closed a protracted meeting; and as it may occasion reports injurious to the cause of Christ, on account of its length and other circumstances, and especially as it has been the means, under God, of the conversion of many souls, I take this opportunity to give you a brief account of the manner in which it was conducted. It commenced on Wednesday, the 30th of January; and with the exception of two days, on which a part of the meetings were suspended, it continued with four exercises in each day till Sabbath evening, the 3d of March, making thirty-three days. Indeed, we continued to have two meetings on each day, till last evening, amounting in all to forty days.

"Reasons for its unusual Length. — Since 1826, there has been a class of men in this village and vicinity, some of which were men of extensive influence, who were so bitterly opposed to all religious effort, that, so far as religious influence is concerned, they were out of our reach. When we saw that God was answering our own prayers, and making the wickedness and opposition of men contribute as a means to their conversion, and that by this means we had a lever under the very foundation of iniquity, we were determined to hold on.

"The Efforts which were Blessed. — The subject of a protracted meeting, as the means of a revival, was kept before the minds of the church and congregation for many weeks, both in the preaching and the public prayers. Committees were appointed by the seniors to visit the parish; and, by dividing it into districts, almost the whole population in the village and adjacent country were visited immediately previous to the commencement of the meeting, and solicited to attend.

"Another means which has contributed in no small degree to the success we have witnessed, and which has preserved, so far as we can learn, the most entire harmony and union in the church, was the adoption, in the most solemn manner, of a series of resolutions. These resolutions bound the members of the church to avoid those things, such as talking about the preaching, the prayers, the measures, etc., by which the success of such meetings is too often prevented, and directed them to look at their own responsibility, and to confine their minds and their labors to their own appropriate duties. Teams were employed to bring such as were poor, and such as had no means of conveyance, from day to day to the meetings. Not a small number of the church were constantly employed in looking up impenitent sinners, and persuading them to attend. From the second day to the close of the meeting the labors were performed by Rev. Jedediah Burchard and myself, and the eldership. For thirty-three days, Brother Burchard attended a meeting of the anxious, which cost him great labor, in the morning, and preached in the afternoon and evening of each day.

"The purposes of God, as consistent with human agency, and as furnishing the only ground of hope, the entire moral depravity of the natural heart, and regeneration by the agency of the Spirit and the instrumentality of the word, were the prominent doctrines which were present in the preaching. Concerning the measures, I would only state — as reports have gone abroad injurious to the character of this people, to the brother that labored with us, and to the cause of religion generally — that they were substantially such as have been practised in the churches in New England for years, such as were adopted with my consent, and such as God has been pleased to bless.

"RESULTS OF THE MEETING. — The meeting, in point of the numbers who attended the preaching, was sustained to the last ; and the church seemed better prepared to carry on the meeting when it closed, than when it had been in progress but a few days. The number of converts, making every allowance, is large ; many of them, however, belong to the neighboring towns and congregations, and will most likely unite with the churches where they live. I shall not attempt to state precisely what the number is, but leave it to the great day to decide. The number that were hopefully the subjects of this work, in each day after the second or third, varied from five to fifteen or twenty. In these are included persons of every age, from that of children up to that of sixty or seventy. Among them are a large number of heads of families, and of young men in the prime of life. Where persons have taken great pains to bring their friends from a distance, their labors have been signally blessed. On the whole, the Lord has done great things for this people, for which we would be grateful, and take our places in the dust at his feet. In some respects it has been such a day as Auburn never saw. The important truth that God is ever ready to bless the efforts of his people, which is to elevate the Christian character, and do much for preparing men for millennial faithfulness and success, has received additional confirmation by this meeting.

"Efforts for the Conversion of Children. — The success which has attended the efforts of Mrs. Burchard, who has labored with a commendable zeal, perseverance, and interest for the conversion of the children, I am not able to state. These efforts, however, have left a deep conviction, that, if a system can be adopted by which the impression of the moral obligation can be planted upon the mind while young, or the mind brought to feel its responsibility to God, it is the most favorable of any period in life to labor for the salvation of souls. That such a system can and will be devised, I firmly believe, and that efforts made with children are soon to be the most successful in the great work of converting the world."

Rev. Wm. Wisner, D. D., of Rochester; wrote in a published pamphlet, the same year : —

"The first week in March was spent by the second church, and by some dear brethren from other churches, as an entire week of prayer for *the salvation of Rochester.* The Monday following was kept as a day of fasting and humiliation before God. Tuesday and Wednesday were spent in religious exercises, and a few were hopefully converted to Christ under the preaching of several of the members of the Rochester Presbytery, which was then in session in this place.

"On Thursday, the 14th of March, Rev. Jedediah Burchard, who had kindly accepted an invitation to assist us, commenced his labors, and the spirit of God seemed to accompany them. In the course of a few days an aspect of seriousness had spread itself very extensively over our village. By the 28th of March, the work had become general; the meetings of inquiry were crowded, and hundreds were already rejoicing in hope.

"There have been, since the 14th day of March, about six hundred persons, who, in the judgment of charity, were converted to God within the walls of the second church, exclusive of the children of Sabbath schools, of whom between two and three hundred are indulging hopes.

"The converts are of all classes, and are by no means confined to the village. The substantial yeomanry of the surrounding country came in to see what the Lord was doing for Rochester; and many of them, when they heard, gladly received the word of life, and returned home to serve and glorify God. Numbers, who were journeying through the place, stopped long enough to become experimentally acquainted with that blessed personage who is yet to 'sprinkle many nations,' and, like the eunuch of old, went on their way rejoicing.

"The instruction given, both to saints and sinners, has been substantially the same that the second church have been in the habit of receiving for two years past. Christians have been taught that the salvation of God must come out of Zion; that revivals did not depend upon the eloquence of the preacher, nor upon any system of measures, but upon the truth of God set home to the heart of the sinner, by the Holy Ghost sent down from heaven; and that this descent of the heavenly Comforter was not to be expected but in answer to the agonizing and believing prayers of God's people.

"The measures, adopted in the progress of this work, have been such as the exigencies of the day seemed to require. There has been, for the most of the time, a prayer-meeting and meeting of inquiry in the forenoon, and preaching in the afternoon and evening. In the meeting of inquiry, sinners have been taught that God was waiting to be gracious, and have been urged to an immediate compliance with the terms of salvation.

"The young converts have been assembled, as far as possible, every morning, in a room by themselves, to receive instruction and be examined in regard to their hope ; and those who have given in this way an opportunity for us to become acquainted with them, appear to have obtained a good hope through grace. One hundred and eighty have already united with the second church, and many have gone to other churches ; while numbers have so much reverence for the *good old way*, that they prefer testing the genuineness of their hope, by living a few months in disobedience to Christ, before they venture upon a public profession.

"CHILDREN. — Upon this subject, the writer is aware that he must go abreast of the unbelief of the church. There are comparatively but few Christians who have faith enough, either to pray for the conversion of little children, or to feel much gratitude to God when these neglected ones profess to hope in Christ. But, notwithstanding all the infidelity which is abroad upon this subject, the Bible looks forward to a period, when Christians 'shall be called the seed of the blessed of the Lord, and their offspring with them.' Of these predicted blessings, the churches in Rochester have received a joyful earnest, in the hopeful conversion of hundreds of the children. In this work, Mrs. Burchard, who had her attention called to the subject by the early death of an only child, has been a distinguished instrument. She, with the aid of a number of the 'mothers in Israel,' had these tender lambs committed to her care ; and the result has been such as before stated in this narrative.

"CONCLUSION. — In closing the narrative of this precious work, the writer would take the liberty of affectionately calling upon his brethren to inquire if something more than is doing may not be done, by the ministry of reconciliation, to bring a deeper work of grace into the hearts of Christians, and to let the gospel have free course, that it may be glorified in the salvation of millions, instead of thousands, of the human family. At the rate that salvation is now flowing, it only requires the arithmetic of a common schoolboy to determine that the millennium can never come in. With all our revivals, and with all the exertions which are making, even in our own favored land, the moral desolations are thickening around us."

Rev. James B. Shaw, D. D., of Rochester, wrote in 1850 : —

"The Rev. J. Burchard labored in my church during the winter of 1841. A powerful revival attended his efforts, and a large number united with the church. These converts appear as well as any similar number of converts that I have ever known, and many of them are now among the most active and consistent Christians that we have. Mr. Burchard's preaching was always sound, occasionally very eloquent. No measures were adopted but such as the pastor approved, as the services were under his exclusive direction. Nor was anything done which did or could grieve any lover of truth and order. During the same winter Mrs. Burchard held meetings for mothers and children, which were highly useful and very discreetly conducted. I know of no female in this department of Christian effort to be compared with Mrs. Burchard, and I hope she may so far regain her shattered health as to resume a work for which she is so peculiarly fitted. Her name among us is still ' as ointment poured forth.'"

From Le Roy, Cazenovia, Camden, Homer, Watertown, and nearly every town in Jefferson and Lewis Counties, from Montpelier, Windsor, and other places in Vermont, from towns far distant from each other, and from different denominations, similar statements were sent to the press. Several of the revivals were of great extent and power. We also quote from the private letters of those who intimately knew Mr. Burchard. Dr. Steele of Auburn writes : —

"In the winter of 1834, Rev. Mr. Burchard preached in our church, and was much blessed in his labors ; many were added to us, whom we trust are or will be saved.

"His manner of presenting the truth was very different from Mr. Finney's ; but his preaching was accompanied with much prayer, and systematic effort on the part of the church from house to house. Sleighs were sent out to bring in the poor, and garments furnished to keep them warm ; and it seemed as though the Lord said, 'According to your faith be it unto you.' For I knew of one of our Christian brethren who went twenty miles to bring in a relative to attend the meetings, feeling that if he would only consent to come he would be converted. He came, and he returned giving glory to God. To-day there are those among us, precious fruits as results of Brother B.'s labors here.

"Many were added to our and other churches here, and numbers as a consequence to the churches in towns around. For it was very much noised abroad, and "many came to hear and see if these things were so."

Writes Rev. O. Parker, one of the earliest converts under his preaching : —

"Mr. Burchard was a man of medium size, of fair, intelligent countenance, dark hair and eyes, very nervous and restless. His conversational powers were very fine and very instructive. A flood of light flowed from his lips in anecdote and historic allusions. He was the life and soul of the social circles. His voice was perfect melody. His descrip-

tive powers were of the highest order. He had perfect
control of his hearers, and would lead them to adopt any
measures he proposed. He had enemies not a few, and had
faults which his friends could see, but no charges against
him of any moral improprieties. During his whole labors
as an evangelist, he met with great opposition from ministers
and others unfriendly to revivals ; and a strong prejudice
was created against evangelists, which has been gradually
giving way. Mr. Burchard had some peculiarities which
were visible to all and made very prominent by overstating
and misrepresentations of his enemies. While laboring
in Vermont, a stenographer followed him from place to place,
taking down his remarks, his prayers and sermons, giving
a burlesque view of his labors, and published them to the
world,—a mere caricature of his work. In his meetings,
there were often much excitement and animal feeling. The
instruction to the inquirers and young converts was thorough and sound; and the most of the conversions were
genuine, and held out well, and made active Christians.
I have gone right over the same track, and have labored
on the same field or near by, and have found much abiding
fruit of his labors in every place. I was passing through
Peoria, Ill., and stopped with Deacon Pettingill, an influential member of the Congregational Church of that place.
In conversation, accidentally, Mrs. Pettingill, a very pious
and intelligent lady, remarked that ' she was converted in
one of Mr. Burchard's meetings in Vermont.' Mr. Pettingill said, ' I was converted in Mr. Burchard's meeting in
Lockport;' and I replied, ' And I was converted in Mr.
Burchard's meeting in Adams, N. Y.' So three old people,
converted in his meetings in different places over forty years
before, met nearly one thousand miles away from them.
I met with many ministers, now living and laboring like
myself, who were brought into the kingdom, and got their
first impulses to preach the gospel from Mr. Burchard.

"Mrs. Burchard always accompanied and assisted her husband in his labors. She was a perfect balance-wheel to him, having lost her only child, a beautiful daughter of seven years, who had sought first the kingdom of heaven, and was thus early prepared to die. Mrs. Burchard's attention was early called to the fact, and the necessity of an early conversion; and she made this her life-work, in which she met with great success. I have often met with gray-headed men, who pointed back to her meeting as the time and place of their conversion. She was a wise, judicious, and accomplished lady, who still survives her husband."

His fast driving, in his travel from place to place, was often made a point of unfavorable remark. That, in obedience to the very law of temperament, he sometimes went over the ground more rapidly than was necessary, is probably true; but that he was ever cruel in this we have not the least evidence. The same mental and physical constitution led him to sudden, and even abrupt, transitions of thought and expression. We recollect a young man who related to us, that, having returned to his native town, where he had known Mr. Burchard, in a revival meeting soon after, Mr. Burchard, while talking with the anxious, coming to him, inquired "when he came back," and of his success, then passed on to the next pew, to renew his spiritual counsel. This was entirely characteristic; and so were his somewhat sensational methods of getting the people to attend upon the means of grace. An illustration of the last eccentricity occurs to us. In the city of Owego, when a series of meetings was opened, at first the attendance was not large; and notice was given that he would preach a "hen sermon," which filled the church. Mr. Burchard gave a gospel sermon on the words of Christ while weeping over Jerusalem: "How often would I have gathered you, as a hen gathers her brood under her wings, and ye would not." The question, including all others, returns : the general results, the effect of his efforts, in the long run, upon the communities in which he was employed by pastors and churches. We are unable to find any disastrous, or even seriously evil, consequences; on the contrary, the testimony of those who are competent judges, if any persons can be, is uniformly favorable, with expressions of confidence in the general fruits of his ministry.

We cannot, therefore, escape the conclusion, from all the evidence before us, that the blessings attending Mr. Burchard's labors cast into eclipse any injurious consequences to the churches or communities to which he was invited. That his style of preaching was adapted to produce the highest results among those well instructed in divine truth, and needing the awakening appeal to move them to decisive action under the Spirit's revealing light, we think is true.

But he was no unimportant actor in the wide-spread evangelism of the second quarter of the nineteenth century. He died peacefully in Adams, N. Y., in 1864, leaving his devoted wife and co-laborer a widow, who still survives him.

Rev. O. Parker, who was converted under Mr. Burchard's preaching, was a co-worker with the brethren departed. His harvest-work has been largely in the Empire State. He has reached a vigorous old age in almost unceasing itinerancy among the churches ; as a rule seeking the quieter parishes, and supplementing very usefully the more conspicuous services of those called to do their work at the great centres of secular and religious activity. He has probably been longer in the field, and conducted a larger number of meetings, than any other American evangelist.

It is also true, that few itinerant preachers have moved more noiselessly over their fields of labor. This evangelist, was born in Methuen, on the 9th of October, 1800, the fourth son in a family of eight children of almost unprecedented longevity, averaging seventy-six years before any death occurred in the circle. Without property, friends, or patronage, Orson carved out his own fortune.

In 1821 he commenced the study of law with the Hon. T. C. Chittenden, of Adams, Jefferson County, N. Y., Mr. Finney being a student at law at the same time in that village. In 1826 Mr. Parker married Celestine Gridley, and became the law partner of Mr. Chittenden. In 1831 he became a Christian, and left the law for preparation to enter the Theological Seminary at Auburn. We give his own account of his conversion and the events upon which his whole subsequent life turned. "In my boyhood I was thrown into the society and under the influence of many professed believers in Universalism, as at that time the doctrine was very prevalent in Jefferson County. I attended their meetings, I read their books and periodicals, I readily embraced their views, and became a believer in and an advocate of their doctrine, and as a general thing I believed as they believed; I fortified myself with their arguments, their books, and their pamphlets, and felt myself strong in my belief. In the hour of present personal danger I felt no misgivings about the stability of my hope, but there were other times when I wavered in view of the permanency of my foundation. I saw that to those with whom I associated, the subject of religion was dreaded, prayer unwelcome, and those things which most comforted the Christian were avoided; and although they might say, ' We are not afraid to die; we are willing to trust ourselves in the hands of a merciful God,' I saw how little Universalism supported them in the final hour. I would ask myself, ' When I am a dying man shall I not feel the need of something I do not possess?' Then again

19

I would dismiss my anxiety, and reason, 'It is very natural that all who have heard about a preparation for death, who are on what others call disputed ground, should have their fears aroused,' and I would settle down and rest all of my vast interest for eternity upon the truth of that doctrine. But while confiding in and advocating that belief, I lost my little boy, and soon my young Christian wife wasted away with disease and urged me to read the Bible and examine my hope of meeting her in heaven. I promised to do so, supposing that Universalism was in the Bible, and that I should find it there. I saw her die a happy death,— her soul launch off upon the ocean of God's eternal love; and though it was transition to her, it was *death* to me. I there saw the power of religion in a dying hour. While I yet believed in Universalism, I rejoiced only in her Christian hope; for I felt that with her all doubt was removed. My belief did not comfort me; I turned to the Bible to redeem my pledge. As I read it unbiassed, to know the truth, although I could find the passages I had so often quoted, in their connection they did not support Universalism. But so prejudiced was I against the orthodox religion, and such my views of God and His character, that I began to question its truth; to believe that if it did not prove Universalism it could not be true, and to find what I called inconsistencies, discrepancies, incredible stories, and apparent sanction of oppression, cruelty, and injustice, till I was on the point of discarding the Bible as a divine revelation, when I decided to attend the protracted meetings which Mr. Burchard, the evangelist, was holding in Adams, and give the subject a fair and candid examination. There I saw that I had embraced a sentiment, but not a Saviour; that I had taken refuge in a mere belief, and not in Christ; and that my superstructure was resting on the sand, and not on the rock. I there came to myself, and saw that like the deranged man, I had reasoned correctly but from wrong premises, which brought me all the time to wrong conclusions. I gave myself to Jesus. I then felt it my duty to go and tell the story to others, and point them to the blood of Christ which cleanseth from all sin."

Mr. Parker soon after left the practice of the law and went to Auburn Seminary, and when licensed and ordained to preach the gospel, labored with Mr. Burchard in protracted meetings, and soon took charge of his old church in Belleville. After laboring there one year he was employed as a missionary evangelist, to hold meetings and build up churches in the bounds of the Black River Association. It was then that he began to hold meetings for the special object of promoting revivals; and as the Lord blessed his labors, he has been constantly engaged in this itinerant work for the last forty years. Although he has held meetings in Boston, Washington, New York, Albany, Buffalo, Detroit, and in other large cities, his labors have been principally confined to the country churches in the Eastern, Middle, and Western States. He has been constantly in protracted meetings, leaving the interest when apparently safe to do so, going directly from one field of labor to another, and without rest from active service during the seasons for holding such meetings.

He has been a man of very great endurance and perfect health. In his seventy-fifth year he commenced preaching in September, and continued till May without a day's rest, except when passing from town to town, averaging fifteen sermons each week, besides attending and taking charge of a daily prayer-meeting. Mr. Parker's success, under God, is due mainly to his strength of endurance and indomitable perseverance, his simplicity in presenting truth, and his remarkable powers of adaptation and illustration. His ability to make every point plain by striking figures and vivid illustrations is seldom equalled.

Mr. Parker is the author of the tract, "The Way to be Saved by One Thirty-five Years in the Inquiry-Room," a work of great merit, and highly recommended for its clearness in answering every objection, meeting every excuse, and removing every difficulty in the way of the sinner, and in leading him directly to Christ.   In anticipation of visiting England, to take part in the great revival in London, many ministers, of different presbyteries and different denominations, gave Mr. Parker the following recommendation : —

"Whereas Rev. O. Parker is desirous of visiting England to engage in the great revival now going on in London, we take pleasure in saying that we consider Mr. Parker one of our oldest, ablest, and most successful American evangelists, and we cordially recommend him to the favor of any church or pastor who may desire the aid of a judicious, experienced, safe assistant in revival efforts."

Mr. Parker says of revival efforts : —

"Ordinarily, no pastor is able to do the whole of the preaching in a special effort and the necessary labor with the inquirers : when he attempts it, without aid, his task becomes too great for him to endure, and he is obliged to submit to a limited blessing ; and when a neighboring pastor is called in, if he has the requisite experience, he cannot often leave his own people long enough to complete the work he begins.   In view of this state of things, I have devoted my ministerial life to the labors of an evangelist.

"I lay no claim to perfection in holding meetings, but I think no pastor can be found who will say that the attachment of his people has ever been weakened, or he driven from his parish, or his church divided, by my labors in his congregation.   I have assisted in settling a thousand difficulties in churches, and I have no knowledge of one ever growing out of my labors with a church as an evangelist.

"Why a revival of religion becomes necessary is, because the mind of the people in the church, and out of it, is turned away from a direct effort of promoting religion, and flows in a worldly or pleasure-taking current, and all the thinking, planning, scheming, and acting is in this direction. Now, before a general revival of religion can be expected, an influence must be brought to bear so continuously and forcibly upon the mind as to turn that current into a new channel of religious talking, thinking, and acting. Get people to think, and they will be convicted. Hold the mind in that state, and conversion will follow.

"The Lord generally comes to the pastor or some faithful watchman of his flock, and often in the darkest time, and 'just before day,' as he did to Noah, Lot, Moses, Nehemiah, Ezekiel; 'Can these bones live?' The set time to favor Zion is when the people have a mind to work, as in 2 Chron. vii. 14. 'If my people, which are called by my name, shall humble themselves and pray, and seek my face, and turn from their wicked ways, then will I hear from heaven and will forgive their sins and heal their land.'

"I use but little machinery in my meetings, depending instrumentally, almost entirely, upon prayer, the preached word, singing, visiting, tract distribution, and those social and home influences which the Holy Spirit, in a noiseless, dispassionate manner, uses to pervade the entire community."

We add a few statements of pastors respecting the work of this evangelist : —

John Ballard, Pastor of Presbyterian Church, Perry, Ill., says, "His labors in my society were very successful, and the result very happy and satisfactory. He leaves a healthy influence behind him, and is remembered by the

people with gratitude and affection. His labors strengthen ·
the bands of union between the pastor and the church, and
leave no wound to fester or give pain after he is gone."

Rev. L. W. Dunlap, Pastor of Presbyterian Church,
Mt. Sterling, Ill., writes, "His congregation was composed of Old and New School Presbyterians, and there is
but one sentiment pervading both classes, and that of
entire approbation and satisfaction, both as to doctrine
and the manner of his conducting his meetings."

Rev. Jeremiah Porter, Pastor of Presbyterian Church,
Green Bay, Wis., February 9, 1857: "Myself and my
church have enjoyed his labors for the past month most
highly. His success in reclaiming backsliders and in
winning sinners to Christ has seemed wonderful Some
one hundred and twenty-five of this class occupied distinctive seats to listen to his counsel and advice to young
converts; forty were men, some of them gray-headed and
far advanced in age."

Rev. S. P. Marvin, Pastor of Congregational Church,
Franklin, N. Y., February 7, 1859: "Rev. O. Parker has
labored for the last four weeks in connection with the First
Congregational Church of this place with great success,
and marked tokens of God's blessing upon his labors.
He is chaste and simple in his style, pure in doctrine,
energetic in delivery, pointed in his appeals, close in reasoning, and eminently felicitous in his illustrations of
doctrines. I shall ever prize the season we have passed
together here as one of the most happy and profitable of
my life."

Wm. M. Martin, Pastor of Old School Presbyterian
Church, Woodbridge, N. J., May 31, 1859: "We have
just passed through the most gracious series of religious
services ever known in this region. We engaged the services of the Rev. O. Parker: the result has realized our
highest hopes. The people of God have been greatly

quickened, and established in faith and duty. From the world, the middle, the aged, and the young have been the subjects of this work. Thirty-five heads of families, some of them the most wealthy and influential in the community, many that had passed through all of the revivals of a lifetime, men of most unyielding resistance to truth in former seasons, have bowed; also between fifty and sixty single persons of all ages, among them several remarkable instances of the power of religion in the young. In all of this work there has been no excitement, — no reprehensible occurrence.

Rev. D. K. Turner, Pastor of the Nehomany Presbyterian Church,* Hartsville, Pa., December 26, 1857 : "Rev. O. Parker, to the success and blessed influence of whose labors so favorable testimonials have been given above, has been laboring in this place for nearly three weeks, and the presence of the Holy Spirit has been with him and has been felt in many hearts. He has deeply interested and profited all who have attended the services in the sanctuary. A precious revival of religion has been commenced, and many have felt, as they never did before, the power of divine truth. Christians have been greatly refreshed, backsliders have been reclaimed, and a large number of the impenitent have been hopefully converted. The entire result of the protracted meeting, in which Mr. Parker has so judiciously and faithfully labored, can only be known in eternity; but his efforts have had the seal of the divine approbation, and the cause of Christ has gained a deeper and stronger hold on the community."

We have not been able to get the history of still another sound and successful worker of the same general period, Rev. Mr. Avery, who did excellent service in New York and also at the West, where we understand he is at pres-

* The Old Church of William Tennant, Sr.

ent residing, nor can we give a record of the many who, by co-operation, and occasional campaigns on their own account, have been a part of this widely-felt instrumentality, to which the churches owe a greater debt of gratitude than not a few intelligent Christian people have been willing to believe.

CHAPTER XVII.

The First Methodist American Evangelist Abroad. — James Caughey. — His Emigration to this Country. — Conversion. — Enters the Ministry. — Deep Experiences. — A Call to England and Ireland. — Marvellous Success. — Peculiarities and Power.

EARLY in the present century a vessel containing emigrants from Ireland brought to our shores a young man destined to return after a lapse of more than thirty years upon a mission of remarkable interest. Soon after his arrival, this waif from a foreign clime came under Christian influences which led him to Christ. Two years passed, and he was a "preacher on probation" in the Methodist Church. In 1834 he received deacon's orders, and in 1836 he was ordained elder. A sentence or two from the works of Dr. Adam Clarke arrested his attention, with wonderful effect. These words of the departed divine stated very forcibly the powerlessness of preaching to accomplish the end contemplated without the presence of the Holy Ghost, until, under that luminous agency, the sinner is compelled to cry, " God have mercy on me, a sinner!" " Save, Lord, or I perish! Heal my soul for it hath sinned against Thee ! " After expressing his " eternal cause of thankfulness that those sentiments ever came under his notice," he says, " On the evening of that never-to-be-forgotten day in which I read them, I took my pen in secret before God, and gave vent to the emotions of my deeply-impressed heart, in language like the following : I see, I feel now, as I have never done before, on this particular subject. From the convictions of this hour,

I hope, by the grace of God, never to vary. I see, I feel :

"1st.   The absolute necessity of the immediate influence of the Holy Ghost to impart point, power, efficacy, and success to a preached gospel.

"2d.   The absolute necessity of praying more frequently, more fervently, more perseveringly, and more believingly, for the aid of the Holy Spirit in my ministry.

"3d.   That my labors must be powerless and comfortless and valueless without this aid.   A cloud without water, a tree without fruit, dead and rootless ; a sound uncertain, unctionless, and meaningless, — such will be the character of my ministry.   It is the Spirit of God alone which imparts significancy and power to the Word preached, without which, as one has expressed it, 'all the threatenings of the Bible will be no more than thunder to the deaf or lightning to the blind.'   A seal requires weight, a hand upon it, in order to make an impression.   The soul of the penitent sinner.is the wax ; gospel truth is the seal : but, without the almighty hand of the Holy Ghost, that seal is powerless.   A bullet demands its powder, without which it is as harmless as any other body.   The careless sinner is the mark ; truth is the ball that must pierce him : but it cannot reach, much less penetrate him, separate from this influence from heaven.   In apostolic times, they preached the gospel with the Holy Ghost sent down from heaven.   (1 Peter i, 12.)   In our day we need an energy from no lower source, to overturn the wickedness of the vile and profane, and to counteract the formality and worldliness which are everywhere visible.

"4th.   I am now fully persuaded that in proportion as the Spirit of God shall condescend to second my efforts in the gospel message, I shall be successful ; nor need I expect any success beyond.   No man has ever been signally useful in winning souls to Christ without the help of the

Spirit. With it, the humblest talent may astonish earth and hell, by gathering into the path of life thousands for the skies; while without it, the finest, the most splendid talents remain comparatively useless.

"5th. The entire glory of all my success shall henceforth be given to the Holy Spirit. By this I shall conscientiously abide, as by any other principle of our holy religion. It is written, 'They that honor me, I will honor.' To this may be added, that righteous, inalienable, and unchanging determination of Jehovah, 'My glory I will not give to another.'"

This was Mr. Caughey's anointing, by yielding to the Spirit's power. Nevermore could he "rest in sound theory instead of steeping his soul in the truth, until it so filled him that he learned, as by instinct,. to lay all the glory of his labors at the footstool of the eternal God." Referring to his partial success in his first parish, because, as he saw afterwards, there was wanting a wise adaptation of the truth and means to secure salvation, he wrote to a brother in the ministry : —

" I now saw the necessity of turning my attention to that style of preaching which would be likely, by the aid of the Holy Ghost, to awaken sinners, and bring penitents to God. Revival artillery I resolved to have. I fasted and prayed, and searched the Scriptures. My reading, thinking, conversation, and all my observations, were laid under contribution to one end, — preparation for soul saving, which I now perceived to be the main end of the gospel ministry. My little stock of sermons suitable for a revival increased rapidly. When a text presented itself as suitable for a revival, my cry was, 'Lord God, open the eyes of my understanding; give me a clear perception of thy meaning in this passage.' A forenoon was generally spent upon my knees, pleading for divisions and subdivisions; sometimes a simple proposition was presented. Having completed my 'skeleton,' I returned to my knees, and pleaded for an introduction, and that flesh and sinews might come upon these dry bones. And the pleading was not in vain ; thoughts of a moving character came into my mind in troops. Having finished the rough outline, it was folded up till next day. On the morrow I returned to my knees, read the subject over, expunged such extraneous and super- fluous matter as only tended to load the memory and encum- ber the subject, but retained all that had point and was likely to do execution among sinners. The Holy Scriptures were then called in, to prove or illustrate the sentiments ; commentators were referred to ; and lastly my private Journal and Common-Place Book. It is proper to remark that I had long attended to that advice given by an aged American minister to a young preacher : 'This I would advise you : wherever you, in any reading, meet with a curious illustration, prize it, seize it, enter it in papers where you may design a lodging for such inestimable jewels. Like Hezekiah, have your treasures for precious stones ; and let these be such unto you. Get such an amassment of them that among them you may be like the king of Tyrus, and "walk up and down in the midst of the stones of fire," when you are upon the holy mountain of God. One of these may be like an ingot of gold, and a whole discourse may be rendered acceptable by having such a jewel studded in it.' After walking thus in the mount with God, among my *jewels* and *stones of fire*, some original, others by right of conquest, and collecting such as were calculated to move an assembly,— supposing I could do nothing more with them at present, the written outline was brought to the footstool of God, thus : 'O Lord God of hosts, God of the armies of Israel, and Head of the Church, I ask thy acceptance of my body, soul, and spirit, and of this my humble offering,— this outline of a sermon, which I now present to Thee. Forgive all that may be

wrong in it, or which savors of human infirmity ; and grant
that, wherever and whenever it shall be preached, the
power of the Holy Ghost may attend it to the hearts of
sinners and believers. Grant that I may obtain, by its
instrumentality, thousands of souls to my ministry, from
the ranks of wickedness, through Jesus Christ my Lord!
For this, and the pardon of all my sins, and the purifica-
tion of my nature, I offer the atonement of the Saviour.
I trust in the blood of Jesus Christ, thy Son ; I cast myself
upon it by faith, and upon the veracity of Christ Jesus in
that promise, 'What things soever ye desire when ye
pray, believe that ye receive them, and ye shall have them.'
I have desired these things, I have prayed for them, and
I do receive what I have asked, agreeably to Thy will.'

"The sermon was then placed among kindred subjects,
and carefully put away, under the label ' REVIVAL '; and
I held myself in readiness to take up another text in a
similar manner.

" But you will inquire, 'Did you not preach them immediately to your people?' Sometimes I did so, but not
always ; nor could I, the ordinary services being so few.
I considered myself only in preparation for a campaign ;
that I was just getting my ammunition and engines of war
in readiness for a great battle."

He then vividly describes an attack upon the " powers
of darkness " strongly entrenched in his field of activity,
resulting in a great victory, and thus speaks of the opposition of some ministers : —

" I am fully persuaded, the reason why some preachers
are averse to what are called ' revival movements' is not
because they have no desire for the conversion of sinners ;
nor from a conviction that God has not called them to
bring sinners to repentance, for they frequently attempt
it ; nor because they have no talents for such an effort ;
but chiefly for the want of proper pulpit preparations

to begin and carry forward a revival. Although they may
have a respectable stock of sermons, which procure them
a rank, deservedly, among the accomplished theologians of
the day, yet the engaging a very few times in preaching
would exhaust their capital; and then, to come forward
with 'long, commonplace sermons,' as unfit for producing immediate and beneficial effect in a revival as snow
upon a harvest-field, would disappoint even the expectations of sinners, discourage penitents, and weary and
unfit believers to enter the prayer-meeting with life and
zeal. Hence the preachers on whom I have ventured to
animadvert are shy of making full proof of their call to
the work of the ministry in this way; and when the matter
is pressed home upon the conscience of one of these, he
usually resorts to the pitiable apology, 'I have no talent
for these revivals. Every man has his particular gift
All cannot be revivalists. I must therefore proceed in
my own way.'

"Let the inquiry be put to his conscience and understanding by a proper person, 'But, my brother, what is
your way? What are you aiming at in preaching? Upon
what principles did you begin to preach at first? Excuse
the inquiry: what were the secret feelings which prompted
you in the beginning of your career in the ministry? If
the immediate conversion of sinners was not your object,
what was it? Why, for what purpose do you yet enter
the pulpit? Is it not to bring sinners to repentance?
But if you are incapable of conducting a prayer-meeting,
and of kneeling down to pray for a penitent sinner, to
whom must the church of God look? If you are incapaci-
tated to point a trembling sinner to the Lamb of God, and
to tell him how to believe, to whom must the unhappy
soul resort? Do you say, 'I make such things known in
the pulpit, and that is the place for the performance of my
duty?' But St. Paul preached Jesus 'from house to house,'

and 'with many tears': is it, therefore, improper to do the same thing in a prayer-meeting under circumstances so interesting?

"I cannot close without an allusion to your mental conflicts. Have you not read Augustine's advice to a young minister, *Prepara te ad pressuras?* To which a good man added, 'When a man enters upon the work of preaching the gospel, he finds himself speedily, as it were, in the wine-press.' It is seldom the following sentiments of one now with God have failed to be realized, in one way or other, in my experience: 'You will hardly ever be engaged in any special service for the kingdom of God, but you will, either just before it or after it, meet with some special trouble, either from some failure of your health, or in some storm of groundless obloquies among the people, or, which is worst of all, some horrid *colaphisations* from wicked spirits on your mind, strongly filling you with consternations and confusions, which, be they ever so unreasonable, yet will be intolerable.'

"It is in the latter way I have hitherto chiefly suffered, although I have had my trials from most of the above sources; but the onsets of those cruel and invisible spirits upon my mind have often been terrible."

Of the progress of another revival, he says: —

"We were not trammelled in our efforts by rich and time-serving professors, nor by any who were anxious we should obtain or retain the approbation of the wealthy. There was no sensation created on the appearance of influential persons in the congregation, lest they might take offence and leave the church, possibly to return no more. We were troubled with no officials cautioning us against giving offence, with a 'Peradventure, such and such persons will withdraw from the church and withhold hereafter their support.'

"Never, I assure you, did a besieging army bombard a

city with greater confidence of beholding a surrender than we felt when beleaguering these sinners. Speculations were never more rife, outside the walls of a besieged city, as to what part of the walls would be likely to give way and cause a breach, than were the speculations among some as to what sinner, or what class of sinners, would first break down under the truth, and cause a gap in the ranks of sin. As the crisis approached, our congregations increased; our all-absorbing feelings seemed to pervade the people; but none had sufficient courage to brave the gaze of the multitude, and separate himself as a stricken sinner.

"Night had succeeded to night, and day to day, without any conversions. The sword of the Lord appeared to us as if blunted against the hardened mass; the arrows of truth rebounded from flinty hearts as if they had been shot against a stone wall.

"The time of extremity was God's opportunity. Is there anything too hard for Jehovah? 'Nothing but quite impossible, is hard.' 'God is terrible out of His holy places,' says the psalmist. He speaks, and it is done; He commands, and it stands fast. 'Pompey boasted,' said one, 'that with one stamp of his foot he could raise all Italy in arms: but God, with one word of His mouth, could raise, not all Italy only, but all heaven.' He is wonderful in working. He humbles human pride, and secures His own glory by rendering our plans and efforts useless for a time, and bringing about His purposes by the humblest and weakest instrumentality. One of our company, a minister, in the course of his visitations from house to house, thought proper to extend his visits of mercy to a black-smith's shop, in which were several men at work, most of whom were very wicked; the voice of profane swearing often sounded out from it horribly. One of the young men was shoeing a horse when our friend entered, and did not observe his approach. He suddenly advanced, and whispered sharply in the ear of the busy sinner, 'You must have *your* feet shod with the preparation of the gospel of peace.' The man was taken by surprise, as much, perhaps, as if the horse had struck him. He hastily raised his head, discovered the author of this strange salute, dropped it again, muttered something, and fell a-hammering a nail into the shoe violently. The word was a nail fastened in a sure place. The Spirit of God was there, and drove it into the sinner's heart. The minister left the shop without saying any more. That night the man mingled with the crowd which entered the church, and at the close of the sermon presented himself as a distressed and condemned sinner, soliciting 'prayer and help.' A number of others, quite as unhappy as himself, were soon by his side, when they all raised their cry together, 'Lord have mercy!' This was the hour of our triumph. Now we witnessed a scene which repaid us for all our toil. The young smith, with many more, obtained salvation the same evening. From that night the work of God went on in majesty and power.

"Let the ministers of any particular church trample under foot that silly objection, that extraordinary means will throw discredit upon the ordinary. Rather let them decide that the former, if successful, must, in the nature of the case, confer honor upon the ordinary services."

Mr. Caughey was soon called to an experience of most extraordinary and affecting interest. It reminds us of those revelations of the divine will not unfrequently recorded in the Word of God; nor can we deny that it is as truly a "heavenly vision," to which he "was not disobedient." Referring to the unbelief that rejects such divine interposition, he says forcibly, "God has ever delighted to humble the pride of man by bringing about the greatest events by the smallest instrumentality. When disposed to smile

20

at the trivial matter which arrested my mind, and which
prepared it to take such an unusual course, I wish you
would reflect on that verse you have heard me repeat, and
which you so much admire : —

> " A pebble in the streamlet scant
> Has turned the course of many a river ;
> A dew-drop on the baby plant
> Has warped the giant oak forever."

At the Conference of 1839 he was appointed to Whitehall, N. Y. He purposed to marry and become settled in
the home field of service for Christ. But he tells us that
from some reasons which he could not explain " the Lord
seemed to depart from him." Gloom succeeded the noon-
tide glory of the divine presence ; nor could he remove
this singular darkness by any plausible explanation of the
cause, which only deepened hourly upon his troubled spirit.
He waited and wondered, while "God was contending
with him." He was sure the Lord, who had so honored
him with displays of loving majesty, was interposing to
prevent his " stepping out of the order of His providence."
The great longing and determination then was to " regain
his former peace and joy in God." We will listen to his
own graphic words respecting this crisis of infinite concern
to him : —

" The world was a blank, a bleak and howling wilderness, to my soul, without the smiles of my Saviour. In
fact, I could not live, but must wither away from the
face of the earth, without His comforting and satisfying
presence. Like a well-chastised son, I came back to the
feet of my heavenly Father, and with many tears I besought
Him to reveal His face to my soul ; that if my purposes
were crossing His, to show me ; and whatever was His will,
I would at once, by His help, yield my soul unto it. ' Lord
God,' I said, ' if my will crosses thy will, then my will

must be *wrong*; for thine cannot but be *right.*' Now I eared not what He commanded me to do, or to leave undone; I stood ready to obey. I felt assured that clear light from God, on some points, would soon reach my soul, and I was fully prepared for it; but I no more expected such an order as came soon after, than I expected He would command me to fly upward and preach the gospel in another planet. During three days I cried to God, without any answer. On the third day, in the afternoon, I obtained an audience with the Lord. The place was almost as lonely as Sinai, where Moses saw the burning bush. It was under open sky, a considerable distance from the habitations of men; steep rocks and mountains, deep forests and venomous reptiles surrounded me. Here, and in a moment, the following passage was given me to plead: ' And the Lord descended in the cloud, and stood with him there, and proclaimed the name of the Lord. And the Lord passed by before him, and proclaimed, The Lord, the Lord God, merciful and gracious, long-suffering, and abundant in goodness and truth, keeping mercy for thousands, forgiving iniquity and transgression and sin, and that will by no means clear the guilty.' (Exod. xxxiv, 5–7.) I took hold of this; many of the words were as fire, and as a hammer to break the rocks in pieces before the Lord. The fountains of tears were opened, and the great deep of my heart was broken up. I left the place, however, without receiving any light; but my heart was fully softened and subdued, and I felt assured I had prevailed in some way with God. I was confident light and direction were coming, but of what nature I could not tell.

"This was on the 9th of July, 1839. The same evening, about twilight, eternal glory be to God! when reading in a small room adjoining my study, a light, as I conceived from heaven, reached me. My soul was singularly calmed

and warmed by a strange visitation. In the moment I
recognized the change; the following, in substance, was
spoken to my heart, but in a manner and with a rapidity
I cannot possibly describe. Every ray of divine glory
seemed to be a word that the eye of my soul could read, a
sentence which my judgment could perceive and understand: 'These matters which trouble thee must be let
entirely alone. The will of God is that thou shouldst visit
Europe. He shall be with thee there, and give thee many
seals to thy ministry. He has provided thee with funds.
Make thy arrangements accordingly; and next Conference,
ask liberty from the proper authorities, and it shall be
granted thee. Visit Canada first; when this is done, sail
for England. God shall be with thee there, and thou shalt
have no want in all thy journeyings; and thou shalt be
brought back in safety again to America.'

"The above is far beneath the dignity and grandeur of
the impression. It came in a way which left no room for
a doubt. A heavenly calm, a powerful persuasion, and an
intense glow of divine love, accompanied the whole. It
was like the breaking forth of the noonday sun at midnight.
I fell upon my knees before the Lord, my whole mind
consenting to the orders, which I believed had come from
heaven. Oh! the sweetness of that communion I then
enjoyed with God! My sky was cloudless, my rest of
soul unutterable. The meaning of many past providences
was now explained. The possession of a few hundreds of
dollars had often made me very uneasy. I doubted the
propriety of laying up treasure on earth. The cause of
missions stood in need of what I possessed, but still I was
restrained. Now I clearly saw that God had provided me
with these funds in order to make me willing to obey the
call, and to save me from embarrassment in my travels.
I could perceive a special reason why I had pressed forward
in my studies for so many years, and why revival texts and

sermons had occupied so much of my time, — that God
had been thus preparing me for a few campaigns in
Europe.

"I arose from my knees under a strong conviction that
God had called me to take this tour. Letters were written
immediately to Canada, etc. The next day my soul was
calm and happy. My books were unpacked, and everything in my study arranged with a glad heart and free.
Eleven months were before me to criticise the impressions
on my soul. With delight I commenced my pastoral work,
visited from house to house, and had the pleasure of seeing
a most powerful revival of religion in my circuit. During
this period, not the least wish entered my heart to form
any connection or engagement whatever that would entangle or hinder me from fulfilling what I conceived to be
the high and solemn commission I had received from the
Lord. I continued to resign the whole matter to God,
entreating Him to overrule all to His glory, and to hedge
up my way, if it were not His will I should leave America.

To a friend, who stated some objections to Mr. Caughey's
view of his call to Europe, he replied as follows : —

"I think I feel the full weight of every question you
have proposed. I have set them down carefully, one by
one, that you may see they have all arrested my attention ;
and that, writing them off, and having them before my
eyes, I might be affected by them, and answer them most
sincerely. I am not aware, however, that they have created the least uneasiness, or in any degree shaken the
purpose of my heart. My call to visit Europe seems quite
as clear as to preach the gospel. It does seem —

    ' A part of my being beyond my control.'

I candidly admit that there is a thick mist spread over my
usefulness on the other side ; but sometimes, through the
haze, I can see great multitudes of sinners coming home to

God through my instrumentality. I have also a solemn impression that the salvation or damnation of thousands may depend upon whether I obey or reject the call. I may also add, my impression is constant that if I refuse to go, God will permit many troubles to come upon me in America, and that I shall, through future life, be ever after sorry I did not obey."

Mr. Caughey's first evangelistic tour was in Canada, where, in a few months of apostolic sacrifices and fearless prosecution of his calling, five hundred professed conversion. The narrative of this campaign is as stirring as any sacred romance. Upon his return, among other incidents mentioned, is that of revisiting the spot which he named "Providence Path," where the revelation of his mission abroad was made, and where he again had a wonderful season of communion.

May 28, 1841, he sailed from Whitehall for Burlington, Montreal, Quebec, Halifax, and England. He preached nineteen sermons at Quebec; and when he had gone on board the vessel to leave, he opened a note, handed him by a messenger at the moment of starting, from Mary McLeod, enclosing a check of sufficient amount to defray the expenses of his trip to England. The "Britannia" bore him from the harbor of Halifax July 19, 1841, and entered the Mersey the twenty-ninth of the same month, after a pleasant voyage of ten days.

He was a little later at a hotel in Liverpool, a lonely man among utter strangers, with unshaken confidence and calm delight in his Redeemer. After much prayer, the same day he started for Manchester, where Conference was in session.

The introduction to English brethren was pleasant, but with his spirit, uplifted in faith for guidance, he turned his steps again towards Liverpool. There the impression that he must go to Dublin became too strong to be resisted. The next morning, after his arrival at the hotel there, he sallied out to find a Methodist preacher. He was invited to preach at the Hendrick Street Chapel, where, for the first time in Europe, he "opened his commission" from John xvii, 1, " Father ! the hour is come." The impression was profound, and " Who is he ? " " Who sent him here ? " and " He should be invited to preach again," were heard on every hand. In the evening he was again in the pulpit of the chapel, and so clearly was the Spirit moving, that a series of meetings was at once decided upon ; and for several successive days the "glory of the Lord filled the house."

In Limerick, Cork, and other cities, and then in Liverpool, Leeds, Hull, Sheffield, and elsewhere in England, it was a repetition in its remarkable interest of Wesley's and Whitefield's careers, till the number of conversions was put as high as twenty thousand during the six years he was abroad.

We regret much that we have not space to describe some of the thrilling scenes which were witnessed abroad, recorded by Rev. Dr. Wise in "Methodism in Earnest," and also to quote passages of great power from his revival sermons. But we pass to a brief account of Mr. Caughey's characteristics, style of preaching, methods, and his peculiar place in the evangelism of the world.

He is self-educated, and has made himself familiar with the best English classics. Few public speakers have had a richer treasure of fine thoughts and illustrations garnered from the field of general literature. Endowed with a splendid imagination, it was uniformly kept within the region of practical impressions and activity. He reasoned well, but his *forte* was an original and vivid presentation of common truths, so as to rivet the attention and stir the conscience and heart. With intense earnestness he would portray the natural man and the requirements of

God's law, then, send forth the most tender accents of persuasion. With a voice, if not musical, of remarkable compass and flexibility, he could fill any audience-room, and reach the most distant circle of an out-door assemblage.

Mr. Caughey's style of proclaiming the gospel message is highly dramatic. "Standing erect in the pulpit, in the majesty of Christian manhood, his left arm stretched out to its full length and his hand pointing to some imaginary eminence in the dim distance, he bids you, in a voice eloquent with emotion, look at that woman who is anxiously watching the retreating footsteps of our Saviour, as he approaches the house of Simon, the rich Pharisee." Then follows a picture so real, imitating Simon's questioning, and the feet-washing by the penitent woman, the hearer seems to be a guest at that table, or a spectator, at least, through some open door. Equally vivid is his description and acting of the trial of Jesus before Pontius Pilate. Men of larger gifts have had small success compared with his. The question and answer of a biographer are natural and pertinent : —

"Whence, then, has his superior power proceeded? Why has he won such victories in the church of God? We must leave this question unsolved, or attribute his surprising victories to the Holy Spirit, who finds His instruments among the herdmen of Tekoa or at the feet of Gamaliel, as His sovereign wisdom may decide. To this source Mr. Caughey himself ascribes the glory of his fruitfulness. We do the same. His success shows the church of God, in her ministry and membership, how she may indeed shine as the light of the world, — the spiritual Pharos of mankind!"

Mr. Caughey was not only charged with enthusiasm on account of his earnestness, but with superstition, because he believed so thoroughly in the revealing of God's presence and will, in answer to confiding prayer. But the church has yet to learn much of the possibilities of faith, and the communion with God it permits, and find a deeper significance in experience than many suppose we are sure, in Paul's uplifting of soul, until he 'knew not whether he was in or out of the body.' In the Methodist branch of the church, Mr. Caughey had a place in the grand work of the undivided Zion of Christ's purchase and love, which Mr. Moody, with his co-worker, Mr. Sankey, have had of late, — the gift of God to repay our indebtedness to Great Britain for the priceless evangelism of a century before in our own new country, whose character was then forming for freedom's conflict and victory. Such a ministry also illustrates the power of entire consecration to the salvation of the lost, and a faith that rests absolutely and habitually upon the divine promise and rule of bestowment, — "According to your faith be it unto you."

Mr. Caughey, who, since his residence abroad, has held successful meetings in his adopted country, is still living, at New Brunswick, N. J., but in feeble health, serenely "waiting till his change comes."

CHAPTER XVIII.

Another remarkable evangelist of the Methodist denomination is comparatively little known outside of it in this country, and we think not generally even in his own church, simply because he has been pre-eminently cosmopolitan in his very effective labors. A more perfect incarnation of original Methodism than Mr. Taylor we think the world has never seen, not excepting Jesse Lee, the founder of the Wesleyan Zion in New England. Jesse Lee left his Virginia home in the spring of 1790, for Boston, and July 13 preached his first sermon to a mixed and curious assembly on the Common, with a table for his pulpit. He was a consecrated and fearless pioneer. Nearly sixty years later, William Taylor went from his Maryland home to the just rising metropolis of the Pacific coast.

December 3, 1849, at three o'clock, P. M., the evangelist stood upon a carpenter's bench in the Plaza at San Francisco. Before him sat Mrs. Taylor, his "sweet singer in Israel," as he fondly called his faithful companion in toil and self-denial, with a few Methodist friends. Around the square were "gambling hells," and the Sabbath was, of all the seven, the favorite day of the lawless revellers. It must be borne in mind that gamblers were no small

portion of the human tide sweeping into the new Eldo-
rado. Suddenly these sporting men, gathered from surrounding towns, are startled by the sound of sacred
music. "Hear the royal proclamation!" rings over the
dens of vice and floats into their polluted air. The sound
of woman's voice reminded some of the inmates of different days and scenes. The crowd thickens, and the
calm, earnest preacher, who with marvellous tact points to
the " Stars and Stripes," and appeals to their patriotism as
a guarantee of order during the services, and then to their
" figuring for the last two months at least under the rule
of 'loss and gain,'" for the appreciation of his text,
" What is a man profited if he shall gain the whole world
and lose his own soul?" A more quiet audience could
not anywhere have been found. That discourse was the
"first of a series of nearly six hundred sermons preached
in those streets, the confluence of all the various creeds
and isms and notions and feelings and prejudices of all
the nations, Christian and heathen."

Such was the decisive and formal entrance upon his
great life-work of a man who years before passed through
deep convictions into a sound conversion, and went about
his Master's business. He quietly sought the neglected
masses, while living in Baltimore, and also in Washington,
attracting the attention of his more conspicuous brethren
to his devoted life.

It was in the autumn of 1848, while passing along Baltimore Street, he heard some one shouting his name; he
turned, when Christian Keener, who was running after
him, said, " Bishop Waugh wants to see you." Retracing
his steps to a book-store, he met the bishop, who told
him he was wanted for missionary work in California.
Mr. Taylor was ready, and made preparations to go.
His public introduction to his field was the meeting in
the Plaza, or "Portsmouth Square." Seven years the

unresting worker blew the gospel trumpet in all accessible places, beholding, with grateful heart, the fulfilment of the prophecy he boldly uttered in the Plaza, as follows : —

"The power of Satan seems at this time in the ascendancy wherever I cast my eye ; but sure as there is a God in heaven, He will turn the tables upon the Evil One, and where now my voice meets naught but scoffs and jeers, with unwavering faith in my divine Master, I hope to labor on to the time when these dens of iniquity shall all be swept away."

Mr. Taylor walked through that square on the Sabbath, when almost New England quiet reigned, while the moving throng were directing their footsteps to the sanctuaries of worship. His record in "Seven Years' Street Preaching in San Francisco" has all the romance of fiction in the narrative of life's soberest facts and of spiritual verities.

We regret the lack of material for a completer outline of his active, eventful, and most useful life. He sailed from New York for Europe, July 17, 1862. After spending about seven months in evangelistic labors in Ireland and England, and another month in Palestine, he journeyed to Australia, where for nearly three years he devoted himself to his revival work in all the principal Wesleyan churches. His family joined him in Australia, and accompanied him to South Africa, where he labored for seven months on a missionary tour. The missionaries there reported 1,200 converts among the English colonists, and 5,000 among the Caffres. Thence Mr. Taylor came to England, remaining about eleven months, laboring in England and Scotland.

Leaving the oldest son in Switzerland, Mrs. Taylor, with the other children of her family, returned to the family home in California. Mr. Taylor proceeded to the West Indies ; but on account of the illness of his son, returned, after three months, to Switzerland. Again, after waiting three months with his sick son, he journeyed to the West Indies, and re-engaged in his revival work. His purpose was to go thence by way of New Zealand to India. Mr. Taylor's great work in India began soon after, and is too fresh in the minds of our readers to need re-stating here. Its methods and success remind one of the apostolic times, and its salutary influence is likely to be most extensive and abiding.

On his way to this country Mr. Taylor spent a few weeks in London, participating in the revival work of Moody and Sankey. His purpose is to spend a few months attending the camp-meetings and visiting the churches in this country. He will soon meet his family, either here or in California. Just now he is looking earnestly for recruits for the mission work under his charge in India, to which country he will in due time return, with the purpose of continuing his labors there until he shall pass from labor to reward.

In connection with Mr. Taylor's return from India, some notice of the best known Brahmin worker there will have a deep interest to Christian people here, who recollect his visit to New York and New England, two years ago, as a delegate to the Evangelical Alliance. He suffered great persecution, upon the profession of his faith in Christ, from his kindred and countrymen. We quote from a letter his own account of his ordinary round of service for Him about whom we heard Sheshasdri preach a precious sermon, from the words, " Full of grace and truth."

" I am thankful to say," he writes, " that I am busy at my own sphere of usefulness from four o'clock, A. M., to nine o'clock, P. M., of course meal hours, bathing time, etc., excepted. Here is the way in which I spend my day : At five o'clock I go out with my evangelistic party, which is formed of the perfect number seven, to some one of our numerous villages in our neighborhood, within an area of ten miles. My evangelists take with them their musical instruments, viz. a drum, a guitar, and a pair of cymbals. As soon as we arrive at the appointed village, our blind minstrel, Bartimeas, sings a Christian hymn to the instrumental music, and as this goes on, men, women, and children collect around us. After singing, one of our evangelists steps forward and tries to set forth the truths that have been sung in as spirited an address as he can. Another hymn is then sung, and a second evangelist gives another address. And what does your humble servant do? His principal business is to supplement the addresses of our young evangelists, and close the whole with a concluding address. This lasts for nearly an hour and a half. We, on the whole, get very good congregations indeed, very orderly and attentive, and respectful. While going to a village, I try to give hints to our evangelists on the art of preaching. After preaching I ride home as fast as I can; that is about nine o'clock. After breakfast I have a class with our medical catechists to read the Word of God. This lasts for nearly an hour. At about one o'clock I go over to the Anglo-Vernacular school, and impart religious instruction to the whole school. After this, at about five o'clock, p. m., I have, twice a week, congregational meetings with our Christian people. At seven o'clock the advanced scholars from the Anglo-Vernacular school come to read Angus's 'Handbook of the English Tongue.' The last class I hear is that of our young masons, who read the Old Testament from 8 to 9 p. m. I assure you I have as much joy and pleasure in this way of working as I used to have when with you. However, with us it is still our sowing time."

Even India has her native evangelist, the sure token of the coming day of Imanuel, when this shall be said of "every kindred, tongue, and people."

CHAPTER XIX.

SCOTLAND'S GREAT EVANGELISTS, REV. WILLIAM BURNS AND DUNCAN MATHESON.— BOYHOOD.— PREPARATION FOR EVANGELISM.— ENGLAND'S MISSIONARY TO CHINA.— THE OPEN-AIR EVANGELIST.—AT PARIS.—IN THE HIGHLANDS.—TRIUMPHANT DEATH-SCENES.

WITH only nine years' difference between their ages, William Burns and Duncan Matheson, like the Haldanes, were providential gifts to Scotland and Immanuel's cause there when greatly needed, and in the good accomplished wrought indirectly yet effectively together. These able and devoted evangelists were in the Scottish field during the years of Mr. Finney's and Mr. Kirk's great usefulness in America.

William Burns was the third son of the Rev. William Hamilton Burns, D. D., minister at Dun in Angus, and subsequently at Kilsyth in Sterlingshire. He was born in the former parish, April 1, 1815. Dun was a "quiet and gentle spot, full of stillness and peace, nestling, with the adjoining church and graveyard, close within the bosom of a romantic dell, amid the shadows of ancient trees, and the hoarse chorus of rooks high overhead, which seemed rather to increase than to break the silence."

In 1821 Dr. Burns removed to Kilsyth, twelve miles from Glasgow, a bustling town of three thousand inhabitants, where around that happy home "the wheels of life moved more swiftly." The devout pastor was a model of dignity and kindness, culture and simplicity, — a fine example of that Christian pastorate which, even in Scotland, is fast passing away.

Mrs. Burns was no less worthy and complete in character, as a pastor's wife and a praying mother, — " the glad sunshine and bright angel of the house."

' William was a young Nimrod with the gun, among the hills, and for long days threw his line in the Carron water beneath their shadow. It was his delight also to swing the woodman's axe against the trees that could be spared from the precincts; and whatever called forth his premature strength gave him real pleasure.

From the parish school, when in his thirteenth year, he went, at the invitation of an uncle in Aberdeen, to spend some time with him and attend the famous grammar school of that city. William always vehemently rejected the idea of being a minister, and said he wished to be a lawyer, because he " saw lawyers rich and with fine houses." This new and wider sphere of culture decided him to enter the legal profession. A consecrated sister was now bearing him on her heart before the throne of mercy, and writing to him words of loving interest in his salvation.

The most direct and recognized means of his awakening was a joint family letter, the reply to which brought the praying band the dawn of hope. It was a small thing of itself, — the mere expression of a tender appreciation of the correspondence, with the request that they would send him good religious reading. This encouragement was followed by a glad surprise.

One day he unexpectedly entered the parsonage with a serious air, while the exclamation burst from his mother's lips, "O Willie! where have you come from?" His answer was gravely, "From Edinburgh."—"How did you come?"—"I walked" (a distance of thirty-six miles). There was then a silence, and standing on the hearth-rug, with his back to the fire, he said, " What would you think, mamma, if I should be a minister after all?" His countenance showed that he was speaking in earnest, and he then told

openly how the Lord had arrested him, and that he had no
rest in his spirit till he should come home and obtain his
parents' consent to relinquish the law and give himself to
the service of Jesus in the ministry of the gospel. In his
journal, he relates his conversion : "Sabbath afternoon, I
think about the middle of December, 1831, an arrow from
the quiver of the King of Zion was shot by his almighty,
sovereign hand through my heart, though it was hard
enough to resist all inferior means of salvation. Although
it was then, I remember, that the light of God first shone
full and transportingly on his Word and in my heart, I
was never, from the beginning, three weeks before, in
utter darkness, but felt that God had been always willing
to save me, that I was a self-murderer, and that now He was,
in His own sovereignty, touching my heart, and drawing me
to Himself for His own glory. I had many fears, and many
awful struggles with sin and Satan, and many sleepless
nights of mingling joy and fear and faith and hope and
love. Ebenezer! Hallelujah! Hallelujah! Amen!"

In the autumn of 1832 he repaired to Aberdeen to enter
with holy enthusiasm upon a course of studies with the ministry in view. His correspondence revealed rapid intellectual and spiritual growth and intense Christian activity.
March 27, 1839. he was licensed by the presbytery of
Glasgow. He had before offered himself to the University
Missionary Association as a missionary to the heathen, and
had been accepted. When preparing to go to India, Mr.
M'Cheyne, of Dundee, desired him to supply the pulpit of
St. Peter's Church while on a tour to Palestine. Feeling it
his duty to yield to the urgent invitation and delay his departure, he took charge of that large and intelligent parish. Of
this beginning of his ministry when a young man twenty-
four years of age, his brother says, "I have heard old members of the congregation tell how their hearts trembled for
him when they saw what seemed to them a mere stripling

21

standing up in the place of one they so revered and honored, and how almost at the first sound of his voice, as he led with such deep-toned spirituality and power the prayers of the sanctuary, their fears vanished, and they seemed to hear the sound of His Master's feet behind him."

Mr. Burns wielded an influence over the masses whom he addressed which was almost without a parallel since the days of Wesley and Whitefield. With him there was no effort at oratorical display, but there was true eloquence. Although he had not the "rich aroma of sanctified poetry and pathos of M'Cheyne, he had strength, clearness, and force," through which the fire of real enthusiasm and the tide of deepest emotion were seen and felt by his hearers.

The subject of a revival of religion as the great want of the time was stirring pious hearts, and nowhere more tearfully than at Kilsyth, which shared so largely in the mighty work of Whitefield's day. The reviving earnestness was increased there by a small but very fervent society of Wesleyan Methodists, with their uncompromising spirituality and zeal.

At this crisis of interest he was appointed to preach a discourse in Kilsyth. A passage in his journal reveals the sources of his power : —

"I preached from Matthew xi, 28. I felt such a yearning of heart over the poor people among whom I had spent so many of my youthful years in sin that I intimated that I would again address them before bidding them farewell, — it might be never to meet again on earth; and that I would do so in the market-place in order to reach the many who absented themselves from the house of God, and after whom I longed in the bowels of Jesus Christ. This meeting was fixed for Tuesday, at 10 A. M."

Before the hour arrived he had wrestled with God and prevailed, and felt a serene assurance that a rich display of His grace was at hand. His thrilling history of that

day is an example of many similar if less powerful revivals, during his career as an evangelist:—

"The morning proved very unfavorable for our assem-
bling in the open air, and this seems to have been a wise,
providential arrangement; for while, on the one hand, it was
necessary that our meeting should be intimated for the open
air, in order to collect the great multitude, on the other
hand, it was very needful, in order to the right management
of so glorious a work as that which followed, that we should
be assembled within doors. When I entered the pulpit,
I saw before me an immense multitude from the town
and neighborhood filling the seats, stairs, passages, and
porches, all in their ordinary clothes, and including many
of the most abandoned of our population. I began, I
think, by singing the 102d Psalm, and was affected deeply,
when in reading it I came to these lines, —

> " ' Her time for favor which was set,
> Behold, is now come to an end.'

That word ' now ' touched my heart as with divine power,
and encouraged the sweet hope that the set time was really
now at hand. I read without comment, but with solemn
feelings, the account of the conversion of the three thousand on the day of Pentecost; and this account, I am told,
affected some of the people considerably. When we had
prayed a second time, specially imploring that the Lord
would open on us the windows of heaven, I preached from
the words (Psalm cx, 2), 'Thy people shall be willing in
the day of Thy power.'

"This subject I had studied and preached on at Dundee
without any remarkable effect; and though I was so much
enlarged on this occasion in discoursing from it, I have
not been able to treat it in the same manner, or with the
same effects, at any subsequent time. I had come to
notice the glorious revelation of Jehovah's right hand

which was given at the Kirk of Shotts in 1630, while
John Livingstone was preaching from Ezekiel xxxvi, 26,
27, when it pleased the sovereign God of grace to make
bare His holy arm in the midst of us, and to perform a
work in many souls resembling that of which I had been
speaking in majesty and glory. And just when I was
speaking of the occasion and the nature of this wonderful address, I felt my own soul moved in a manner
so remarkable that I was led, like Mr. Livingstone, to
plead with the unconverted before me instantly to close
with God's offers of mercy, and continued to do so until
the power of the Lord's Spirit became so mighty upon their
souls as to carry all before it, like the rushing mighty
wind of Pentecost. During the whole of the time that I
was speaking, the people listened with the most riveted
and solemn attention, and with many silent tears and inward groanings of the spirit; but at the last their feelings
became too strong for all ordinary restraints, and broke
forth simultaneously in weeping and wailing, tears and
groans, intermingled with shouts of joy and praise from
some of the people of God. The appearance of a great
part of the people from the pulpit gave me an awfully
vivid picture of the state of the ungodly in the day of
Christ's coming to judgment. Some were screaming out
in agony; others, and among these strong men, fell to the
ground as if they had been dead; and such was the general
commotion that, after repeating for some time the most
free and urgent invitations of the Lord to sinners (as
Isaiah lv, Revelations xxii, 17), I was obliged to give
out a psalm, which was soon joined in by a considerable
number, our voices being mingled with the mourning
groans of many prisoners sighing for deliverance. After
Dr. Burns and my father had spoken for a little, and
prayed, the meeting was closed at three o'clock, intimation
having been given that we would meet again at six.

"To my own astonishment, during the progress of this wonderful scene, when almost all present were overpowered, it pleased the Lord to keep my soul perfectly calm. Along with the awful and affecting realization which I obtained of the state of the unconverted, I had such a view of the glory redounding to God and the blessings conferred on poor sinners by the work that was advancing, as to fill my soul with tranquil joy and praise. Indeed, I was so composed that when, with the view of recruiting my strength for the labors still in view, I stretched myself on my bed on going home, I enjoyed an hour of the most refreshing sleep, and rose as vigorous in mind and body as before."

Prayerful caution was needed to guide such intense and wide-spread feeling, and clergymen of experience came from "all parts of the country, especially from Glasgow, to help the overtasked pastor and give stability and spiritual substance to the movement." Mr. Burns returned to Dundee to find that the tidings from Kilsyth had deepened the interest begun there. A few weeks later he left for Kilsyth to witness the work of the Spirit, which continued until the Sabbath air seemed to pervade the place all the week.

At Dundee, Perth, Aberdeen, and adjacent towns, he repeated his labors only to see attending them the same victories of the Lamb. In 1814 Mr. Burns heard from the glens and slopes of the mountains of Scotland the call to leave the exhausting excitement of cities, and proclaim among them the gospel message. He obeyed, and never was happier than when "kneeling in lonely prayer in some forest thicket by the river or mountain side, or standing up before those arrested crowds that hung upon his words silent and solemn as the mountains around. His very eyes left their light with you after he had gone. There was an Isaiah-like grandeur about his expositions of the gospel."

In his journal he has the following passage : "July 1.—I spent the day chiefly alone seeking personal holiness, the fundamental requisite in order to a successful ministry. Before me I had, to the right Queen Mary's Island in Loch Leven, and to the left the Lomonds, where the Covenanters hid themselves from their persecutors. The scene was solemn and affecting, and I trust the everlasting Imanuel was with me. Oh that I had a martyr's heart, if not a martyr's death and a martyr's crown!" Around Loch Lomond and other romantic lakes, in solitary, romantic churchyards, and among wild heights, he preached and prayed, and directed souls to the Lamb of God.

In 1841, from the Highlands he returned to the great centres of human activity, to reap down abundant harvests. In Newcastle, Edinburgh, and Dublin he lived over again life in Aberdeen, Dundee, and Perth, sometimes in danger of death from the "wrath of man," which God in the end made to praise Him.

Mr. Burns had kindred in the British colonies in America, and in 1844 the proposal was urgently sent him from leading clergymen and others to extend to them his evangelistic field. He sailed in the autumn of 1844 for Quebec, and continued for about two years his chosen service for Jesus in Canada, often in a tumult of Irish and French Catholic opposition quite as threatening as that raised by Pharisees and Sadducees around the heroic Paul.

Upon his return to Scotland in 1846, while his mind was again turned to foreign missions with peculiar interest, the inquiry reached him from the English Presbyterian Missionary Committee for a man to go as their first herald of Christ's salvation to China. With joy he offered himself, and for sixteen years was a pioneer missionary of unflagging zeal and abiding success. We must pass over the deeply interesting record of his fidelity and achievements in the "Celestial Empire," but we cannot deny the reader his sister's simple story of the unexpectedly hurried departure : —

"Having heard that some timid persons were daunted by some difficulties that stood in the way, he said, ' That's the very thing that makes my call clear to go,' and at once packed his little carpet-bag to start for Newcastle. The day he went off he was long in papa's study in prayer, and then coming out he silently wrung my hand and looked solemnly round, as if taking a farewell look of the house ; he had his Breadalbane plaid over his arm, and after reaching the front door he turned and hung it up in the lobby, taking one belonging to his mother instead, and giving me an expressive look as he did so. I was very much overcome, and watched his receding figure with the feeling that he would not return. I went into the study to give vent to my feelings, and found the Bible left open at Isaiah xliv : ' Oh, that Thou would rend the heavens !' etc. On going up to the drawing-room I found the Gaelic Testament and psalm-book neatly put into one of the shelves, as if he had done with them, and I then said, ' William will return no more.' In a very few days, as you know, it was all decided, and the first announcement we received was from Mr. Irving, of Falkirk, who kindly came straight from the synod meeting to give us the tidings."

The years of his holy activity were at length numbered, and this distinguished servant of the Lord, who cared so little for human applause and so much for that honor which comes from God only, passed on to his eternal reward. Exhausting toil, with severe colds, induced fever, which entrenched itself in his system ; and in the springtime of 1868, he sank gradually to the last sleep of his worn-out body. Sweet words of promise and triumph were often on his lips. April 4, after a religious service in his room at Nieu-chwang, he suddenly repeated with thrilling emphasis, as his last utterance before he entered the splendors of the King's throne, "For Thine is the kingdom and the power and the glory!"

While Mr. Burns was doing the self-denying, toilsome work of a missionary evangelist in China, the lay-evangelist who so nobly and wonderfully supplemented his labors in Scotland was engaged in scarcely less trying, heroic, and exhausting service among the common people of their own countrymen.

Duncan Matheson, whose loving biographer, Rev. John Macpherson, was a faithful and very successful co-worker with him, was born Nov. 22, 1824, in Huntly, Aberdeenshire, a quiet town, famous in ecclesiastical history on account of the free-church movement more than thirty years ago. His father was a "mail runner" between Huntly and Banff,— a plain, godly man, whose Celtic blood gave to his son that fire of his race which, in after life, "fused all his powers into one great passion."

The Haldanes had stirred the heart of Scotland; but the northern part, in the matter of religion, presented the same prevailing deadness of faith and reliance upon works and forms which has so generally preceded a great spiritual awakening. Hirelings were in the pulpit, some of whom called praying people hypocrites, and others boldly confessed their dislike to the returning Sabbath by applying to it the term "hanging day." There were exceptions beneath the upas shadow of that boasted "moderation" which meant "a religion without earnestness and a gospel without grace"; for the spirit of Chalmers was abroad, and there were earnest listeners wherever they could hear the story of the Cross.

Rev. George Cowe, who was grand-uncle of Duncan Matheson, and whose character as a man and a preacher strikingly reappeared in that of the latter, was among the faithful few. Because he admitted James Haldane into his

pulpit, he was thrust out of the secession church. Himself
a pastor-evangelist, he was mobbed repeatedly by the haters
of evangelical truth. To hear him, the spiritually hungry
people came from " the midst of the wilderness of peat-moss,
where the only sign of life was the blue smoke curling to
the sky, and from the lonely glen, where the silence was
seldom broken save by the cry of the wild bird." These
caravans of broad-shouldered men, with blue bonnet and
plaid, and thoughtful matrons with Bible and psalm-book,
would pause by the way to rest, lift the song of praise,
then kneel in simple pleading prayer. We must quote a
single brief petition, which a hearer has recorded : —

"O God, oor souls are jist as dry as the heather ; oor
herts are as hard as the granite stane ; but Thou that gi'est
the draps o' dew to the heather, gie us the drappins o' thy
grace this day, and let thy ain love licht upon oor hard
herts like the birdie sittin' singin' on the rock yonner ; an' fill
the souls o' thy fowk this day wi' peace and joy till they're
rinnin' o'er like the water-spout on the brae. Lord, it'll
be nae loss to you, an' it'll be a grand bargain for us, an'
we'll mind ye on't tae a' eternity. Amen."

When the " disruption " burst suddenly upon the church,
Strathbogee, near Duncan's home, became the scene of
the opening conflict, and drew to it, from Dundee and other
towns, gifted and devoted men, who held meetings in the
open air. Here a powerful sermon from Robert M'Cheyne,
who preached " with eternity stamped upon his brow,"
brought the youthful hearer to the threshold of the kingdom ; but a hesitating companion tempted him to grieve
the Spirit. He was now sixteen years of age, and declined
a collegiate course, for which he was prepared, because of
certain conditions imposed ; and knowing that he was
unconverted, " he would not be a minister because he could
not be a hypocrite."

His mechanical genius turned his attention to architecture, and he was apprenticed at Kilrumin to chisel his native sandstone. Dissatisfied with his occupation, in which he received no encouragement, God met him again there by a pulpit appeal which deeply affected him. In October, 1845, he was called home to see his mother die, with the land of Beulah full in view. Taking his hand, she entreated him to seek Christ, bade him farewell, and left him once more weeping over his guilt and peril, only to repeat the experience of declining feeling and delay. One year from the date of that death a searching and alarming discourse by Rev. A. Bonar, Robert M'Cheyne's biographer, revived his former convictions, and he sought relief in the promise to enter upon Christ's service twelve months from that time. But the Holy Ghost was engaged in the conquest of that procrastinating sinner ; and even the perilous counsel of a minister who commended him for his right feeling and bade him hope, instead of believe, failed to bring peace. We will give the story of salvation from his own pen : —

"I was standing, on the 10th December, 1846, at the end of my father's house, and meditating on that precious Word which has brought peace to countless weary ones : 'God so loved the world, that He gave his only begotten Son, that whosoever believeth in Him should not perish, but have everlasting life.' (John iii, 16.) I saw that God loved me, for I was one of the world. I saw the proof of His love in the giving of His Son Jesus. I saw that 'whosoever' meant anybody and everybody, and therefore me, even me. I saw the result of believing, — that I would not perish, but have everlasting life.' I was enabled to take God at his word. I saw no one but Jesus only, all in all in redemption. My burden fell from my back, and I was saved. Yes, saved!"

Terrible temptations were permitted to assail him, that he might not only learn the wiles of the devil for the sake of those for whom he was to labor, but to lead him to that rest of faith, that happy confidence in the Lord, which fitted him for the work of an evangelist and sustained him amidst many labors and trials. The joy of the Lord was his strength, and true of him were these lines : —

> " There are in this loud and stunning tide
>   Of human care and crime,
> With whom the melodies abide
>   Of the everlasting chime;
> Who carry music in their heart
> Through dusky lane and wrangling mart,
> Plying their daily task with busier feet
> Because their secret souls a holy strain repeat."

Matheson was ready for the field of toil and conflict. At Burntisland he obtained permission to teach drawing in the school gratuitously, that he might gain access to the pupils and lead them to Jesus. Returning to Huntly, he began to go over his native town, with Bible in hand, reading, talking, and praying, wherever he met an unsaved soul. His helper and friend, Mr. Macpherson, gives an account of his first preaching : —

"One day Miss Macpherson, a devoted Christian, who had been his friend, counsellor, and good angel throughout the period of his protracted spiritual conflict, requested him to address a company of aged women whom she had gathered together. Matheson declined the invitation. He 'could not preach.' Miss Macpherson reasoned, urged, and entreated ; but all in vain. Finally, demanding what he would answer at the great tribunal for a neglected talent, she charged him not to refuse lest souls should perish in consequence. This was more than he could bear. He went to the meeting, though with the greatest hesitancy and fear. Opening the Bible at Isaiah xxxii, 2, 'Tremble, ye women that are at ease ; be troubled, ye careless ones,' he spoke with great freedom and power. Both the text and matter of his address seemed to be laid to his hand; and such were the results that he felt assured the Lord was calling him to this work."

The Duchess of Gordon heard of the young evangelist, and sent for him, and offered to give him forty pounds a year that he might fit himself for his work. He accepted it, but spent nearly all of the small sum in the purchase of tracts and in the relief of the poor. Not satisfied with this, he found an old printing-press, repaired it, learned to print by patient effort after repeated failures, and printed his own tracts. He wrote on the press "For God and Eternity," and prayed daily for skill to use it. He said the sight of that inscription inspired him with fresh zeal when discouragement seemed near despair.

At this time the perishing millions of China lay heavy on his heart, and he longed to go forth and preach the gospel in the land of Sinim. Much did he "sigh and cry" about the heathen, and often did he say in his inmost heart, "Lord, here am I; send me."

At this crisis of experience the war in the Crimea was calling for men, and he saw a beckoning hand of divine pity inviting to the plains of death, to seek there and save the lost. We cannot even take a glimpse of the tireless and glorious toils of the evangelist in the trenches, in hospitals, on ship-board, and in the very smoke of battle. His chosen companion there was Hector Macpherson, drum-major, 93d Highlanders, a soldier both of his country and of the Cross, of whom our missionary used to tell the following story: One day a chaplain, newly arrived, called on the sergeant and asked his advice as to the best method of conducting his work. "Come with me," said Hector, "to the hill-top. Now, look around you. See yonder the pickets of Liprandi's army; see you batteries on the right, and the men at the guns; mark yon trains of ammunition; hear the roar of the cannon. Look where you may, it is all earnest here. There is not a man but feels it is a death-struggle. If we don't conquer the Russians, the Russians will conquer us. We are all in earnest, sir; we are not playing at soldiers here. If you would do good, you must be in earnest too. An earnest man will always win his way." Such was the advice of Queen Victoria's servant to the servant of Jesus Christ.

Hector and Duncan, on the first Sabbath after the arrival of the latter, retired to a ravine, and there, amid the deafening roar of cannon, which the missionary thought was always worse on the Lord's day, they read and prayed, and sang together the old battle-song of David and Luther, —

> " God is our refuge and our strength,
>   In straits a present aid ;
>   Therefore, although the earth remove,
>   We will not be afraid."

In Turkey, France, and Italy he scattered the truth, and leaving the latter country in March, 1857, reached home early in the summer.

Invigorated by his native air, he prepared to enter again without delay upon his labors as an evangelist. The first pulpit he entered was that of the Free Church at Insch, at the request of the pastor. An awakening followed. In October the rector of the Episcopal Church at Whiteham sends for Matheson, when he began to preach every day, — the rule of his after life. Here he began to publish "The Herald of Mercy," which was greatly blessed to the conversion of souls and of which there was a monthly circulation of 32,000. The issuing and scattering of these papers and personal efforts to save men occupied the following months till the autumn of 1858, when he was requested by Lady Pirrie to visit Malvern. On a green hillside there he held his first out-of-door service, the

success of which was to him a special call to this means
of reaching the masses, and henceforth he gave himself to
preaching in the open air, "By day, by night, beneath the
summer sun, out in the drenching rain or piercing cold of
winter, in the remote glen amidst the bleating of the
sheep, at the sea-side where the singing of David's psalms
mingles with the still more ancient harmonies of the great
ocean, on the crowded street, in the noisy fair, beneath
the shadow of the scaffold, in the face of the raging mob,
— everywhere, in short, as far as in him lay, he strove to
preach Christ to perishing men. In this way his voice
reached many who otherwise would never have heard the
glad tidings of salvation."

On February 2, 1859, he was married at Weston-super-
Mare to Miss Mary Milne, a Christian lady whom he ever
regarded as an invaluable gift bestowed upon him in
answer to prayer. Not one day was withdrawn from
labor.   Exuberantly social and tenderly affectionate
though he was, the winning of souls was to him infinitely
more than the most endearing relationship or the most
hallowed earthly joy. "We'll get settled up yonder in
the Father's house," he said to her; "meanwhile let us
work and win souls."

In the spring of 1859 Mr. Matheson returned to Scotland and took up his residence in the city of Aberdeen.
The great religious awakening of that period was just
beginning. Tidings of the work of grace in America and
Ireland stirred the hearts of Christians, and many were in
expectation of a similar blessing. The spirit of grace and
supplication was poured down, and many a blessed scene
was now witnessed. The winter was indeed past and the
time of the singing of birds was come. The months succeeding were made memorable by the displays of redeeming power.

Towards the close of 1859 he began to extend his evangelistic itineracy to Banffshire, preaching for the most part in the towns and villages along the coast. His labors were specially blessed in the burgh and seaport of Cullen. This little town is situated on the brow of a hill, looking full in the face the blue waters of the Northern Sea.

"Early in 1860 the whole place was moved as by an earthquake. Fear took hold on the sinners in Zion; trembling seized the hypocrites; careless ones, whose shadow had not darkened the door of God's house for many years, found their way to church or chapel; and even worldly men talked to one another about the great question upon the streets. At first the awful shadow of an angry God coming to judgment fell on many, and it seemed as if there was one dead in every house. Awakening was followed by conversion; the thunder of Sinai gave way to the peaceful sunshine of Calvary. Christians who had never known the liberty of the gospel were suddenly delivered from the spirit of bondage and ushered into the glorious liberty of the gospel.

"To see the great crowd kneeling reverently on the grass amidst the deepest silence, broken only by a groan, a sob, a loud cry for mercy, to be followed by fond, enthusiastic demonstrations of love and hearty songs of praise, characteristic of these impulsive children of the sea, was a sight impressive beyond description and never to be forgotten. From such scenes Duncan Matheson, like one refreshed with the new wine of the kingdom, was wont to come away singing his favorite Psalm, —

> "When Zion's bondage God turned back,
>   Like men that dreamed were we;
> Then filled with laughter was our mouth,
>   Our tongue with melody."

The landward parishes were not overlooked by the great Redeemer as He marched along the sea-coast in glorious majesty; from His bountiful hand the blessings of His grace were now being scattered far and wide. The reapers on the field, from the master to the gleaner, were known to lay aside at noonday the urgent labors of the harvest to attend to the more pressing business of the soul. Jesus was gathering golden sheaves into His garner. Matheson at this period, strong to reap rather than patient to sow, lent his powerful aid in every place. Few in all that region missed hearing the jubilant voice of our sturdy reaper, and seeing the gleam of his sharp sickle among the yellow corn."

One Sabbath he preached in Dundee, from Matthew xxv, 46, with such an attending power of the Spirit that at the close the vestry and session-room were thronged with the anxious, sobbing in penitence, crying out with alarm, or silent and pallid with despair. Suddenly one arose, exclaiming, "I have found Him! I have found Him! I never saw the way before." The effect was overwhelming upon the convicted, seized with the fear they should be left unsaved. They reproached themselves, fell on their faces in an agony of prayer, till one after another found peace in believing, and praises succeeded the cries of conviction.

The Huntly meetings, held in Castle Park, July 25 and 26, 1860, and renewed for the three succeeding summers under the patronage of the Duchess of Gordon, were suggested by Matheson, and to his wise, untiring zeal owed much, under God, of their marvellous success. Never, perhaps, was more of romance, in natural scenery, variety of persons in social position and character, and in modes of travel, associated with the worship of God, the proclamation of his great salvation; while the spiritual harvest was glorious. Amid wildest highlands, in regions " of beauty, yet of tempest and storm," and in remotest lowlands, Mr. Matheson was the same loyal, holy ambassador for

Christ, although without "the laying on of priestly hands."

In the autumn of that year, 1860, the open-air meetings were held in Barrack Park, of that town. The second day several of the pastors, with others, fearing the blessing might not come, retired to a grove, and spent two hours in wrestling prayer. At the close of this pleading faith, that would take no denial, the heavens gathered blackness and the rain fell in torrents. The people began to disperse, when Duncan Matheson's voice rang over the multitude: "Perhaps God is trying us by the rain. Let us wait a little." Quiet was soon restored, and while the services were continued the sun burst through the clouds, the rain ceased, and the divine glory mantled them. Pentecost was repeated, and the work went on with overawing majesty.

One part of our evangelist's mission deserves special mention,— preaching at village fairs. A Scotchman, Mr. Macpherson, describes these occasions: —

"The feeing-market, at which farmers engage their servants from one half-year to another, is a long-established institution in the northern counties of Scotland. It is usually held in the street or neighborhood of some little town or village. Early in the morning of the market-day there is a wonderful stir in the erection of refreshment tents, booths for the sale of sweets, trinkets, and all things dear to a ploughboy's heart, shows, and all the other paraphernalia of a village fair. Soon after breakfast the market is crowded by farmers and their wives, ploughmen, female servants, and all who have business to do. Besides these there is a general assembly of all the idlers and ne'er-do-weels in the country-side; tramps, tinkers, ballad-singers, fiddlers, rogues, beggar-women with starving babies, the man who is "out of employment" because he will not work, the shipwrecked sailor who never was at sea, the veteran soldier who has seen no service but the devil's, —

22

in short, all the scoundrels within a radius of thirty miles.
No time is lost; the whole machinery of the market is set
a-going. All the animal spirits of half a score parishes
and villages are now crowded into one place. There is no
restraint; universal freedom reigns. Wild hilarity, roar-
ing frankness, outrageous demonstrations of friendship,
characterize the scene, and a tumult of varied sounds fills
the air. Underneath all this, however, there is an eye to
business, its very life being in noise, excitement, and
uproar. Towards evening the more respectable people
take their way homewards, carrying with them all sorts of
useful household articles purchased at the fair. Among
the remaining portion the drinking and quarrelling go on
apace; coarseness, profanity, and violence increase, till at
length the deepening shades, not a moment too soon, cast
the mantle of God over a very hell of riot, charged with
all the elements of misery and ruin. It was a bold idea
to introduce the gospel here. It was like David's attempt
to save the lamb by attacking the lion and the bear.

"Nature and grace conspired to make Duncan Matheson
a prince of market-preachers. His handsome, well-knit
form impressed the sons of the soil with a sense of his
great strength; his frank, straightforward manner commanded their respect; his ready wit captivated a people
whose genuine humor is proverbial; his voice, rising above
the din, summoned them, as with a trumpet, to listen; his
manifest superiority to all fear made him a hero in their eyes;
and the grace of the Holy Ghost, with the truth as it is in
Christ Jesus, did the rest. In this self-denying work he
was nobly assisted by several ministers of the gospel and
other right-hearted servants of Jesus Christ.

"Sometimes when a hearing could not be obtained, and
further prosecution of the work seemed an utter waste of
energy and time, Duncan would start up and begin thus:
'I will tell you a thing that happened when I was in the

Crimea.' Immediately there is a respectful silence; the audience seem as if spell-bound, while the preacher proceeds to tell his story, which is only an introduction to the gospel.

" Prudence and tact were needed as well as courage. Sometimes he deemed it right to buy up the showmen; by giving them a fair day's custom he procured their silence.

" In a 'Special Call for Prayer,' he says, ' These markets are fields of deepest trial. For long they have been left in the power of the Wicked One, and thousands of souls have been ruined for eternity. Surely, we shall not ask for prayer in vain; and when the banner of Christ is unfurled, shall there be one living soul found shrinking from the fight, or refusing to cry from the depths of their hearts, ' Awake, awake, put on strength, O arm of the Lord'?

" The 'Special Call for Prayer' was accompanied by the use of other means, such as the following advertisement in a newspaper : —

'MARKET PREACHING.

'If the Lord permit, the Everlasting Gospel will be preached at Longside, Ellon, Aberdeen, Turriff, Inverury, and other feeing-markets.'"

To gather the inhabitants of obscure and out-of-the-way places, he purchased a bell, and would ring it up and down the streets, quietly telling the astonished spectators that he, the bell-ringer, would preach at the cross or market-place. This was not a trick of eccentricity; on the contrary, his sensitive nature shrank from it, extorting the confession, " I never knew how little grace I had till I did that." Powerful effusions of the spirit attended many of these endeavors to save men, while persecution and insult were not infrequent. But his most trying opposition came from Christian people by profession. We quote a single instance related of a clergyman : —

"He was accustomed to pray for a revival of religion. But the 'Great Awakening' in America was 'too American,' and the minister went on praying as before. The work of grace in Ireland followed; but it was 'too Irish,' and he went on praying as before. Remarkable movements occurred in various parts of Scotland; but it was 'wild-fire, and he would have none of it.' The Spirit of God began to work in his own town, very much through the instrumentality of our evangelist; but in the opinion of the minister the instruments were contemptible and the whole thing of doubtful tendency, and he now began to pray for a true revival. At length members of his congregation were converted under the preaching of Mr. Matheson, who said to them, 'Go and tell your minister what the Lord has done for your souls; it will cheer his heart and do him good.' They went, some to ask direction, and some to acknowledge grace received. The minister was angry. Next Sabbath he said it was all excitement and delusion, and he stamped with his foot as if he would stamp out the spiritual rinderpest. The excitement and delusion seemed to be all his own. His prayer had been answered, but he would not accept the answer in God's way. The work of grace stood before him, but he knew it not. Jesus came to His own, but His own received Him not, because His visage was so marred. The Holy Spirit came to the minister, but the minister disowned and rejected Him because He came in a garb of humiliation offensive to human pride.

"Some opposed the work because they had no scruples of conscience, and others because they had too many. Certain religious people have more scruples in their conscience than conscience in their scruples. To those who in effect said, 'Sermons, sermons are our business!' his reply was, 'Souls, souls are mine!' His constant cry, 'Eternity! eternity! Souls are perishing!' was a cutting rebuke to mere sermon-makers and sermon-hearers. He did not practise trumpet-blowing for a bit of bread. His was not the soft serenading of lovers but the sounding of shrill battle-blasts. He refused to say, 'Peace! peace!' when he ought to cry, 'Fire! fire!'"

The scene was very touching when, at his request, Macpherson went with him to visit St. Andrews for the refreshing inspiration of the hallowed associations. After seeing the place where George Wishart "was turned to a light to Scotland, to the end of time, and where Knox thundered defiance to Rome," they lay down on Rutherford's grave and wept and prayed, then sung "Rock of Ages," and "Rest for the Weary." It was a time of new consecration, which marked an era in his spiritual history.

He addressed the Perth Conference on Evangelism, from which we take a few suggestive and forcible extracts: —

" God has raised up not a few evangelists, who go hither and thither. I call the majority of them irregulars, free lances, knowing no church, understanding nothing of parochial divisions, subject to no master but Christ, and, it cannot be denied, wielding a mighty influence on not a few.

" There is much in their freedom of action fitted to help on the work, and also snares which only grace can deliver from. It is likely their numbers will be greatly increased; and if the Lord shall use them as sharp sickles for gathering in souls, surely every Christian will, from the inmost soul, bid them God-speed.

" With such of them as have a single eye in seeking the salvation of the lost (and I think life is nobly spent if spent for this), living ministers can have no difficulty in working. Co-operation with the dead on either side is out of the question; co-operation with the living is to be sought after by every possible means.

" Usually evangelists go to places to which they have been invited by one or more living souls. Their work is to 'preach the gospel.' I have preached in many lands, and in this dear land of ours I have proclaimed salvation in its crowded cities, lowly hamlets, by the side of its wimpling burnies and on its mountain-sides, and no one dare charge me with making one proselyte to my views or spending my time on aught else but the one theme.

"William Burns, that man of God now in glory, was once asked by a lady many things as to how he felt when preaching to the millions of China. After a pause, and fixing his eye on her, — an eye that was always full of pity, — he said, 'I never think but of one thing, — the lost and a Christ for them!'

"I have been told that it is a sacrifice preaching always to the unsaved. I grant it. We lose much joy in always dwelling about the temple-door, and not rising to proclaim higher truths, in which our souls would luxuriate. But if we speak of sacrifices, let us think of the tears wept over Jerusalem, of the sore agony in dark Gethsemane, of the dying love on the cross, and then say if life itself is not worth the giving, if we may but win one jewel for Immanuel's crown.

"Bless God for Scottish caution! but it is often at fault. When an evangelist comes to a place, there ought at first to be a 'trying of the spirits.' Standing on etiquette must be laid aside. Evangelists, if full of power, need not to be patronized. Earnest ministers are not to be ignored. They meet on a common platform, they serve the one Christ. Stereotyped modes of action, if need be, must be laid aside, and the ministry of the Spirit must be recognized."

On his journey to the Orkneys, the middle of January, 1867, he was completely prostrated; and in his delirium, fancying he was addressing the students of the New College, Edinburgh, he exclaimed, "Young men, young men, down with books and up with Christ! Souls are perishing,

souls are perishing! Up, and aim at saving sinners!"
Rallying, he goes for his health to Limpley Stoke near
Bath, and in April writes to a friend : —

"Like an old hulk disabled, I lie passive,—no easy
thing for a restless Bedouin like me. I am in a new
school, and if I learn my lesson well I may be able yet to
comfort many and give them a lift Zionward. Rutherford says, 'Oh, how much I owe to the file and hammer
of the dear Lord Jesus!' Can we not say the same?"

The following month he tries beautiful Jersey, and then
St. Serrau, Normandy, writing to his family and friends
letters full of sweetest resignation, gems of holy thought,
and the unquenchable love for souls, returning to Scotland
in July with the fatal grasp of disease still upon him.
The following winter was passed in the south of his native
land, and in the spring he repaired to Carlsbad, Bohemia.
He then went to work to secure translations of the "Blood
of Jesus" and similar pages into the language of the
people there. In September, 1869, he returned to Perth
to rejoin his family and go to his eternal home.

"'Give my clothes to the poor,' he said to his wife ; it
was almost the only legacy he had to leave. To his
friends at parting he spake words of joy and triumph.
To Dr. A. S—— he said 'Resurgam!' to Mr. M——, an
evangelist, 'You are going to speak of the King, but I am
going to see Him.' To his old Crimean friend, Mr.
Hector Macpherson, whose emotion was too strong for
even the soldier's firmness, he said, 'Do not weep for
me; I have only to die once that I may live forever.'
To another, who found him making arrangements for a
series of evangelistic services to be held at Hillhead, near
Glasgow, he said, 'I should like to die planning revival
services.' The services then planned by him were in
progress at the time of his death; the word was in demonstration of the Spirit, and a considerable number of

persons were converted. To another friend he said, 'I got the victory long ago, when the Lord first forgave my sins. . . . You have nothing now to ask for me but that I may have an abundant entrance.'

"To Mrs. Sandeman, Springland, he said, 'It's all love, it's all well. Reality is the great thing. I have always sought reality. . . . I have served the Lord for two and twenty years; I have sought to win souls,— it has been my passion, — and now I have the fruit of it. One of my spiritual children went the other day as a missionary to China, and many others of them are preaching the gospel. . . . Well, at least you can say you have seen the vanquished the conqueror.'

"When alone, he was often heard saying to himself, with a quiet jubilance of tone, 'Victory!' and often too, in soft, rapt whispers, 'Jesus only!' Again to his wife he exclaimed, 'Mary, this room is filled with the heavenly host. Had I strength how we would sing!' On this he repeated the last three verses of the 72d Psalm in metre, coming back with rapt delight on the last four lines,—

> ' And blessed be His glorious name
> To all eternity!
> The whole earth let His glory fill.
> Amen, so let it be!'

"He now appeared to be filled with the Spirit of glory and of God, and as if already triumphing amidst the heavenly host, his voice gave out with exultant tones the words of Psalm lxviii, 17, —

> ' God's chariots twenty thousand are,
> Thousands of angels strong;
> In 's holy place God is, as in
> Mount Sinai them among.'

"To Macpherson, his old comrade in the Lord's battles, he said, 'Man, I don't get singing enough. I want to sing :

will you help me?' I agreed to sing with him the hymn,
'Shall we gather at the river?' But before singing he
insisted, with that warmth of genuine hospitality that
characterized him, on my partaking of refreshment. Just
then he was seized with cramp. We seemed to hear a
voice saying, 'The Master is come, and calleth for thee.'
Quickly his wife and sister were by his side. 'Our friend
is in deep waters,' said his kind Christian physician, whom
I ran to fetch. So indeed it was; but his feet were firm
upon the rock; the everlasting arms were underneath
him. 'Lord Jesus, come quickly! Oh, come quickly!'
he several times exclaimed. Quickly the Lord Jesus came
and took him. Our hymn was not sung. He went to sing
by the river: we were left to weep.

"His grave is marked by a plain monument on which is
inscribed, as prepared by himself, the following epitaph :—

In Memory

OF

DUNCAN MATHESON,

Editor 'Herald of Mercy,'
and
Evangelist.
Born at Huntly, Nov. 22d, 1824.
Born again, Oct. 26th, 1846.
Died Sept. 16th, 1869.

And they that be wise shall shine as the brightness of the
firmament; and they that turn many to righteousness as the
stars for ever and ever." (Dan. xii, 3.)

No reader will doubt that Duncan Matheson was an evangelist appointed and anointed for his work by God; nor
that his success was mainly owing to his communion with
God, through which was poured upon his heart the baptism
of the Holy Ghost; and as another result, his clear views of
truth. Sin, the sinner and his guilt and peril, Christ and
his salvation, were real to him. What an example and a
rebuke!

CHAPTER XX.

Rev. A. B. Earle has earned the title we give him of " union evangelist." He has been a pioneer in this special form of revival efforts. It has not been merely a willingness to have Christians of different denominations unite, but he aims at the outset to secure this concert of action. It seems to be of little consequence to him in what sanctuary he begins a series of meetings, if it be the most convenient for all the people. We shall let him be heard on this topic : —

" I will mention a few reasons for my confidence in the usefulness and propriety of union meetings when special efforts are to be made for a revival of religion. They lead Christians to speak more kindly and tenderly of what they call each other's errors. As they work together they come to a better understanding of each other, and learn how few things there are in which they differ, and how many in which they agree. So that when Christians unite in labor for a revival, everything is at work removing the disposition to speak of others in any way but kindly and lovingly. Oh, that the sweet influences of these seasons of refreshing might permanently abide in the hearts of all believers !

" Union meetings convince the unconverted of a reality in religion. A well-known gambler in Massachusetts was brought to Christ through just this influence, and said to me, ' Mr. Earle, wherever you go, tell the world of my conversion; tell them I could withstand the appeals of each denomination when they worked separately, but when they united in a meeting, and I saw the Spirit of love prevailing among them, I felt its power, and gave myself to the Saviour.'

" The Spirit of God, I believe, is moving the denominations in regard to this subject, — not only in favor of protracted effort for the salvation of men, but united effort.

" My own denominational sentiments have ever been dear to me and never more so than now, and so I think it should be with every one; but as I have labored, and wept and prayed with thirteen or fourteen different denominations, in our own country and the British Provinces, I have learned to love all in whom I find the spirit of Christ. And as I cannot and must not be the judge of their hearts, I concede to them, what I ask them to concede to me, — the credit of entire sincerity.

" If, as some maintain, the churches strive wrongfully to secure for themselves the new converts, the blame must rest where it justly belongs. But I see no reason for unkind feeling between the different denominations, although each preach and practise what they believe to be right.

" I am accustomed in every revival to urge the converts carefully and prayerfully to search the Scriptures, that they may learn the will of Jesus, and, having learned it, to go and do what they believe He would have them.

" Beyond this it does not seem necessary for me to go, nor can I think it would be wise."

Mr. Earle has not yet given to the world a biographical sketch of his life previous to his entrance upon his itineracy, and it is not likely to be written while he is living.

His birthplace was Charlestown N. Y. in 1812. Upon his conversion he joined the Baptist church, and his thoughts were directed to the ministry. Soon after his license to preach, he was settled in the pastoral office. At Amster-- dam and Oneonta, N. Y., he had charge of the Baptist churches, the latter, we believe, his last settlement. Like Rev. Jacob Knapp, he was led by the blessing attending his labors to give himself wholly to revival efforts.

His experience was one of believing prayer and cheerful consecration to his work, but this did not satisfy him. About fifteen years ago he gave himself earnestly and decisively to the attainment of that higher privilege of the Christian, an habitual, victorious abiding in Christ. He calls it, in the title of a small volume on the subject written by him, "The Rest of Faith." After the heart-searching struggle before the blessing was received, and the revelations made by the Spirit of an unsanctified nature, he wrote of the victory : —

"With this mingling of faith, desire, and expectation, I commenced a meeting on Cape Cod. After re-dedicating myself, in company with others, anew to God, I was in my room alone, pleading for the fulness of Christ's love, when all at once a sweet, heavenly peace filled all the vacuum in my soul, leaving no longing, no unrest, no dissatisfied feeling in my bosom. I felt, I knew that I was accepted fully of Jesus. A calm, simple, child-like trust took possession of my whole being; I felt that if I had a thousand hearts and lives I would give them all to the Saviour; my grateful love to him found expression in those glowing lines, —

> 'Oh, for a thousand tongues to sing
> My dear Redeemer's praise,
> The glories of my God and King,
> The triumphs of His grace!'

Then, for the first time in my life, I had that rest

which is more than peace. I had felt peace before, but feared I should not retain it; now I had peace without fear, which really became rest."

We shall give from his own pen some glimpses of the union evangelist in the field of spiritual harvests. In Albany, the capital of his native State, he held early and successfully a series of meetings. Of these efforts he records : —

"In this city I have labored in two meetings ; the first was held in Washington Avenue, in a hall fitted for the purpose. Ten or twelve members from different churches in the city had united in forming a mission-station in this street, and I was invited to hold a series of meetings there. This was in 1859. So much interest was manifested that several times when we closed our evening meeting at nine and a half o'clock, and a part of the audience left, there were enough outside about the doors to fill all vacant places in the hall. On one occasion I said to the congregation, 'If any of you feel that you are sinners, and will do anything you can to find Jesus, I will stay with you until you do find Him. I feel safe to take God at His word.' Six men and five women took the front seats, feeling that they were great sinners. This was after dismissing the congregation twice. After all but a few who remained to pray had retired, and the way of salvation through Jesus had been pointed out, we all bowed in prayer for the immediate conversion of these eleven individuals, they having said, 'We will pray for ourselves, and as far as we know will give ourselves now to the Saviour.' It was a moment of deep solemnity. The Holy Spirit was there to enlighten and lead the blind to Jesus. Within two hours every one of the eleven had found Jesus.

"This work continued four weeks with increasing interest, and many hearts and homes were made happy in

Albany.   Out of this revival grew the Washington Avenue
Baptist Church, since known as the Calvary Baptist
Church."

After holding successful meetings in less important
towns, he went to New England   In East Bridgewater,
Mass., he found a Methodist class, numbering about
twenty persons, who had hired for a place of worship the
meeting-house belonging to the Universalist society.   He
records : —

" At this early period in their history I was invited to
labor with them.   From the commencement, God was with
us and blessed our efforts.   The town seemed to be shaken
to its very foundation by the power of God's Spirit working
upon the hearts of men ; and sinners by scores flocked to
the fold of Christ.

" The 'Abington Standard' published the following,
in regard to the spiritual condition of this town at the
time of the revival : ' There is one event in the religious history of East Bridgewater which seems worthy
of notice.   When the celebrated Whitefield was in this
country, some one hundred and twenty years ago, an
effort was made to secure his services at that village,
and he himself expressed a strong desire to labor there,
for even then the place was notorious for its wickedness.
The effort, however, failed, and an old gentleman publicly prophesied that there would not be a revival there
during that generation.

" Until the present time there has been none ; and during the century and over that has intervened, that part of
the town has been known by its own inhabitants as the
' God-forsaken village.'   Now a change has taken place.
Meetings are crowded, and many are turning from their
evil ways."

In Chelsea, a "union meeting held in the spring of
1866 was blessed with a deep and far-reaching work of

grace. There was a marked spirit of unity and harmony among Christians of different denominations; they seemed to feel that they were indeed members of Christ's family, and were laboring for a common cause."

In Springfield, where he was invited to labor directly with Dr. Ide's church, the meeting soon became, in spirit and form, a union meeting, embracing the different evangelical denominations of the city.

" City Hall, the largest audience-room in the city, was secured for many of our meetings, where were sometimes gathered as many as three thousand persons, while many were obliged to turn away, being unable to get in.

" As the interest was not denominational, so it was not sectional; but throughout the entire city the great subject of conversation was 'the meeting.' War was not the all-absorbing question, but men found time to talk about religion.

" The awakening was not confined to Springfield, but, to an extraordinary degree, was felt in many of the villages and towns in the surrounding country.

" The 'Daily Union' of March 17, 1864, made the following reference to an evening meeting in City Hall: ' Strong men, in the pride and strength of manhood, were led to inquire what they should do to be saved. No one who was there could doubt for a moment the reality of religion. There was no excitement, no shouting, no noisy demonstrations; but every one was calm, thoughtful, and deeply impressed with the solemnity of the occasion."

Adds Mr. Earle, "The Spirit of God reached all classes. Workmen connected with the U. S. Armory at Springfield were constant attendants of these meetings, and manifested their interest in them, and in the subject of religion, by sending the following petition, signed by nearly six hundred of their number : —

" ' SPRINGFIELD, March 9, 1864.

" ' REV. A. B. EARLE :

" ' *Dear Sir,* — Are you willing to hold a meeting at City Hall, some evening during your stay in our city, with special reference to the men connected with Armory where we are employed ? '

" This petition is in my possession, with that long list of names as they were signed upon one roll, very much soiled by the finger-marks of those workingmen, and I prize it just as it is."

In compliance with this request the meeting was held, and it was a solemn, heavenly season, — one which we may believe many of those noble men will look back upon from eternity with great joy. It was thought over four hundred persons rose that evening, and requested the prayers of Christians that they might be brought into the fold of Christ.

" Without attempting any estimate of the number of conversions, some idea may be gained from the words of one of the pastors : ' As the fruit of this meeting, over six hundred united with the churches.' A new Baptist church sprang up from that meeting, and has been a growing, working church ever since, and is exerting a deep and wide-felt influence throughout the city. Many converts were also gathered into the churches in adjoining towns as the result of that meeting.

" In the summer of 1858, after a year of hard and constant work in the States, during which I had preached more than five hundred sermons, I went, with my family, to one of the British Provinces, hoping to find retirement and rest for a few weeks on those quiet, healthy, hospitable shores.

" The steamer in which we embarked at Boston landed us safely at the wharf in St. John, New Brunswick, Friday evening, July 23. Before I had been three days in the

city I commenced preaching, and went on from that time,
until within about five months I had preached, in different
parts of the Province, over three hundred times, and trust
fifteen hundred or two thousand souls had been 'born
again,' as the fruit of our meetings. I found a kind and
generous-hearted people there, everywhere welcoming me
as a servant of Jesus."

At Haverhill the interest was deep, including in its
range Bradford Female Seminary, nearly all of whose
pupils, before impenitent, were hopefully converted.

Fall River was the field of one of the most powerful displays of the divine presence that attended his preaching.
The first service was opened with seventeen persons; the
last closed with not less than seventeen hundred.

We quote from a letter written to "The New York
Observer," Feb. 21, 1863 : "We are enjoying a glorious
work of grace in this city. It commenced in one of the
Baptist churches with the labors of Rev. A. B. Earle, whose
success as an evangelist has for several years past been so
great. All classes and all ages were alike moved, from
the little school-child to those who had grown gray in the
service of Satan. Such was the power of the Spirit that
the strong oaks of Bashan were made to bow with as
much ease as the willows by the water-courses. It is 'the
Lord's doing, and is marvellous in our eyes.'"

It is believed that more than a thousand souls were
born again as the fruit of this meeting, and more than
half that number connected with the churches in the city,
and many with those in the vicinity.

Mr. Earle was in Washington, D. C., at the time of the
second inauguration of Abraham Lincoln, "and yet was
crowned with a large blessing. There were not so many
conversions as in many other places, about one hundred
having given me their names as among the converts; still
I think the work was glorious in its results. A few days

23

after leaving the city there came to me the following cheering letter : —

"WASHINGTON, D. C., March 25, 1865.

"DEAR BROTHER EARLE,—

"Good news for you! Night before last Hon. Amos Kendall rose in our meeting and said he believed he was converted many years ago, but obstacles arose which placed him in the dark. Since the meeting you held, he had been very much exercised.

"After giving his views of religion, and the duty of all believers in Christ, he said he was determined for the balance of his life to be known as on the Lord's side, and wished to unite with the church. He referred to your sermon of last Sabbath, from the words 'Almost thou persuadest me to be a Christian.'"

In 1866 Mr. Earle was called to California by the Ministerial Union, which included nearly all the Evangelical ministers of San Francisco and vicinity. A repeated discussion of the great question, "Our duty as ministers to the masses of the city who are unreached by the gospel," led to the invitation to the evangelist to come over and help them. Mr. Earle states the effect of this communication on his own mind : —

"Could duty lie in that direction? For a time it seemed not : but something began to change convictions; friends, too, began to say, 'God is in it'; Dr. Kirk, Dr. Bright, Dr. Backus, and others who are wont to watch the leadings of Providence from a high standpoint, said, 'Go.' At length, on my knees, in my study, in prayer, with my wife, the answer came ; light from the golden gates of the New Jerusalem fell upon the path over the seas into the Golden Gate of the Pacific; my way was clear ; and without hesitation I telegraphed, 'I will come. Will sail September 11.'"

The evangelist incidentally refers to another, whose serene trust and clear judgment are appreciated by all who knew her : —

"Grateful I shall ever be that my wife accompanied me ; for whatever success attended my labors was due, in no small measure, to her cheerful presence, her faith, ever bright and strong, her clear and comprehensive views of truth, and her serene and close communion with God."

Farewell services were held in Strong-Place Church, Brooklyn, N. Y., on the evening before his departure. Mr. Earle says of his arrival in California : —

"My welcome at San Francisco was warm and hearty, making me sure the promise of co-operation would be carried out to the fullest extent. Immediately on my arrival, one common union meeting was established as the working-ground and rallying-point for the various denominations and churches connected with the Ministerial Union. For this purpose the Union had secured Platt's Hall as the regular place of meeting, and the occasional use of Union Hall, because these were much larger than any of the churches ; and the expense of hiring these halls — some fifteen hundred dollars — gives an idea of the heartiness with which the people entered into the work. The same spirit was manifest in all they did : in the crowded attendance, in their thoughtfulness as hearers and promptness as doers of the Word. Very soon deep, quiet feeling was manifest over the entire city ; men were awakened to the solemn issues of life as never before ; the Unseen seemed to sweep over and sink out of sight the Seen ; people felt they were living for eternity.

"Some idea of the extent of the work, even at the end of the first two weeks, may be obtained in the following extracts from an article in one of the daily papers, 'The Alta' : —

"'A religious revival, such as has never before been

experienced on this coast, is now in progress in this city.
. . . Mr. Earle arrived in this city a little over two
weeks ago. . . . He commenced his services on Sunday, October 7, in Dr. A. L. Stone's church. On Monday, the 8th, he preached in Dr. Scudder's church. On
Tuesday, in Dr. Cheney's; and most of the time since has
been preaching in Platt's Hall, twice each day; on Sunday, at Union Hall.

"'The congregation which assembled, on Sunday evening last, at Union Hall, was the largest ever collected
under one roof on this coast; every available space for
standing room was occupied; there could not have been
less than three thousand auditors present, and there were
at least one thousand who could not get into the hall, and
were obliged to leave without hearing Mr. Earle.

"'But the number attending these services is the least
remarkable thing about them. The interest pervading
the assemblage, amounting even to solemnity of devotion,
is extraordinary, and the quiet order and reverence displayed is astonishing.'

"I continued my labors here five weeks, preaching twice
each day, on Sunday three times. The Spirit reached,
with His convicting, converting power, people of every
age and condition, in every part of the city; converts multiplied by hundreds."

From Sonora and Columbia, Mr. Earle went to Oakland, across the bay from San Francisco, the educational
centre of that region and the home of many of the business
and professional men of San Francisco. He says: —

"I spent the next ten days in a delightful season of
labor with the different denominations. The windows of
heaven were opened wide; the revival spread not only
among the permanent inhabitants of the town, but also
through the schools and seminaries, bringing many of the
scholars to the feet of the Great Teacher, where they

learned the alphabet of all true knowledge, — 'the fear of the Lord,' which ' is the beginning of wisdom.' "

Since Mr. Earle's return to this country, his course has been the same as before. 'He has held meetings of great interest again in New York, New England, and the West; among them, the last spring, was one in Chicago.

We think Mr. Earle is the first evangelist who has told us of the peculiar trials of the calling: " One great trial in this work is the necessity of being from home most of the time. Home has so many sweet and soothing associations, so many holy, purifying influences, which are just what a minister needs in his work. To be deprived of all these for so great a portion of the time is no small sacrifice. Oh, the joy of my bounding heart, when, after weeks, and perhaps months, of unceasing toil and anxiety, I turn towards my home, weary and worn ! I have often, at such times, repeated the expressive lines, —

> ' What do we reck on a weary way,
>   Though lonely and benighted,
> When we know there are lips to chide our stay,
>   And eyes that will beam, love-lighted? '

" Another of the evangelist's trials is the distrust and prejudice cherished, even among good men, in regard to his work. Many pastors feel such a prejudice towards this department of ministerial labor, that they say, ' I will never invite an evangelist to assist me'; and not a few of their members sustain them in this position.

" This is, no doubt, in part the result of misrepresentation, and the want of a careful examination of the subject, and much, no doubt, is chargeable to the want of wisdom and prudence on the part of some of us who are attempting to perform the difficult work of an evangelist; yet, like the pastoral office, it must be perpetuated, notwithstanding its faults, and therefore, those who are called to this work must go forward in it, no matter what its trials.

"Years ago I made up my mind to go on with this work, and do what I could in the great harvest-field, and bring as many souls to Jesus as possible, without stopping to defend it against prejudice or opposition. And yet no one feels more keenly than myself an unkind word or look or act, or is more sensitive to the touch of distrust or prejudice.

"The burden of soul at certain stages of a meeting is sometimes almost crushing. No one can realize this who has not borne the responsibility of conducting a series of revival meetings. It is often necessary to converse and pray with different inquirers many times in a single evening, until nature seems unable to endure more.

"It is a trial to be obliged to part with friends almost as soon as their acquaintance is formed. Habit does not render it any easier. It is just as painful now, after having held about two hundred series of meetings, in different parts of the country, to part at the close of these seasons, where we have wept and prayed and rejoiced together, as it was many years ago. Oh, the strength of friendship formed at Jesus' feet!

"Such are some of the trials in the work of an evangelist; but they are far outweighed by its joys, the greatest of which is the necessity of living near the Saviour, if he would have success." He alludes glowingly to the delights of holy friendships and heavenly prospects of reunion.

Rev. Dr. Hague, in the "Watchman and Reflector," gives us a pen-picture of the evangelist : —

"Again and again have we been asked by friends, far and near, 'What do you think of Mr. Earle as an evangelist and a co-worker? Does he exert an influence that is healthful and enduring? Wherein lieth his power?' First of all, you will say to yourself, he is honest, he is in earnest, he is simple-hearted, he believes what he says, he is a transparent character; he has gained your sympathy and confidence. Next, you are consciously inclined to give him your attention, and yield yourself to his friendly suggestions, that seem so apt, so judiciously put, so exactly adapted to your condition. They reveal you to yourself; they touch the points of your own unexpressed experiences; they meet your deep heart needs. All at once, ' before you know it,' as one said, you will respond to his appeals. You forget he is a minister, so far, at least, as to regard him officially; you think of him as a good man, a fellow-sinner, a loving brother, a joyous Christian, who has a heavenly treasure that he desires to impart, and that you would receive. If you must tell somebody where his power lies, you will say it is in his simplicity and godly sincerity, and a profound heart experience, which tells its own story and wins you."

Mr. Earle resided for several years after coming to New England in Abington, but since has purchased a beautiful yet not expensive residence in Newton, the present family home.

A little earlier in the evangelistic service, and yet contemporary with Mr. Earle, was the Rev. Emmerson Andrews, a man of eccentric, off-hand, self-reliant character, an uncompromising Baptist. That he was greatly useful and sowed no seeds of discord is quite evident from his narrative of his manifold labors. He was born in Mansfield, Massachusetts, Nov. 24, 1806. His early life was passed quietly on his father's farm. His religious convictions began while a boy, and at times were very deep. Preparatory studies for college were pursued at Chesterfield Academy, N. H., and later, at Kimball Union Academy, Plainfield, the same State, where, having heard some time before a sermon from Dr. Nettleton from " Quench not the Spirit," which had a subduing effect, he openly espoused the cause of Christ.

September, 1831, he entered Union College, graduating in 1834. While there he united with the Baptist church. He had felt before a call to preach, and very soon to the work of an evangelist. In 1845–6 he spent a year with the church at Reading, Pa.

Beginning at Lee, N. Y., in 1838, he has been engaged in holding protracted meetings in the Middle and New England States, meanwhile visiting Europe, first in 1846, as delegate to the Evangelical Alliance and World's Temperance Convention. His labors have been confined to his own denomination, but have been distinguished by thoroughly Evangelical preaching, earnestness, and the advocacy of every true reform. He records of himself, "I have travelled and preached in twenty-eight States of our Union, in Canada, in Europe, in Africa and Asia. I think about forty thousand have been truly converted in meetings where I have labored, of whom I have immersed some thousand in pools, rivers, lakes, and waters from the Atlantic to the Pacific. I have been called to pastorates, eight of which were in cities. To God be all the glory!"

Rev. A. P. Graves is an evangelist of considerable success, but of whom we have been unable to get any account beyond the general report of his faithful, untiring efforts to bring men to Christ.

Rev. Edwin Burnham, also Baptist, is one of our ablest preachers, and has done good service as an evangelist, but no record of his itineracy has come to hand. Independent, fearless, and somewhat eccentric, he always commands attention. His residence is at Newburyport, Mass.

Mr. Whittier, of Lowell, Mass., is also a successful evangelist.

Rev. R. A. Patterson has for several years been in the field of evangelism, and is now preaching successfully at the West. He expects to return soon to engage in similar labors in his native Scotland.

CHAPTER XXI.

The Children's Evangelist, Rev. Edward Payson Hammond. — His
Early Experiences. — College Life. — Goes to England. — Engages
in Study. — Begins the Work of an Evangelist. — Revival Services and Scenes. — Testimonies to his Usefulness. — Returns to
America. — Experiences Abroad repeated here. — Marries, and
visits Palestine. — Activity since his Return. — Underwoods.

We call Mr. Hammond the children's evangelist, because, as Mr. Earle has been the champion of union revival
meetings, he has given special attention, and certainly with
singular success, to the children. This prominence occupied by the young in his ministry has been far from exclusive ; on the contrary, it has been made by him preparatory
to, and auxiliary in, carrying forward his efforts in connection with pastors among the adult population. In this
method of labor he is quite alone, and, according to pastoral testimony, rarely, if ever, has made a failure. The
wonderful interest he awakens in the juvenile people not
only does not absorb and distract attention, but with a
recognized harmony contributes to the general development and progress of the awakening. After making a
brief record of his life till he began his evangelistic career,
we shall let sketches of his varied and multiplied labors,
and the statements of clergymen and others concerning
their character and usefulness, speak for the evangelist.

Edward Payson Hammond was born in Ellington, a
quiet town in the valley of the Connecticut, Sept. 1, 1831,
but passed his boyhood and youth in Vernon, Conn. He
was a child of prayer, consecrated to God by parental piety ;
especially was he nurtured with holy fidelity under the

wing of maternal love. At the age of seventeen he attended school at Southington, where had been a powerful revival of religion, including in its sweep nearly all the youth of the place.

Mr. Hammond, in his addresses, sometimes refers to the story of his conversion, and relates it thus : —

"The first Sabbath of my stay in Southington was the communion. This was held between the services, and all who were not Christians were in the habit of going out. As I looked about, it seemed that all my friends and relatives and new acquaintances were gathering around the table of the Lord. Among the few who passed out were none whom I knew. The thought of the judgment day flashed across my troubled mind, and the awful scenes of that final separation passed like a panorama before my view. On returning to my boarding-place that night, a lady handed me James's 'Anxious Inquirer' to read. I glanced my eye hastily over a few of its pages, but thought it too dry a book for me, and I angrily threw it down. But this did not extract the arrow of conviction that had pierced my heart. I felt that I was a sinner, hastening on to the great judgment day unprepared. Little did I know of the earnest pleadings that were daily ascending from a mother's fond heart. Day by day my convictions deepened. My heart rebelled against God. I disputed His undivided claim to my heart.

"During these dark days I read James's 'Anxious Inquirer.' I used to study it by the hour with my Bible, looking out all the passages referred to. I thus saw more and more of my deceitful and polluted heart. At first, it was thoughts of the judgment day and the sight of the wicked going away into everlasting punishment that alarmed me ; but afterwards it was the sight of myself that alarmed me most. I was led by the Holy Spirit to look on Him whom my sins had 'pierced, and . . . mourn.'

(Zach. xii, 10.) I began to understand those words in Acts v, 31 : ' Him hath God exalted with His right hand to be a Prince and a Saviour, for to give repentance.' I shall never forget that calm autumn morning when I fell upon my knees in my little closet and repeated the hymn my mother had taught me, —

> ' Alas, and did my Saviour bleed,
> And did my Sovereign die?
> Would He devote that sacred head
> For such a worm as I?
>
> ' Was it for crimes that I had done,
> He groaned upon the tree?
> Amazing pity! grace unknown,
> And love beyond degree ! '

"I then saw that God ' might be just, and the justifier of him which believeth in Jesus' (Rom. iii, 26), and that I must

> ' Cast my deadly doing down,
> Down, down at Jesus' feet' ;

And with tears in my eyes I exclaimed, in the words of the last verse of the hymn which I was repeating, —

> ' But drops of grief can ne'er repay
> The debt of love I owe.
> Here, Lord, I give myself away,
> 'T is all that I can do.'

"It was then the Holy Spirit, that had so long been striving with me, took of the things of Christ and showed them unto me ; my blind eyes were opened. I saw that God was satisfied with what Christ had done ; that Jesus had paid the debt, and I had only to trust Him for it all."

He subsequently completed his preparation for college at Phillips Academy, Andover, Mass. There, as wherever he went after his conversion, God blessed his faithfulness

to the conversion of souls in the institution and in neighboring villages, in which, with other students, he established meetings. He entered Williams College in 1854.
Without neglecting his studies, as his instructors testify,
he labored earnestly and successfully for the conversion
of his classmates. With Henry Hopkins, the president's
son, he attended meetings in Pownal, Vt. The little
company of seven or eight Christians there was increased
to a prosperous church. In the spring of 1855 he went,
in behalf of the American Sunday School Union, among
the Alleghany Mountains, and planted several Sunday
Schools during his vacation, which in some instances proved
to be the nucleus of churches. He received his degree,
with an appointment for Commencement, in 1858, and in
1861 the degree of A. M.

The desire and intention to be a missionary had been
cherished by the young disciple; but God otherwise
ordered his useful life. In the year 1858 he became a
student in Union Theological Seminary, New York, and
in that great city continued with unflagging zeal his home
missionary work among the destitute.

Having planned a trip to Europe, he sailed in the noble
ship "Edinburgh." Spending a few weeks in England and
Scotland, Mr. Hammond went to Ireland to witness and
enjoy the wondrous displays of divine grace on that island.
At Ballymena he addressed large audiences, triumphantly
vindicating the American revivals from the charge circulated abroad by their enemies, that they had proved a
failure. The two weeks' experience in Ireland was a fresh
preparation and impulse in the life-work of saving souls.

Returning to Scotland after a tour on the Continent, Mr.
Hammond failed to receive remittances from America, and
was disappointed in his expectations of sailing for his native
land. Unexpectedly God's kind providence opened the
way for resuming and prosecuting his theological studies in

the Free Church College in Edinburgh. Dr. W. L. Alexander requested him to supply the destitute town of Musselburgh, six miles from Edinburgh. Of the results a few months later Dr. Alexander said : —

" I think no impartial and grateful person will say that the soil in Musselburgh has been one favorable to the growth of a vital spiritual piety. When I heard of and saw crowded gatherings of people, evening after evening during the week, assembled to hear plain, earnest, and faithful addresses on the concerns of their soul; when I saw the deep, unmistakable earnestness of groups of inquirers; when I listened to the sobs and cries of men and women,— some of them as unlikely to be moved to such displays of emotion as can be well conceived ; when I found that night after night the work of conversion was apparently going forward, and many who had been not only careless but profligate were giving evidence of being born again; and when I heard of large meetings during the day and numerously attended meetings in the street for religious purposes, — I felt that indeed new and strange things had come to pass, and I could only bow my head and say, ' It is the doing of the Lord, and it is marvellous in our eyes.' "

A call was extended to Mr. Hammond by the church in Musselburgh to settle over them as their pastor, but his heart was in the work of the evangelist. Six churches and five ministers of Haddington united in extending the invitation to commence a series of meetings there, and he at once accepted. For a week they were held in the different churches. The old cathedral where Dr. John Brown, the great expositor, and John Knox preached, seating fifteen hundred, was filled. The Holy Spirit was present, and a number were led to the Lamb of God, while Christians were refreshed and rejoiced together in His saving presence.

Mr. Hammond went to Huntly, in the north of Scotland, to speak in the open-air meetings held for two days under the patronage of the Duchess of Gordon, who expended $2,000, it was stated, in defraying expenses of trains going to and returning from the grounds, and other demands upon her liberality. It was the inauguration of a series of similar gatherings in the kingdom, attended with incalculable good.

In one of the large churches of Aberdeen, crowded to its utmost capacity, after an earnest appeal the expressions of anxiety were so general and thrilling that one of the elders, standing in the porch, called Mr. Hammond to the door, and said the congregation must be dispersed, — he did n't want such excitement. But the people would not go till they were driven away, and flocked to another temple where an inquiry-meeting was in progress, and enjoyed an awful, yet glorious and memorable season.

October 8, 1860, Mr. Hammond went to Edinburgh to supply the pulpit of Richmond place Chapel for four weeks, and addressed meetings every night during that time with an increasing measure of the Spirit's influence.

In Mr. Hammond's first memorandum of the New Year he writes, "It is safe to record that, after careful calculation, about seventeen hundred profess to have been awakened and found Jesus within the past year."

We have a strong confirmation of the reality and greatness of the blessing enjoyed in Annan from the pen of Rev. Mr. Young, which we give. It was written, as the date shows, more than a year after the revival scenes described, and addressed to a friend in America : —

"I have the most lively and happy recollection of Mr. Hammond's coming to Annan. Of his peculiar qualifications for an evangelist, I place in the foreground his humble, child-like confidence in the Lord. Believing that God has given promises, he expects Him to keep them. This expectation gives the tone to his prayers, and helps him greatly in all that he undertakes. Whenever he came among us he urged us to look for great things, and quoted oftener than once, and with excellent effect, these words of God by Jeremiah : 'Call unto me, and I will answer thee, and shew thee great and mighty things which thou knowest not.' (Jer. xxxiii, 3.)"

Mr. Hammond commenced his labors in Dr. Buchanan's beautiful church, whose congregation represent much of the wealth and culture of the city. He afterwards preached for a number of evenings in Hope-street Church. The awakening spread through the town with great power.

We cannot omit a pleasant note from Rev. Mr. Bonar, the well-known and admired poet, whose lines are more frequently quoted, perhaps, than those of any living religious writer, feeling quite sure it will interest the reader, and inspire confidence in his friend : —

KELSO, April.

I have been following your footsteps with interest in many quarters, and I now write to ask you to visit the borders. I would earnestly entreat you to come to our help here. This is the centre of a very populous district. Many of our villages have been visited with blessing. As yet Kelso has only received a few drops. We are waiting for the shower. Will you not come and help us? Do try. I need not use arguments. I commend the matter to God, and remain yours very faithfully, in the bonds of Christ,

HORATIUS BONAR.

Worn down with his labors, he left them the forepart of April, 1861, for a tour on the Continent. Before leaving for America, a *soirée* presentation meeting, presided over by Robert M'Cowan, Esq., was held in the City Hall, containing 4,000 people, which was packed; and it was believed three times that number would have been present had there been room.

Upon Mr. Hammond's arrival in America, he began to labor again in Pownal, Vt., and other places, finding it difficult to realize the first intention to rest and recruit exhausted energies. He received invitations to labor in different fields, when, incidentally visiting Boston, early in September, he preached in the Salem-street Church. Interest was apparent, and prominent pastors of the city urged the continuance of the meetings, and took part in them. Rev. Geo. Dunham, who had supplied the pulpit in the pastor's absence, wrote the following sketch for the "Congregationalist" : —

"It seems very evident that God is in the assemblies, doing His great work, convicting sinners, and delivering them from bondage and death. The great and peculiar feature of the movement is found in the inquiry-meetings that follow the preaching. At the close of this service all Christians that are willing to converse and pray with anxious sinners, or to unite in praying for them, are invited to repair to the lecture-room, and take with them as many, who are willing to be conversed with personally, as they can persuade to go.

"The meeting is opened with singing, and some short addresses and prayers. At this point it is always instinct with interest and solemnity. It afterwards becomes informal and social, the brethren and sisters speaking a few words of inquiry, counsel, or encouragement to each other, and searching out such as are yet strangers to the peace of God, conversing with them, striving to deepen their feelings, and point them to the Saviour; they kneel together in little groups about the room and in adjoining rooms, and pray individually with such as are willing to be prayed with. These personal and close dealings often culminate at once in hopeful conversion. Many souls have been led at once directly to Christ, and have obtained a sweet relief. Sometimes eight or ten groups will be conversing and praying together at the same time, in low and earnest tones; and instead of the confusion that might be apprehended, the effect is not unlike the order of a Sabbath-school recitation.

"Of an open-air meeting on the Common, the 'Boston Journal' contained this notice : —

"'Rev. Dr. Kirk conducted the services, and after a few remarks, stating the meeting to be one in which all denominations could unite in seeking religion, he opened with prayer, and introduced Rev. E. P. Hammond, who followed with an impressive discourse for nearly an hour, and with simple statements of the vast amount of evil daily practised by us, impressed his hearers with the truth of their sinful state, and invited them all to seek the forgiveness and grace of God.'

"For a further history of the revival, we have a sketch from the pen of a reporter of the 'Traveller,' of a meeting held Oct. 5 : —

"'Rev. Dr. Kirk, who was present, then rose and addressed the large company before him. Every eye was fixed upon the speaker, and the deepest solemnity pervaded the entire audience. He commenced by saying, "What a sight! What are you all here for? What do you want?" After a few words upon the immense importance of the occasion, he asked those present who hoped they had recently found the Saviour to rise. A large number stood, including whole seats of young men and some young children. He then prayed for them, and afterwards addressed those present who were seeking the Saviour, in his usual impressive and earnest manner.

"'Rev Mr. Hammond then requested Christians either to assist him in conversing with inquirers or to repair to an adjoining room for prayer. An interesting scene then followed. The whole company were at once engaged in praying, talking, and praising God. In one corner were four or five ladies kneeling and praying around an anxious soul. In another was a group of little children, who

24

were addressed by an elderly man, and exhorted to give their hearts to Christ. In another place was a young man rejoicing, who a few days ago was a Catholic.'"

From Boston Mr. Hammond went to Portland, Me., with Rev. Mr Moore of the Union Church. We take extracts from a letter addressed to a well-known pastor, in accordance with his request, which appeared in the " Congregationalist " : —

PORTLAND, Dec. 11, 1851.

REV. DR. KIRK:

My Dear Brother,— You have asked me to recall and state the circumstances that preceded and introduced the remarkable work of grace now advancing in our city. Soon after the pastor's return from Boston, he learned that Mr. E. P. Hammond had been invited by a young clergyman of this city to spend a week with his congregation. The invitation was accepted. Mr. Hammond spoke each evening throughout the week, and by the blessing of God upon his labors, much good, it is confidently believed, was done. The pastor of the Second Church attended some of the meetings, encouraged his people also to attend, and eventually suggested an invitation to Mr. Hammond to labor in the Second Parish.

With the exception of ten days' absence, Mr. E. P. Hammond has been indefatigable in his labors. To his honor be it spoken, he has in no instance attempted to invade the prerogatives of the pastor, has readily adopted every practical suggestion as to methods of procedure, and has proved himself, in all respects, a workman that needeth not to be ashamed. The seal of divine approval has been most unequivocally affixed to his unwearied labors.

Pray for us, dear brother, that the Word of the Lord may have free course and be glorified.

Many sheets might be filled with accounts of specific cases, but these, for the present, I reserve.

Yours most fraternally,
J. J. CARRUTHERS.

From Bethel, a romantic town twenty miles from the base of the White Mountains, and a place of considerable resort in the summer, the pastor wrote of Mr. Hammond's labors to the "Christian Union" early in January, 1861, after daily meetings had been in progress nearly a week : —

"God is pouring out His Spirit upon us in Bethel. Many hope that they have been 'born again.' Many are asking what they shall do to be saved. Our meetings are solemn, well attended, well sustained by the prayers and efforts of God's people."

From Bethel Mr. Hammond went to Gorham, a village among the White Hills, — "peace reposing in the bosom of strength," — where as the result of the merciful visitation of the Spirit a church was formed, and a neat, pleasant temple dedicated to the worship of Him "who touches the hills and they melt, who taketh up the isles as a very little thing."

The city of Bath, whose population had never the reputation of being excitable, but staid in character and devoted to the business of a sea-port town, was stirred with scenes of unearthly interest during the months of January and February, 1862. Rev. J. O. Fiske, in a communication to the "Christian Mirror," said : —

"From the very first, special attention was given, in meetings Saturday and Wednesday afternoons, and in the other meetings, to the children. They were all very deeply interested, and one of the best features of Mr. Hammond's labors among us was his unintermitted, skilful, and believing zeal for the conversion of children. Quite a number of these lambs of the flock we hope have passed from death unto life, and a few of them between the ages of twelve and seventeen years have been received into our church. No meetings that I have ever attended have been more delightful and solemn than some of these children's meetings."

South Paris, a village on the Grand Trunk Railroad, between Portland and Bethel, received a great and abiding dispensation of the Spirit.

Farmington, a delightful village, where Rev. Mr. Howard, the brother of Gen. Howard of the army, was pastor of the Congregational Church, had a glorious refreshing, during which a hundred and fifty were, it is believed, brought to Christ.

In the providence of God, the writer, seeking health, went to Plymouth, Mass., in the autumn of 1861. With all descendants of the Pilgrims in natural or spiritual lineage he felt a deep interest in the Old Colony, with its beautiful bay, where the "Mayflower" rocked, Burying Hill where their ashes lie, and the church they planted, with sacrifice and suffering without a parallel since the days of the apostles.

Errors were rife in the community, and too often the Zion, which should beat them back, had slept while her adversary sowed the tares. The parish was visited, church fasts appointed, and the necessity of a revival kept before the people on all occasions. The aspect of the congregation gradually changed to a marked seriousness, and indications of unusual interest were apparent among the impenitent. At this crisis, attention was turned for help to Mr. Hammond. The church invited him to come; and he held the first services on Sabbath-day, the last of March.

The work in a brief time assumed a decided form and power. Although he remained less than three weeks, the house of God was opened nightly for almost nine weeks, during which were witnessed scenes of stirring interest. In the town between two and three hundred expressed hope in Christ, many of whom, at least, have continued to walk according to the gospel.

While in Plymouth, a call from the city of Lewiston, Me., the united voice of the pastors of the various churches, came to Mr. Hammond, to labor in the whitening harvest-field. Five hundred persons were hopefully converted,

— as we find in the "Lewiston Herald," from the pen of one of the ministers.

In early summer, in obedience to the repeated call of Christians in Brunswick, the beautiful seat of Bowdoin College, and twenty miles from Lewiston, the evangelist entered upon a course of systematic effort there, to concentrate and use for the salvation of souls the faith and working power of the churches. There had been a burden on the hearts of some connected with the college, both for it — consecrated to Christ by prayer — and the people of the town, perhaps never known without a blessing near.

Dr. Adams's large and beautiful church was soon thronged; and with him, on the platform, were gathered the Faculty of the college.

It was the writer's privilege to go amid the memorable scenes of that deep and blessed work of the Spirit; to meet with the students when the heavenly influence pervaded the college; to stand with the pastor, who has long been over the flock of Christ, in the sanctuary of God, and in the open air, when none could doubt the presence of the Most High. More hallowed hours, fresh and fragrant still in memory, we have never known in all the experiences of Pentecostal blessings.

After Mr. Hammond's marriage about ten years since, he sailed for Europe *en route* to Palestine, where he spent several months, and wrote upon his return a poetical narrative of his tour through the Holy Land.

Since his return to this country, he has been devoted to itinerating from New England to Oregon, and is on that western border of the republic while we write.

Before he went to the Pacific coast, he conducted meetings of deepest interest in Nashua, N. H., and other places at the East, in Cincinnati, St. Louis, Mo., Lawrence, Kansas, and many towns besides in the great West. The narrative of the work in Lawrence fills a goodly pamphlet,

and the published accounts of revival scenes elsewhère
would make volumes.

At San Francisco the awakening was very extensive.
Rev. A. L. Stone, D. D., formerly of the Park-street
Church, Boston, united heartily in the movement, as did
nearly all the pastors. Mr. K. B. Fisher, we believe, an
Oakland pastor, gives a sketch of his methods and success
there, which is a very good account of his freedom in the
use of means to reach the masses : —

"Oakland is a conservative city, the Athens of the
Pacific. This spirit extended even to our churches; yet
they resolved to lay aside all personal prejudice and aid
Mr. Hammond in his labors, which God had so signally
owned elsewhere. The interest so increased that it was
evident some larger place of meeting must be provided.
The Committee of Arrangements therefore caused to be
erected a large pavilion, capable of seating 3,500 people,
and affording standing-room for 1,000 more. Our dear
brother has conquered prejudice and won for himself our
warmest personal affection. Not long ago a beloved pastor, professor in our theological seminary, a man scholarly
and conservative in an unusual degree, rose in one of our
morning meetings, and said in substance, 'I desire to
thank God for the variety of ways in which He speaks to
the sinner's heart. ' Words that would fail to impress me
bring other souls to Jesus ; and men whom I might preach
to for years without effect are persuaded by the earnest
call of our dear brother to choose the better way.'

"The same pastor said on another public occasion that
these meetings had done very much to wean him from his
old forms and methods, and bring him into greater freedom and liberty.

"One evening, a severe shower came up. The frail roof
flapped in the wind, and through its worn seams torrents
of rain descended on the worshippers. A few who had

umbrellas raised them, and the rest edged away from the intruding streams as well as they could. I think under any other leadership the meeting would have been broken up; but Mr. Hammond said a few inspiring words, and bade his choir of three hundred sing 'Hold the fort.' When they had gone through the four stanzas and chorus, he ordered it repeated, and his own powerful voice led the chorus to every verse : —

> ' Hold the fort, for I am coming,
>   Jesus signals still.
> Wave the answer back to heaven, —
>   By Thy grace we will.'

Overhead the rain fell in torrents, the canvas flapped in the wind, the tent-poles swayed to and fro, people moved and rustled in their seats, but not more than fifty left the place ; and the great choir never paused, and the volume of song rose above the war of the elements, till at last the storm subsided and the service went on.

" The most doubting among us are ready to confess that this is indeed God's own work. We have felt His presence in the solemn hush of the assembled thousands, when His claims were urged upon them, and when in tears of joyful thanksgiving, hearts overflowing with love to Jesus told in broken accents of His conscious indwelling."

We give two interesting incidents, as pleasant glimpses of some results in Stockton City : —

" In a court-room in Stockton, California, May 26, an important case was to have been tried. When the hour for commencing arrived, one of the lawyers arose and addressed the judge as follows : ' May it please your Honor, you are perhaps aware that there is an eminent evangelist in our town who has been doing all in his power as a peace-maker among our citizens. As a conse-quence of his labors, the plaintiff and defendant have met, and settled in an amicable manner this perplexing suit, which has already had two trials; and it is now, therefore, taken out of court.' At this, the judge, who was a Christian man, rejoiced, and the jury were especially delighted that they were released from the irksome task of hearing the witnesses and pleas.

" Another fact of interest was related yesterday morning in the prayer-meeting. A lady said that last week she was at the governor's banquet, where wine was flowing freely. One of the speakers, while making an exciting speech, said, 'If there is any one present who was ever happier in his life than he is to-night, I call upon him to at once arise and say so.' A young man sprang to his feet and said, 'I was very much happier in one of Mr. Hammond's meetings than I am here.' It produced a profound impression on that gay audience."

The intelligence from Portland, Oregon, respecting his labors in that region is not unlike that from different parts of the land nearer home.

Mr. Hammond employs the inquiry-meeting, especially a general one at the close of service, when all who are willing to have religious conversation are requested to remain. This solemn meeting sometimes continues for two hours. He expounds the Scriptures at almost every meeting, adding illustrations with excellent effect. His vacation home is Vernon, Conn., where a widowed mother died ten years ago, and a sister resides.

Rev. J. D. Potter is widely known among the churches, mainly outside of our cities, apparently preferring to labor in parishes where he, in connection with one or two pastors, can employ with more freedom and success his methods of reaching the population as a whole, among whom he labors. In some respects he resembles Dr. Nettleton. If for lack of co-operation or any serious hinderance to the work in a church, he sees little prospect of success, he suddenly departs to another field. Dignified, earnest, and thoroughly evangelical, he commands attention, and is straightforward in dealing with the people.

Mr. Potter does not wish a public record made of his long services until the night of death has closed it. His home was in Brooklyn. That Mr. Potter has been instrumental in the conversion of a multitude is undeniable, nor have we heard of any deprecated results from his labors of twenty years or more.

While in college Mr. Potter passed through a crisis of religious experience which cleared his views of truth, settled his faith in the atoning sacrifice, and led him into itineracy, to which he has been wholly devoted. Denominationally he is a Congregationalist. A few years since he married, and has a pleasant home in Westboro', Mass. A Baptist brother, with whom he was associated in meetings, after speaking of his marked peculiarities, which sometimes create prejudice, writes as follows : —

" As to his preaching, for which he is most distinguished, I love to speak, and it is embodied in the few words that he preached Christ and Him crucified as the only hope of perishing man. He is different from some evangelists, being a man of culture with a classical training, which makes his sermons instructive as well as awakening ; his sermons are rich with the doctrines of grace. I should say he was a sound Calvinist and believed the truth of the Bible. He approaches nearer to Jacob Knapp than any other man to whom I ever listened. His illustrations of gospel truth are wonderful, and are rich food for every believing soul, while the truth of man's lost and helpless condition is so faithfully set forth that it seldom fails of fastening conviction on a guilty conscience. While he preaches so plainly and pointedly he does not scatter, but draws people most wonderfully to the house of God. The largest sanctuaries are nightly filled to listen to the burning words of truth falling from his lips. His sermon on the Prodigal Son I consider one of the most able and stirring appeals on the sin of intemperance ever given by man. His manner of preaching is entirely destitute of what is called sensationalism, is calm, with little bodily motion or physical effort, but is a plain, direct appeal to the judgment of the hearer. On the terrors of the Lord, he is fearfully solemn, while the love of God, as manifested in Christ, brings Calvary very near to the sinner and leaves him without excuse.

"From the public to the private life we come to find more of the man and learn the secret of his success. He is a man of fervent piety and strong faith, a man of prayer, wrestling with God for souls ; he reads the promises, and believes them as given for all time and claims them as his. I never shall forget a season of prayer with him when the room seemed to be filled with a holy atmosphere and the glory of God filling every soul. Evidently, prayer is his great dependence, and the armory from whence he draws his weapons for the slaying of souls. The man is to be commended for his freedom from the love of gain ; no planning for a great collection, but the simple offerings of the people, and that known only to himself. May the Lord spare him to lead many to Jesus ! "

Rev. Charles Nichols, of Boston, Congregationalist, who is also in full sympathy with the evangelists of the "higher christian life," has been and is doing quietly a good work in the churches where he has labored. He is still in the field.

Rev. Almon Underwood, who was born in Munson, Mass., in 1808, and a graduate of Amherst College, has been a very useful evangelist, and is still in the field. He was a settled pastor for several years in Poughkeepsie, N. Y., and Newark, N. J. From his pen we have a sugges tive volume entitled "Millennial Experience." He also wrote three volumes of commentary on the Bible, which he intended to make his life-work, but felt called to give up all for his present calling. Thoroughly evangelical and judicious, he is remembered in many churches with confidence and grateful love.

Rev. Rufus S. Underwood, son of the above, born in Newark, N. J., 1846, from his earliest recollection has been a child of God; but when thirteen years of age passed through a new crisis in his religious experience into the "full assurance of faith," and gave himself unreservedly to the Lord. He began his evangelistic work while in college, and has been engaged in it almost constantly since he entered the ministry in 1867. He has held meetings in New York State and New England, especially Massachusetts and Connecticut. With no fixed, uniform plan of labor or measures, he employs such means as the particular field in which he labors may require. He is now conducting services in the Park Street Church, Boston.

CHAPTER XXII.

Evangelism of the Protestant Episcopal Church. — Rev. J. W. Bonham. — The Late Great Awakening in England. — The London Mission. — The Work in this Country. — Lord Radstock. — In England. — In Russia. — Reginald Radcliffe, Esq.

WE have a remarkable confession in a London editorial upon the great awakening in the Established Church in connection with the protracted meetings and evangelistic labors there during the winter and spring of 1874 : —

"It is almost impossible not to see that if such an outlet for enthusiasm had been possible in the days of Wesley and Whitefield, their preaching might have simply produced that revival *within* the church which they originally contemplated, instead of leaving behind it a new sect."

To this, Rev. J. W. Bonham, Church evangelist, adds the following : —

"It has been said that England has starved some of her great men, but erected costly monuments to their memory after their decease. The offer of a place in Westminster Abbey for a monument to the Wesleys is an acknowledgment now of their ability and usefulness."

This mission movement, or evangelism, began about ten years since in parishes where evangelists proposed it. In 1869, the memorable twelve days' mission was held in sixty of the largest London churches; but the growing interest culminated in the great metropolis during the few weeks preceding Lent of the year 1874, when there were simultaneously, in nearly all the churches, special services for ten consecutive days. Of this extraordinary development of spiritual activity, Mr. Bonham, who was present, writes in the " Church Journal and Messenger " : —

" It marks a new era in the history of the Church of England. It was a bold religious measure, but the results justify its wisdom and importance. For some time the flame of revival had been gradually growing brighter. The awakened clergy prayed, —

> ' Revive Thy work, O Lord!
> Disturb this sleep of death.'

Here and there slumberers were aroused, and quickened parishes no longer resembled cemeteries filled with the dead. The bishops, wisely discerning the signs of the times, boldly met the emergency. To keep the increasing flame of revival within the church, they said to the evangelists, Go forward with your mission work, and we will labor with you.

> ' Zion hears the watchmen singing,
> Her heart with deep delight is springing,
> At once she wakes, she hastes away.'

" In the presence of fifteen hundred clergymen, the Bishop of London urged the value and importance of special services to save the lost and quicken Christians. The Bishop of Winchester portrayed the power and need of that love to souls, which goes after them. He said, ' We have tried police-courts, jails, and penitentiaries, but how little the true light of Christian love has penetrated into the hearts of the poor!' The Bishop of Rochester spoke forcibly upon the necessity of definiteness in sermons. ' The preacher should make the hearer feel as David felt when Nathan said, " *Thou* art the man!"'

" Through God's blessing the London Mission has been successful. The noble attitude of the bishops and archbishops showed their willingness to co-operate in every good work, displayed the aggressive spirit of the Anglican Communion, and recognized 'the need of evangelists to conquer, as well as pastors and teachers to retain and organize, what is won for Christ.'

"In one of the mission sermons preached in Westminster Abbey, Dr. Vaughan declared that enthusiasm is an element of power, and protested against the idea that enthusiasm is foreign to the spirit of the Church of England. The London Mission was a practical demonstration of the efficiency of holy fervor. What, through God's blessing, evangelists melted, rectors are now moulding; and the multitudes first aroused, and then won, will now enjoy the blessings of church nurture."

Of the extra means which were employed at London, Mr. Bonham says : —

"That the various classes in London may be benefited, special services are provided and appropriate addresses delivered. To seek and save the lost, unusual means are used and gospel appliances concentrated. Outcasts hear the echo of the Saviour's gracious voice, 'Thy sins are forgiven thee ; go, and sin no more.' Men and women visit neglected districts, sing a hymn to arrest attention, and then announce the service at the nearest church, and invite those gazing from doors and windows to attend. In some regions this is done by a company in cassock and surplice, in what is called 'a processional'; in other places by a company in ordinary attire, clustering around a lamp-post to see their hymns. Last night, at the last stopping-place before going to the church, the lay leader requested me to give the notice, as his throat was tired. Of course I complied, and after singing —

> ' Hark ! hark ! Hear the blest tidings !
>   Soon, soon, Jesus will come.
> Robed, robed in honor and glory,
>   To gather His ransomed ones home,'

I cried with a loud voice, 'Behold, the Bridegroom com-
eth! Go ye out to meet Him!' and invited the people to
the sanctuary.

"The service was at St. Jude's, Islington; the mission
preacher, the Rev. Mr. Aiken. The sermon I will not
attempt to describe. The vast audience were moved by
the truth, and the power of the Holy Ghost. Many
remained for the instructions after the sermon."

Truly there is the dawn of a new era in the activity of
the Episcopal Zion, if these, as we believe, are foretokens
of the future. Mr. Bonham remarks in a note, "The
great mission doubtless prepared the way for Moody and
Sankey."

It will be noticed that the same reasons given for the employment of evangelists have always been found to exist,
and indicate that their divine appointment is discovered
at length by even our more conservative Episcopacy. The
bishops in England discountenance "sacramental confession," and the free interchange of their clergy with those
upon whom their hands have not been laid, but "they
decline to lay down special rules" for them, while the
pastors "are now too busy with the real work of the mission to discuss the proper pronunciation of 'amen,' the
length of surplices, and the color of stoles."

Rev. Mr. Bonham, who is wholly and earnestly devoted
to his work, is about forty-five years of age. He wears
no beard, and his usual manner is calm and quiet. When
he is fired with the enthusiasm of his chosen work, his
whole nature responds to the silent appeal of perishing
souls.

Mr. Bonham has crossed the ocean thirteen times, and
travelled extensively. He has held services in various
places in England and in America. He was present in
Ireland and in Scotland at the time of the great revival a
number of years since. He has also visited France and

Italy, and was in Paris during the revival conducted by Reginald Radcliffe, Esq., the eminent lay evangelist of the Church of England. For several years Mr. Bonham was rector of a church in Philadelphia, Pa. When he resigned the rectorship of the bishop's church in that city, he took charge of St. Paul's Church, Peoria, Ill., where he published a parish paper and other issues. For several years he has declined to settle as rector of a parish, in order to travel and do the work of an evangelist.

In 1873 he was appointed by the Rt. Rev. F. D. Huntington, D. D., diocesan evangelist of Central New York, and held missions in various places.

In January, 1874, with letters commendatory from Bishops Whitehouse and Huntington, he crossed the ocean to be present at the great London Pre-Lent Mission, held simultaneously in two hundred and forty-eight of the largest churches. Since his return to the United States he has visited about twenty dioceses to set forth the importance of special missions as a supplementary agency in harmony with the parochial system.

February 23, he wrote of the efforts to reach the most degraded by holding midnight meetings, " devoted Christian men have gone from street to street, distributing cards, inviting them to the gospel feast, and a goodly number accepted the invitation." The largest and most impressive scenes were witnessed in St. Peter's Church, which stands near the principal centres of fashionable revelry. Mr. Bonham describes them graphically, but we can quote only a paragraph : —

" At midnight, the multitude in the dazzlingly-bright and richly-decorated 'Argyle Casino,' the most fashionable one in London, excited with wine and the whirl of the mazy dance, enter their respective carriages beneath the glare of the dazzling front-lights, turning night into day, to retire to the more private haunts of sin. Though no

cards of invitation have been distributed nor any out-door
effort made, as they pass St. Peter's Church, the tolling
bell arrests their attention. Many wonder and pass by,
but some remain. Women and their sinful companions
enter the church. Within a short time the church is filled,
and the vestibule and entries are crowded. But oh, how
solemn the scene! Girls of tender age, and some of the
fairest daughters in the land, beautiful in person and gor-
geously attired in the most costly fabrics, and decorated
with diamonds and costly jewelry, are for once seated at
midnight in the holy sanctuary, with their handsome and
fashionable companions in guilt! Their natural beauty
and gorgeous attire would cause a stranger to conclude
that they were the guests of a royal wedding or grand
reception. But alas! the women are 'strange women,'
who, with their companions in fashionable dress costume,
are on their way to hell! In words of affectionate and
earnest warning, different speakers address this strange
assembly. Some listen attentively; some look downcast;
some look defiant; some sneer. As all are supplied
with hymn-books, the majority sing. Some sing well, and
have evidently sung the hymns before, but purposely some
make fearful discord. During and after the addresses,
clergymen and devoted sisters go from pew to pew, urging
the fair but deceived daughters to accept the Saviour's
offered mercy, forsake the path to woe, and go to homes
provided."

In America, Mr. Bonham has visited about twenty dioceses North and South. We regret exceedingly that the
reports of the missions held in numerous places were
received too late for the space their interest demands.

In Louisville, Ky., Mr. Bonham held a mission in Grace
Church and Calvary Church, which lasted eighteen days.
Included in the series were sermons on "What shall it
profit a man," etc., on "Foreshadows of Future Retribu-

25

tion," from 2 Peter ii, 4–9, and also upon the fatal decision of Felix; "Christ the Revealed Deity," and "Looking unto Jesus." He excels in descriptive power, and is often eloquent. But higher than all mortal gifts and graces are his sources of success, — the presence of the Holy Spirit, in answer to prayer.

The mission commenced in the Church of the Holy Trinity, April 4, was one of unusual interest. Though announced to continue but one week, it was continued four weeks, and at its close the interest was greater than at any previous time.

The 9 A. M. meeting for inquirers and Bible instruction was conducted by the rector of the parish, the Rev. S. H. Tyng, Jr., D. D. Morning after morning for over four weeks a large number assembled, and as the services drew to a close, additional seats were needed, and some listened standing in the chapel entrance.

The afternoon Bible readings for ladies were conducted by two ladies of the English Church and the wife of the evangelist. A great interest was awakened, and a fresh impetus given to woman's work for Christ. Many ladies in the region have ample time to spare, and ability to work for Christ, and a number have resolved to thus use it.

The evening preaching service was held in the capacious church. The mission sermons were preached by the evangelist, the Rev. J. W. Bonham. The instruction was given by the rector of the parish, who also ably conducted the after meetings. At nearly every service some decided to accept the salvation that is in Christ Jesus, and those who for years had rejected Him were by the Holy Ghost bowed down to receive Him.

On the first three Sunday evenings of the mission period, the sermons were preached by the rector of the parish to between 2,000 and 3,000 persons. At two of the after meetings between five and six hundred persons remained. The Sunday on which the mission closed will be a day long remembered. At the morning service, after a sermon by the rector on assurance of salvation, about one thousand persons received the Holy Communion.

At the anniversary of the Sunday Schools with which are connected over 2,700 children, the rector, superintendents, teachers, and children seemed very, very happy, and lustily sang "Oh, that will be joyful When we meet to part no more!"

The mission was closed by a special service for the people in the evening. The evangelist delivered a lecture on the great awakening in the Church of England. Over two thousand persons were present at the closing service of the mission. Though all benefited by it will not be confirmed, the class for confirmation numbers about one hundred. Though the interest was still great, the strength of the rector and evangelist would not allow them to continue the mission longer.

On Sunday evening, one hundred and six persons were confirmed. The church was crowded, and interesting addresses were delivered by Bishop Potter and Dr. Tyng, Sr.

Early in August, with students from the "House of the Evangelists," he went to different centres on Houston and Staunton Streets, and in the square at Suffolk. The services were opened with singing, the Scriptures were read, and a sermon or address followed. Sometimes, besides the immediate crowd, the heads at the windows of the tenement houses, eight stories high, reminded one of "the people in the galleries of a theatre, towering tier above tier." He has since extended these street services with excellent effect, imitating the proscribed Whitefield and Wesleys in obeying the divine mandate, "Go into the streets."

The evangelist has also delivered several times a lecture upon "The Great Awakening in the Church of England in the Eighteenth Century, and the Results of Parochial Missions at the Present Time." An editorial hearer said of it, "Viewed as a literary production, it was an admirable discourse. As a word-painter, the reverend gentleman has few equals in the church of his faith; and his vivid description of the Anglican Church in the sixteenth and seventeenth centuries, and its awakening to new life through mission work in the eighteenth century, will not soon be forgotten by his audience." Mr. Bonham delivers another lecture of great practical interest on "John Wesley's Position in the Church," and one on "London Clerical Work at Midnight for the Fallen." He is at present the Head of the "House of the Evangelists."

Lord Radstock is an English nobleman, about forty years of age. With himself, like Robert Haldane, he gave his fortune to Christ, distributing it largely among the poor, and devoting his whole time to evangelistic efforts, with much success, among the higher classes. He has been for a few years past a great deal upon the Continent, where he met many travelling Russians, and won influential converts to the Lord Jesus, both then and when in England. By them he was led to extend his itineracy to St. Petersburg; the results here were extraordinary. He preached in the American church in the English and French languages, and daily received half a score of invitations "to hold forth in aristocratic saloons the doctrines of Christ."

The best testimony to his labors and the reality of the awakening is found in an extract from a popular Russian paper not in sympathy with the movement: —

"To be an eye-witness of one of the assemblies opens the mind to a good deal. At an early hour the room is filled to overflowing with princesses and countesses. They are all clad in black or gray, are accompanied by their little children, and hunger and thirst after the spiritual food they have come to receive. Lord Radstock first kneels down with his back to the assembly, entreating Christ to inspire him with fitting words. Then, rising and turning round, he says, 'Let us pray,' an injunction which is immediately obeyed by all present. After this he opens the Bible, reading the first text upon which his eye happens to fall, and commenting upon it in eloquent and impressive language. The ladies are gradually excited to the highest pitch of religious enthusiasm. As they sit weeping before him, they resemble so many heathen women admitted to the first knowledge of Christ by the powerful teaching of St. Paul. The close of the discourse is marked by loud sobbings. The fair devotees rise from their seats, and crowding round the evangelist lord, thank him in passionate terms for showing them the way of salvation, and directing them and their children into the paths of peace. Every now and then it happens that one of the children present, startled by the contrast between the language of Lord Radstock and that of the Russian clergy, asks his mother whether it is necessary to attend the teachings of the orthodox pastors at all, after this attractive experience of the foreigner's religion. 'Ah,' she says, 'you had better look to the dear Lord.'

"It is well known that in Southern Russia, too, whole villages have been lately embracing Protestantism, and that a seminary is forming at Berlin for the purpose of teaching German Protestant clergymen the Russian language, and educating them to act as missionaries among us. Worse than this, there is Countess M——, a Russian orthodox lady, and the mother of four children, who, the other day, told Lord Radstock that she had only learned to love Christ from his exposition of the Anglican doctrine; that the Greek Church was so stiff and cold, and that she only now knew what it was to be really a Christian. Princess G——, another Russian orthodox lady, and the mother of two children, after attending Lord Radstock's Bible-class, has been heard to exclaim, 'I only now know what the religion of Christ really is. It is Protestantism!' 'Yes,' added another orthodox lady, Princess P——, 'Protestantism is the only religion I ever understood. It is based upon love, not upon rite and ceremony, as is ours.' 'My dear lord, oh, pray teach me how to love Christ! Tell me, my dear Lord Radstock, how to make the necessary and proper distinction between the love I feel for my husband and the love I owe to Christ.' These words have recently fallen from the lips of Princess D——, likewise an orthodox lady, and the mother of four children. The above few authentic utterances will give the reader an idea of the religious condition of St. Petersburg society, early in the year 1874. Balls are forgotten and fine dresses discarded, the fair owners having taken to loving Christ and receiving religious instruction from a modern English apostle. Even the male portion of our fashionable society is beginning to be affected with a predilection for Protestantism."

Lord Radstock, although he has not accepted all the views of truth they preach, has co-operated earnestly with Mr. and Mrs. Boardman, R. Pearsall Smith and Mrs. Smith, and also has been in sympathy with the great awakening in England. His personal appearance is excellent and his manner winning. He is manifestly called of God to the work he has chosen.

Reginald Radcliffe, Esq., an eminent lawyer of Liverpool, England, has for years conducted a large legal business by means of assistants, while *he* has devoted much time to travelling as a lay evangelist and holding special services. An account of his successful labors would fill a volume.

CHAPTER XXIII.

Woman as an Evangelist. — Mrs. Maggie Van Cott. — Her Birth, Childhood, and Youth. — Conversion. — Death of Her Husband. — Remarkable Executive Ability. — How she became an Evangelist. — Success. — Bishop Haven's Estimate of Mrs. Van Cott and Her Work.

WITHOUT venturing an opinion, in the absence of sufficient light to do so, upon the providential need and call of woman in the evangelistic department of Christian activity, our record would be incomplete without a sketch of the pioneer American evangelist of her sex, and the views of a popular Methodist bishop upon the subject.

Mrs. Maggie Van Cott was born in the city of New York, March 25, 1830, and was the daughter of William K. Newton, a fine, dignified gentleman. He at one time was manager of the real estate of John Jacob Astor. The family attended the Episcopal Church, in which Maggie was confirmed when eleven years of age.

At twelve years of age Maggie was engaged, and all the arrangements made for the wedding, to be followed by a trip to Europe. The affair reached the good mother's ear, and she broke up the match.

Soon after, the dwelling was disturbed by those singular phenomena which were known in Epworth Rectory, and have elsewhere appeared, and out of which came modern Spiritualism.

Mr. Newton removed to Williamsburg, where the Episcopal Church was two miles away and a Methodist sanctuary very near. Maggie's mother opposed her attendance at the Methodist Church, and she would hide away in the cupola of her home to hear the songs and earnest words of the worshippers.

January 27, 1847, she married Mr. Peter P. Van Cott, a merchant in the same city. The years passed swiftly, and sorrows succeeded the joys of domestic life; death and business failures came, and with them the development of a rare executive power in the heroic wife and mother. Not only so, but at length God's discipline drew her thoughts to Him, till one day, while crossing Fulton Ferry, "she heard the Saviour saying, 'You must decide to-day. Now is the accepted time; behold, now is the day of salvation. Why longer delay?' Suddenly, as if awakening from a dream, with her heart trusting, praying, believing, she cried out, 'Lord, if Thou wilt accept the sacrifice, I from this moment give Thee my body and soul. I will be wholly Thine, and by Thy grace I will never turn back.'"

The remarkable experiences of Mrs. Van Cott, the burdens of business, the exultant faith through all her exhausting exertions, till her husband, who had gradually wasted away, died in holy triumph, and then afterwards in the unaided management of her large affairs, read like the story of some heroine invested with more than mortal energy and sustained by a faith stronger than that which sang in the fires of ancient martyrdom. Her earliest service for Christ was in the Sabbath School, where she took a class reluctantly on account of her conscious need of teaching in the oracles of God. She next accepted, under the protest of friends, a request to connect herself with the Five Points Mission, and soon her efficient help was widely felt in the extending work of benevolence. Here she passed through a fearful struggle before God, with prejudice against color, when called to a post of duty among poor negroes; and a joyful victory of faith and love followed the conflict. Her lips were opened, and in the

humble circles around her, from time to time, many souls
gave evidence of a saving trust in Jesus.

The tidings of her earnest activity and appeals went
abroad ; and when in February, 1868, she visited friends in
Green County, N. Y., her host, the venerable Rev. John
Battersby, told her she must preach in the school-house
the evening following her arrival. Mrs. Van Cott stoutly
refused, and the minister as firmly but tenderly urged,
until, convinced it was her duty to speak according to the
appointment he had made, she wiped away the tears, and
retired to prepare her first sermon. The hour came, and
many were unable to get within the door of the place of
meeting. Then she must preach in the Baptist Church,
a mile distant ; and so she has been doing ever since,
going from place to place amid revival scenes of which
we cannot even give an outline sketch.

That she is not a logical preacher we suppose all will
concede ; but that she does reach a certain class of minds
and do good, is equally evident. Of these facts we will
let the excellent Bishop Haven, the enthusiastic champion
of woman's civil rights, speak in her behalf. We quote
from an extended introduction to the " Life and Labors of
Mrs. Maggie Van Cott " : —

" The lady who commenced her labors in the city of
Boston in the African church is fair to look upon, of
large frame, of full form, of small, delicate features, light,
clear complexion, an eye of melting blue, with the pose
and ease of a queen of the drawing-room. Her dress is
elegant to the top of propriety, but not a whit beyond ;
it shows the womanly elegance of her nature ; it disarms
criticism as to her boldness in entering the pulpit, and her
modes of discourse and of appeal, by which she wins such
multitudes to Christ. She is mistress of their eyes before
she opens her lips. Grace is in her face and her apparel.
As becomes the king's daughter, 'all her garments smell

of myrrh and aloes and cassia'; they conform to the laws of beauty and propriety.

"She refused to attend class-meeting until a few years ago, because she said it was a shame for a woman to speak in such places. Enticed to one by an invitation to sing, and a promise that she should not be compelled to speak, she broke forth, on the privilege being offered, in a fulness of testimony and power that carried all the class captive, and at once made her leader of the leader.

"When, after her first success, ministers said, 'You must do the work of an evangelist,' she answers, 'I cannot; my business is on my hands. I must get my living.' But she follows the voice, gives up a lucrative business, and devotes herself wholly to the work. They say, 'You must be licensed as a local preacher.' Again she objects, again submits. Thus every step in her public career has been forced upon her, and thus every step has been a victory.

"It is not our purpose, nor have we space here, to discuss the questions involved in the labors of this elect lady. That they have taken the Church by surprise is true. It did not expect to have this duty set before its face; it did not dream that it would be called to license women as preachers, to ordain them as such, to station them as such. The Methodist Episcopal Church and all its affiliated branches, as well as its parent stock, give women large liberty in its services. Born of a woman, — Susanna Wesley being almost as directly the mother of Wesleyanism as of Wesley, — it from the start encouraged woman in all works of spiritual activity.

"He who had made all England accept a non-canonical clergy as the most approved before God and all the people of any in the realm with his latest breath, hardly a month before he died, threw the door wide open to all those called of God to this ministry, and answered all objections of his own followers at least, if not of any, in any church, who might still be possessed of the spirit of the persecutors of Miss Cambridge. There was a good stroke of satire, too, in his advice to her not to preach when a preacher was preaching at the same time, lest 'she might draw away his hearers,' — a stroke not inapplicable to some modern objectors to the modern Miss Cambridge, who would be sure to have a very empty house if they should dare to hold meetings near her own.

"Methodism has ever accepted the clear leadings of Providence. Its success has been largely because of this acceptance. Has He called women to preach? That is the question and the only question. If He has, every true son and daughter of His will say, 'Amen. So let it be. Come in this way, if so Thou wilt only come, Lord Jesus!'

"Men who have not been inside of a church for a score of years come, hear, tremble, fall before the Lord, and come forth new creatures in Christ Jesus.

"Mrs. Van Cott is, without doubt, to-day the most popular, most laborious, and most successful preacher in the Methodist Episcopal Church. She has more calls, does more work, and wins more souls to Christ than any of her brothers. She does this by her genius and her faith. Genius is naught without faith; faith is not all-powerful without genius.

"Her sermons are not finished orations: Peter's were not, nor Paul's, nor Christ's; it is doubtful if any true gospel sermons should be. 'Sermon' means 'conversation,' and a sermon should be a conversation on Christ. Her learning is not of the schools; she knows little about theology as a science, probably nothing, scholars being judges; she never had the least 'theological education,' so called, which is often an education without theology; she never was trained to public speaking. She prepares no discourses, in the usual sense of pulpit preparation.

"She is as dramatic as Gough or any actor, but she is no actor. It is dead earnest with her. Her appeals are more thrilling than her descriptions, nor does she content herself with pulpit efforts. These are only preliminary to her prayer-meetings and altar work. She is over all the congregation, addressing every one she can reach, and gathering more to the Lord by personal address than by her pulpit portrayals and appeals. She leaves no stone unturned to save souls; ceaseless in prayer, spending whole nights on her knees, visiting from house to house, holding meetings all the day through, instant in season and out of season, she tires the stoutest man with her immense capacity for work, as well as astonishes all by her ease and felicity in doing it.

"To her Master she stands or falls. She feels a call higher than any of earth: she obeys, and all recognize its authenticity. She has made a name in the church annals that will not die."

CHAPTER XXIV.

Independent Evangelists of Faith and Bible Reading. — Henry Morehouse.— George C. Needham.— H. Grattan Guinness.— Rev. A. N. Somerville. — Edward Wright. — Other and Youthful Evangelists.

We have used the term "independent evangelists" because the principal men whose names appear in this chapter are strictly so. In accord with the Plymouth brethren more nearly than any other body of Christians, especially on the subjects of faith and the Lord's second coming, they keep aloof from all denominational connections whatever. And this position is taken in order to be unembarrassed in their movements, — working wherever they can have an audience, and without any sectarian odor upon their garments.

Henry Morehouse was born in Manchester, Lancashire, England. He was converted in a circus under the appeals of some plain lay preachers on a Sunday night. He then joined them in their efforts, and not long after gave up his business situation and devoted himself to evangelistic work. Christians in Dublin became interested in him, and through them he was led to study the Bible for himself, and he has kept to that one book ever since. He has visited America four times, and has been greatly blessed. In the West, Christian people think highly of him. Mr. Morehouse is a little over thirty years of age. His power is felt in his Bible-readings, where he has, perhaps, no superior. We have not had the opportunity of listening to him, but have the spirited report of an admiring hearer at Rochester, N. Y., who says : —

" He spent two weeks in this city last February, holding daily and nightly service, and in spite of the intense cold of that month — the thermometer often standing from ten to fifteen degrees below zero — the people thronged to hear him. Those services had so won all hearts to him, the warmest of welcomes awaited his second visit. And we count it the richest spiritual blessing of our lives to have heard him.

"Youthful almost to boyishness in figure and appearance, you wonder at first where lies the spell that draws people so irresistibly. But one look into those clear gray eyes reveals such earnestness, sincerity, and perfect transparency of soul, you trust him without an instant's questioning. His whole face wears the calm, untroubled look of a soul at perfect rest in God. His voice is clear and winning, his delivery rapid, especially in his readings, as if the time were all too short for what he has to say. And all too short it is for those who hang with breathless interest on his words.

" A full and free salvation he preaches, and preaches with all the earnestness of his soul ; but not a salvation that involves no Christian living. In this he is emphatic.

" His readings are marvellous. His unbounded love and reverence for the Bible, and its constant study, have given him a deep insight into its very heart. And the freshness, beauty, and originality of thought in these readings are a constant surprise, sometimes making every verse of a psalm, that from childhood has been familiar as the alphabet, a new illuminated text.

" The flashes of genius all through his readings and sermons ; the wonderful aptness of his illustrations, driving the truth home irresistibly, and linking both truth and illustration so perfectly that one can never be recalled without the other; his astonishing memory, that carries a score of texts, perhaps, at a single reading, scattered from Genesis to Revelation, naming book, chapter, and verse, that the congregation may follow him in their own Bibles, and not a bit of paper to aid his memory, and never an instant's hesitation in recalling a text or expressing a thought of his own, — these all give him great power over an audience.

"His intense love for souls and his boundless love for the Master are the key-notes of his life. And the tender, beseeching earnestness with which he strives to win even the most fallen and depraved to him, and the startling power with which he speaks to the conscience of those who have already named the name of Christ, will never be forgotten by those who heard him.

"The last service on Sabbath evening drew by far the largest congregation ever gathered within the walls of the Brick Church. Before seven o'clock the entire audience-room was filled, the galleries crowded to their utmost capacity, the aisles below filled, and every inch of standing room taken, while hundreds went away who could not gain entrance anywhere.

"Mr. Morehouse has carried with him to his English home the loving gratitude of thousands of Christian hearts who have been made better for a lifetime by his visit."

Mr. Morehouse will always have peculiar interest to Christian people in this country because closely associated with Mr. Moody. In Chicago, before the latter left for Britain, and since this English evangelist's return to his own realm, he has rendered invaluable service to his American brother by his scriptural knowledge and spirituality.

Mr. Moody does not hesitate to acknowledge his great indebtedness to Mr. Morehouse, who unfolded with wonderful clearness and force the Bible method of dealing

directly with human souls, as the earnest evangelist, ever
eager to learn of Christ and how to lead men to Christ,
had never seen and felt the way and the truth before.

The providential ordering of the blessing is very interesting. Soon after Mr. Morehouse came to this country
he sent word to Mr. Moody that, if he desired it, he would
preach for him. It proved to be God's voice through the
human agency. Saturday came, and he said to his wife,
when leaving to attend a convention, "Harry Morehouse,
an Englishman, who calls himself 'the Boy Preacher,' will
preach for me to-morrow if I wish it. It is too late to get
any one else, and if he makes a failure, tell the deacons to
find some one else for the evening, or hold a prayer-meeting." Upon his return he inquired about the stranger's
success, and found that he had preached all day from
the text, "God so loved the world," etc., making a very
deep impression, and that the deacons had invited him
to preach every night during the week. The "Boy
Preacher" did so, and from the same text, and closed
the seventh discourse with the following climax : —

"If I were to die to-night, and go up to heaven, and
there meet Gabriel, who stands in the presence of God ;
and if I were to ask him how much God loves sinners,
this is what I think he would say : 'God *so* loved the
world that He gave His only begotten Son, that whoso
believeth in Him should not perish but have everlasting
life.'"

When the meetings were over, Mr. Morehouse said to
Mr. Moody, "You are sailing on the wrong tack. If you
will change your course, and learn to preach God's words
instead of your own, He will make you a great power for
good."

Whatever the general results, Mr. Moody's whole ministry was shaped by the evangelist, who learned his spiritual lessons from the Plymouth brethren. He was led into

the "hidden mysteries of the Word," and felt the power
of a single passage as never before, "I charge thee before
God and the Lord Jesus Christ, who shall judge the quick
and the dead at His appearing and His kingdom, PREACH
THE WORD." Mr. Moody had been advised to enter
upon a course of reading, but had not found time to do it.
Mr. Morehouse said to him, "You need only one book
for the study of the Bible." The reply was, "You have
studied many books to gain your knowledge of it." Mr.
Morehouse answered, "No ; since I have been an evangelist
I have been the man of one book. If a text of Scripture
troubles me, I ask another text to explain it; and if this
will not answer, I carry it straight to the Lord."

At Mr. Moody's suggestion, a Bible-reading was ap-
pointed at his house, and the idea of "every man his own
theological seminary" became to him intensely practical.
This was one of the first meetings of the kind in America.
Mr. Morehouse also introduced into Mr. Moody's tabernacle, or hall, the Scotch custom, which should be universal, of hearers taking their Bibles with them to church.
The radical change wrought under the guiding Spirit by
Mr. Morehouse in the views and methods of labor for
Christ in saving men of our lay-evangelist has been the
secret of his marvellous achievements more than any other
instrumentality employed by God.

Rev. George C. Needham was born in the south of
Ireland, in the parish of Templenue, county of Kerry,
not many miles from the famous Killarney Lakes. This
portion of the county, although Catholic, is inhabited by
several Protestant families, nearly all of whom belonged
to the Church of England. His parents and relatives
were members of that church, and at the proper age he
was baptized and confirmed according to its order. At
one time, when about fourteen years of age, he was powerfully affected by a sermon from 1 John i, 7, preached

26

in the large hall of Dramore Castle, by that honored evangelist, H. Grattan Guinness, who was then beginning his evangelistic career. No one spoke to him on his spiritual condition, and for three years more he continued in an unconverted state.

The revival of 1859, which stirred the whole of the north, had not as yet visited the south of the island. But now the day of gladness had come, and the meetings, which began with only two, increased in numbers until probably every Protestant in the community had been led to attend them. A few gifted laymen, converted at the time, gave themselves to the work of expounding the Scriptures and appealing to the unconverted. In two weeks after the first meeting held, and at the second one at which he was present, he was enabled to see Christ as his substitute, putting away his sin and by His blood giving him pardon. He joined in the work of holding meetings around the neighborhood, and with other young men established cottage prayer-meetings in other parishes, a few of them meeting once a week, for Bible study. This study and investigation of God's truth equipped a band for evangelistic work. Mr. Needham often worked all day, and then walked nine miles to a meeting, preached, held an after meeting, dealt personally with souls, and walked home again; and others of the converts frequently did the same. "During the first year after his conversion he had rejoiced only in the pardon of sin, but did not realize his complete justification before God. The discovery of this truth and of the indwelling of the Holy Ghost in believers, coupled with the hope of the Lord's second coming, inspired him with fresh vigor and filled him with deeper peace and joy." The second year of his conversion found him in an office in Dublin, where, as cashier and bookkeeper, his time was so occupied that he had little or no opportunities for preaching except on the Lord's day. After much prayer and thought he resigned his position, and while serving as bank-cashier he felt called to give himself wholly to the work of an evangelist. About two weeks after this step was taken, he was holding meetings near Dublin.

At this early age, and with but little experience, he entered the work of a voluntary evangelist, without salary, income, or resources, save only as the Lord supplied his daily need; and by His grace he continued. He says, "I have worked on this plan unto this day. For nearly twelve years I can testify to the goodness of the Lord in supplying all my necessities, and day by day fulfilling His own word in my case. I preached for a year in the south, east, middle counties, and north of Ireland, in streets, fields, churches, halls, court-houses, school-rooms, and other places where the people could be gathered. Hundreds were hopefully converted, churches were revived, and believers helped to a life of victory and joy in the Lord."

Early in 1868 he came to the United States, landing at Boston, with an introduction to the Young Men's Christian Association from Mr. Spurgeon. Having married an American lady, who has also given herself to the work of the Master fully, he felt it a duty to remain in this country, and help on the cause as best he could. Since his arrival here he has labored North, East, West, and South. He preached for Mr. Moody several months in Chicago, and labored with him in that city. Besides his evangelistic work and Bible-reading, he edited for nearly two years from the start "The Times of Refreshing," having commenced the paper with Dr. Cullis. For three years he edited "The Testimony," a gospel paper which had many subscribers in Canada also. He has for several years given Bible-readings, being one of the first to introduce them in this country. Philadelphia is now his home, where his family remain during his evangelistic tours.

A leading paper of London, Canada, furnishes a pen-picture of this evangelist : —

" Mr. Needham's accent is broadly Irish ; he is exceedingly fluent, and he cannot help being witty. Moody's illustrations are not more rough and ready and eccentrically original. In appearance he is young, fresh, Spurgeon-looking, almost jolly, — a man 'one would expect to find very genial in private intercourse. His sentiments are eminently sound, and we should judge him calculated to do much good."

Mr. Needham has never solicited compensation for his services, nor even hinted that he wanted any, depending wholly on a providential supply of his need through those who freely give for the spread of the gospel. His faith has not been disappointed. Although resources have been cut off, relief has come. He was a pioneer among English evangelists to the South, and goes forth from his chosen and quiet Philadelphia home, with his large tent, to proclaim a full salvation, and read to the gathered throngs his fresh expositions from the living oracles.

Rev. A. N. Somerville, of the Free Church, Glasgow, Scotland, during the past year represented the Anglo-Indian Christian Union in India. The object of his evangelistic mission, in his own words, "was to win souls to Christ, and, by God's blessing, to aid in vitalizing, stimulating, and uniting all the churches." A resident there writes : —

" His methods resemble Mr. Moody's, in whose work in Scotland Mr. Somerville has been a hearty sympathizer and helper. Large numbers are drawn to his preaching, and, what is very cheering, Christians of all denominations, lay and clerical, are rallying round him for prayer and hearty co-operation. Let praying ones in America join with us in India in imploring the divine blessing upon these revival meetings· in Calcutta! A great and thorough work there must reach the native churches, and through them make itself felt throughout the whole country. These revivals in Calcutta, Bombay, Madras, and other Indian cities are preparing the way of the Lord in this pagan land."

Rev. H. Grattan Guinness has been for several years a prominent evangelist, and well known in the English metropolis in connection with his erection and management of the East End Training Institute. Of his early history we have no data. He is able with voice or pen, deeply spiritual, and intensely in earnest. There is a Pauline heroism about him, and a yearning fidelity to souls. Many in this country have felt his hallowed power.

Dr. T. J. Bonardo is also a very efficient evangelist. But taking his whole history together, there is no more remarkable man among the London evangelists than Edward Wright, or " Ned Wright," as he is called. He was born at Lambeth, July 24, 1836, in humble life. Reading "Jack Sheppard" literature led him to imitate the heroes of vice, and he became a lawless, thieving, desperate young man. Converted in a theatre under the preaching of a lay evangelist, he became one himself, to the very class among whom he had lived, and now occupies platforms with the most distinguished workers for Christ.

Robert Anan, " the Christian Hero," and others we cannot even name, of blessed memory, have "ceased from their labors, and their works do follow them."

We justly enrol among true evangelists Rev. William Reid, M. A., and Rev. W. P. Mackay, editors of "The British Evangelist," and authors of various spiritual issues.

Their able and most excellent paper is an evangelist of wide and widening influence for Christ, recording faithfully the harvest-work of the human agencies; their pens are employed in other forms of enduring usefulness; and they have done precious service for the Master with the voice.

The Conference of Christian Workers, which holds quarterly meetings in London, is in reality an association of evangelists. February 27, 1874, the meeting in Henry Varley's West London Tabernacle, Notting Hill, was a memorable one. Stirring addresses were made by Mr. Varley, who presided, Mr. Benjamin Scott, F. R. S. A., Rev. H. Grattan Guinness, Dr. T. I. Benardo, "Ned" Wright, and others. Seldom in any assemblage of ministers and laymen does the spirit of apostolic consecration pervade more sensibly an atmosphere of prayer. It is, perhaps, a singular fact that this association of Christian workers, many of them possessing rare gifts and graces, agree with the Brethren in the doctrine of Christ's second coming.

The Evangelization Society of London, on whose committee are the Earl of Cavan, the Marquis of Cholmondelry, and Lord Radstock, is a quiet but far-reaching power for Christ, which, during the year 1874–5, visited with evangelists about five hundred places outside of London. The Hon. Secretary is Capt. W. E. Smith, 57 Charing Cross, who has sent forth a very timely and thoughtful address to evangelists.

CHAPTER XXV.

EVANGELISTS OF THE HIGHER CHRISTIAN LIFE. — REV. W. E. BOARDMAN. —
MRS. M. H. BOARDMAN. — R. PEARSALL SMITH. — MRS. H. W. SMITH. —
DR. CHARLES CULLIS. — HENRY VARLEY.

THE peculiar and quiet evangelism of what is known
as the "higher Christian life" has become of late a very
powerful spiritual agency, particularly abroad.   The term
which designates it has been widely criticised, and quite
unjustly, it seems to us.   The matter of terminology is a
very unimportant thing unless it misrepresent essential
truth or is clearly in bad taste.   While it should not
obscure vital doctrine or duty, it certainly ought never to
be an excuse for neglecting to examine and feel the force
of either.   And does any intelligent person misunder-
stand the meaning of a higher Christian life, — an advanced
position in the soul's relations to Christ?   That erroneous
views sometimes are expressed, no one doubts ; for truth
is always in danger of unconscious misrepresentation
through the imperfect human agency, and is not presented
by different minds in its original purity.   But if this fact
be an objection, it covers the whole field of inquiry and
experience.

The recognized pioneers in this aggressive movement
are Rev. W. E. Boardman and Mrs. M. W. Boardman.   A native of New York State when an infant, Mr.
Boardman just escaped alive from the upsetting of a
chaise at "The Narrows," on the banks of the beautiful
Chemung River, horse and carriage, parents and child,

rolling down a steep declivity to the water's edge. He lived to be an ambitious, sceptical young man, under the influence of a congenial room-mate. Several years later he was travelling through "The Narrows" again with a brother who had made a profession of religion, when Mr. Boardman introduced and expatiated upon his cherished Pantheism. He turned to his brother for his expected reply. To his surprise he got silence only. Then he appealed, saying, "Well, what do you think of all this?"

"Oh, it is all very plausible, but then it is not true."

"Not true? How do you know that?"

"Oh, I *know* your theory for conversion to be untrue, by my own experience."

The brother then gave a very clear statement of the Holy Spirit's work upon his heart, proving its supernatural origin.

Mr. Boardman was convicted on the spot, and he said to himself, "I will prove it all, and know it to be true, if it is so, in my own experience." Upon returning to his place of residence, revival meetings were appointed there, and he resolved to attend them. Time went on, the last night came, and his soul was not saved. In his deep earnestness he sought the lowliest seat, and there hid his face in his hands between his knees, and had it out with the Lord. Very soon the decision was made, the matter settled, and his soul was free. Marvellous things were unfolded to him. From that night commenced wonderful manifestations of God to his soul, sometimes in the church, sometimes in the fields, sometimes in the prayer place, sometimes on his journeyings, sometimes from the Word, at others from the works of God. He was a new creature in a new world.

Soon came to him the question of leaving a promising business for preparation to enter the ministry. He decided for the gospel, and to his surprise, his partner proposed one day to buy Mr. Boardman's interest. He sold, and commenced his studies, only to abandon them for a very lucrative offer in trade. He married, and worldly gains and pleasures were theirs. Mrs. Boardman was not a Christian, but, satisfied with her own virtues, calmly contemplated death, which a fever brought very near. Not long after her recovery, she heard in the house of her husband's relatives that he had made a profession of faith in Christ. When she asked him about it, he confessed it all, making a deep impression on her mind. She resolved to know by her own experience what he had told her of himself. Not long after, they looked at night upon a burning hotel, and the loss of thousands invested in it, followed by a failing bank, which involved him in still further losses. He said to Mrs. Boardman, "I deserve it all, for the life I have lived." The confession smote her with deep conviction, because if she had been living right, conscience said, he might not have gone astray. So deep was her distress she was laid upon a bed of sickness; her husband bowed there in prayer, and they consecrated themselves and their home to Christ. When, subsequently, they removed to the prairies of the West, among the tracts they took with them was that wonderful letter of J. Brainard Taylor upon his entrance upon his higher life of peace and joy. Mrs. Boardman called the attention of her husband to it, but expressed her doubts whether such an experience were possible for ordinary Christians. He listened till she finished reading it, and then exclaimed, "There! that is just what I need and must have." She met a minister who had a similar testimony, and she said to herself, "This is very reasonable. I know that if I am ever saved from these things, Christ must save me, and if He is to save me He can do it at once. I could never go through such a long struggle as my husband has; I

should die before I came to the end. I will commit it all
to Jesus." And she did, and was happy. Then came up
the question, "Will you confess what the Lord has done
for you?"

"Where, Lord? Where can I? There is only one
place, and that is in a little meeting in a private house this
afternoon, of those who belong to another denomination."

"Well, you can go there and witness for Jesus."

"Yes; but that would be altogether out of place for
me, a woman, and belonging to another church. I can't
do that."

This quenched the light in her soul in a moment. She
rose, and walked the floor, and finally took to her knees
with the prayer, "Lord, make me willing." And in a
moment the struggle was ended and the peace of Christ
filled her soul.

Upon Mr. Boardman's return from a meeting, she told
him with tears of joy of her great blessing. He, never
thinking that she could have so quickly come into the
experience he had been so long seeking in vain, yet filled
with joy that she was now in full sympathy with him about
it, and would no longer stand in his way, exclaimed,
"The Lord be praised! Maybe you will get hold of it
now before I do."—" Get hold of it? Why, there is nothing to get hold of. It is just letting all go, and trusting
all with Jesus." He was bewildered, and knew not what
to say. But light sprang unexpectedly from the darkness.
In a meeting wretchedly conducted, he was tempted to
unholy indignation, when the question how Jesus would
act, were He present, calmed his spirit, and " Lo I am with
you alway " made Christ *real* to the eye of faith. This
manifestation was followed by a revelation no less clear
of the truth, "Thou shalt call his name Jesus, for He *shall
save His people from their sins.*" The last burden and the
last cloud were gone, and gladness filled his heart.

At Lane Seminary which he entered, he led earnest souls to restful trust. While engaged in Sabbath-school work at the West, he suggested the first convention in behalf of the cause. He removed to Gloucester City, near Philadelphia, where at Mrs. Boardman's urgent desire, he wrote his first book, "The Higher Christian Life," of which over sixty thousand copies have been sold, and richest blessings have attended it, whatever of criticism it has encountered.

When our terrible civil war was opened, Mr. Boardman was ready to enter the chaplaincy, that he might gain access to the army. The Christian Commission was formed, and Mr. Stuart accepted Mr. Boardman's offer to go as delegate in response to an earnest appeal. His services as Secretary of the Christian Commission, were second to none in exhausting number and variety. His physical frame was prostrated and he went to Europe. Upon his return he wrote his second book, "He that overcometh, a Conquering Gospel." Soon after, business matters led him again to England, where, for a year, he held meetings almost daily. When he reached this country once more with Mrs. Boardman, the strong desire matured into a purpose to devote the remainder of their lives directly to higher life evangelism. At the same time he commenced writing his third volume, "Gladness in Jesus," in monthly contributions to the "Times of Refreshing," — perhaps the clearest presentation of the richer experiences which are the theme of his ministration than any other.

The next autumn Mr. and Mrs. Boardman opened their union conventions in connection with the Young Men's Christian Association, at Newark, N. J., with deepening interest. They were living by faith alone, without any salary or provision for their support, and have found God faithful to his promises in supplying *all* their need. In

1871 they separated themselves from all associations, working independently so far as any formal or financial connections are concerned. The itineracy from this time was constant, and the strain so great, Mr. Belden, who accompanied them, was paralyzed upon reaching home, and Mr. Boardman brought near to death.

In the summer of 1873, with Mrs. Boardman, he sailed again for England, in company with Dr. Cullis' family, and friends. In London he was joined by Mr. R. Pearsall Smith from the Continent, who a few months before had held meetings, and soon others were called in his name and those of Mr. Boardman and Mr. Varley. At length, under the active mangement of Mr. Smithies, they met two thousand independent ministers with prominent laymen, in divisions of from forty to sixty, at breakfast, in the rooms of the Young Men's Christian Association. The work went rapidly forward, including in its sweep ministers of all denominations, and even members of Parliament.

They were invited to hold similar meetings at Lady Beauchamp's mansion, and also at the Admiral Caffin's, and other homes of no less distinguished Englishmen. With the autumn came the great Oxford union meeting, which drew together prominent pastors and laymen, not only from Britain, but also from the Continent. The record of the ten days of crowded halls, pervaded by the Spirit's presence, fills a handsome volume. Besides Mr. and Mrs. Boardman, Mr. and Mrs. Smith, Lord Radstock conducted meetings. The very heart of Christian England was stirred.

During the winter of 1874–75, Mr. and Mrs. Boardman held many meetings of great interest in Cannon-street Hotel, Stoke-Newington, and Agricultural Hall at Broadlands, the princely estate of Hon. Cowper Temple, formerly Lord Palmerston's, Southampton, and Uxbridge; in the latter city the gatherings were especially fruitful, and attended largely by clergy of the Established Church. Mr. and Mrs. Boardman returned to this country last spring, and resumed their labors here.

At the request of Mr. R. Pearsall Smith, we omit a brief sketch, gleaned from authentic sources, of himself and Mrs. Smith, and confine our record to a simple notice of his work. His home is in Philadelphia, where from early life he has been a successful business man. Mr. and Mrs. Smith's evangelistic labors have been the most remarkable of any kind or period. We have alluded to those in England, where, as elsewhere, the services conducted by Mrs. Smith were special occasions of the Spirit's revealing light. Their published books and tracts, particularly the "Record of a Happy Life," have been scattered the world over. Their experience is given in "The Way of Righteousness" and "Jesus a Saviour from Sin," published by the W. T. Society.

In France Pasteur Monod's services followed the great meeting in February at Montmeygran in the Dome. In old Strasburg, seared with War's missiles of destruction, crowds gathered to hear of that peace too deep and perfect for the tumult of earth or rage of hell to disturb. At Bordeaux the interest was very intense both among Christians and the impenitent, and a number of conversions occurred. From March 7th to the 12th was a memorable time in Geneva, Switzerland. The evening meetings held in Reformation Hall were attended by 3,500 persons. Mr. Smith had the effective co-operation of the gifted and beloved Theodore Monod. "Many pastors were revived. Some who came with a prejudiced mind testified that they had found Jesus to be a present Saviour, and the source of strength, of peace, and of joy. Beginning with humiliation, then with consecration, they went on to enter into the current of benediction, and returned home with light hearts to commence their ministry of rest under the rays of the Sun of Righteousness. On Friday, the last day of the meeting, 1,200 came forward to partake of the Lord's Supper. It was a memorable season, when many expressed their desire to love the Saviour and abide in Him."

The last of March, at the invitation of one of the court chaplains, he went to Berlin. The chaplain at whose house Mr. Smith made his home, had written to the emperor to ask the liberty of using his great Soldiers' Church, holding five thousand people, and in the afternoon the emperor sent for him, listened with interest to the account of the work, and granted the church very cheerfully.

On the 2d of April a meeting was held in the drawing-rooms of Baron Bulow, the Minister of Foreign Affairs, the baron expressing at the close his warm thanks for the blessing brought to his house, and saying he could never forget that hour.

In the evening the emperor's church was opened, and it was estimated that about four thousand people were present. It was a wonderful time of the presence and power of the Spirit. One striking thing about these meetings was, that quite a number of plain peasants walked long distances to attend them, some even sixty miles, bringing their meals with them. It is thought that the religious part of Berlin has not been so deeply moved through and through during this century as in this wonderful week.

A union meeting was opened at Brighton, May 29, of similar character and wonderful spiritual power, of which we cannot give here even an outline. Admiral Fishbourne said at Hull that it was supposed that a thousand persons definitely found " the rest of faith."

Dr. Charles Cullis is so intimately connected with all the activities of this life of faith that the chapter would be incomplete without some account of him and his work. He was born in Boston, March 7, 1833. From birth an invalid, his frail life, while yet a boy, nearly went out by drowning when bathing with a companion. At fifteen he was clerk in a mercantile house in his native city, intending to prepare there for his future calling. At the end of three years, with the failure of general health, his voice became a whisper, and books were his only companions. A physician, interested in the young man, invited him to ride with him on his round of professional calls. Reading medical books followed, with timely aid financially, until he commenced practice, remaining with the physician with whom he had studied. Meanwhile, the question of personal salvation was pressed upon his conscience and heart.

He discovered a similar condition of feeling in a friend who had assisted him pecuniarily and had great influence over him. They both decided to make a profession of their faith, — Dr. Cullis uniting with the Episcopal Church, while his friend became a Baptist. Soon after he married a lady related to and in the family of the physician with whom he was associated. This very happy union was soon broken by death. He found his religious experience had been superficial: he needed something better. Alone in the room where the coffin of his idol lay, his bowed and breaking heart consecrated all his future worldly gains to Christ. For this purpose he began a separate practice. Then the expenses attending the established agencies of benevolence gave him dissatisfaction, which led him to consider the cause of a conscious unrest of heart and failure to keep holy resolutions. He found he was living more under the law than under grace.

He had reached a crisis where he could not long remain. The transition to rest and gladness is recorded in the four pages of "Keeping Power of Christ" issued from his press, and the volume which bears the title of "Faith-Work." The spiritual sky once clear, there arose the longing for a definite object of consecrated life. After fervent

prayer, like a new revelation came the words of Scripture,
"Every man to his work." Subsequently there was a
providential call by a stranger, for aid in behalf of a poor
consumptive, which was attended by a voice that said,
"Here is your work." Two years of waiting upon God
brought small contributions, increasing in number and
amount, till the Willard-street houses were successively
purchased, the wards crowded, the tract-rooms opened,
and at length the ample and beautiful buildings, including
the chapel, at Grove Hall were finished, and finally the
Beacon-place Chapel, Training College, Book-Rooms, and
other means of carrying forward the faith-work followed.
Dr. Cullis is the preacher at Grove Hall, occasionally doing evangelistic service elsewhere, while his Lay College
is designed especially to promote true spiritual evangelism.

Whatever may be said of the appeals made to the public by Reports of the Home and other ways of public
information, two facts remain : one is, there is the noble
work of a single unpretentious, quiet Christian man,
monumental in its greatness and beneficence ; the other is,
if so easily done on his plan, all benevolent institutions
have before them a method by which a vast amount of
expensive machinery can be saved. To exclude faith is
certainly to deny the power of it as revealed and illustrated in the oracles of God. Dr. Cullis has put the
Home out of his hands, excepting his personal control
of it while living. Mrs. Cullis is an efficient co-worker
with her husband.

Henry Varley was born in the year 1835 in London.
He is known in this country as an able, impressive ex-
pounder of the Bible, and evangelist of a full salvation.
He early became a member of the Baptist Church. When
a boy of fifteen he chose the business of the market-place
for his own, and ripening youth found him driving a prosperous trade in meats. He was most happily married

when twenty-two. So actively was he engaged in religious work that he began to attract the interest of those who had been long in the field. With the remunerative growth of business, his devotion to the spreading of a saving knowledge of Christ among the masses surging around him steadily increased. He soon felt the necessity of a central fortress of aggressive movement upon the kingdom of darkness, — a concentration of spiritual force at some natural locality for more effective operations.

In 1860 this zealous yet prudent young man opened in a school-room at Kensington Potteries, lying on the western border of London, his first regular preaching-station, the commencement of his mission enterprise, of whose future importance he could have had but a faint conception. The mixed, attentive assembly outgrew in numbers the humble school-room, and to his eye of faith rose a spacious edifice, to which he consecrated five thousand dollars of his future income; his father-in-law pledged an equal sum, and then each added to his gift, until the Western London Tabernacle at St. James Square invited, through its open doors, two thousand people to hear the call of mercy to the perishing. Henry Varley could now sympathize with Whitefield in his joy when he stood before the larger throng in his Tabernacle at Moorfields nearly a century and a quarter before.

On the Sabbath days it has been his custom to hold three or four services, retiring to rest about eleven o'clock at night, only to rise at a quarter before four o'clock Monday morning, at the ringing of the servants' bell. Soon a fleet horse was bearing him to the city market to purchase supplies for his own. At eight o'clock he was home again to breakfast, and then in the midst of business till two o'clock, which was dinner hour, followed with a nap. The rest of the day was given to the poor, inquirers, Bible study, tea, and evening meetings.

27.

Thus his busy, useful life was passed, till, about ten years later, he had a new and deeper spiritual experience, the narrative of which is given in one of the small issues of the Willard Tract Society, entitled "Trust in the Living Father."

After visiting Canada in the autumn of 1874, holding deeply interesting services, he repeated these meetings with wonderful effect in New York, and in April he reached Boston. The crowded churches to hear his discourses and Bible readings, one occasion filling Music Hall, his farewell in Tremont Temple, with the eloquent addresses of Rev. Dr. Webb and others, are fresh in the memory of all who heard them, and have become an important part of the religious history of the city. The fine physique of the man, and his skilful use of his native tongue, are wellnigh faultless. His face wears uniformly a smile of peace and joy. But some of his expressions were condemned, and the old charge of egotism preferred against him because of his frequent reference to his own experience and to his home. All testimony of experience includes personal allusions. Who ever had more of them than Paul? These are too inconsiderable in importance for a moment's discussion, before the real question, — the general results of his evangelism. We think there is a tendency to create false impressions, in the direction of the very faith in which he glories; presenting it too strongly in the light of simply an intellectual assent to truth and too exclusive of verities that search the conscience and the heart, and show the worldly Christian and dreaming sinner the necessity of an intelligent self-surrender to God in Christ and entire consecration to Him. When new, glorious light comes to the soul, we are likely to forget, in urging it upon others, the steps by which we were led to it.

That Mr. Varley's work is divinely appointed and great in fruitage we judge no impartial observer can doubt.

The Bible, to use his own words, is "brought to the front," whenever he deals with men. God is honored in His Word, and souls pointed to it as the only fountain of spiritual light, life, and joy. People turn to their neglected Bibles. "Faith, without which it is impossible to please God," is the great theme and end of his preaching; and that measure of it which shall make Christian life a delight, and a power in the world.

CHAPTER XXVI.

Methodist Evangelism of Holiness. — Dr. W. S. Palmer. — His Conversion. — Christian Activity. — Mrs. Phœbe Palmer. — Her Useful Life. — Death. — Rev. J. S. Inskipp. — Rev. William Macdonald.

Dr. W. C. Palmer is a native of New Jersey, and was born February 9, 1804. While an infant, his parents removed to the city of New York, where he still resides. When, on his thirteenth birthday, the serious impressions which he had long cherished ripened into conversion, he was pleading for assurance of acceptance, repeating the words, " My Saviour, save me, *me!* " Then his Sabbath-school superintendent knelt by his side, saying, " My little son, is He not your Saviour? " Exclaimed the lad, " Yes, He is my Saviour! " while the joy of realized salvation filled his heart. After completing his academic studies, he pursued medical studies, and entered with honor his chosen profession. September 27, 1827, he married Miss Phœbe Worrall, of New York, whose father, when fourteen, joined a Methodist society in England, under the care of John Wesley. Dr. Palmer was identified with all the rising reforms of the times, and active in Sabbath Schools.

Phœbe Worrall, the fourth child of Henry and Dorothea Worrall, was born the 18th of December, 1807. She could recall no hour or day, perhaps no year, when she was translated into the "kingdom of light," but she knew she was there. With a conscience of great tenderness and longings after holiness, she erred at first in comparing her joys with those more rapturous in other experiences. In her " Way of Holiness," she graphically describes the

Gethsemane experience through which she entered upon a life of holiness to the Lord. She was one of the founders of the Five Points Mission, and, with her husband, among the few who pledged a thousand dollars each to establish the first Methodist Mission in China.

For about thirty-five years a weekly meeting has been held at their house, for the "promotion of holiness," on Tuesday afternoon. Sometimes England, Ireland, and America, including the British Provinces, have been represented in these deeply-spiritual gatherings. Never did hearts beat and work more in harmony, than those of Dr. and Mrs. Palmer in all their manifold services for Christ. Writes a clergyman of the same denomination of Mrs. Palmer : —

"In addressing an audience her position was erect. In spirit, subject, and manner she indicated no confusion. Her intellect and action revealed discipline and self-control. She had enough gesture for either vivacity or effect, and it was easy and appropriate. She never appeared to be in a hurry, though not tedious in any of her exercises, and felt that if eternity compensated the time consumed the outlay was not unwise. Her articulation was distinct and deliberate, and her voice that was clear has sufficient compass for the largest churches in which she officiated. She was calm and free from vociferation, and was rarely vehement. Her style was clear, concise, and colloquial. The public labors of Mrs. Palmer have been attended with wonderful success. In single charges, where her services and those of her husband have extended over three or four weeks, three or four hundred souls have professed pardon, and an equal number have asserted their experience of purity of heart. In England, Ireland, Scotland, and Wales, as their published volumes show, about twenty thousand persons declared, through their instrumentality, the remission of their sins, and ten thousand made profession of the blessing of perfect love. This work was not confined to any class of society or denomination of Christians. Ministers and members alike testified their experience of the deep things of God."

In prose and poetry Mrs. Palmer has been an attractive and popular writer, always moving her ready pen for her adored, ever-present Redeemer. But there came at length the bankruptcy of nervous energy, when failure is inevitable. She writes, August 23, 1874 : —

"Since my return from my fruitful journeys abroad in Ohio, Illinois, etc., my health has been failing yet more seriously. Disease in complicated form, like so many hands, is ever most busily and rapidly at work in taking down this earthly tabernacle. Three years the demolition has been progressing. It was then that the prophetic words were inspoken by the tender, all-gracious Holy Spirit to my heart, with a significance deep and abiding. 'For we know that if the earthly house of this tabernacle were dissolved, we have a building of God, a house not made with hands, eternal in the heavens.'"

Her sufferings were very great, but amid it all she would cry out, "Alleluia, Alleluia, Alleluia! Precious Jesus, precious Jesus!" She frequently repeated, "Thy will is best; Thy will, not mine, be done." During the first part of her severe illness she said, "I want to say that my teachings have been correct, and I am now testing them in this hour of extreme suffering, and find that I am fully saved; not a shadow of a doubt. The altar is a beautiful type; it is a scriptural figure, and I am resting upon it. And the altar, which is Christ, sanctifies the gift. The blood of Jesus cleanses me from all unrighteousness" ; and then the exclamation, "Glory, glory!" burst from her lips. "The Word of the Lord is a sure foundation for faith; it is solid rock. I am resting on the Word."

Music was soothing beyond expression to her, and the songs of holy joy dulled the edge of pain.

During her last night on earth she said : "Is it not wonderful, wonderful that this body is a temple for the Holy Ghost? And if this body is a temple, then Jesus knows all this body suffers." When the verse was repeated, "If we suffer with Him, we shall also reign with Him," she replied, "That is a sweet thought. All Thy rich promises in me fulfil!" At another time, "When shall these sightless eyes behold the King in His beauty?" The chariot of her King drew near, and ecstacies fell from her dying lips. Then suddenly a convulsive quiver of the frame, and in the arms of her devoted husband she passed away at $2\frac{1}{2}$ P. M., November 2, 1874. Three days later, in the Methodist Episcopal Church, corner of Fourth Avenue and Twenty-Second Street, a large concourse gathered to mourn for their loss, which was her eternal and glorious gain. A pure, intensely active life of evangelism, in which Dr. Palmer always accompanied her, a legacy of hallowed pages from her pen, and a death of unclouded victory, was, in a sentence, the history of Phœbe Palmer.

Mr. Inskip and Mr. Macdonald are widely known, particularly so from their connection, from its origin, with the National Camp-Meeting Association, whose object it is to promote "Scriptural holiness" among Christians. Their evangelistic labors are distinct from it, although they have the same general end in view. Mr. Inskipp was born August 10, 1816 ; converted in 1832 ; licensed to preach in the Philadelphia Conference in 1836 ; engaged in the camp-meeting enterprise in 1867, and entered fully the field of evangelism four years later. They are not entirely in accord with the majority of their denomination, while substantially in agreement and fellowship.

"Mr. Inskip is a right sturdy specimen of an old-fash-

ioned Methodist preacher, — one by nature well endowed
with vitality and with courage sufficient to enable him to
face without fear anything that might come in his way.
His voice is strong and passably clear, and when he wills,
it has a volume that is really tremendous.   He is earnest
in manner and enthusiastic in his expressions.   When
moved with feeling his utterance is rapid, loud, and yet
under perfect control.

"Rev. W. Macdonald, who is about the same age, is his
counterpart, — cool, calm, logical, and persuasive.   From
Maine to California, and as far south as Tennessee, they
have labored with a diligence and zeal worthy of the best
days of Methodism.   They have faced and conquered
the worst mobs of Salt Lake City, of Sacramento and
San Francisco ; and wherever they have been, the blessing
and presence of God have ever attended them, and they
have deserved the praise and prayers of all good people
elsewhere."

These co-workers hold protracted meetings in churches
wherever invited, requesting them to have, before they
commence, a week of prayer.   Their sermons and efforts
substantially harmonize with those of Phœbe Palmer.

CHAPTER XXVII.

EVANGELISTS OF THE PLYMOUTH BRETHREN. — MR. J. N. DARBY, THEIR
FOUNDER. — HIS REMARKABLE LIFE. — MR. WILLIAM KELLEY. — MR.
C. H. MACKINTOSH. — LORD A. P. CECIL. — REV. WILLIAM REID ON
THE ACCUSERS OF THE BRETHREN. — THE UNITED BRETHREN. — COUNT
ZINZENDORF. — THE FRIENDS. — D. P. UPDEGRAFF. — ELIZA P. GUR-
NEY. — RACHEL S. HOWLAND.

THE Brethren, as they call themselves, are indeed " a
peculiar people, zealous of good works." They are peculiar in origin and present position ; and their zeal for God's
Word and the spread of the gospel in its purity makes
them an association of evangelists. We have, with considerable care, become acquainted with their history and
relation to the progress of a spiritual Christianity. We
shall quote substantially from Mr. Darby's account of his
own religious experience, which, although not intended for
the public, can have no other effect than to correct false
ideas and impressions concerning the Brethren.

He was born at 10 Great George Street, Westminster.
The family, though very orderly, was entirely worldly.
He was at Westminster, a great public school in England.
His father, having very considerable property in Ireland,
would have him called to the bar there. He graduated in
Dublin, and entered his profession just when he was converted. He was three years at the bar, with good prospects. He was converted by the Scriptures while studying for it, having never to his knowledge heard the gospel.
Awakened a little before, he remained from twenty-one
to twenty-seven under the law, having passed through the

deepest possible convictions. After three years he felt, though not set free, that he owed himself and his all to Christ, and gave up the bar. His father at that time opposed; though afterwards he died in the Lord, and left John to shift for himself for twelve years. Friends, though he felt little disposed to it, persuaded him, when inclined to work about among the poor in Ireland, to be ordained as an Episcopal clergyman, but that could not go on. Even then he declined a salary, and within two years and a half left. He had an accident which laid him by, and then it was he found he was in Christ, and got settled peace as being in Christ. This made him apprehend that that was the church, *i. e.* the body of Christ, — those thus united to Him; the parish was not, nor were the Dissenters (sects) the unity of the body. At the same time he got hold of the Lord's coming and the re-establishment of the Jews. That was in 1827, and in 1827–8, when, under a surgeon's care in Dublin, and after five months' exercise, he began to break bread with three others, with no other thought than the unity of the body, and thinking where two or three were gathered together in his name, to enjoy Christ themselves, He in their midst, apart from evil. Thence it spread. The evangelization soon became active, the brethren in England, where it began in 1831 at Plymouth (whence the name), preaching in fairs, markets, races, and wherever they could get a hearing. For a year or two Mr. Darby preached also in churches when allowed, " but could not get on long with it." In Ireland, a little later, they set up a home mission over all the country. What essentially constituted the change after deep legal experience was Christ, the head in heaven, and so union with Him by the Holy Ghost down here, and the coming of the Lord to take us to be with Him; the Lord's Supper being the symbol and expression of this unity between His first coming and work in death and His second to receive us.

The clergy disappeared, or, rather, were a false thing as such for him, because he "believed in a ministry by the Holy Ghost come down from heaven." He wrote a tract on the nature and unity of the Church of Christ. The doctrine of the church as the house or habitation of God by the Spirit came in very much later. He had many particular trials needless to relate, and many ways of divine teaching. His going to Ireland, and then leaving it again, tended to isolate him more, breaking up any friendly associations that might have formed themselves, which he mentions as a part of God's ways. When he got peace, while laid up by his accident, he went through a "remarkable inward testing process as to the divine and sure authority of God's Word, which has always held its place with divine authority in his soul since, and he has never found it fail him." He says, "I have been a poor, feeble, failing creature,—I know it well and confess it to the Lord; but since 1821 I have never had any object but the Lord. A large number of sailors in the fleet have been converted, and have breaking of bread in Japan, Malta, and wherever their vessels are stationed." Mr. Darby has travelled through Europe in his work, on foot, and harvested nearly every land.

It will be seen from the narrative that the Brethren claim simply a return to primitive Christianity, protesting against the present church and parish system, regarding it as Zion externally "in ruins." They call the rest of faith "deliverance," holding to the believer's privilege of settled peace in Christ through an appropriating faith, which leaves no doubt of His finished work and perpetual priesthood for His redeemed people. The millenarian views of the Lord's second coming, held by many in all denominations of Christians, are accepted by them.

One of the most active evangelists of the Brethren in America, Lord C. P. Cecil, who is understood to be "godson" of Queen Victoria, a converted officer of the English army, has been for several years in Canada, where, we learn from a note recently received from him, the field of successful labor is widening, with increasing interest.

Mr. William Kelly and Mr. C. H. Mackintosh, so generally known and appreciated as expounders of the Word, are gifted evangelists, and men of the highest culture.

Rev. William Reid, author of the "Blood of Jesus" and other works, has written a neat little pamphlet on the "Accusers of the Brethren," and another upon their "Literature and Mission," which are carefully considered, and warm in their defence of these Christians, who are attracting, with growing regard, the attention of religious people.

The United Brethren, or Moravians, who had their origin in Moravia, are among the oldest and most spiritual religious organizations of the world, and have been devoted almost exclusively to evangelistic and missionary fields of martyr-like consecration to Christ. Their apostle of the last century, an evangelist, who, like Paul, was brought before kings for "irregularity," the founder of wonderful Hernhut, the maker of hymns, and patron of music, was Count Zinzendorf. The narrative of his career in Bost's "History of the Moravians" reads like the annals of Luther in moral sublimity. The Wesleys were moulded in Christian character by the United Brethren, and borrowed their love-feasts from them.

Felix Neff, the Genevan evangelist, after wasting toil among the high Alps, seeking among wild, secluded valleys, beneath eternal snows, the scattered flocks of a persecuted people, was compelled to yield his life, and died triumphantly. The echoes of his saintly voice linger still around the peaks which lifted his soul adoringly to the God in whom was his delight.

The Friends have in their quiet religious activity a system of evangelism which has been greatly blessed among them; indeed it is a part of their settled order of denominational life.

D. P. Updegraff, of Mount Pleasant, Ohio, is one of the most influential workers in this service, a gentleman of worldly means, and a devoted preacher of Jesus, often with Mr. and Mrs. Boardman in conventions for the promotion of "scriptural holiness."

Born in August, 1830, he was nurtured in the fear of God by devout parents. His mother, Rebecca T. Updegraff, was one of the most successful evangelists of her people. Writes a Presbyterian clergyman of her: "She was one who would have attracted attention in any assembly, anywhere. Of a slight and delicate figure, but still not feeble-looking, there was something in her manner, as well as in her still, beautiful face, and her marvellous voice, which made an indelible impression on my mind." Mr. Updegraff's grandparents were "eminent ministers." His own conversion he dates to the spring of 1864, but his reluctance to speak in public — self-pleading for indulgence — led him, in 1869, "to resolve to have the victory or die." He bowed in prayer for hours, when the joy of full salvation filled his heart; "for days he sailed through seas of heavenly bliss." Since that hour he has been an evangelist wonderfully blessed of God. For four years, annually, powerful revivals have attended the series of meetings held at Mount Pleasant, in which all denominations united.

I. H. Douglass, a co-worker with Mr. Updegraff, who has been in the service since he was nineteen, is one of the most extensively known evangelists, and highly favored of God. Writes one who shared in the glorious scenes of 1875: "Mr. Douglass is a man in the prime of life, — not a common-looking man: he is one who would attract your attention in a crowd, — tall, slender, with a wonderfully spiritual face, deep-set dark eyes, and wears his brown

hair and beard long and flowing.   He has a pleasant voice
and a calm, graceful manner; his deep earnestness im-
presses one as soon as he begins to speak, and as with
burning words he unfolds the message of good news we
feel that he is God's anointed messenger.   D. B. Updegraff is too well known for personal description; he is a
deep thinker and a convincing reasoner; wholly in earnest, and striking at the very root of the disease.   He waits
for nothing; into the inmost recesses of your heart he
will go, and will drag thence any unclean thing he may find
lurking there, and show it to you face to face.   These devoted men are doing a wonderful work wherever they go."

Eliza P. Gurney has long been a gifted, impressive
minister among her people.   There is an unpublished
scene in her history of national interest.

During the darkest period of the late civil war, she
called upon President Lincoln.   After a few moments of
general conversation, Mrs. Gurney, having removed her
bonnet, commenced by saying, in the most beautifully
distinct and modulated tones: —

"It is with no feeling of idle curiosity that I have
sought this interview, but in the name and love of the
blessed gospel of our Lord and Saviour Jesus Christ,
breathing a spirit of peace and good-will towards all men.
In unison with the feeling of the people of my persuasion,
my heart is in full sympathy with the chief magistrate.
I believe him weighed down by cares and responsibilities
of no ordinary magnitude, and desirous, as he is, to pre-
serve a conscience void of offence both before God and
his fellow-men, I would encourage him not to be careful
for things over which he has no control, but to place his
trust on Him who is mighty and able to save.   I have
rejoiced and been made thankful in common with good
people on both sides the Atlantic that our President has
been able to keep the true fast, and to let the oppressed

go free ; I believe that generations yet unborn will call
him blessed for this magnificent deed. Yet he will find
that all will suffer persecution who attempt to hold a just
and true balance. How blessed, therefore, the promise
to the believer, given us from on high, 'Therefore will
we not be afraid though the mountains shall be removed,
and though they be cast into the sea.' There is a river
the waters whereof shall make glad the whole city of God,
and the breathing of my spirit is that our President may
daily, and oftener than that, drink from those living waters
that his spirit may be strengthened and refreshed, and
that he may be largely instrumental in hastening that day
when He shall reign throughout the whole earth forever.
May our President seek that wisdom that is from above,
first pure, then peaceable, gentle, and easy to be entreated.
And while he is subject to burdens heavy to be borne,
how sweet to the believer to know that he shall abide
under the shadow of the Almighty. He shall cover him
with His feathers, and under His wings shall he trust.
How great are the promises to the believer in Jesus, how
calculated to strengthen and support us, —a very present
help in time of trouble.

"And now, my dear friend, if I may be allowed to call
thee so, may the Lord lift up the light of His countenance
upon thee, may every effort to strengthen the cause of
truth be increased ; may He help thee in thy heavenward
way, and when thou shalt have served thy generation in
this thy day and appointed time, through His atoning
mercy may He receive thy ransomed spirit into that glorious company of victors around the throne, standing on
the sea of glass, bearing in their hands harps of gold, and
singing, 'Blessing and honor and glory and power be
unto Him that sitteth upon the throne and unto the Lamb
for ever and ever.'"

After a moment's intermission, Mrs. Gurney kneeled

and uttered a short, fervent, and comprehensive prayer, that light and wisdom might be shed down from on high to guide our President through the troublous times.

After a brief pause the President replied : —

"I am glad of this interview, and glad to know that I have your sympathy and prayers. We are indeed going through a great trial, — a fiery trial. In the very responsible position in which I am placed, being an humble instrument in the hands of our Heavenly Father to work out His great purposes, I have desired that all my works and acts may be according to His will, and that it might be so, I have sought His aid ; but if my efforts fail, I must believe that for some purpose unknown to me, He wills it otherwise. If I had had my way, this war would never have been commenced. If I had had my way, this war would have been ended before this. Mysterious and unknown to us His purposes, and though with our limited understanding we may not be able to comprehend it, yet He who made the world still governs it."

The President was deeply affected. When he commenced speaking, he stood holding her hand for some seconds before he could speak ; his eyes filled, his lip quivered, and his voice was choked with emotion.

Sarah Smiley was born and educated a Friend, and became a preacher among them. Her burden of preaching is faith, illustrated with great enthusiasm by Old Testament narratives, perhaps sometimes straining a type or symbol or hidden meaning a little, but always instructive and impressive. Her countenance is radiant with quiet joy. Thousands think of her gratefully and lovingly. She has a cottage at Saratoga.

Rachel S. Howland, of New Bedford, and Esther Tuttle, are widely known as very devout, persuasive preachers of Jesus, whose name falls like heavenly music from their lips.

CHAPTER XXVIII.

"WHAT changes a few years bring!" is the exclamation
of Rev. William W. Patton, D. D., of Chicago, in a recent
article on "Lay-Evangelists." He then relates the experience of a theological student (whom we suspect was himself) who ventured to hold a series of services in a rural
parish which were attended with a precious harvest, upon
whom the Presbytery let fall their wrath. His defence
was the following passage: "The Spirit and the bride
say, Come! *And let him that heareth say, Come!*"
Reference is also made to a volume, whose authorship is
unknown, published in 1823, with the title, "A Defence
of Lay-Teaching," — an able and unanswerable discussion
of the subject. But the voice of that solitary advocate of
Christian liberty died away under the silent protest of
ecclesiastical law. Dr. Patton adds forcibly, "But a half
century has witnessed brave progress of thought and practice on this subject, and now our religious newspapers are
largely occupied with recording the labors and success of
lay-evangelists on both hemispheres."

28

While we are aware of the difficulty of making a just comparison between the pastoral and evangelistic ministry, inseparable as they are in their work and fruitage, the conviction has deepened with the progress of this volume, that the world is more indebted to the latter for great spiritual impulses and movements in the churches and society at large, than to any other class of men among the clergy or laity. This view was sustained by a passage in Rev. Dr. Taylor's impressive sermon in the Central Church, Boston, August last, from the text, " What do ye more than others? " When dwelling eloquently on the spirit of self-sacrifice for souls, which is the central force of Christianity, he inquired, Where would have been the cause of missions and other benevolent agencies, had there been only a well-settled, easy-going ministry, without our Whitefield and Wesley, and kindred servants of Christ, whose love to Him and to humanity sent them forth with consuming zeal to labor and to suffer reproach?

The Church is in the midst of a twofold religious revolution, or a readjustment of its inner life and outward activity. The divine possibilities of faith and agencies largely unemployed hitherto are stirring her heart with increasing and practical interest; and we are evidently on the eve of a new epoch in her aggressive influence upon mankind. To meet the tendencies to worldly compromise and laxity of belief, God seems to be preparing the way for the displays of His glorious majesty, by the use of means which rebuke a merely professional estimate of the office of His ambassador, humble ecclesiastical pride and all forms of selfish ambition, compelling the sceptical and unbelieving to see His hand, while Jesus wears the crown of victory. We turn to our sketch for the latest and most remarkable illustration.

A few miles north of Greenfield, Mass., the very beautiful shire-town of Franklin County, lies the quiet and delightful village of Northfield, in the same unrivalled valley of the Connecticut. The rich farms sloping down to the river, the clean, shaded streets, the clustered dwellings of the business centre, and the encircling hills, make a charming picture of rural life. In one of those peaceful homes, amidst broad fields spreading away towards the mountains, on the fifth of February, 1837, was born Dwight Lyman Moody, the sixth of nine children, two of whom, a pair of twins, were born after his father's death. January 3, 1828, Mr. Edwin Moody married Betsey Holton, a descendant of the original settlers of the valley. He was a mason, and died suddenly May 28, 1841, by the bed which he had attempted to reach. Mrs. Moody is still living with her daughters in Northfield. The boy went early to the common school, and was also sent to the Sabbath School of the Unitarian Society, with which the family was connected.

After his mother became a widow, with small means and a large family, Dwight lived among relatives much of the time. With no paternal oversight and naturally high-spirited, he became unsettled in aims and wayward in his general conduct. Studies were neglected, and the mother's heart became deeply anxious over his prospects. When sixteen years of age, his uncle, Samuel Holton, a shoe-merchant in Boston, who went there a boy, and worked his own way in the world, visited Northfield. Dwight asked for his aid in procuring a situation in the city; but his inclination to throw off restraint being a serious objection, nothing was done for the lad. This was in midwinter. The next spring, to the surprise of Mr. Holton, Dwight one day entered his store. He had started out on a pilgrimage to find employment, trying at Clinton, Worcester, and other places on the route, in vain. The times were dull and no opening offered. He was plainly clad, and had a boil on his neck, setting his

head awry, when he reached the New England metropolis.
That night he found a home at the house of Mr. Holton,
in Winchester. In the morning, when invited to join
in reading the Bible in turn, at family worship, he was
unable to do so without difficulty and mistakes, giving to
a word unpronounceable by himself some convenient sound
and passing on to the next. He now began to look through
the business streets for employment, too proud to make any
further application to his relative for assistance, who felt
that the discipline of failure was indispensable until the
boy was willing to put himself more directly under his
guidance. From irritation, Dwight's feelings changed to
right views of the matter, and he sought counsel. Assistance was granted conditioned upon his attendance on Dr.
Kirk's church and Sunday School, and accepting a boarding-place selected for him. These preliminaries settled,
Dwight began his clerkship, "and," remarked his employer, "soon could sell more goods in three months than
other clerks in a year. He was self-reliant, always naming
a price sufficiently high to ensure a fair profit if he went
below his first figures."

In the Sabbath School, when Moses was the topic, and
his teacher, Mr. Kimball, unfolded the grand qualities
of the Hebrew leader's character, Dwight, with surprise
and admiration, exclaimed, "Don't you think that Moses
was a pretty smart man?" His teacher little thought that
the questioner would one day be leading a mightier host
to the promised land than any other living inhabitant of
the globe. The boy became serious, and when one day
Mr. Kimball asked him into his store, and laying his hand
on his shoulder inquired if he would not then give his
heart to Jesus, his conviction became decided and deep.
That gentle touch yet remains as fresh to his consciousness
as when, with the question that followed, it thrilled him
with a mysterious power. But he was very reticent respect-

ing his religious feelings. At length, May 16, 1855, he asked for admission to the church. So unsatisfactory were his statements of experience, partly owing, it may be, to the common neglect, too, of sufficient personal attention to his case, that the admission to communion was deferred. On presenting himself again to the committee, he was received into the communion of the church on March 5, 1856. Soon after, attending a church prayer-meeting, he rose and spoke briefly. At the close of the service, the pastor took him aside, and kindly told him that he had better not attempt to speak in the meetings, but that he might serve God more acceptably in some other way. He attended other meetings, and delivered short addresses; but the strongest impression he left upon many good people by these efforts was that he ought not to attempt public speaking at all,— that it was not in his line; and they frankly told him so.

Now came business changes. Dwight went with another uncle to manage a branch-store on Court Street, but, not satisfied with his success, removed, September, 1856, to Chicago. He joined the Plymouth Congregational Church. But he was a stranger and lonely; and this solitude in a city stimulated his desire to engage in active service for his Master. He hired four pews and filled them with young men. In the prayer-meetings his voice was heard, sometimes with dissatisfaction because of his directness and faithfulness. Wanting more work, he took a Sabbath-morning class in the First Methodist Church.

The next move was in connection with a small mission Sunday School in North Wells Street, where the only thing offered him by the superintendent was the privilege of getting and teaching new scholars. The next Sabbath he appeared with eighteen ragged street-boys.

In the spring of 1857, while distributing tracts and Testaments to the sailors in port, he met Mr. J. B. Stillson, a Presbyterian elder from Rochester, N. Y., who was building the Chicago Custom House, engaged in the same work. They joined hands in goodly fellowship and labored for months, — a profitable experience for both, especially for the young evangelist.

Urged forward by success, he planned a larger field of his own. There stood near the North-side Market a deserted saloon, in sight of nearly two hundred others which were occupied and in "full blast," and in this forbidding place he gathered a motley crowd of juvenile humanity. He found it embarrassing, on account of his very defective education, to study God's Word as he desired; indeed, sometimes he had to spell out the long words while teaching the neglected youth around him.

The work grew upon his hands, and by permission of the mayor he removed his school to the large hall of the North Market, which was used on Saturday nights for dancing; and after the gay crowd had dispersed, Mr. Moody with his associates spent the time into the early hours of Sunday morning, in putting the room in order for the morrow's work. The school was held in this hall six years, amidst marked encouragements and discouragements. Finding it difficult to hold prayer-meetings or Sabbath-evening services in this hall, Mr. Moody rented a saloon that would accommodate about two hundred persons. Here, in a dismal, unventilated place, where during service he found it necessary to have policemen to guard the door, he collected the poor and the vicious, and offered Christ to them.

The wholesale merchants in whose employ he was, while appreciating the good achieved, complained that customers who desired to trade with him often found him absent. Mr. Moody, therefore, set a time when he would be in, and wrote his friends accordingly. But his field of usefulness extended on every hand; even neighboring parishes sent for him to address the Sabbath Schools. In the winter of 1857–58, the revival led to the formation of the Young Men's Christian Association in Chicago, and the establishment of a daily union prayer-meeting. He was most active in this meeting; and at a time when the interest had flagged so that but three or four persons attended it, he by his personal efforts induced more than a hundred to join the praying band.

He at length determined to give God all his time. When asked how he expected to live, he said, " God will provide if He wishes me to keep on, and I will keep on until I am obliged to stop." Since that day he has received no salary from any individual or Society, but God has supplied his wants, often in most striking ways.

Converts were now multiplied under his ministrations; revivals were started and promoted by his zealous labors; the Young Men's Christian Association was raised out of a state of dulness and torpor to great activity and power in the city and State. For a glimpse of Mr. Moody's service for Christ in the late civil war, which soon after burst upon the country, we are indebted to Rev. William Burnett Wright, of the Berkeley-street Church, Boston. He says : —

" He never lost an opportunity for work. While we waited in the depot at Pittsburg, an angry hackman was cursing, vociferously, near the platform. Moody dropped my arm, drew near him, and spoke to him. Presently the swearer was gently talking about his mother.

" We reached Hampton. He moved and spoke among the sick as though the special study of his life had been the wants of sick men.

" The man's humility was as marvellous as his tact. When he was not preaching, he was asking questions to get material for preaching. Morning, noon, and night I have heard him uttering the same request, — ' Now tell

me something I can use for Christ, something about the
Bible.' His friends used to speculate how he could be
happy in heaven, where he would find no sinners to convert. Some answered, 'He will never get through with
asking the angels to tell him something he can use for
Christ.'

"Shortly after leaving Hampton, he was preaching at
City Point. In the near vicinity of this place a number
of ministers from all parts of the country were gathered.
It was a hospital station, and near the front. The number
of troops was great. It soon became evident that Moody's
methods were not wholly acceptable to the brethren who
had been in charge of the station. Moody learned it with
sorrow. He had been preaching three times a day. The
effect had been amazing. A powerful revival was in progress. The instant the state of feeling was known to him,
he said to me, confidentially, 'We must have no dissen-
sions among the Lord's people. Let us put these meetings in charge of ——. We can work outside, and help
make his meetings successful, without seeming to inter-
fere.' I confess I was indignant, but he was not. For
days he attended the meetings without speaking once. He
was diligent in speaking and praying with inquirers who
remained for that purpose ; he was indefatigable in visiting the sick in hospital. It was not long before his sweetness and his humility so won the hearts of those who
opposed him, that they requested him to resume charge
of the public services, and became to a man cordial co-
workers, cheerfully accepting his leadership."

Mr. Moody's army work in field, camp, and prison was,
like the rest of it, untiring, and adapted to the conditions
of mind and body of those with whom he had to do. When
his almost unnoted, unrecorded usefulness on our battle-
fields was over, "he began to question books as closely as
he had questioned men. For five to seven hours daily he

shut himself up with books, refusing to be interrupted, rising at five o'clock, and often at four, and studying until breakfast. The result is, that few men are more deeply read in the best pulpit literature than he. It is true that the single aim of his studies has been mastery of the Scriptures. But to master these he has recognized his need of learned help."

When he gave himself, his fortune, and his honors to Christ, the entireness of the consecration was expressed in the few words, "I have but one passion; it is the love of *Him*, — nothing but Him."

Mr. Moody was married to Emma C. Revell, August 28, 1862, and went to housekeeping in a snug cottage after he had a home for his North Market Mission School. They are a happy family of four, — a boy and girl completing the consecrated circle.

In 1863 a large chapel, with spire, was erected in Illinois Street, near the Market Hall, at the cost of $20,000, collected by Mr. Moody. He later became pastor of an organized church, in polity Congregational, but without having an ordained clergyman; in its spirit and management open to all believers; practically, an independent body of Christians. It was a warm centre of a saving activity, which became justly very dear to Mr. Moody's heart, and a priceless treasure to the New York of the West.

At length a new building for the Young Men's Christian Association became a necessity, and how should money be raised? Elect Mr. Moody president of the Association, was the reply of one of the brethren; and September 29, 1869, "Farwell Hall" was dedicated, with very impressive ceremonies. George H. Stuart, Esq., made an eloquent address, which opened with the following words, "I have travelled eight hundred miles to be present at the dedication of the first hall ever erected for Christian young men."

John V. Farwell, Esq., gave him a house, which friends
beautifully furnished.   But the great conflagration of
1871 swept over both the tabernacle and the home, and
left only dust and ashes around the unsightly ruins.   The
evangelist escaped with his family and what he would
part with last of all, — his Bagster's Bible, indexed and
filled with short notes of incidents and illustrations.   He
then made a visit to England for the cause in which he
then labored.   Fifteen months later the second Farwell
Hall rose upon the ruins of the first.   Mr. Moody's convention labors were limited only by the number of rapidly
increasing associations.   In the midst of them, when the
meeting of the American Board was held in Chicago, Dr.
E. N. Kirk was invited by Mr. Moody to spend a few
days at his house.   He went, and enjoyed, as such a
devout, working spirit would, his communion with the
brother and his companion worthy of him.

Upon Dr. Kirk's return he made a powerful appeal to
his church, in view of the fact that this brother, once so
humble a member of their communion, through the faith
and love of Christ, should be doing such a work for Him,
while they were accomplishing so little.   This suggests
the most instructive, wonderful thing respecting Mr.
Moody's career, — the sovereign grace of God in select-
ing a plain, uncultivated young man, so far as "the
schools" are concerned, untitled and unaided in the out-
start, and crowning him with such honor in extending His
kingdom in connection with the "sweet singer" of our
modern Israel.   "What is the secret of power?" we asked
one who has known him from his birth.   "The Bible and
close communion with Christ," was the reply.   His book
of theology and of preaching is the Word of God, and
his aids in its study such profound expounders as he found
among the Plymouth Brethren.   His source of power in
wielding the Scriptures and of humble walk with God

amidst unequalled successes and popularity, is prayer, — a life of believing prayer. God means the Church to ponder well the history of such a man,.

Upon one occasion, while spending a Sabbath with a pastor, the brother criticised his grammar. "Yes," replied Mr. Moody, " I know I fail there, but I am trying to serve my Master ; and what, brother, are you doing?" There was no reply to the gentle rebuke. His glad human life appears in the playful overflow of feeling. Two or three years since, when visiting the old home in Northfield with his uncle, the family group arranged a picnic upon the neighboring hills. A pair of oxen were yoked to the wagon, and the party were scarcely safely in it before Mr. Moody seized the whip, and sent the astonished cattle galloping away with their equally surprised yet happy load. Such playfulness was only the sparkle and ripple of the current setting ever with steady sweep towards the ocean of infinite love.

The singing evangelist, Mr. Sankey, has ancient precedent for making music the medium of the gospel message. The Hebrew prophets not unfrequently accompanied their announcements in poetical form with such music as the instruments of their age might furnish. Whitefield, the Wesleys more largely, Dr. Nettleton with his "Village Hymns," and indeed nearly all evangelists, Mr. Finney, perhaps, less so than any other one, have relied upon sacred melodies both to awaken and deepen religious impressions. But it remained for Mr. Moody to introduce in its distinct character and conspicuous importance, as the preaching power of a co-worker, the use of our popular tunes. There is nothing like it in the history of the religious world ; it marks an era in the pentecostal service of the church ; and no man can foresee the ultimate results of this extraordinary departure, not only from the original American evangelism represented by Dr. Nettleton, but of all later harvest-workers. Singing has been hitherto an accompaniment and auxiliary to the practical prose of aggressive gospel agencies; but in this ministry of salvation, we think that very often it would be difficult to judge through whose instrumentality, that of Mr. Moody addressing the people with prayerful simplicity upon sin and redemption, or that of Mr. Sankey, when from his lips of song the tender warning or appeal floats over the tearful multitude, the deeper impression was made.

The ancestry of Mr. Sankey on the paternal side was English, and on the maternal, North-of-Ireland Irish. Mr. Sankey's father was a public man for several years, and successively member of both Houses of the Legislature. He has also been president of a bank in New Castle, Penn., where he resides. In the Methodist Church, of which he is a member, Mr. Sankey has served it usefully as a licensed exhorter.

Ira David is the eldest living son of David Sankey, and was born on the 28th of August, 1840; he has two brothers and one sister living, and four brothers and three sisters in heaven, most of them having died in infancy. Ira was converted under the pastoral labors of Rev. H. H. Moore, of the Erie Annual Conference of the M. E. Church, when sixteen years of age, and connected himself with the church at what is known as King's Chapel, three or four miles north of New Castle. Edinburg, the place of his birth, is in the same county (Lawrence), which at that time was Mercer County.

His father writes: —

"There was nothing very remarkable in his early or boyhood history. The gift of singing developed in him at a very early age. I say gift, because it was God-given; he never took lessons from any one, but his taste for music was such that when a small boy he could make passable music on almost any kind of instrument. He not

only attended musical conventions, Sabbath-school meetings, and associations of that character, but by invitation
frequently attended and sang at political gatherings. But
for several years past he has sung nothing but sacred
music. Ira being a worker in the Y. M. C. A., was sent
as a delegate to a National Convention of Y. M. C. A.'s
which met at Indianapolis, Indiana, March, 1872. Mr.
Moody being engaged in the same work, they were thus
thrown together. Mr. Moody, attracted by Ira's singing, at
once, in his Yankee style, commenced to persuade him to
give up his business in this place, and go with him to
Chicago, and continued his importunity unceasingly, until
Ira yielded to his solicitations, and went. They sailed
from New York for Europe June 7, 1873."

Said a well-known layman recently on a public occasion, "The revival under Mr. Moody was suggested by a
remark of Mr. Varley's, while walking with Mr. Moody
two years ago in a garden, in Dublin : 'It is yet to be
seen what the Lord will do with a man wholly given up
to him.' Mr. Moody returned to America, but he wrote
to Mr. Varley, 'I have been thinking of that remark,
and have given myself wholly to God, and am coming back
to Europe to see what the Lord will do with me.'"

When asked why he returned to England so soon again,
he answered, "To win ten thousand souls to Christ."

The invitation to go to England had been extended by
Rev. Mr. Pennyfeather, rector of Mildmay Park Church,
London, and Mr. Cuthbert Bainbridge, an influential Wesleyan layman and merchant. He reached Liverpool June
17, 1873, ten days later. The friends alluded to were
dead. But another invitation from Mr. George Bennett,
of York, Secretary of the Young Men's Christian Association, was accepted. In reply to the secretary's assurance that York was so dead it would require a month to
prepare for the revival meetings, Mr. Moody telegraphed,

"I will be in York to-night"; and arrived in the city accordingly at ten o'clock. On Sunday morning, in one of the small rooms of the Association, four persons gathered — the first of a series of meetings which closed with an attendance of many thousands.

The old story of a cold reception from the clergy on account of irregularity and new measures, overcome only by the power of God which was with them, was repeated. Then in New-Castle-on-Tyne, Stockton-on-Tees, Carlisle, Edinburgh, Glasgow, Paisley, Greenock, Dundee, Aberdeen, Eton, and several of the country towns of Scotland; Belfast, Londonderry, and Dublin, in Ireland; Manchester, Sheffield, Liverpool, and Birmingham, in England, reaching London in March of this year, occurred a succession of revival scenes, unknown since the days of the Wesleys and Whitefield. In each place, the largest churches or halls were crowded to their utmost capacity by throngs anxious to hear the Word of Life expounded with the earnestness and simplicity that characterize Mr. Moody's services, and the sweet gospel invitations sung so effectively and winningly by Mr. Sankey.

Besides their public services, numerous daily prayer-meetings were established, and a system of house-to-house Christian visitation, similar to what had been introduced in the other cities where they labored, was inaugurated, whose results were most encouraging. "People of all ranks, from the highest of the nobility and even from the families of royalty, the dignitaries of the church and those occupying the most eminent social positions, have felt the influence of this religious work, and have helped to swell the throngs, and to aid in the public services. But one sentiment has pervaded all classes, that it was without doubt the work of God, and men have stood in awe and reverence before the evidence of the Divine Presence."

When the visit to London was first announced, it was

proposed to divide the city into sections, and give a month
to each. Arrangements were made for the use of the
Agricultural Hall for the north, which would hold an audience of 20,000, the Opera House for the west, the Bow
Road Hall, built especially for the occasion, for the east,
and Victoria Theatre for the south. This plan was carried
out, only it became necessary to build the tabernacle for
the south district. The throngs that crowded the Agricultural Hall were scarcely greater than those that went
away unable to gain admission.

Rev. H. M. Field, D. D., the editor of "The Evangelist," New York, under date of June 10, 1875, gave a very
full and graphic account of the first great meeting held at
the south of London, in the tabernacle built for Mr.
Moody on Camberwell Green, not far from Mr. Spurgeon's church. This famous preacher and pastor warmly
favored the movement, urging his people on the previous
Sabbath, "instead of standing aloof and criticising, to join
heartily in the effort, which he believed would result in
great good." Dr. Field started for the tabernacle an hour
and a half before the time of service, and yet upon reaching one of the half a dozen entrances, he found the gates
shut and guarded, because the edifice was full, while a
living tide was surging against the enclosure. His ticket,
indorsed by the Hon. Arthur Kinnaird, M. P., secured
his admission; but the moment the gate was ajar the
excited throng swept in, and the officers were like straws
upon a rushing current. Mr Field was borne onward,
equally helpless, to the end of the audience-room, precisely opposite to that in which was the seat assigned
him. The spectacle within he describes as follows : —

"It was indeed wonderful. The building is somewhat
like Barnum's Hippodrome, though not so large, and of
better shape for speaking and hearing, being not so oblong,
but more square, with deep galleries, and will hold, I

should say, at a rough estimate, six or eight thousand people. The front of the galleries was covered with texts in large letters, such as 'God is love,' 'Jesus only,' 'Looking unto Jesus, the Author and Finisher of our faith,' 'Come unto Me all ye that labor and are heavy-laden, and I will give you rest.' At each corner was a room marked 'For Inquirers.' At length Mr. Moody appeared. The moment he rose on the stand in front of the platform there was a movement of applause, which he instantly checked with a wave of his hand, and at once proceeded to business, turning the minds of the audience to something besides himself, by asking them to rise and sing the stirring hymn, —

" Ring the bells of heaven! There is joy to-day! "

The whole assembly rose, and caught up the words with such energy that the rafters rang with the mighty volume of sound. A venerable minister, with white locks, then rose, and clinging to the railing for support, and raising his voice, offered a brief but fervent prayer."

Mr. Moody presided, speaking briefly, and Mr. Sankey thrilled the vast congregation with

" Nothing but leaves! The Spirit grieves
Over a wasted life."

Mr. Spurgeon made the closing address with his usual impressiveness, and wealth of apt illustrations.

The farewell service in the Opera House, with its five galleries, which was occupied for eight weeks, was held on Monday noon, May 31, and the place was literally packed from floor to roof.

The exercises, naturally enough, took the form of a praise-meeting, conducted by Mr. Moody. He thought they had much to praise God for, since there had been everything to encourage and nothing to discourage them in their efforts, though they came here with a good deal of trembling. Mr. Sankey, who can talk as well as sing, referred to their first meeting when they started in York nearly two years ago. There were four persons present then, he said, and here there were thousands. After singing, —

"There is a land that is fairer than day,"

The meeting closed with "Old Hundred" and benedictions. The occasion was one of profound interest, and will long be remembered by those present.

The Lord Chancellor of England, a short time since, said of Moody, "The simplicity of that man's preaching, the clear manner in which he sets forth salvation by Christ, is to me the most striking and the most delightful thing I ever knew in my life."

Adds another : —

"Is there not in this an element of mighty power and strength which is largely overlooked by the ministry of the present day?"

The very impressive thanksgiving-meeting which closed the labors of Messrs. Moody and Sankey, was held in Mildmay Conference Hall, on Monday afternoon, July 12, and six hundred clergymen were present.

Mr. Moody having read verses from Psalms cv, cvii, and Luke xvii, made a few remarks, in which he declared the purpose of their coming to have been not to glorify man but God; to Him alone belonged all honor and praise for the work accomplished, and to Him was heartfelt gratitude due for His goodness, mercy, and care.

Mr. Sankey then sang, "Oh, 't was love," after which Mr. Stone, Chairman of the Central Committee, gave a summary of the work in which they had been engaged since September last.

He was followed by Dr. A. A. Bonar, of Scotland, Rev. Archibald Brown, of the East London Tabernacle, and many other prominent clergymen, all of whom united in testifying to the spiritual quickening of Christians, the almost countless conversions among the impenitent of all classes, and the greater denominational unity which, by the Holy Spirit's power, had been brought about during the sojourn of Messrs. Moody and Sankey in Great Britain.

Mr. Varley, in his remarks, urged the most tender and watchful care of new converts. Lord Shaftesbury said that nothing but a positive command from Mr. Moody — and he felt bound to obey a command from such a man — would have induced him to speak before so many members of the clerical order, and when he was almost the only layman to speak. He felt the deepest gratitude to Almighty God for having raised up such men with such a message, and to deliver it in such a manner. He had received a letter from Manchester, which stated that Mr. Moody's preaching was still at work among the most wretched people, and was "like the leaven in that magnificent lump." From Sheffield he had also heard, and it was said that if a million tracts were sent there it would fail to satisfy the public appetite for spiritual food. If Mr. Sankey had done no more than teach the people to sing " Hold the Fort," he would have conferred an inestimable blessing on the British Empire. Mr. Moody rose to speak after Mr. Sankey had sung "The Ninety and Nine," and was visibly affected. He wished to return thanks to the public and ministers for the sympathy they had extended towards him during the past two years. He had received nothing but kindness. He wanted to thank the committee publicly. For four months he had received nothing but love and kindness from them. Their love and their kindness had broken his heart. He had been asked to speak on that occasion, but he did not dare trust his feelings. He said he never could bear to leave his home, the parting used to be so hard, and now it was like parting with his own family, the friends had become so dear to him. He wanted to thank the stewards, for he had received nothing but kindness from them. He also would like to thank the reporters. He had made mistakes, but the reporters had been so kind they had not spoken of his failures. He also wanted to thank the policemen. They, too, had been so kind — in fact, all had been kind. London was on his heart, and whenever he heard the name of London mentioned, he would think of the warm friends, and of the four happiest months of his life which he spent in that city. He wanted God to use them in America, and would ask the friends to pray for them.

After an interval of silent prayer, Rev. Newman Hall led the devotions, the meeting being brought to a close at half-past five with the doxology, and benediction pronounced by Dr. Kennedy. The evangelists hurriedly left the hall to avoid anything like a demonstration.

Just as the audience was about to retire, Rev. Marcus Rainsford suggested the raising of a money testimonial for Mr. Moody, as a memento of his visit. Mr. Stone at once came forward, and said he knew Mr. Moody's feelings on such matters, and felt sure that nothing would give their brother greater pain than the carrying out of such a proposition. As Mr. Moody's nearest friends stoutly opposed the suggestion, the idea was at once abandoned.

At the close of the London meetings, the evangelists took a short vacation before returning to America, — Mr. Moody going to Wales, and Mr. Sankey to Switzerland. The former arrived at Bala, July 26, accompanied by the Rev. Mr. Aitken, Episcopal, who has been for several months associated intimately with him in his work. The people thronged him, the town crier with his bell sometimes giving notice of meetings at eleven o'clock at night, for the next day; on one occasion a large multitude gathered from the country to see and hear him. Early in August he left the enthusiastic Welsh.

Messrs. Moody and Sankey reached New York August 14, 1875, by the steamer "Spain." The former was accompanied by his wife and two children, and the latter by Mrs. Sankey and three children. Among their fellow-passengers were Rev. J. Sabine Knight, English evangelist to the Southern freedmen, and a brother of Mr. Sankey. As soon as the approach of the vessel was announced, a party repaired to the quarantine in the custom-house barge to meet her, consisting of Mr. George H. Stuart, of Philadelphia; Mr. Rowland, Secretary of the Philadelphia Young Men's Christian Association; Mr. Robert R. McBurney, secretary of the New York Young Men's Christian Association; Mr. McWilliams, superintendent of the Sunday School of Dr. Cuyler's church, Brooklyn; Rev. G. C. Needham, the Irish evangelist, of Philadelphia; and Mr. John V. Farwell, of Chicago. The evangelists were very joyful on reaching home after their long absence, and brief thanks and praise were offered at the dock for their safe arrival. Mr. Moody is not a good sailor, and both he and Mr. Sankey were in need of the rest they immediately sought at their respective old homes in Massachusetts and Pennsylvania. At three o'clock the former left by rail, reaching Springfield, where he remained over Sabbath at the Massasoit House. Mr. Sankey spent Sunday with Mr. McWilliams, and attended the Classon-Avenue Church (Dr. Duryea's).

Major Whittle, of Chicago, a devoted, unassuming layman, taking the hint from Mr. Moody's method, itinerates with Mr. Bliss, the well-known musician, and made a very successful tour in the Southwest. In St. Louis the interest was like that in some of the English cities of late. He left a salary of $5,000 per annum, in the office of the Elgin Watch Company, through the influence of Mr. Moody, to become with him a lay-evangelist.

September 6, 1875, Mr. Sankey left New Castle, to

rejoin Mr. Moody at Northfield. On the 9th they held
their first meeting since their return to this country,
followed by another on the 10th, of increasing interest ; Mr.
Moody making a touching exposition of the prodigal son.
He went on to show that people are all the time forgetting
that " God takes the place of the seeker." The first thing
after the fall of Adam, God went about searching for
him, when Adam should have gone up and down crying,
"Where, oh where, is my God ?" He was followed
by Major Whittle, who, with Mr. Bliss, had joined
him. Mr. Moody then preached from the story of blind
Bartimeus.

On the 11th, the Sabbath, the people came from all the
country round, so that the Orthodox church proved too
small. Mr. Moody spoke from the church-steps to an audience of a thousand people in the morning. At three
o'clock Mr. Sankey and Maj. Whittle, of Chicago, talked
to the children in the church, and Col. Fairbanks, of St.
Johnsbury, and D. W. McWilliams, President of the
Young Men's Christian Association of New York, organized a meeting for the crowds waiting for the evening
service. At five o'clock Mr. Moody preached again to an
audience of two thousand people. The feeling of the
large assemblies revealed itself often in tears, and sometimes in sobs.

The spiritual campaign will doubtless erelong be continued down the Connecticut Valley, extending to Boston,
New York, and other places, to which, by the vote of
pastors, they have been invited.

Looking over the vast amount of evangelistic labor
represented in the brief sketches we have made of its
workmen, how varied appear their gifts, characteristics,
and methods ; nor less various have been the classes
reached, and the general results. But who is prepared

to say that any one of the laborers had been better left out of the field of the world? Who can doubt the infinite good, whatever may have been directly or incidentally evil, because human depravity loves occasion for self-justification or profounder indifference to spiritual realities? No man is competent to say, as did an honored divine who opposed Mr. Finney's evangelism, that "the conversion of a soul may cost too much"; it is declaring that the Holy Ghost is sometimes extravagant in the use of His converting energy. Earnest Christian people are looking forward over the months to come, and inquiring, "Watchmen, what of the night?" Shall we have the "times of refreshing," preparing the country, especially the "City of Brotherly Love," for the influx, another summer, of foreign population, with their Continental Sabbath and easy conscience touching religious obligations and moral restraints? And yet how many, from the "conservative" pastor to the "lover of pleasure more than of God," dread the excitement, labor, and possible irregularities and reactions of a harvest-work of the Holy Ghost like that of Whitefield's day!

A true-hearted young minister recently referred to this subject in connection with a course of lectures delivered by a physician before the theological students of the seminary where he studied, one of which we heard, on the influence of the nervous system, in connection with the imagination and emotional nature, upon religious experiences, giving certain statistics to show us how large a percentage of hopeful conversions were superficial and of short duration. While the doctor is instructive and at home on his subject, the effect practically, it seems to us, upon the young men, will tend to extreme conservatism. God does not apply a scientific gauge to that Power which comes and goes, like the noiseless wind, where He listeth, any more than to the prayer of faith. Not only so, but He has taught us in His Word that if men will slumber till they awake in hell, or grieve the quickening Spirit by a partial surrender under unusual excitement, the responsibility is their own. And that the latter often and even largely will be seen, is contemplated in His Word. The parable of the ten virgins ; the experience of Jesus, to which reference has been made ; and the complaint of Paul to Timothy, " All they which are in Asia be turned away from me," are a few pointed illustrations.

The enemy of souls could desire nothing more than to have Christian ministers and laymen, the moment a charnel-house-quiet is disturbed, in which for the unsaved a hopeless eternity is only a question of time, sit in frowning judgment upon the men and means employed by the Holy Ghost, and refuse to co-operate without the assurance that none will be awakened nor moved except those whom He soundly converts. There is something fearful in all this ; for if the Spirit moves at all, He requires a recognition of the fact, and most prayerful caution how we regard His sovereign pleasure. Human precedents and judgments in such a time may do far more mischief to souls than any peculiarities of the instrumentalities God deigns to employ, or the falling away of those whose promise of good withers under the heat of congenial temptations. A prudence, like that in our early war campaigns a few years ago, which so feared the loss of life that the watchful foe gained advantage that later cost a greater sacrifice, is not unfrequently seen in the army of the living God.

We stood by the coffin of Whitefield in the church-vault, and laid a hand upon the skeleton brow, beneath which the active brain had wrought so fearlessly and tenderly for human salvation, and thought of the contrast between his life-work and the legacy to the world he might have left, — that of the accomplished conservative pulpit orator, — the admired favorite of a large and, in its general aspect, prosperous parish. He may, as stated, have taken lessons of a tragedian to make his elocution more effective, but it was only to forget the instrument in the passionate love for Jesus and the souls for which He bled. He was " dramatic, but not theatrical." How mournful in what it suggests was the criticism of Betterton, the actor, to the Bishop of London : " The dulness and coldness which empties the churches would empty the play-houses if the actors spake like the preachers."

Moody and Sankey have been called of God; not only to reap down harvest, but to rebuke a fruitless ministry, which we are sure will be represented by those graduates of a New England college who turned their faces towards the Theological Seminary, experts in card-playing for amusement. The Lord will set aside such instrumentalities, and put the honor of winning the lost to Him upon the humblest herald of His mercy who goes forth from the " Holy of holies" with the blended glory of Sinai and Calvary upon his brow, and his lips touched with the living fire from the altar of God.

Since the first edition of this work was published, these evangelists have held a limited series of meetings in the " Rink " at Brooklyn, N. Y., with good but not great results. Christians were quickened and souls saved. Could the effort have been continued, we may believe there would have been a mighty work. Early in November following, services were commenced in Philadelphia.

The old freight-depot at the corner of Market and Thirteenth Streets was purchased and fitted up by the well-known and devoted layman, Mr. Wanamaker, who, with Mr. Stuart, in this and all other activity and giving for the Lord's cause, is never found wanting. It seated ten thousand people.

December 23 a correspondent of the "Congregationalist" gave its readers an excellent picture in a brief sketch
of the work and workers, as the former reached its high-
water mark. He wrote : —

"A long, low, worn-looking building, close by the
Mint, and the stupendous City Building, with huge bills
along the walls, is the place of the Moody and Sankey
meetings. Go in, and the craven old depot is as a palace ;
new floors, matted aisles, brightly-whitened walls, and
roof-timbers striped blue ; gas circlets and clustered burn-
ers, and eleven thousand new unpainted chairs, fastened
in cross lines of two, three, and four hundred feet long,
please the eye. Seventy-five feet from the rear wall a
platform four feet high, rising to twice that as it recedes,
holds several hundred chairs, labeled 'Committee,'
'Clergy,' 'Choir,' etc.

"Look now. Every chair filled, a thousand and more
persons lining the wall-aisles standing, and within a four-
inch railing about five feet square, with a slight desk on
the right-hand corner, stands Dwight L. Moody. You
saw him years ago. He is in face the same, with hair
cropped, and beard like Abimeleeh ; in form stout, almost
to clumsiness. He speaks. 'T is the same voice you used
to hear ; tone cadences, rush-motion the same, the ragged
edge a little more so ; and soon the winning touch and
pathos of the inner tones, so to call them, more marked
than years ago. That vast *prairie* of people are in silence,
all eyes fastened on the wondrous man ; and as your eye
traverses the realm of faces, the tear will swell through it.
Such a spectacle ! Such attention !

"Sankey sings. The first strains seem superhuman
almost. They sweep over that vast expanse, seemingly,
as if it was a boudoir. Tears are visible in eyes all about
you, *if* you can see through your own. Prayer is offered.
The assembly rises and sings, with choir enrolled as con-

tributed by all the churches. That 'tide of song!' I
never heard its equal. Mr. Moody opens his hand Bible,
reads, and from a swift comment or two passes into an
address, — neither a sermon, too informal; nor a harangue, too curt and cutting; nor a discourse, too fiery,
tempestuous, and personal. Spear-points of truth taken
out of the Divine Word, and fastened to handles made of
rustic forms of speech and examples always human and
ever quite this side the miraculous, and then hurled
with loving vehemence, convincing without cauterizing
the hearer, and fastened like 'nails in a sure place,' is
one way of describing it. The first week, the steadfast
aim was to waken God's people to working life. Now,
poor lost souls are entreated and won in numbers. Two
large rooms, one on either side the platform, 'Inquirers'
Rooms,' receive all at the end of each meeting who seek
further help towards the cross.

"The crowds are so great, divisions are made, — Men's,
Women's, Parents', Non-church-goers' meetings. Tickets
are given to the latter class. ''T was the best day I ever
had in America,' said Mr. Moody of last Lord's Day.
Results are not to be seen yet. Processes, work, now
engages us. A meeting of young men, in a church near
by, follows the evening service. I saw five hundred there
last evening with John Wanamaker leading them. The
churches for miles outside the city feel the impulse, and
scarcely a church have I heard from in which special
interest is not seen.

"If this is not the finger of God, what is it?"

Another adds, "An interesting feature of the meetings
has been the hearty participation of Rev. Dr. Newton, a
widely-known Episcopal clergyman of the city. On one
occasion Mr. Moody gave a fresh proof of his readiness
and decision in meeting awkward emergencies. A colored
woman had broken out in the midst of the sermon with

screams and shouts in true camp-meeting style. People got up all about to see what was the matter. Mr. Moody stopped short and said, 'The ushers will take that person out of the room immediately. Let us all rise, and sing "Rock of Ages."' At a wave of his hand the congregation rose and instantly joined in the hymn. The shouts of the woman as she was taken out were of course drowned in the torrent of song. When two verses had been sung, Mr. Moody waved his hand again, the audience resumed their seats, and after a few pleasant words about people having full liberty to shout 'Amen' on their way home, the preacher resumed the thread of his discourse."

A novel and thrilling aspect of the work has been the Friday noon temperance meetings, when, at the request of Mr. Moody, all bowed in silent prayer; the requests for prayer were then read from parents and children for the loved and ruined, — "a long and terrible roll of anguished hearts pleading with the prayerful to beseech God's mercy for them." The climax of overwhelming interest was reached when the "reading, which sounded like the wail of muffled drums," was followed by Mr. Sankey's "Rescue the Perishing," which swept over the tearful throng.

The results have been great, and constantly increasing. The city is not only moved on the subject of personal salvation, but the circles of awakening influence are widening away from it. How far they will extend none on earth can tell.

January 19 and 20 were held the sessions of the Christian Convention, which called together ministers and laymen from the surrounding region and also from other States. At appointed hours, evangelistic work, the prayer-meeting, training of young converts, how to expound and illustrate the Scriptures, and other topics, were discussed with great animation and profit to all.

In the evening twelve thousand people thronged the

vast audience room, while the crowds outside fairly blocked the tracks of the street-cars. It was the twenty-first anniversary of the Young Men's Christian Association, and Mr. Moody's theme was "Daniel," one of his ablest discourses. At its close he made an appeal for funds to pay the debt on the new and beautiful edifice of the Association in that city; and $100,000 were subscribed, $70,000 of which were given by three gentlemen. A diamond ring, presented to Mr. Moody by a mother whose son was converted, was sold for $1,000, and the sum added to the building fund. The touching farewells followed, and Mr. Moody left to visit Florida on account of the health of a son, before beginning a similar spiritual campaign in New York, whose head-quarters were to be the Great Hippo-drome built by Mr. Barnum. This building is six hundred feet long by two hundred broad, enclosing an area quite too vast for one man to fill with his voice. It is divided in two by a double partition, the walls of which are twenty feet apart, thus making two rooms, each capable of holding eight thousand people. The double partition allows of distinct services being carried on simultaneously without interruption. The space between the partitions is utilized for committee rooms, etc., and by means of doors, access will be easy from one side to the other. Thus Mr. Moody can preach and Mr. Sankey can sing to two con-gregations at the same time.

As these pages go to press, the multitudes are moving in converging tides of humanity towards the doors of the gigantic tabernacle; the army of ushers, singers, and Chris-tian workers are in their places, and countless prayers are going up to God that our nation's metropolis, like that of Britain, may have a glorious Pentecost, which shall be repeated in the Puritan capital of New England, and be felt in every part of the land.

In Pittsburg and Lancaster, Penn., during months past,

Mr. Hammond's labors have been attended with a mighty outpouring of the Spirit; and at Cleveland, Ohio, Troy, N. Y., and in New Brunswick, Mr. Earle has witnessed similar harvests of the Holy Ghost. Other evangelists sketched in these pages are reaping largely in their fields of labor for the Master.

In closing these narratives, it may be of practical interest to briefly notice the different methods of labor employed by evangelists. Whitefield had really, it seems, no plan beyond preaching the pure gospel to the multitudes that everywhere thronged him. He exposed formalism, unmasked hypocrisy, and in the light of the Law and of Calvary, swept away the excuses for impenitence, while with tears he expostulated with sinners. His personal directions to the awakened were pointed and tender. Nettleton, Finney, Kirk, Baker, Knapp, and others, devoted their first efforts in a parish (unless the way was already prepared) to Christians, often holding days of fasting, confession, and prayer, till they were consecrated fully to the salvation of souls. The way to Calvary is through Gethsemane, where Zion, in sympathy with Jesus, prevails with God. This general order of successful labor is evidently the Divine appointment. In presenting the truth, evangelists who have been greatly blessed have had a threefold object in view in dealing with the impenitent, — to awaken, convict, and lead to Christ. We think that the cause of failure sometimes has been just here, — overlooking the indispensable conditions of the Spirit's working, preparation, and thorough instruction to the unconverted; and thus attempting to reap before the harvest was ripe. All evangelists have had "measures" of some kind. The inquiry meeting has uniformly been employed. Other expressions of interest have frequently been asked, to develop and deepen feeling; among these have been designated seats for the anxious, rising for prayers, and

requesting those in the congregation willing to have religious conversation to remain at the close of the preaching
service, with Christians, and so have a general meeting for
inquiry, personal appeal, and prayer. We have witnessed
scenes of great power of this last character, attended with
sound conversions on the spot.

Whatever the means, the secret of success, reveals that
of failure to a great extent, in the ordinary routine of the
parish, *seeking immediate results,* and adapting the gospel
messages, and all the Christian activity to the grand
design of the ministry and of the church itself. A farmer
may scatter seed till the ground is covered with it, but to
secure harvest is another matter. Mr. Moody's plan includes all these considerations, and even turns from the
costly temple for the rich, to the plain tabernacle for the
people. He resembles Mr. Finney in his general method,
spending weeks in a city; and although he frequently calls
upon the anxious to rise for prayer, he relies mainly upon
the inquiry meeting in rooms fitted for this object, after
the public worship. He also is not unlike that unrivalled
messenger of God since Whitefield's days, in the incisive,
searching, fresh, and telling presentation of the Word.
We add extracts from a letter written by the venerable
evangelist, Rev. Almon Underwood, just received, which
throws interesting light upon the experience of those called
to this service for the churches : —

"DEAR BROTHER,— My labors have been more abundant
in New England than anywhere else. Three seasons I
have spent at the West, in Illinois, Wisconsin, and Iowa.
My summers have been spent at home, in the bosom of
my family, often performing but little ministerial labor.
During this time I have never spent a day on my back
from ill health, and scarcely taken a particle of medicine.
I have found it emphatically healthy to serve God. 'They
that wait upon the Lord shall renew their strength, they

shall mount up with wings as eagles, they shall run and not be weary, they shall walk and not faint.'

"I found the few years I spent as a pastor very useful to me in enlarging my views of truth and in giving them a more general application to the various vicissitudes of human life. It cannot be denied that the life of an evangelist has a tendency to circumscribe one's views of truth. He has necessarily to go over the A, B, C of religion again and again; like one teaching, he must repeat lesson after lesson, till the whole becomes as familiar to him as his own breath. While there may be a circumstantial variety, there is a general resemblance in the different fields occupied. There is a class of truth adapted to awaken and interest the mind, there is another to convict and alarm, and still another to convert and save. All these do not furnish a long range of truth, and they are about the same wherever the evangelist goes. The pastorate furnishes a wider and a more general range of truth, adapted to strengthen and confirm the believer, to instruct and improve the intelligence of a community. In this way I found it serviceable to my own growth and helpful to me as an evangelist in giving others a more enlarged view of truth. My life has been emphatically one of trial and also one of blessing. I cannot conceive how any one can engage in such a work without often feeling an intense burden, an agony of spirit, that no one can tell who has not endured it. He will have his faith tried again and again all along his course. Then, again, one will feel to triumph and exult. Who ever heard of a victory without a battle, of a triumph without a conflict? 'As our sufferings abound so our consolations abound.' My last twenty-five years of evangelical labor commenced and have been continued as much for the benefit of believers as for the conversion of sinners. While I have labored to promote revivals as a necessity for the perpetuity of the church, I have constantly taught them a more excellent way of abiding in Christ, of ' committing the *keeping* of their souls unto God as unto a faithful Creator.' This has been a kind of specialty in my work, and I believe without an exception greatly prized in the fields where I have labored. They have received the word of *faith* with all gladness, and it has been greatly blessed to the emancipation of the church from bondage, to a new departure in the way of holy living. In connection with revivals, I believe the Lord intends to introduce the church into a Pentecostal experience, and thus harbinger forth the millennial reign of Zion, ' when the sun shall no more go down nor the moon withdraw its light, but the Lord shall be her everlasting light and the days of her mourning shall be ended.'

"ALMON UNDERWOOD."

Never, we think, was the need of true evangelists, to assist pastors in the gathering of spiritual harvests, greater than now.

The three or four thousand hopefully converted in Philadelphia, the deepening interest at New York, in which the leading pastors, among whom are Drs. Hall, Crosby, and Tyng, are active, indicate very clearly this return to an instrumentality ordained of God, but to a great extent ignored in the past by the churches.

Miss Drake has just reached India, the first evangelist of the faith-work under Dr. Cullis who has gone from the home field to that of independent missionary labor. From abroad and in our own land come unanswered calls for help.

Surely in these times of humiliating betrayal of trust in the churches, and declining morality, does our country need a baptism of the Spirit of God, which shall still the scornful lips of the " enemy and the avenger," and save His own people, that through them the openly ungodly may be saved.

9 783382 831998